EveryWoman's
EMOTIONAL
WELL-BEING

EveryWoman's®
EMOTIONAL
WELL-BEING

Carol Tavris, Editor

Contributors

DIANNE L. CHAMBLESS, FAYE CROSBY, ELIZABETH DOUVAN, JUDY IWENS EIDELSON, CYNTHIA FUCHS EPSTEIN, IRENE HANSON FRIEZE AND MAUREEN C. McHUGH, JOEL GURIN, ELIZABETH HALL, RACHEL T. HARE-MUSTIN, HARRIET GOLDHOR LERNER, AYALA M. PINES, KAREN ROOK, CARIN RUBENSTEIN, LINDA TSCHIRHART SANFORD AND MARY ELLEN DONOVAN, NANCY SCHLOSSBERG, PHILLIP SHAVER AND CARY O'CONNOR, STEPHANIE A. SHIELDS, LEONORE TIEFER, LILLIAN E. TROLL, CAROLE WADE

Drawings by Sandra Forrest

Doubleday & Company, Inc., Garden City, New York

Library of Congress Cataloging-in-Publication Data
Main entry under title:
EveryWoman's emotional well-being.
    (EveryWoman's library [superscript registered
trademark symbol R])
    On t.p. the registered trade mark symbol R
is superscript following EveryWoman's.
    Includes index.
    1. Women—United States—Psychology—Addresses,
essays, lectures. 2. Women—Mental health—United
States—Addresses, essays, lectures. 3. Life cycle,
Human—Addresses, essays, lectures. I. Tavris, Carol.
II. Chambless, Dianne L., 1948–   . III. Series.
HQ1206.E94 1986   305.4   85-29395
ISBN 0-385-18561-8

Contributors

Editor *Carol Tavris*, Ph.D., social psychologist; writer; lecturer, Human Relations Center, New School for Social Research; former Senior Editor, *Psychology Today* magazine; New York, New York

Authors

Dianne L. Chambless, Ph.D., Director, Agoraphobia and Anxiety Program, Department of Psychology, American University; private practice, Washington, D.C.

Faye Crosby, Ph.D., Professor, Department of Psychology, Smith College, Northampton, Massachusetts

Mary Ellen Donovan, writer, New York, New York

Elizabeth Douvan, Ph.D., Professor, Department of Psychology, Co-director, Women's Studies Program, University of Michigan; Research Scientist, Survey Research Center, Institute of Social Research, Ann Arbor, Michigan

Judy Iwens Eidelson, Ph.D., Clinical Supervisor, Department of Psychology, University of Pennsylvania; Clinical Assistant, Department of Psychiatry, University of Pennsylvania School of Medicine. Private practice, Philadelphia, Pennsylvania

Cynthia Fuchs Epstein, Ph.D., Professor, Department of Sociology, Graduate Center, City University of New York; Resident Scholar, Russell Sage Foundation, New York, New York

Irene Hanson Frieze, Ph.D., Professor of Psychology, Business, and Women's Studies, Department of Psychology, University of Pittsburgh, Pittsburgh, Pennsylvania

Joel Gurin, Editor, *American Health* magazine, New York, New York

Elizabeth Hall, writer; former Managing Editor, *Psychology Today* magazine; former Editor, *Human Nature* magazine; Waccabuc, New York

Rachel T. Hare-Mustin, Ph.D., Professor, Department of Counseling and Human Relations, Villanova University, Villanova, Pennsylvania; private practice, Wayne, Pennsylvania, and Westport, Massachusetts

Harriet Goldhor Lerner, Ph.D., Senior Staff Psychologist, The Menninger Foundation, Topeka, Kansas

Maureen C. McHugh, Ph.D., Assistant Professor, Department of Psychology, Duquesne University, Pittsburgh, Pennsylvania

Cary O'Connor, doctoral candidate in Social Psychology, Department of Psychology, University of Denver, Denver, Colorado

Ayala M. Pines, Ph.D., Research Associate, Department of Psychology, University of California at Berkeley; private practice, Berkeley, California

Karen Rook, Ph.D., Professor, Program in Social Ecology, University of California at Irvine, Irvine, California

Carin Rubenstein, Ph.D., social psychologist; writer, North Tarrytown, New York

Linda Tschirhart Sanford, Lic.S.W., psychotherapist; director of a sex-abuse treatment center; private practice, Boston, Massachusetts

Nancy Schlossberg, Ed.D., Professor, Department of Counseling, College of Education, University of Maryland, College Park, Maryland

Phillip Shaver, Ph.D., Professor, Department of Psychology, University of Denver, Denver, Colorado

Stephanie A. Shields, Ph.D., Associate Professor, Department of Psychology, Director, Women's Studies Program, University of California at Davis, Davis, California

Leonore Tiefer, Ph.D., Clinical Associate Professor of Psychiatry, Department of Psychiatry, New York University School of Medicine; Psychologist, Department of Urology, Beth Israel Medical Center; private practice, New York, New York

Lillian E. Troll, Ph.D., Professor II, Department of Psychology, Rutgers-The State University, New Brunswick, New Jersey

Carole Wade, Ph.D., psychologist; teacher, College of Marin; writer; Larkspur, California

Acknowledgments

My real recommendation for emotional well-being is to work with people you enjoy, who stimulate ideas, and who make you laugh. In this respect, the people who worked with me on this project contributed to my emotional well-being no end. First and foremost, I was fortunate to have had the help and counsel of Barbara Greenman, editor of the EveryWoman's Library. Barbara has great patience, unflappability, and skill. The contributors did include many of her suggestions for tranquillity in life ("it is not necessary to change the bed linens *every* week"), even though they missed one critical one (we couldn't really have a whole chapter on the importance of vacations).

Your well-being will also improve remarkably if you can find a Beth Margolis. Beth organized us, kept track of authors and manuscripts, attended meticulously to every detail as well as the larger picture, and offered excellent editorial ideas. Although she decided to abandon psychology and publishing for law, Beth saw this book through to the very end.

All editors of collected works, of course, risk special mental-health hazards by having to chase after their contributors, waving various combinations of carrots and sticks to get them to turn in their work on time. The contributors to this volume were alarmingly on schedule—even ahead of schedule. Even more shocking, they did just what they were supposed to, and they did it well. For making my task so easy and for preserving my mental health, my heartfelt thanks to the authors.

Next, my thanks and appreciation to Sandra Forrest, whose lively illustrations blend just the combination of humor and perspective we hope the book conveys.

Finally, I thank my husband, Ronan O'Casey, who sees to my well-being every day, in ways beyond words.

—Carol Tavris

Contents

EveryWoman's®
EMOTIONAL
WELL-BEING

A Note to the Reader

Most books on "mental health" concentrate on emotional problems, stress, and the headaches of life. They look at the components and causes of illness and symptoms of distress. But as medical sociologist Aaron Antonovsky observes, few researchers and members of the public consider the components and causes of *health*. Scientists are so busy looking for the "high-risk" factors in disease and distress that they forget how many people, under the worst possible stress, do *not* succumb. What protects them? "Everyone, by virtue of being human, is in a high-risk group," says Antonovsky. "The question is no longer 'How can we eradicate this or that stressor?' but rather 'How can we learn to live, and live well, with stressors, and possibly even turn their existence to our advantage?' "

This book seeks to answer that question. Readers will not find in its pages "Ten Simple Steps to Dealing With the Blues, the Blahs, and the Bores," although they will find plenty of practical suggestions and wise advice. The twenty-three eminent contributors to this volume offer a strategy, a philosophy, for approaching life's difficulties and delights. "Emotional well-being" is a state of mind, one that, surprisingly, is independent of physically being well. The contributors to this volume investigate the most important ingredients of well-being, which include a sense of humor, the ability to see things in perspective, self-esteem without self-absorption, not taking oneself too solemnly, and understanding that facts alone do not wisdom make. But the recipe for putting them together is up to us.

Each chapter represents a refreshing look at the continuing concerns that affect women's lives and well-being. Each contains up-to-date research findings and, I believe, a wise interpretation of them. The chapter on the psychology of humor is, amazingly, funny. The essay on sex ought to drive a stake once and for all through the heart of that old "am I normal" question. The chapter on motherhood actually will not make a mother feel guilty that whatever she is doing, it is wrong. The chapter on diet and exercise doesn't sternly warn women to do both—in fact, it explains why "overweight" is not nearly as dangerous as dieting. The discussion of old age is neither sentimental nor pessimistic. And the consumer guide to therapy questions whether one needs it and whether it will help, as well as evaluating what works.

The book is divided into four sections. Part One considers self-esteem, love, work, sex, friends, and what "emotional" well-being means. Part Two examines the major transitions in women's lives, from adolescence to old age, with the milestones of marriage, children, and work along the way. Part Three reports the latest research on coping with everyday problems and occasional disasters. And Part Four considers dilemmas of change, emotional disorders, and the question of therapy.

Readers can approach the collection two ways: to look for information on specific issues, and to gain a general understanding of the nature of well-being. Those who are interested in particular problems are advised to consult both the table of contents and the index, since the topic may be discussed in several chapters. For example, different aspects of loneliness are dealt with in several places, including Chapter 6, on friendship, and Chapter 9, on marriage. Different aspects of the perennial female worry about weight are covered in Chapter 2 (the relationship of body image to self-esteem); Chapter 8 (adolescent eating patterns and physical changes); and Chapter 16 (fact and fiction about "overweight," diets, and exercise). Chapter 5 discusses special issues of work for high-achieving career women, and Chapter 11 considers the pros and cons of paid employment for women in general.

But, basically, I recommend that readers dip in and browse around, because answers to questions may turn up in unexpected chapters. In this book, as in life, well-being doesn't divide up neatly into discrete packets. Nor do solutions to the surprising choices that life continually plunks in one's path. A woman who wants to make changes in her life might profit from reading Chapter 12, on the nature of transitions throughout the life cycle, and from reading Chapter 18, which explains why change is both appealing and difficult. A woman who is feeling depressed might do well to understand the reasons for her feelings (Chap. 2) as well as the therapeutic methods of changing them (Chap. 19).

So perhaps the best starting point is the introductory chapter, Rachel Hare-Mustin's essay on "The Impossible Pursuit of Perfection." The message she offers is, I think, the best advice of all: Relax. Perfect well-being, like the perfect marriage or the perfect sex life, would drive us mad with boredom. Perfection, like happiness, is worth pursuing, but only if we realize that getting there is all the fun.

Carol Tavris

Groundhog Day, 1986

PROLOGUE

1

The Impossible
Pursuit of Perfection

RACHEL T. HARE-MUSTIN

The story is told of a poor scholar who was famished yet had no money to buy food. He went to a bakery on a crowded street. On catching sight of the rolls on display, he gave a loud scream, started to run away in fright, and fell to the ground.

The crowd gathered and asked what he was frightened of. "Those rolls," he replied. Everyone laughed; they had never heard of such a thing. The owner of the bakery was incredulous, but he wanted to test the poor man. He induced the scholar to go into a room where he placed a pile of rolls on a plate. Then the baker left and watched through the keyhole.

The scholar happily dug into the pile with both hands and began to stuff himself. Greatly touched, the baker rushed into the room and said kindly to him, "Is there anything else you are afraid of?"

"Now I am afraid of a really good cup of hot tea," replied the scholar.

This is a story told nine hundred years ago. What this tale from an eleventh-century Chinese philosopher tells us is that sometimes the best way to achieve one's goal is to run away from it. Stanislavski, the director of the famed Moscow Art Theater, understood that one cannot chase success. He once told a student, "If you want to catch a squirrel, you do not chase it. You lie down in the sun with a nut on your outstretched hand and wait."

One Right Way to Be

How can it be that we can achieve a goal without pursuing it? We have learned in school that logic and being rational, the methods of science, are the ways to solve problems. And we have learned that there is one right answer, one right way to do something which is "the truth," and we must find it.

But suppose I am arguing with you and you get the better of me. Does that mean you are right and I am wrong? Or if I get the better of you, does that mean I am really right? Why must one of us be right and the other wrong? Can't we both be right, or even (horrors) both be wrong?

Not only do we assume that there is one right way to be, one right way to solve our problems, one right way to achieve our goals, but we suspect, as women, we will never be able to "get it right." We have even been told that right time, right place, right people equals success. Yet it is wrong time, wrong place, and wrong people that equals most of the real human story. Even to see both sides of a problem is the surest way to prevent its solution, because there are always more than two sides. As Kipling said, "There are 101 ways to trap a tiger, all of them equally good."

My mother understood such possibilities very well. I remember once complaining to her, "Nobody likes me." She replied, "Don't say that—everyone hasn't met you yet."

If we assume that one way is right, the other wrong, we are led to what is called the fallacy of opposites. That is, if something is bad, we assume its opposite must be good. But as G. B. Shaw cautioned, "There are two great tragedies in life. One is not to get your heart's desire. The other is to get it." Rather we would do better to accept things as does the simple sheep who says, "I always look at alternatives: I can munch and I can bite." In this way we can avoid a view of life as a contest between differences, a view that has led us to believe that one way is winning, another losing.

Utopia—the Road to Nowhere

In past times people had simple and basic goals: to lead a decent life, to eat, to sleep. But our age is the age of utopia. Because there is a word for perfection, people imagine it is attainable. Recall that Utopia, the magical place written about by Thomas More in 1516, means "nowhere." Are we trying to achieve goals and solutions when there are none? Are we on the road to nowhere?

What are the utopian goals that are dangled before us in our modern age? Self-actualization, individuation, identity, happiness, the meaning of life. These tantalize us, like the parched wanderer in the desert following a mirage which recedes as we approach. Can one ever find "complete meaning" or "ultimate happiness"? We are so seduced by the utopian goals put forward by the sages of our time that we forget the little pleasures of the moment. As that great wanderer Robert Louis Stevenson discovered, it is better to travel than to arrive.

Women and psychotherapy, our modern-day religion, have had a strange relationship. It may be that psychotherapy could not have developed and flourished if it were not for the pervasive and chronic unhappiness of many women. Therapy has promised freedom from anxiety and depression and has fostered the belief that the "ultimate good" is attainable. Perhaps in his heart Freud knew better when he said that psychoanalysis merely makes neurotics into ordinary unhappy people.

Many human qualities are elusive and cannot be captured or measured. We can measure achievements, but not curiosity, imagination, or creativity. We can measure productivity, but not determination, unpredictability, or vanity. We cannot really describe our dreams or our pain. We cannot measure fear or courage, anger or despair or hope. We cannot measure beauty. We cannot measure happiness. Or progress.

In considering progress, economist Charles Issawi proposed the Law of Conservation: Most things don't change. He pointed out that the total amount of evil in any system remains constant. Hence, any diminution in evil, such as reduction in poverty or unemployment, is accompanied by an increase, for example, in crime or air pollution. He further noted that most things get steadily worse. This does not contradict the first principle because a few things have become much better, such as surgery, copying machines, and long-playing records. A particular application of his principle is that most people get worse with age, because they become more like themselves.

As American as the Pursuit of Happiness

Even the American Declaration of Independence assured the early colonists that they were entitled to the pursuit of happiness. We still feel we are entitled to it, or at least that we can buy it. In the frontier days before the closing of the West, endless expansion held the promise that everyone's dreams could be attained. With this goes our belief that anyone who works hard can win, and the belief that what works is right. The pragmatic American view further implies that self-improvement can overcome the limitations of class, race, and gender.

The themes and premises distinctive to American life include:

- Emphasis on work rather than on relationships and love.
- Self-direction and independence rather than interdependence and acceptance of guidance from others.
- An attitude toward time as passing and used up rather than an ahistorical view of time.
- A focused individual consciousness rather than a social consciousness.
- A problem-solving, cerebral approach to life's conflicts rather than one that emphasizes absorbing and integrating experience.

Having learned these American principles, we all try to excel at everything we do. In this way we have turned even play into work. I find it amazing to see people who hate work go to Herculean labors in the name of play. Now we cannot just engage in recreation for enjoyment, but we must constantly improve ourselves. We buy manuals that tell us how to get better at sports and hobbies, how to play tennis, how to garden, how to have sex, how to do it better, how to measure our progress. Self-improvement has truly entered the world of play. We dress like cowboys and workers when we prepare to have fun. Fashion advertisements for "adventurous play separates" show workers' "canvas pants with tool pockets," and "canvas overalls with suspenders and painter's pockets."

Our ideals of independence and opportunity have not only led us to work at playing, but according to social commentators such as Irving Howe, the pursuit of excellence has led to the dominant themes of our time being the politics of macho swagger, possessive individualism, ideological narrowness, and social meanness. Is this what we are seeking?

As women we too have accepted the American ideals of a society where one's value is measured by the money one earns. But where productivity is linked to monetary rewards, those who do not earn money—women, children, old people—have an ambiguous status in the society. I suggest that in a goal-oriented society that sets impossible utopian goals, it is the goals that may be the problem, not the failure to achieve them.

How can we learn to accept minimal or small goals? In a tale of enlightenment, Idries Shah tells of the simple man who lay under a cherry tree and, glancing at some enormous watermelons growing nearby, mused, "How is it that an immense, impressive tree like the cherry brings forth such puny fruit? And the miserable, weakling creeper produces such huge and delicious melons?"

As he was pondering the question, a cherry fell and landed on his head. "I see," he said. "That is the reason. I should have thought of that before."

Self-Blame and Self-Help

Show me a woman who doesn't feel guilt and I'll show you a man. Utopian goals and the ideal of American opportunity lead us as women to blame ourselves for our shortcomings rather than blaming the standards of our society. Freudian theory has explained this as women being innately masochistic, full of self-hatred. Some of Freud's early followers tried to put forward a different view, a view that the problems women face are due to the pressures of the society they live in, but the dominance of Freudian theory meant that anyone with a different point of view was ostracized and ignored. All of which proves that no good deed goes unpunished.

Although humanist and Gestalt psychotherapy do not have such sexist theories of the inferiority of women as Freudian theory does, in practice they have been highly patriarchial. They do not question the sexism in society and women's lives. This supports the Law of Inverse Fun: The more fun a therapeutic approach is, the less justification there is for using it.

Most people who study behavior focus on what goes on in the individual rather than how the individual is influenced by others. But as women we have been raised to believe we should meet the expectations of others, and that if we don't fulfill those expectations, there is something wrong with us. We are avid supporters of the advice industry. We devour self-help books, and if we fail, we never blame the book but blame ourselves. Rarely do we believe we can reject others' advice.

If we do succeed, we fear that there will be a price down the road. Erma Bombeck, the humorist, expressed the fear: "I always think everything good is going to evaporate overnight." We may not even be on the right road, like the pilgrim going to Mecca who was told, "You will never reach Mecca, I fear, for you are on the road to Damascus." Feeling inadequate and bad is like a familiar old friend we can return to again and again.

Sometimes women's lack of success is obscured, and attributed to women's being more emotional and less able to "handle power" than men, rather than to women's opportunities being limited. But what is power? Power is merely the ability to get others to do what you want. The dominant group defines the acceptable roles of the less powerful. Universally, these are activities that the dominant group does not choose to do, like housework. You wonder why a woman's work is never done.

Conflicting Demands on Women

Ideals of perfection are held out for women, but are they ever attainable? Women are to be soft and charming, ideal marital and sexual partners, but at the same time responsive to children's needs, good cooks and housecleaners, career women, and all in a life span that is measured by men's lives. It is hard to be an optimist about these expectations, but then a pessimist is only an optimist with extra information.

THE PERFECT WOMAN

Women are constantly exhorted to remake themselves, to improve their appearance, mind, house, temperament, and use of the telephone. Perfumed, shampooed, slim, smiling, receptive, "a good sport," we see the perfect woman's life as she runs through fields of daisies to serve sugared munchies to her children, polish her kitchen floor, accept her husband's sage advice, and, as she ages, keep her dentures gleaming.

Since women's identity has depended on the appraisal of others, women are more vulnerable to others' opinions and the pressures to change. Women's complaints are trivialized into thousands of small things, as if they were really separate problems each woman should solve one after another. Because women are unsure of themselves from trying to satisfy others, they seek legitimation from experts such as clergymen, doctors, teachers, and therapists, who tell them how they should be. I have observed that when the ignorant become numerous and powerful enough, they have been referred to by a special name. This name is "the Wise."

The standard of living and social status women have are derived primarily from their relationships with men, first their fathers, then their husbands. Women who have no men, such as old women and single mothers, are the most likely ones to live in poverty. (This confirms the Golden Rule: Those who have the gold make the rules.) When women do have importance in the family as mothers, they are easy targets for everyone's complaints because of overexposure and overresponsibility.

When women go to work, they find that, relative to men, they are worse off in wages than they were thirty years ago. Yet men still think they are being flooded by inferiors—women, blacks, ethnic groups, lower classes. In fact, only a few members of these groups are rising, and they are highly visible, such as Geraldine Ferraro, who finally broke the barrier to be the first vice presidential candidate to be Italian-American. Or Sandra Day O'Connor, who became a Supreme Court justice. (Maybe we should have a woman President. She would save the country money because she would make only half what a man makes.)

In a recent public address Justice O'Connor said young women planning both a career and family can "have it all." "Women have a great deal of stamina and strength—it is possible to plan both a family and career and enjoy success at both." But she cautioned against expecting equality. Many social scientists have found that men have learned the *language* of equality, but little else has changed.

WOMEN'S DEVELOPMENT: OFF THE TRACK

Despite stamina and strength, women are beginning to suspect that many of them are not going to be able to overcome the handicap of starting the race from behind, because the race is not their race. It is on men's development that theories of human development have been based, and on the bodily differences between the sexes, with women considered biologically inferior. Little attention has been given to the fact that women experience unique and dramatic bodily changes and role changes in the course of their lives. Yet failure to acknowledge differences where they exist is but another form of prejudice.

The eight stages of identity development devised by psychoanalyst Erik Erikson, for example, are based on the typical male experience. What attention he gives to women's life cycle is primarily to say that women's identity will be achieved through the man she marries. Other popular theories of development (Daniel Levinson, George Vaillant, Gail Sheehy) are based primarily on men's careers and the stages for men in choosing jobs and advancing in their work lives. This is not surprising; for the most part, men are defined by their occupations, and the dominant themes of society are male themes. After all, fathers are Republicans, mothers are Democrats. Fathers will say, "Show me. Prove it. And then when you grow up, I'll buy you a rocket." But mothers will care for you and give you a pony whether you deserve it or not. Women have been raised in both modes. Women are raised in the male culture where the dominant themes are individuality and achievement. But women are also raised in the female subculture where caretaking, sacrifice, and domestic values are extolled. As a consequence, women are more variable than men because of the dual and often conflicting value systems they have learned. Further, women keep trying to find new ways to please others who define what they should be.

As women we assume excessive responsibility for relationships and attribute failures in relationships to our own shortcomings. Theories like psychologist Carol Gilligan's—that women's essential nature is to emphasize compassion and social relations, whereas men's nature is to emphasize justice and higher principles—encourage this responsibility. In point of fact, men and women alike have been found to be both principled and relational when faced with moral dilemmas. Whether one way is more important than the other ultimately depends on the situation and the power the person holds. In conflicts the powerful person tends to claim that logic and rationality are crucial, the weak one that relationships and caring are most important. Thus, in husband-wife conflicts, husbands point to principles, wives to loyalty and compassion. In parent-child conflicts, parents emphasize the rules, children appeal for understanding. Because emotions are less trusted in our society than intellect, the rational mode is seen as superior to the relational, but its use is associated with who has the power, not primarily with being male or female.

In regard to feeling and thinking, women are trained to be emotional and to be the cheerleaders rather than the ballplayers in the society. It reminds me of the story of a local chief who was invited by the British to a great military display. Every time a shell hit its target, the British officer shouted enthusiastically, drawing the chief's attention to it. Subsequently, the British were invited to visit the chief. He took them on a tour of his stables. As a horse was being fed, the chief roared, "Look, how he eats!" Another horse was being exercised. Clapping his hands, the chief exclaimed, "He can actually walk and run!" The visitors thought their host must be mad.

As they were leaving, the chief said, "You have guns which do exactly what they were designed to do—hit the target. I, too, am surrounded by things which do what they are intended to do. What I have learned from you is to get excited about it." Women, too, have learned to get excited. There are over 40 miles of nerves in the human body, which means a possible 211,200 feet of frazzles.

In addition to their cheerleading function, women have a different way of talking from men: We are always explaining ourselves. But counter to the stereotype, women have not been found to interrupt as much as men do. On the other hand, our vaunted verbal ability may not stand us in good stead, because the person who shuts his mouth and withdraws in arguments is the winner, thus demonstrating that silence can be more powerful than noise. Actually, I have found a marvelous remedy for many forms of deafness. It is called "praise."

Until recently, little was written about the role of friendship in human experience, because it does not seem to figure prominently in men's development. But women's friendships have been important to them. As a consequence, women are deeply affected by the loss of friends or by being excluded. It is truly said that one hundred friends are not too many, but one enemy is. And two enemies together feel like an army.

A FIVE-POUND SOLUTION

No other achievement matters if a woman is not thin. That is the lesson constantly drummed into women. Fat is a female issue. Pejorative male terms for women are "fatty," "piggy," "cow," and "blimp." The medical and psychological professions have shown little understanding of why women differ in the degree of comfort with their bodies or how their body weight is distributed. The "problem" of weight control for women has become big business. The majority of behavior modification groups are directed at women's weight control. Women's magazines today show the same regimen of exercises my sister and I faithfully carried out when we were in high school. For a five- or ten-pound difference, our society's prescriptions for ideal weight have made many women's lives miserable. The widely advertised standard of beauty for women involves social pressure on many women to achieve unrealistic standards of slimness. Certain occupations, such as fashion modeling, actually require women to maintain weights at anorexic levels.

Why don't we question treatments that utilize shame, that imply lack of motivation when weight loss is not enough, or that result in levels of constant hunger for women? It has been found that moderately "overweight" women are not at greater health risk than so-called normal women and do not have shorter life spans as do overweight men. On the other hand, how can we understand that obesity among women is 70 percent higher than among men?

Anorexia nervosa frequently has its onset in early adolescence in girls who start a course of dieting to achieve the much advertised ideal of bodily beauty. Among the various eating patterns associated with anorexia nervosa is bulimia (binge eating followed by purging or vomiting). These problems receive less attention and research funding than hypertension, heart attacks, smoking, alcoholism, and other problems that affect our congressmen.

THE MARRIAGE BOND

The bond between couples is often a puzzle. In every couple there is a relatedness that defies understanding. One of my favorite stories is of a man who returned home one day to find his wife packing.

"What are you doing?" he asked.

"I can't stand it anymore!" she said, "All these years of fighting, arguing, bickering—I'm leaving."

He watched her for a moment, bewildered as she struggled through the door with packed suitcases. Then he ran to the closet and snatched out a suitcase. "Wait a minute," he cried. "I can't stand it anymore either. I'm coming with you."

Oh well, it takes two to tangle. Or, better the first quarrel than the last.

Marriage is a fragile and delicate relationship. How it blossoms and grows is a mystery. But the little knowledge about what actually goes on inside marriage means this mystery often does not bloom for very long. The only thing some couples have in common is that they were both married on the same day. Marital problems are the most common problems people bring to therapy. Of course, in Freud's day psychoanalysis lasted only a year and marriage lasted a lifetime. Now it is just the opposite.

Successful marriage involves a give-and-take—once wryly described as "You give and he takes." The myth is that women benefit more from marriage than men, but to the contrary, married men have better emotional and physical health than single men or married women. The commitment in marriage can lead to individual resiliency and relief from outside pressures, but also to toleration of undesirable behavior, and a greater sense of loss at the marriage's ending. I have noticed that divorce per se does not undermine the family, but serves as a safety valve for the institution of marriage by allowing intolerable marriages to be terminated.

As women we feel the responsibility for making marriage work. In any relationship the person who is more in love has less power because of being more dependent on the other one. Women have found that they can sometimes exchange love for power, even without being a "Total Woman." Other ways women have found to counter men's power include appealing to uncontrollable causes such as one's illness, helplessness, anxiety, or depression. Milan Kundera's *The Book of Laughter and Forgetting* suggests that the struggle of people against power is the struggle of memory against forgetting. Perhaps that is why, as T. S. Eliot wrote, men live by forgetting, women live by memories.

Men and women differ in many other ways, which makes marriage even more of a challenge. Men's and women's bodies are adapted for reproduction differently. Men's and women's influence in religious, economic, academic, sports, media, professional, cultural, political, and international life is different. We all have our favorite differences that I won't go into, such as that men prefer to read in a sitting position, and no woman can enjoy a book in that posture.

In acknowledging differences I don't want to ignore the common humanity of men and women, but does "common humanity" mean anything more than that most people watch TV an average of five hours a day? You can't have revolution with everyone glued to the tube.

To the man who says he is looking for the perfect woman, the only appropriate response is that you are looking for the perfect man. Or one who can be made perfect: I have observed that a loving wife will do anything for her husband except stop trying to improve him.

For others there can be a give-and-take, as shown by one wife's experience. One day she had cooked some eggplant, which her husband found delicious. He asked her to serve it every day. "Isn't this the best vegetable in the world!" he exclaimed.

"The very best, dear," she replied.

After five days of eating eggplant every day, he complained, "Take this away, I hate it."

"Yes, it is the worst vegetable in the world, dear," she agreed.

"But last week you said it was the very best."

"It is true, I did," she replied. "But I am your wife, not the wife of the eggplant."

HOME IS WHERE THE HEART ACHES

What happens in the family is a microcosm of what happens in the world at large. The family is the primary beneficiary and focus of women's labor as well as the source of women's most fundamental identity, that of mother. Today the family has become a hot political issue, perhaps because only 7 percent of American households still consist of the traditional family with a working father, a mother at home, and two school-aged children. We long for the family of the past, an idealized family that never was. When someone makes a statement about the family, Letty Cottin Pogrebin suggests substituting "male supremacy" for "family" in order to understand what profamily advocates are really concerned about. The family is not separate from, but supports, the social order. If the father is the good provider and the mother the servant of the family, the children, says psychiatrist Thomas Szasz, are the prisoners of the family. He notes that if they run away they will be captured and returned to the family. In some countries they say, "Be a dog, but don't be a daughter or a younger brother."

The family is where we learn to be what we are. Within the family we all face the problem of how to balance independence and autonomy with the intimacy we also long for. As women we have found that individualism is in conflict with service to others (called social responsibility). Housewives are taught to accept the view that their needs are less important than those of others; they are expected to be the caretakers for children, husbands, the old and the sick. Women who question whether they should engage in this self-sacrifice are accused of being selfish.

The privacy of the family has led to isolation that has increased the emotional overload on the family, particularly on women, at the same time that the family may have gained some freedom from public observation. Often the family, in seeking harmony, suppresses differences among its members. But the privacy of the family also leads to abuse. We do not permit among strangers the violence permitted in the family.

Housewives have been described as remaining at a preindustrial stage, doing work in the private family sphere that has no exchange value in the marketplace. We may not recognize that women in the family have an overload of decision making, because the decisions women make, although time-consuming, are regarded as "unimportant." As women in the home we often feel the lack of personal space and personal privacy, our space being associated with household work, like the kitchen or sewing room. It is time for women to turn over a new leaf on life—or at least take a new lease on a private room.

The myth of motherhood is a powerful myth, trailing clouds of glory, yet women who have had children are often ready to admit that a mother is happiest once her children are in school. Mothers are seen as totally responsible for the way their children turn out; almost every psychological problem is attributed to a dominant mother and an ineffectual father. Many people have read about it in *Portnoy's Complaint*. But how many have read

Portnoy's Mother's Complaint? Society is beginning to espouse equality for women, but not yet for mothers. Children can be fun, but they make many demands—as one of my children said, "If you didn't plan on buying me a dog, why did you ever have me in the first place?" Mothers must creatively combine their housework and child care. One mother I heard of taught her children to swim while she was waiting for the plumber.

Women's mothering role is idealized, but there is consistent evidence that children have a negative effect on the emotional well-being of women. The much feared empty nest when the children are grown is actually a time of low stress for women; the birth of a child is a time of high stress. Mothers are widely scapegoated in our society. But then so are nonmothers, all of which is very evenhanded. How can women who care about their children and their families not devalue themselves in a society which devalues them, and devalues their work? Yet it is still true that old people die calling for their mothers.

HALF-TIME WORK

The most dramatic change in America in this century may be that the majority of American wives now work outside the home. Why do women work? Women work for the same reasons that men work—economic need and personal satisfaction. But the demands at home have not changed, so women exhaust themselves trying to work and meet family needs without inconveniencing men. It's as if she can work outside the home as long as she fulfills her primary role within the house. There has been a lot of resistance to child care for working women and maternity pay because people fear that every Tom, Dick, and Harry will get pregnant.

Women's depression is often associated with women's being bored by the mindless routines of housework or by not feeling appreciated. Of course, the beauty of housework, as every woman knows, is that you only have to work half-time. And it doesn't matter which twelve hours a day you work.

What men do affects women, who are their subordinates, more than the converse. Thus, men do not observe carefully many aspects of women's behavior. They assume their greater accomplishments are the result of in-born superiority. The corollary is that they are more aware of the burdens of being dominant than the unearned advantages. Our ideas of inborn superiority need modification. Someone went back and reexamined Sir Francis Galton's famous studies of the inheritance of genius. The results showed that heirs of geniuses who did not inherit money did not become geniuses.

Not everyone is born with a silver platter in the mouth. Still, a male high school dropout can look forward to greater lifetime earning than a female college graduate. Women still earn less than men on the average *even* in the same positions.

Greedy occupations in America's technological economy cause stress, which falls more heavily on women than men because a man is more likely to have a wife to maintain a household for him and look after his needs. Husbands of employed wives do as little at home as husbands of stay-at-home wives, averaging about an hour and a half a day, including yard and car maintenance. Yet, despite overload, employment outside the home is associated with improved emotional health among married women. Such women achieve a sense of greater satisfaction and self-acceptance despite the fact that "having everything" does not mean equality, as Justice O'Connor noted.

A "Glory-to-Work" ratio has been devised by psychiatrist Ellen Berman to help guide women who try to "do it all" from chasing after the chimera of perfectibility. In order to deal with the choices involved in having everything, she suggests a method for calculating the amount of glory in relation to the amount of work. First, if enough money is offered for you to do a job, say yes at once. Otherwise, compute the amount of work: Estimate the time you will need to complete the task—and then double it. Glory is more difficult to calculate. Glory involves the number and status of the people who will be involved, the enjoyment of the job, and an aspect that is hard to evaluate and that women often exaggerate, the moral righteousness of a "yes" decision. Here women must be very cautious. If you have no problems, it is all right to take on a few. But as they say in the countryside, if you have no troubles, buy a goat.

AGE AND THE TIMING OF LIFE EVENTS

Is it better to be young or old? Well, to be old is to have less time in front of you and more mistakes behind. I leave you to decide whether this is better than the reverse.

Over the life span, age periods define what we are allowed to do—drive a car, stay out late—and what we are required to do. Age combined with gender controls our access to certain groups, clubs, roles, social situations, and rewards. Because the typical age progression is defined by male development and male careers, the *timing* of women's life events may not fit the pattern. Whether a woman is "on schedule" influences the degree of stress she may feel.

As women we have a briefer interval when we are the "right age" than men. We are treated as more youthful, childlike, and immature when we are young; thus, we are still called "girls." Conversely, women are perceived as being "too old" sooner than men. A man may be viewed as at the height of his powers when he is fifty years old, but a woman at age fifty is seen as too old. A woman arrives at adulthood late and moves on to old age too soon. I confess, now that I am over forty, I have put away childish things, including the desire to be a grown-up.

When being old is no longer looked down on, women will feel free to tell their true ages. At least for the present, there is some virtue in consistency:

Upon being asked her age, a woman replied, "Forty."

"But you said the same thing last time I asked you two years ago!"

"Yes, I always stand by what I have said," she replied.

Age-related decisions exist with regard to education, marriage, employment, residence, retirement, friendships, and leisure pursuits. Postponement of childbearing may make pregnancy impossible. Career tracks may be difficult to break into after age thirty-five. Late career decisions can mean forgoing the earlier chance for job experimentation.

Women born during the high fertility period, from 1947 to the early 1960s, are the baby boomers now in early adulthood. Because of the size of this cohort, all members will face greater competition for fewer opportunities than their predecessors did or their successors will. Women in this cohort are in a marriage squeeze, because women tend to marry older men. For them the eligible men are members of a smaller birth cohort conceived during the 1940s. Eight million more women than men are now in the twenty-eight-to-thirty-five-year age cohort.

Women experience more stressful events over their life span than men because typically women have more changes in the course of their lives. Full-time employment gives way to full-time housekeeping and parenting, and then to part-time work and full-time housekeeping and parenting, and then to another round of full-time employment. There are many complicated role combinations and changes for women. The expectation that women will adjust to men's patterns and give up their activities and places of residence starts at marriage. Sylvia Plath once said, "My only free act is choosing or refusing a mate."

Do human companionship and love sustain life? Does familiarity breed content? Married people live longer than unmarried, women live longer than men, the educated live longer than the uneducated, the rich live longer than the poor. As Mark Twain said, "Getting old is not so bad when you consider the alternative."

One Thing After Another

What is life? As the philosopher Ludwig Binswanger said, life is one thing after another. The many conflicting demands that women face, reviewed above, are collective problems shared by many women, not just problems of a single individual. The common experiences associated with being female are so much a part of our lives, they encompass us like the air we breathe. We have trouble seeing them for the common problems they are, just as the fish is the last to discover the water.

In the face of these patterns in our lives, we become demoralized, feeling bewildered, deprived of courage, thrown into confusion. As women we fear we have failed to meet our own expectations or those of others. We feel powerless to change the situation or ourselves. In the face of such loss of control of our lives, our need is to regain a sense of control. It is important to realize that blaming the system rather than oneself leads to higher self-esteem and better emotional health.

Perhaps we first need to make a distinction between difficulties and problems, for sometimes we cannot see the forest or the trees. Difficulties have been described as the common life situations we all experience as undesirable. They can be resolved through commonsense action and knowledge. However, for some difficulties, such as the generation gap, no solution exists. They must simply be lived with. Of course, one must be cautious about appeals to common knowledge, as it is more likely to be common than knowledge. No real knowledge is common.

Problems, on the other hand, result from mishandling difficulties. Sometimes this is due to a failure to take action when one should. Or sometimes problems can result from taking action when one should not, such as when the situation is unchangeable, when there actually is no problem, or when the goal is utopian and therefore unattainable.

At times we feel impelled to interfere with a natural process of change that is already occurring, to hurry it up or shift it. But society is a mule, not a car. If pressed too hard, it will kick and throw its rider. It is interesting that schizophrenics have a better chance of recovering in simple societies where there is little treatment because no one interferes with the natural healing process. In our own medically oriented society, the discovery of a new treatment defines the illness, and there is increased pressure to use the drug. Thus, the discovery of Thorazine led to more diagnoses of schizophrenia, the discovery of tranquilizers led to more diagnoses of anxiety, Ritalin led to more diagnoses of childhood hyperactivity, and behavior modification has led to more diagnoses of antisocial problems. I would like to suggest that sometimes in psychotherapy the chief function of the therapist should be merely to keep the patient amused while the patient gets better.

Difficulties and problems are a way of communicating our experiences. They are a way of getting a certain response we may want. If we cry, we get sympathy. If we feel sick, we get concern. People often say they want help when they really want attention; they say they want to listen when they really want to be heard. Faced with an overload of conflicting demands, women are tempted to rush to solve problems. But you don't cure malaria by jumping in bed with the patient. Nor do you solve problems by rushing headlong to take action.

In John O'Hara's tale "Appointment in Samarra," a merchant sent his servant to the marketplace. The servant soon returned in fear and trembling, saying, "I saw Death in the marketplace and he looked at me strangely. Oh, give me a horse that I may flee to Samarra." So a horse was brought and the man quickly mounted and rode toward Samarra.

Then the merchant went down to the marketplace, and when he found Death there, he asked, "Why did you frighten my servant?"

And Death replied, "I did not mean to frighten him, but I was startled to see him here, for I have an appointment with him tonight in Samarra."

The lesson for us is like the one I learned from a woman who was fearful of wasps and carefully avoided them. As it turned out, wasps did her no harm. But she was stung by a scorpion.

WHY SHOULD YOU CHANGE?

Before rushing to take action, we need to ask, Why should we change? To please someone else? Because we have learned to be dissatisfied with ourselves? If we are perfect, people probably will not want to be with us. Again, we need to sort out what are difficulties and what are problems. Can we accept reality, that there are some things that we may not be able to change: What is is, what ain't ain't. A common misconception is that if one makes some desired change everything else in one's life will fall into place. This, of course, is a utopian error. Denying or getting mad about what is or insisting it should be otherwise is as fundamental an error as assuming that we can make others into what we want. As baseball manager Yogi Berra said, "If people don't want to come to the ballgame, nobody's going to stop them."

Attempts to change relationships with others need to be approached with caution, because such attempts will stimulate action to reestablish the relationships as they were. Often we see life as a contest between the forces for change and the forces against change. But the fact that individuals do not change merely means that there is a fit between them and the pressures in their situation to remain as they are, so they may just go on being themselves. People say they want to change, but many are like the person who wanted knowledge and was told to read a book. She refused, saying, "No, I tried it once and it didn't work."

Still, we may feel that our emotional well-being depends on making changes. What brings about change? Some difficulties can indeed be changed through efforts at self-improvement. The essential ingredients include having someone who supports the change you are working on; a clear definition of what's to be changed; a study of the possible solutions; the setting of a definite goal and a plan to reach it; and the expectation that you will succeed. This approach can be used successfully for some difficulties (such as stopping smoking), but it may not work for complex problems. Failure to alter difficulties with this kind of effort leads women to assume they did not try hard enough. So we mistakenly try harder. It is our efforts which end up becoming the problem. In fact, the obstacle may be that we did not correctly understand the problem. As H. L. Mencken said, "For every complex problem there is a solution which is simple, elegant, and wrong."

Another bad outcome occurs when we engage in a battle or a contest to produce change, for we risk becoming what we hate. That is the history of revolutions. The humanist movement arose to counter Freud and behaviorism, and it thought it was creating a new vision and "potential" for the self. Actually, it led to a stereotyped self; its view of emotional "liberation" has become regularized through techniques that are now part of management training. Ivan Illich's anarchist view of free education and society has led to the voucher system in education. Mao Tse-tung thought he was creating a religionless society in China; instead, he created the largest Puritan state in history. Our democracy, in the name of peace, has become the most powerful militarist state in history. We have become our enemy. They say it takes all sorts to make the world. This may be true, but if it is, where are they? Every innovation becomes conservative over time, so when we try to change, we may end up back where we started. Remember the man who picked up a talisman that was inscribed, "Talisman for transforming stones and gold." He took the talisman to a place that was covered with stones, and said in the approved way, "Talisman, do your work!" In a twinkling of an eye, the talisman had turned into a stone. So be careful what you ask for; you may get it.

Rather than seeking perfection, I think as women we need to focus on how to avoid being perfect.

The Paradox of Change

At some point in my childhood I stopped taking my doll to bed with me. I don't know why. It was a spontaneous change that occurred without my effort or understanding. It did not fit with any attempts to change. It was counter to theories of change. We have been taught that to change, we must look at our past, and once we understand and resolve issues around past traumas, we will be prepared for all time to deal with the world. This assumes, of course, that the world is a stable order. But dealing with one's past is as impossible as dealing with one's future. The past has changed in our recalling it. History is stories. That is why we try to understand life through stories—the stories people live, and the stories people tell.

SPONTANEOUS CHANGE

Change can come in many ways. Change can come through a chance visit, a word of praise, a disappointment, a victory over someone else, a change of seasons. Sudden and dramatic changes cannot be explained by adding one step to another as in learning the letters of the alphabet. Falling in love or learning to ride a bicycle are not step-by-step changes, but sudden, mysterious transformations. Just as a symphony cannot be comprehended as one note following another, such changes are not rationally deducible from their parts. To say we "nearly understand" this is like saying something is "almost an apple." The whole cannot be broken into its parts and still retain its nature, for the nature of things is to be complex and interrelated. Often a state of confusion should be welcomed, because it may lead to an openness to a new solution or a new way of seeing things.

Sometimes the best way to influence others may be by yielding to them, just as in judo the opponent's thrust is not opposed by a counterthrust, but rather accepted, and even exaggerated, by yielding to and going with it. An old man in a folk tale used such an approach. He was bothered by some noisy boys playing outside his house. So he called the boys to him and told them he liked to hear them play, but he was getting deaf. If they would come and play noisily every day, he would give them each a quarter. The next day they played noisily and the old man paid them. The day after that they came and played, but he only gave each boy fifteen cents, explaining that he was running out of money. The following day he said he regretted he would have to reduce the payment to five cents on the subsequent day. The boys became angry and refused to come back because it was not worth the effort to play noisily for only five cents a day.

We observe that things can get better when you try to make them worse. I have learned that you can defeat a pessimist by becoming more pessimistic. If a person you are with behaves like a baby, you, too, must behave like a baby. If a person has foibles, you, too, must have your foibles.

BEING WHAT ONE IS

When common sense, serious efforts, and advice have not worked in making changes, it is time to try reverse psychology. Rather than trying to change, continue to do what you are already doing. This has the advantage of not compounding the problem as many other "solutions" do. In trying not to change, we can continue to take care to view our problems seriously until at some point the humor of the situation may dawn on us. We do not need to try to hurry through transitions, but can just go slowly and monitor any changes as they easily occur. Sometimes just keeping track of and gathering information about a problem without trying to solve it will bring surprising results. Perhaps we need to accept the fact that our problems may be special and set us apart, so we can further try to preserve them with practice. Change will occur when one becomes what one is, not when one tries harder to become what one is not. Restraining oneself from changing removes a sense of urgency and leads to a new perception of things, so to be yourself I suggest you make no effort to modify yourself or your personal views of yourself.

Another way to create the conditions for spontaneous change is through reversals, the seeking of those experiences we fear and avoid. Rollo May has called this confronting one's demon. Women who are exceedingly responsible—that is, most women—can try in a small way to act irresponsibly and observe the consequences. If we fear criticism, we can seek a little criticism, even going into a Mexican restaurant and asking for an egg roll or standing on a street and asking a passerby where that street is. But is that being genuine? Deliberately choosing to play a different role is no less genuine than playing one imposed on us by the way we have grown up and lived. If you cannot start a behavior you want to stop, how can you expect to stop it?

Such approaches to the process of change are not rational or logical, but they do emphasize the positive. Often they are accompanied first by confusion and bewilderment, then by a cognitive startle, a new perception, and new understanding, humor, or anger. Sometimes they are not. But they allow us to see things in a different way. It is not totally foolish to say that the moon is more useful than the sun because we need the light more at night than during the day. What works may be more important than the truth or falsity of a theory.

SIMPLE THINGS ARE THE HARDEST

A unique human trait is that we remain in an unending state of development. Yet we talk about growth and development as we talk about an ingrown toenail, as if it is bound to be painful. Life, the quality of being alive, is mysterious, despite what we try to make it.

To tell someone to be spontaneous is a paradox, because spontaneity cannot be achieved at someone's direction. Similarly, to tell someone to relax is a paradox, because relaxing cannot be ordered. In like manner, you cannot be sincere by trying to be sincere. You may wish to serve your friend tea with sincerity and honesty. But if you are trying to be sincere and honest, you are not. The simplest things in life are the hardest to do.

Detachment gives us greater freedom than trying too hard. As we step out of the tragic action we as women sometimes seem caught in, we can observe ourselves and our intensity and laugh. Thus, comedy avoids evil, it is an outlet, a way out. While tragedy confronts evil directly, there are costs in tragedy. Comedy, a sense of humor, is a healthy thing, a way of stepping back and gaining a more detached and distant view of one's life. In addition, I have found that humor and tact are valuable because they mitigate the need for lying.

But I am not an authority on other's lives. You know yourself best. As for giving advice, women (unlike men) do not expect their good advice to be followed. In any case, I have learned that truth is unpopular. There is a Yugoslavian proverb that says, "Tell the truth and run."

So I will end with another of Issawi's laws: "Not everything has to go wrong, and anyway, nothing is 'the end' of anything—it has happened before and will happen again."

What do you want to be? Perhaps that is what you already are. You may ask, Have I got a chance? Rather, I would say, Have you seen your chance? And finally, yes, be a tiger—if you are ready for a tiger's problems.

RACHEL T. HARE-MUSTIN is a clinical psychologist who has been on the faculties of Harvard University and the University of Pennsylvania. She is currently a professor at Villanova University. She has published widely on women and psychotherapy, ethical issues, and family systems, and has carried out research on attitudes toward motherhood here and abroad. Her observations while working in Asia and Africa have contributed to her skepticism about there being one right way of approaching problems. In regard to the pursuit of perfection, she reports that she started slowly, then tapered off. In addition to a career, Dr. Hare-Mustin has raised four children, so she has experienced firsthand the conflicts for women in seeking and avoiding perfection. She notes that few things work as well in practice as they do in books, but she does find truth in stories like *The Wizard of Oz*. She likes to recall that when Dorothy reached the Emerald City and saw what a fraud the Wizard was, Dorothy said to him, "You are a very bad man!" But the Wizard responded, "Oh, no. I'm a very good man; I'm just a very bad wizard."

Further Reading

Brodsky, Annette M., and Hare-Mustin, Rachel T., eds. *Women and Psychotherapy: An Assessment of Research and Practice.* New York: Guilford Press, 1980.

Frank, Jerome. *Persuasion and Healing.* Rev. ed. Baltimore: Johns Hopkins University Press, 1973.

Herrigel, Eugen. *Zen in the Art of Archery.* New York: Vintage Books, 1971.

Pogrebin, Letty Cottin. *Family Politics: Love and Power on an Intimate Frontier.* New York: McGraw-Hill, 1983.

Shah, Idries. *Reflections.* Baltimore: Penguin Books, 1972.

Thompson, William Irwin. *Evil and World Order.* New York: Harper & Row, 1976.

Thorne, Barrie, and Yalom, Marilyn, eds. *Rethinking the Family: Some Feminist Questions.* New York: Longman Group, 1982.

Wallach, Michael A., and Wallach, Lisa. *Psychology's Sanction of Selfishness: The Error of Egoism in Theory and Therapy.* San Francisco: W. H. Freeman, 1983.

Watzlawick, Paul; Weakland, John; and Fisch, Richard. *Change: Principles of Problem Formation and Problem Resolution.* New York: Norton, 1974.

LOVE, WORK, AND SELF-RESPECT

2

The Elements of Self-Esteem

MARY ELLEN DONOVAN AND LINDA TSCHIRHART SANFORD

Do you sometimes feel inadequate and worthless? Do you dislike your body? Are you nagged by the fear that you don't really deserve to be happy and successful? Do you frequently compare yourself to others and come up short? When things go wrong, do you automatically blame yourself? Do you often feel vaguely depressed, and wake up dreading another day? Do you view life as basically beyond your control, something that just happens to you?

If you can answer yes to one or several of these questions, you're probably suffering from low self-esteem, a problem that plagues large numbers of women. Low self-esteem affects all types of women, regardless of race, ethnicity, age, economic and job status, religious background, sexual preference, or personal family history.

Some women assume that the problems they have with self-esteem aren't very important. Many say something along the lines of, "So big deal that I have low self-esteem. What does it really matter?" The answer is, *it matters plenty*. Our level of self-esteem affects virtually everything we think, say, and do. It affects how we see the world and our place in it. It affects how others in the world see and treat us. It affects the choices we make—choices about what to do with our lives and whom we'll be involved with. It affects our ability to both give and receive love. And it affects our ability to take action to change things that need to be changed, whether in our own personal sphere or the larger world around us. If a woman has low self-esteem, she will not be able to act in her own best interest, and she will have little chance of living to her full potential and experiencing happiness. And if a woman has no self-esteem at all, she will become overwhelmed and immobile, and eventually give up.

A lot of women accept their low self-esteem as a seemingly unalterable condition of life. While working on our book *Women and Self-Esteem* (Penguin, 1985), we conducted numerous eight-week-long self-esteem enhancement groups. Inevitably, at the first meeting some participants would ask, "But isn't low self-esteem something you're born with?" The way these women saw it, having low self-esteem is like having a certain shoe size—you got what you got, and like it or not, you just have to live with it. Nothing could be further from the truth. No one was born with low self-esteem and no one has to live with it. If a woman sees herself as flawed, inadequate, and just not "good enough," it's because she *learned* to see herself that way. And if a woman learned to have low self-esteem, she can learn to have higher self-esteem. It might not be easy and it might not happen overnight, but it is possible.

"What does it matter that I have low self-esteem?" and "Isn't self-esteem something you're born with?" are only two of the many questions we've found women have about self-esteem. Other questions crop up time and again wherever we go. Women from all over, it seems, want to know the same things about self-esteem. Here are a few of them:

Why focus on women and self-esteem? Don't men have problems with self-esteem too?

Yes, many men do suffer from low self-esteem, and this is a problem that deserves attention. But we focused on women because the life experiences of men and women in our culture tend to be completely different. From the moment one infant is placed in a blue blanket and another is placed in a pink one, they will be treated so differently that it's almost as if they were living in two separate worlds. As a result, while a man and a woman can have equally low levels of self-esteem, they typically do so for very different reasons. Further, men and women in our culture generally learn to deal with their self-esteem problems in radically different ways. Men, for example, are encouraged to mask their feelings of inadequacy by being competitive and macho, while women are encouraged to wear our feelings of inadequacy on our sleeves, so to speak, by being passive and self-deprecating.

Another reason we focused on women is that, overall, men in our culture have tremendous advantages over women when it comes to developing high self-esteem. In general, it is a lot easier for a male to develop high self-esteem because the world we live in is one that constantly affirms the worth of males while negating the worth of females.

A final reason we focused on women's self-esteem is that women in a male-dominated world face many obstacles men do not face, and we'll only be able to overcome these obstacles if we see ourselves as persons of worth and great capabilities. When one woman suffers the unhappiness of feeling that she isn't worth much, nor capable of much either, it's easy to say hers is an individual problem. But when thousands of women suffer from lack of self-worth and have limited views of their capabilities, then we are talking about a group problem of enormous political implications. Low self-esteem and the ancillary problems it gives rise to—among them depression, passivity, fear of taking risks—help to perpetuate women's secondary status in a male-dominated world. Only by raising ourselves in our own estimation can we begin to bring all women up.

Understanding Self-Esteem

Can you be more precise about defining self-esteem? "Self-esteem" is one of those terms that people throw about loosely, often using it interchangeably with the terms "self-concept" and "self-image." In fact, these are not interchangeable, although they are closely related.

The self-concept or self-image is that package of beliefs about yourself that you carry around inside, and which you take for granted as the real truth about yourself. Usually, a wide variety of beliefs and images are contained in the package. Some of these are simple statements of fact whose accuracy is easily verifiable: I am a woman; I am five feet five; I am black; I am a mother; I am a student; I am a lesbian; I am a secretary; I am broke. Others refer to less tangible aspects of the self, and their accuracy is not so easy to verify: I am smart; I am ugly; I am incompetent; I am sexy; I am unlovable; I am worthless; I am no good.

In addition to having a set of ideas about who we are, each of us has a set of ideas about who we should be. These ideas about who we should be make up our ideal self. Typically, we constantly compare our image of who we actually are to our image of who we should be. If we feel our real self falls far short of the person we should be, we'll disapprove of ourselves and our self-esteem will be low. By contrast, if there's a close alignment between the way we feel we should be and the way we think we actually are, we'll probably like and approve of ourselves, and our self-esteem will be high.

Self-esteem, then, can be defined as the measure of how much we like and approve of the person we perceive ourselves to be. Or as we've heard it put, "Self-esteem is the reputation you have with yourself."

Aren't certain components of our self-concepts—such as the knowledge that we are a certain gender or a certain race—with us from birth?

No. All the various beliefs and images that go into our self-concepts were acquired through learning. None was with us at birth. To be sure, everyone is born with concrete physical characteristics and undiscovered capacities. But no one is born knowing she is male or female, black or white—just as no one comes into the world already thinking she is stupid or smart, pretty or ugly, shy or outgoing, strong or weak, lovable or unlovable, generally inadequate or basically okay. As far as ideas and impressions of herself are concerned, the newborn can be said to begin life with a "blank slate." Everything she eventually comes to believe about herself—whether it be the belief that "I am a girl" or "I am klutzy"—is something she has been taught.

None of the ideal standards which make up the ideal selves that we judge ourselves by was with us at birth either. Just as no one comes into the world already thinking of herself as a girl, no one comes into the world with any idea whatsoever of what it means to be a good girl. We had to be taught to believe we should be a certain way, and the specific ideals and standards by which we judge ourselves vary from culture to culture, and even from individual to individual within the same culture.

Is it possible to like parts of yourself but still have low self-esteem?

Yes, and this is because the way we assemble or structure our self-concepts is as important as what beliefs they contain. When we put the various images and beliefs we have of ourselves together in our minds, we don't give each one equal weight and prominence. Rather, we put the various components together so that the self-concept resembles a collage. Those beliefs and images that are most important to our identity and sense of self-worth (for example, I am a woman; I am a mother; I am incompetent/competent; I am pretty/ugly) will be placed in the center and foreground of the collage, and constitute the core self-concept. Those beliefs and images that are less important to our identity and sense of self-worth (for example, I am a good cook; I am left-handed; I am unathletic) will be placed toward the periphery of the collage, outside the core of the self-concept.

Because of the way we structure our self-concepts, it is possible to have a self-concept containing mostly positive beliefs—a positive self-concept—and still lack self-esteem. No matter how many positive images and beliefs a woman has of herself, if she puts them off to the side of her self-concept, downplaying their importance, low self-esteem will result.

This brings us to an important point: There are actually two types of self-esteem—global and specific. Global self-esteem is the measure of how much a person likes and approves of herself as a whole. Specific self-esteem is the measure of how much she likes and approves of a certain part of her perceived self. If a woman places a high value on a certain aspect of herself (her looks or intelligence, for example), her global self-esteem will be greatly affected by her specific self-esteem in that one area. But if a woman doesn't care much about a certain aspect (her cooking skills, for example), her specific self-esteem in that area won't have much impact on her overall or global self-esteem.

Is it possible to have high global self-esteem without being an egotistical, selfish, narcissistic, and arrogant braggart?

Yes! Many people think having high global self-esteem means being arrogant, vain, conceited, egotistical, selfish, narcissistic, and feeling superior and insensitive to others. But this is not the case. Such traits are most common among people with *low* self-esteem. A person who has high self-esteem does not vainly consider herself the center of the universe or see herself as better than others, but she also doesn't see herself as a valueless, inconsequential creature who is worse than others. She simply knows many aspects of herself, has respect for herself, is aware and appreciative of her own worth. She knows she has good qualities, but she doesn't delude herself into believing she is perfect. Rather than seeing her flaws and mistakes as representative of her worthlessness as a human being, however, she sees them as representative of the fact that she is human.

The Effects of Low Self-Esteem

If a woman has low self-esteem, how is it likely to be manifested?

One problem that virtually all women share is negative body image. Not one woman we interviewed really liked and accepted her entire body. And a lot of women spend a huge amount of time and effort worrying about their bodies, hating them, and trying to change them. It is an incredible waste of energy.

Many people would like to think that a negative body image comes first, and low self-esteem follows—and that therefore the way to improve women's self-esteem is to improve women's bodies so that they look better. But we discovered that it's often the other way around—low self-esteem gets instilled early, and later general feelings of self-loathing get translated into specific loathing of the body. This dynamic is dramatically illustrated in anorexia nervosa, whose victims, mostly female, act out deep-seated feelings of self-hatred by becoming totally obsessed with their weight and with trying to control it.

The prevalence of negative body images among women underscores the role that culture plays in generating low self-esteem. Men with low self-esteem are not encouraged to see their bodies as the cause of their problems; they are taught to look for external sources of blame (their "domineering" mothers or "castrating" wives, for example). But women are encouraged to see their bodies as the principal cause of all their problems, and in our culture women are *expected* to be unhappy with their bodies.

Two purposes are served by encouraging women to focus on their bodies as the source of their problems. First, it's good business; the profits brought in by the cosmetics, fashion, diet, plastic surgery, and exercise industries would drop considerably if women suddenly decided that maybe they didn't look so bad after all. Second, when women focus on their bodies as the cause of their problems, they are blinded to the cultural beliefs and the social, political, and economic inequities that are the true source of women's low self-esteem. Ironically, feeling bad about their bodies offers women an illusion of control. If a woman thinks "My problem is my hips," she will feel a lot less overwhelmed than if she thinks "My problem is that I live in a culture that had caused me to hate my hips."

As to the issue of whether it helps to look better, the answer is often, "Yes—but not that much." Although a lot of women think that their feelings about themselves and their lives would improve dramatically if they just fixed whatever is "wrong" with their bodies, we have found that a better body doesn't necessarily bring a dramatic increase in self-esteem—or a better life. The self-esteem problems that led to the poor body image in the first place will usually manifest themselves in another way; and all the other problems a woman has will remain, too.

In addition to poor body image, a woman with low self-esteem is likely to practice certain ways of thinking that inevitably reinforce her negative feelings about herself. These negative thought habits are among the most obvious symptoms of low self-esteem. Here are the more common ones among women:

Black Clouds. A black cloud is what a person creates when she takes a specific piece of criticism, insignificant mistake, or passing comment and blows it up into a reflection of, or attack on, her overall self-worth. A person with this habit will translate a remark such as "You look tired today—are you okay?" into "You look like a total mess. It's obvious your whole life is a shambles."

Critical Tapes. These are powerful, negative statements—or sometimes upsetting visual images—that run through a person's mind constantly. Sometimes they're set off by a particular event, but other times they just appear seemingly out of the blue. Common examples: "I'm so slow and lazy, I never get things done." "I'm so ugly, I should be in a circus freak show." "I'll never be happy." "No one will ever love me."

Chronic Comparisons to Others. A person with this habit sees the world as a rigid hierarchy, and she spends a good deal of time figuring out how she rates in comparison to those around her. Her self-esteem is entirely dependent on her rating at any given moment: if she rates herself as better than others, then she feels good about herself; but if she sees herself as inferior in some respect, she feels rotten about herself.

Expectations of Perfection. A person with this habit measures herself against a standard of perfection that is impossible ever to achieve. And the all-or-nothing thinking she practices leaves no room for a middle ground: if she's not perfect, then she must be utterly worthless—there's no in-between. She must rate an A to measure up; if she gets a C instead, she views it as if it were an F. She's got to be in perfect shape; if she's not, she sees herself as *totally* out of shape or *grossly* fat, never as a bit out of shape or ten pounds too plump.

Expectations of Doom. A person with this habit sees disaster around every corner. No problem or challenge is too small to bring the threat of total doom. If she has a headache, she doesn't think, "I have a headache. Maybe it's the weather or I'm getting a cold." Instead, she assumes the worst: "It must be a brain tumor. But I'm not ready to die—I don't even have a will. But then I don't have anything to leave anyone. And if I did have something to leave, who'd want it? No one wants me. I'll bet no one will come to my funeral. . . ."

Inability to Accept a Compliment. Tell a person with this habit that you like her dress, and she will say, "Oh, this old thing? I've had it for years, and look—it has all these little stains on it." Or she might say, "You really like it? I think it makes me look fat." Or she might launch into a long-winded story about what happened the day she bought it or the first time she wore it. All these responses serve the purpose of deflecting attention from the fact that someone has said something nice about her. It never occurs to her to simply say "Thank you," accept the compliment, and then let it go.

If a woman has low self-esteem, how will it influence her behavior?

The negative thoughts and feelings a woman has about herself often directly translate into self-defeating behavior that reinforces her low self-esteem. People with low self-esteem tend to have a knack for creating self-fulfilling prophecies. They do this by acting in ways that are sure to "prove" that their negative beliefs about themselves are accurate after all. Beginning with hypotheses such as "No one will ever love me" or "I have to do everything myself, no one will ever help me," they will set out to prove the hypotheses correct. The woman who believes she will never be loved will do everything in her power to keep others at bay, and she will show an eagle eye for reading rejection in even the friendliest gestures. The woman who believes she will always have to do everything herself will similarly refuse anyone's attempts to help her; then when she ends up doing everything herself once again, she will have the satisfaction of saying to herself, "See, I was right." Like everyone who creates self-fulfilling prophecies as a way of coping with low self-esteem, these women would rather be right than happy.

Many others further perpetuate their low self-esteem by basing their actions, sometimes their entire lives, on "if-then" schemes such as these:

- If I am really generous and nice and helpful, then everyone will like me.
- If I am beautiful and sexy, then I will never be alone.
- If I am really smart, then I will be valued.
- If I can make people laugh, then they won't dislike me or get angry with me.
- If I am supercompetent, then all career opportunities will be mine.
- If I lose weight, then I will be worthy and everything in my life will be fine.

Unfortunately, women who believe in these equations tend to postpone real life until the condition set by their "if" is fulfilled. The woman who believes "If someone loves me, then I'll be happy" will tell herself that until a lover comes along her life doesn't really count. She therefore doesn't take steps to make herself happy; all her energy goes into waiting and fantasizing about that magical moment when her life will be transformed.

"If-then" schemes tend to be unrealistic, unlike their realistic counterparts:

- Lots of people take advantage of generous people—they don't like them at all; they think they are foolish.
- Many beautiful, sexy people end up alone.
- Not everyone values intelligence, especially in women. A lot of people resent it.

- Everyone's idea of what's funny is different, and it is easy to unintentionally offend someone with certain types of humor.
- Promotions often have nothing to do with competence. There is such a thing as nepotism. And ageism, racism, sex discrimination and other forms of prejudice often get in the way. There are no guarantees in the work world.
- If you lose weight, you'll still have the same personality.

How does low self-esteem affect our relationships with other people?

There's a lot of truth to the old saw about not being able to give or receive love from others until you love yourself. Many people with low self-esteem take their hatred of themselves and turn it against other groups—e.g., Jews, women, Hispanics, "liberals," foreigners—and sometimes the entire world. Hating others serves the purpose of distracting them from their own deep-seated self-dissatisfaction. It is convenient to have someone against whom they can ventilate pent-up negativity, and to have scapegoats for their problems. Moreover, it is culturally accepted, even encouraged, for people to take out their feelings of inadequacy by hating, scapegoating, and oppressing others, by practicing what we call the bully approach to self-esteem. Many people, in fact, believe that the only way to feel good about themselves is to set themselves up as superior to others. They then guard their self-esteem by making sure that those under them remain there.

On a more personal level, women with low self-esteem frequently feel that they must have a romantic relationship in order to be worthy and complete, and we have found this holds true for lesbian as well as heterosexual women. This belief is inevitable considering that from childhood, girls have been told time and again in millions of different ways that we're nobody until somebody loves us. But a woman who expects a lover to make her feel worthy ultimately will be sorely disappointed. No one can make another person worthy. A woman needs to find out for herself that she is of worth, and then, and only then, will she have a chance of building a satisfying relationship with someone else.

Have you found similarities in the way women see themselves?

Yes, we found that many women think about themselves in one of six distinct ways:

For some women the issue is that "there's not much of a self there." Although in an ideal world everyone would reach mid-life with a pretty clear idea of who she is and what she's about, in our world women traditionally have not been encouraged to "know thyself" as men have been admonished to do, and women historically have been denied the opportunities for self-discovery that many men take for granted. As a result, many women we interviewed had great difficulty describing themselves at all. These women felt "shot full of holes," and because they lacked sufficient knowledge of who they are, they felt they really didn't have selves to like and value.

Others are in the habit of thinking, "I'm a good woman—so what?" These women have well-defined self-concepts but still lack self-esteem because their sense of who they are has been greatly constricted by sex role stereotypes that define men as having one set of highly valued attributes and women as having another, less valuable set. Many women have internalized our culture's devaluation of women, women's work, and the attributes commonly associated with women. As a result, we rarely heard women say, "I'm a good mother and housewife; it's too bad this culture doesn't value that." Instead, women were far more likely to say in self-deprecation, "I'm *only* a mother and housewife." Similarly, we heard very few women say, "I'm a terrific secretary; it's really unfair that secretarial work is considered so unimportant." Instead, we heard many women say, "I'm *just* a secretary. Big deal."

Some women have the "but let me tell you what I'm not" syndrome. Asked to describe themselves, such women immediately launched into a string of negatives. "Well," a woman with this problem would say, "I'm not all that attractive, not all that smart, not very good at sports, not as capable as the other women who work in my office, not as well-informed as my husband, not as much fun to be around as my friend Anne, not as caring as I should be, not as involved in community activities or as well read as I should be. . . ."

Still other women are in the pattern of thinking, "If I'm good at that, then it really can't matter." Such women usually know they have many positive attributes; they are well aware that they "measure up" in a variety of respects. The problem for them is that they have trouble convincing themselves that their good qualities matter as much as their flaws and failings, and so their self-concepts lack structural balance. "Oh, I know I've got a nice face, that I'm pretty bright, a good teacher, a kind person and all that," a woman might say. "But," she is quick to add, "I should lose ten pounds." In this woman's self-concept collage, those ten pounds occupy the most prominent position, and they loom so large as to make all the positive images and beliefs she has of herself pale by comparison.

Research suggests that this preoccupation with flaws is peculiarly female. Men tend to focus on their positive attributes and to overlook their flaws. According to the studies, if a man excels in a certain area—athletics, say— he is likely to value that area highly and to give his athletic self a prominent position in his overall self-concept, thereby enhancing his self-esteem.

Among women, however, the opposite tends to be the case. "If I'm good at that," many women say, "then it really can't matter."

Some women once felt okay about themselves, but they are currently going through a period of significantly lowered self-esteem. Some of them are experiencing "self-concept dislocation," which occurs when a major event in a person's life forces her to change the way she looks at and thinks about herself, sometimes radically. A woman who has recently lost her job or gotten divorced, for example, may go through self-concept dislocation, lamenting, "I'm not the person I used to be."

Self-concept dislocation can be a problem for two reasons. First, it often takes a while to integrate a new set of beliefs about the self into the self-concept. Second, even when the new beliefs have been integrated, it can take a long time to convince oneself that the new self is okay.

Any time a woman goes through a major change in her life—whether by moving, going back to school, having a baby, or changing jobs—her concept of herself will be forced to change, and she may have difficulty adjusting to the new image she has of herself. Aging in itself is bound to bring about a certain amount of self-concept dislocation, particularly in a culture that so dreads it (especially in women); and our self-esteem may shift as we go through different stages of life (see Chaps. 12 and 13).

Finally, some women worry that "I'm not sure who I should be anymore." Consider, for example, a woman who was raised with the rigid expectation that she prove her worth by getting married and having children. At first, she rejects this ideal, choosing instead to remain single and to pursue a career in advertising, something she goes on to do with success. Throughout her twenties and early thirties, she is happy with her choices, and because she's lived up to her ideal self—successful, independent career woman—she is happy with herself.

As she nears her late thirties, however, this woman begins to question the value of her profession, and more and more often she thinks that maybe she should put her energy into political activism. At the same time, as she approaches the end of her prime childbearing years, she has begun to wonder whether she might not want to have a baby after all. To exacerbate her confusion, her father died two years ago, now her mother is seriously ill and needing considerable care, and she is wondering if she shouldn't go back to her hometown to nurse her mother. A part of her feels she should care for her mother, just as a part of her feels she should change careers and another part feels she should have a baby while she still has time.

The woman we have described is a woman whose ideal self is in transition. When she compares her self-image to her old ideal—independent, successful career woman—she feels good about herself. But when she starts comparing her image of herself to all the other ideal images that are now running through her mind—the ideal of herself as a political activist, the ideal of herself as a mother, the ideal of herself as a good and nurturing daughter—she feels rotten about herself. Until she's able to decide what new ideals she wants to pursue, and until she starts taking action that will bring her closer to those goals, she will probably continue to experience low global self-esteem.

The Sources of Self-Esteem

What role do parents play in determining their children's self-esteem?

A major one—but not the only one. Most people get their most basic, fundamental sense of who they are and whether they are worthy during childhood. This is a crucial time for self-esteem development, and childhood families, particularly parents or surrogate parents, are the most influential teachers. Through the way they treated us, what they told us about ourselves, and the examples they set, they gave us our basic sense of identity, what we are like, what we are capable of, and whether we are worthy, just okay, or totally worthless.

Parents who raise children to have high self-esteem are aware that children are learning beings who lack the knowledge and skills adults take for granted. They know that as a child grows up she will learn by trial and error, and that she will inevitably behave in ways they don't like—that she will be slow at times, will make mistakes, even misbehave, throw tantrums, and otherwise be a brat. But such parents will not withhold their love when the child misbehaves; they will let her know that they might dislike her *behavior,* but they won't communicate to her the message that she is bad because she has done something bad. Many women, though, grew up in situations where love was given when they were "good" and withdrawn when they somehow fell short of their parents' often unreasonable expectations.

We found that there are five principal things that children need in order to start off with a solid foundation of self-esteem.

- *A sense of significance*—the sense that they matter as people, that they are worth paying attention to and giving love to. The amounts of nourishment, physical affection, and attention that young children receive all affect their sense of significance.

- *A sense of competence*—the sense that they can *do* things and make things happen. Unfortunately, many women did not gain a sufficient sense of competence. The range of activities they could master was restricted by overprotectiveness ("You'll hurt yourself"), sex role stereotypes ("Little girls don't do that"), or parental lack of confidence ("You're such a klutz, you'll just blow it anyway—so why even try?").

- *A sense of individuality, balanced by a sense of connectedness to others.* Males in our culture tend to grow up with a strong sense of the ways they are different from and separate from others. But often their sense of individuality is so exaggerated that they are blind to the many ways in which they are like other people, and the many ways that they are connected to others and dependent on them, too. By contrast, females in our culture tend to grow up with a deep-seated, strong feeling of connectedness to others, but an insufficient sense of individuality. In many families girls have been taught not to develop too strong a sense of autonomy because their self-identities would eventually be defined by the men they marry. Enormous problems result from this training, for to have self-esteem a woman first must have a solid sense of self.

- *A sense of realism about oneself and the world.* It doesn't help a girl to be told that she is a genius or the pinnacle of perfection when she is not. Nor does it help to be told that the world is a wonderful fairyland where Prince Charmings and happy endings abound. Then again, it is no help for a child to be told that she is the worst child on earth or a total moron—or that the world is a snakepit where the only thing you can count on is misery and victimization. To have high self-esteem, children must learn to be realistic in their perceptions of themselves, their abilities, and how they fit in in the world.

- *A coherent set of values and ethics.* What is right, what is wrong? What is important in life? What do I personally value? High self-esteem rests on the ability to answer these questions with certainty and security. Unfortunately, some families are so intent on foisting all their own frequently inappropriate values on their children that they cannot accept their children's attempts to find their own values. And in other families, children are fed values that are contradictory. One woman we interviewed, for example, was told not to worry about having pimples because "it's what's inside a person that counts." But she was also taught that people with different color skin are inferior and can't be trusted.

Even if your parents did not instill an adequate foundation of self-esteem, keep in mind that this wasn't necessarily by design. No parents ever leaned over their infant's crib and said, "Boy, if we play our cards right, this kid will really hate herself when she grows up." Many parents have low self-esteem themselves and didn't know any way not to pass it on. Others may have been so overwhelmed by their own problems that it was beyond them to give their children the support they needed.

By emphasizing the importance of what happened in childhood families, are you saying that all self-esteem problems are our parents' fault?

No! Parents and other close family members aren't the only ones with influence over the way women see and think about themselves. Other people outside the childhood family—friends, schoolmates, and other relatives and, later, lovers, spouses, work colleagues, etc.—affect our beliefs and attitudes about ourselves, too, and their influence typically increases as we grow older. Generally, the more we care about a "chosen intimate," the greater his or her impact on our self-concept and self-esteem.

In addition, women are also enormously influenced by the world outside the intimate sphere: attending church, going to school, hearing the radio, watching TV, reading, going to the movies, and observing what goes on around us. The often negative impact of such outside influences makes it clear that a girl can grow up in an extremely nurturing family and still end up with self-esteem problems. Because her parents have given her a solid foundation of self-esteem, her self-esteem problems probably won't be as severe as some other women's—but it's likely that she will still have some.

Do you really think our culture is all that damaging to girls' and women's sense of worth?

Yes—but we don't just think it; it has been demonstrated by research in the social sciences time and again. A few years ago, Dr. Alice I. Baumgartner and her colleagues at the Institute for Equality in Education at the University of Colorado asked two thousand children in grades three through twelve how their lives would be different if they woke up tomorrow and found themselves transformed into the opposite sex. The boys consistently portrayed the change as one for the worse—a "disaster," a "nightmare." They saw that being a girl would mean losing the freedom to enter a range of occupations, losing the esteem of their parents and peers, and losing self-respect. "If I were a girl," said one third-grade boy, "everybody would be better than me, because boys are better than girls." In contrast, the girls consistently felt that their lives would be much improved if they were boys. They reported that as boys they would *gain* in freedom, social status, self-worth, and value in the eyes of their parents. "If I were a boy," said one third-grade girl, "my daddy might have loved me."

The children's reactions are not surprising considering the overwhelming antifemale, promale biases that run through every major institution in our society. Take, for example, the lessons promulgated by the three most influential religions in the United States today. Protestant Christianity, Roman Catholicism, and Judaism differ from one another in countless ways, yet each is designed to affirm the significance and worth of men and to negate the significance and worth of women. In every one, men hold the positions of authority. Women traditionally have been and often still are subordinated, in some cases even segregated, and women have also been deemed inferior, tainted, unclean, and responsible for bringing evil into the world. Over time, women have managed to salvage a lot of positive things from the Judeo-Christian tradition, but this does not compensate for the damage to women's sense of self-worth this tradition has caused. Perhaps the most damaging religious belief is that God is a male and that only men are really created in His image. The young boy who sees pictures of God as a male, and who hears God referred to as He and the Father, has his sense of self-worth bolstered immeasurably. The girl who is taught to think of God as a male, by contrast, has her self-esteem diminished accordingly.

Experiences in school often undercut female self-esteem, too. This has changed somewhat in recent years, but for most women school was a place where the chances of developing a sense of competence were restricted by sex role stereotyping (sports, shop, and the sciences were for boys; cooking and typing were for girls). And our sense of significance was hurt by much of what we were taught: a version of human history in which males and male achievements were showcased, while women and women's experiences were rendered practically invisible; a version of literature in which the focus was almost exclusively on male writers. Thus, the false impression is created that history and literature are made by men and men alone, and that women are not significant—never were, and never will be. (Some history books talked about "the brave pioneers and their wives"—as if the wives were not also pioneers!)

The impact of religions and schools tends to be doubly damaging to girls and women who are black, Hispanic, Asian, or Native American, and this is often true in the case of those who are homosexual or have physical disabilities as well. The major religions don't just portray God as a male, they portray him as a *white* male, and for centuries racism and homophobia have been fostered in the name of religion. The history taught in our schools is not just the history of males, it's history as seen through the eyes of *white* males (history, of course, is written by the winners). As a result, it is history that typically demeans and portrays as inferior, even evil, those on the losing side. For a child to hear her teachers portray herself and her loved ones as "primitives," "savages," "emotional children," "mental inferiors," or "heathens" can be devastating.

For most girls and women the damaging lessons of childhood and adolescence are reinforced by adult experiences. Despite the social changes that have occurred in recent years and all the steps forward that women have made, men still run the major institutions of the world, and they still regard women as a subgroup that is of lesser value and importance. This message is communicated to women in their day-to-day experience—in the lower salaries and lower status they receive for the work they do; in the violence committed against them; in the insulting way they are depicted in the press and the entertainment media; in the demeaning experience of being hassled on the street; in the frustrating experience of trying to get a point across to a man, only to be constantly interrupted. (Studies of what happens during conversations, by the way, show that men interrupt women far more often than they interrupt other men, and far more often than women interrupt anyone.) For women of color, lesbians, and women with physical disabilities, daily life typically brings even more disrespectful treatment, which can further damage self-esteem.

What about economics—does this play a role, too?

In childhood it's the quality of the parent-child relationship, not the family's economic standing, that matters most. We interviewed women from well-off homes who had extremely low self-esteem because their parents were abusive, alcoholic, or otherwise unable to give much emotionally. And we interviewed women from poor backgrounds who had high self-esteem because their parents or surrogate parents had been much more loving and, moreover, had encouraged them to develop their competence.

In adulthood, however, economics does seem to have a more direct impact on women's self-esteem (see Chap. 11). Many women, particularly those with young children, are entirely dependent upon their husbands for food, shelter, and the other basics of life. And more and more women, from the young unwed mother in the ghetto to the once well-off widow now in old age, are sinking into poverty. Without a basic minimum of money and security, it's impossible to have a sense of control over one's life. Without that sense of control, a woman is bound to suffer anxiety; anxiety in turn undercuts self-esteem.

Improving Self-Esteem

What can an individual woman do, beginning now, to improve her self-esteem?

Many women are overwhelmed by the prospect of even starting to change their negative views of themselves. This is understandable, because there are no easy, overnight, surefire cure-alls for women's self-esteem problems—problems rooted in our cultural institutions, our economic structure, and our social and political systems. Nevertheless, and this is a crucial point, there *is* a lot that individual women can do, starting now, to begin to improve their self-esteem.

The following exercise, for example, can help a woman to break the habit of thinking of herself in self-deprecating ways. You will need a friend. Sit back in a chair, get very comfortable, and close your eyes. Your friend is to read the following instructions and then lead you in the exercise.

> Tell your friend to think her self-deprecating thought—whatever comes into her mind. Tell her to really get into it, to think very hard about it until she really feels terrible about herself.
>
> When you trust she is really immersed in her negative thought and really feeling rotten, pick up a book and slam it down, yelling *"Stop!"* Your friend will be startled and will probably have a nervous reaction such as laughing, clutching her throat, or even crying. Don't worry; she is fine.
>
> Ask her now if she stopped thinking her negative thought, if she was able to suddenly snap out of it. When she says "Yes" or "Of course," point out to her that her thoughts do not have wills of their own, that they can be controlled. She does not need to be controlled by them.

You will most likely have to do this exercise half a dozen times to get the system down. Then you will be able to do it for yourself by simply saying to yourself, loudly and firmly, *"Stop!"* when a self-deprecating tape begins to run in your head.

Exercises such as this may seem silly and trifling. But this simple little technique does work and can make a large difference. When you catch yourself in a pattern of self-deprecation, saying to yourself "Oh, there I go again running myself down, I'd better stop" will *not* be effective. A firm and loud *"Stop!"* will give you the physical sensation of pulling yourself up short and is the most effective method of snapping out of a pattern in progress.

Once you've mastered the "stop" technique, try to replace the old thought with a more accurate and positive one. For example:

> "I'm such a worthless mess, I always screw things up." *Stop!* Take a deep breath, relax, and tell yourself: "I'm human, and part of being human is making mistakes. *Everyone* makes mistakes, and there's no reason I shouldn't be allowed to, too."
>
> -or-
>
> "I'm so ugly I should be in a circus freak show." *Stop!* Then take a deep breath, relax, and tell yourself: "I'm really not so hideous as I used to think. A lot of people think I'm interesting-looking, in fact."

The stop technique is also effective with all-or-nothing thinking. For example:

> "I'm so grossly obese it's disgusting." *Stop!* Take a deep breath, relax, and tell yourself: "I'm stocky and plump, not the mountain of blubber I've been taught to see myself as."

Be careful, though, to keep your replacement thought *realistically* positive. It just won't work if you try to replace "I'm so ugly I should be in a circus freak show" with "I'm so gorgeous Christie Brinkley would die if she saw me." You'll end up feeling ridiculous if your replacement thoughts are unbelievable.

For women who tend to focus on their flaws as if they were the most significant aspects of their existence, the following meditation exercise can be of help. It will help you to see yourself in realistic perspective, not in the distorted way you have learned to see yourself.

Make a list of three flaws or negative attributes that play a dominant role in your self-concept. Then make a list of three of your positive attributes. With each, repeat the following:

My _____ is a part of me; I am not my _____.

For example, a woman might say:

My <u>bad temper</u> is a part of me; I am not my <u>bad temper</u>.

My <u>pretty face</u> is a part of me; I am not my <u>pretty face</u>.

This meditation will help you accept that no one aspect of yourself, no matter how much you like or dislike it, is in itself representative of you. A woman who tried this exercise in our self-esteem groups elaborates:

> I have no problem saying, "My bad temper is a part of me; I am not my bad temper," or "My fragility is a part of me; I am not my

fragility." But when it came to things like my intelligence or accomplishments or emotional strength, I thought, "Wait a minute, *I am too* these wonderful things." I really resented the notion that those parts weren't the whole story. But then I saw that it's the type of thinking that keeps me from accepting myself. When my bad temper or fragility was revealed, I used to think, "Oh, God, this is all of me." If I continue to boost my ego by sometimes thinking my achievements or intelligence are all of me, I'll still be vulnerable to those times when I think I'm totally defined by the other real but not so wonderful parts of me.

These are only two of the many exercises we found effective in our self-esteem groups. (Many more can be found in *Women and Self-Esteem.*)

What advice can you give a woman who wants to improve her self-esteem?

First, remember that change *is* possible. Some women think it is too late for them to change. They have gotten to a certain point in life, they say, and they figure that they are beyond hope. Others think it is too soon to change; they have gotten this far with little self-esteem, so they figure what's the use of shaking things up now? But at any age it is within a woman's power to examine her beliefs about herself, determine where they came from, and replace those that are inaccurate with more accurate and perhaps more positive ones.

Second, keep in mind that people are complicated and *change takes time.* Even after a woman has identified and intellectually rejected a belief about herself, it can still be operating. For example, a woman who was taught that she needs a man to be worthy and complete might consciously reject this belief, calling it stupid, archaic, and wrong. But at some level she still might believe it. Have patience: No woman should berate herself for not being able to rid herself easily and quickly of the beliefs and feelings that have been entrenched for years.

Third, look at the role that low self-esteem has played in your life, and consider what the payoffs in holding on to it are. Odd as this might seem, women often have apparently sound reasons for not wanting higher self-esteem. Giving up low self-esteem means they have to change fundamental ideas about themselves. It might also mean losing certain friends who feel good when a woman feels bad. It might mean losing social approval (in many circles a good woman is still a woman who sees herself as less valuable than men and who "knows her place"). It might upset the balance of power in a woman's relationship with her spouse or lover. Low self-esteem can protect a woman from taking risks, and can also provide her with easy excuses for both her and the world's shortcomings. Giving it up can be scary. (See Chap. 18.)

Fourth, women can take some of the talent many of us have developed for self-criticism and begin to put it to use in taking a critical look at the world. Women tend to be quick to ask, "What's wrong with me?" But they are often reluctant to ask, "What's wrong with this world that's caused me to feel so bad about myself?"

Fifth, remember that you are not alone; don't hesitate to reach out to other women. Many women feel that they are the only ones who feel this way about themselves, and they are afraid that others might laugh at them or think ill of them if they knew how they really felt inside. But we found that women who came to our groups were pleasantly surprised to discover how much in common they had with other women, and this sense of commonality in itself helped to boost their self-esteem. Support groups, whether formal or informal, can be extremely helpful to women seeking to increase their self-esteem. Working together, women can succeed at tasks that would overwhelm any one individual, and have some fun, too.

Finally, have some compassion for yourself. Women tend to be very good at showing compassion for others, but not very good at feeling similar compassion for themselves. Many of us have no trouble doling out sympathy for another person when that person is sick, exhausted, or grieving, but when we are in the same situation, we berate ourselves for being self-pitying or not strong enough. We find it easy to forgive other people's shortcomings, but can't forgive our own. Learning to have the same compassion for ourselves that we would feel for someone else in the same situation is an important step in building higher self-esteem.

We are well aware that it is not easy to change one's basic self-concept, but obviously we believe it is worth it. And that you are worth it, too.

MARY ELLEN DONOVAN and LINDA TSCHIRHART SANFORD are coauthors of *Women and Self-Esteem: Understanding and Improving the Way We Think and Feel About Ourselves* (Penguin paperback). As part of their research, they conducted interviews with more than three hundred women and dozens of self-esteem enhancement groups for women.

Ms. Donovan, a former newspaper reporter, currently lives in New York City, where she does freelance writing, teaches English to newly arrived refugees from a variety of countries, and is on the staff of *Newsweek* magazine. Her articles have appeared in a number of publications, including *Harper's Bazaar* and *Ladies' Home Journal.*

Ms. Sanford, a psychotherapist, is also author of *The Silent Children: A Parents' Guide to the Prevention of Child Sexual Abuse* (McGraw-Hill, 1982) and coauthor of *In Defense of Ourselves: A Rape Prevention Handbook for Women* (Anchor Press, 1979). She currently resides in the Boston area, where she coordinates a sex abuse treatment center. She also lectures and provides training for mental health professionals nationwide.

Further Reading

Arcana, Judith. *Our Mothers' Daughters.* Berkeley, Calif.: Shameless Hussy Press, 1979.

Briggs, Dorothy Corkille. *Celebrate Your Self.* Garden City, N.Y.: Doubleday, 1977.

——. *Your Child's Self-Esteem.* Garden City, N.Y.: Doubleday, 1982.

Eichenbaum, Luise, and Orbach, Susie. *What Do Women Want: Exploding the Myth of Dependency.* New York: Berkley Publishing Corp., 1984.

Gilligan, Carol. *In a Different Voice: Psychological Theory and Women's Development.* Cambridge: Harvard University Press, 1982.

Miller, Jean Baker. *Toward a New Psychology of Women.* Boston: Beacon Press, 1976.

Moraga, Cherríe, and Anzaldúa, Gloria, eds. *This Bridge Called My Back.* Watertown, Mass.: Persephone Press, 1981.

Rich, Adrienne. *Of Woman Born.* New York: Norton, 1976.

Rubin, Lillian. *Women of a Certain Age: The Midlife Search for Self.* New York: Harper & Row, 1980.

Ryan, Mary P. *Womanhood in America.* 2nd ed. New York: New Viewpoints, 1979.

Schulman, Michael, and Mekler, Eva. *Bringing Up a Moral Child.* Reading, Mass.: Addison Wesley, 1985.

3

"*Am I Normal?*":
The Question of Sex

LEONORE TIEFER

Three times in my career I have written regular columns on sexuality for the public—a weekly column for six months for a New York City newspaper, and monthly columns for two nationwide magazines. In each case I received stacks of letters from readers. The ones below, taken from the newspaper job, are representative:

- "My name is Arlene. I am eighteen years of age, I have a friend who we have become very committed to each other in a friendship way, but he thinks that because we have developed this friendly relationship we ought to have a sexual relationship, too. But I am a bit confused [as] to what to do first before I have a sexual relationship with him. I am not sure if I really love him enough. What I am really afraid of is that once I get involved with him, all he will want to do is just have sex, and not be friends anymore."

- "I am forty-nine years old and my husband is fifty-five years old. My problem is that we have had sex twice in fourteen months. When I bring the matter up, which I have done twice in this period of time, my husband insists that there is nothing wrong, not in any way, physically or mentally. He says that he is more tired lately, or that our twenty-four-year-old daughter may come in . . . Two years ago I had a hysterectomy and we both joked about freedom from contraceptives and how we could look forward to 'really enjoying it.' But, to the contrary, our sex life is almost nil. I miss those intimate moments, preliminary caresses, and the feeling of being desired."

- "I am a divorced woman who, in addition to a ten-year marriage, also has had two other sexually satisfying relationships. So I know I don't have a problem. In the past year, however, I have met several seemingly nice men who just don't make love very nicely and it has created anxieties in me which were never there before. How common are things like this, for example?

"a. Food, which I believe belongs in the kitchen, not on the body. (This man thought I was unimaginative and unenlightened.)

   b. Such a preference for oral and manual sex that I felt like a masturbating machine, not a lover.

   c. The weirdo who refused to ejaculate inside me, even with rubbers 'for the first two or three months until we know each other better.' All he could say was, 'Look, I've always done it this way. It frustrates me as much as it frustrates you, but I prefer not to just yet.'

"I know all about 'consenting adults,' but are these men normal?"

- "God forbids all sex outside marriage—but you encourage it! Which leads to promiscuity and all sorts of trouble. Are you proud of yourself? Someday God will judge you. He will hold you accountable for everything."

There are three things to notice about these letters. First, typically, they don't reveal that the writer herself has a problem, but rather that her partner has a problem (2 and 3), she has a problem only because of her partner (1), or I, the expert, have a problem (4). This pattern also holds true in questions from magazine correspondents, and in questions I've received during radio and TV shows. Partly, people are defensive and don't like to admit something is wrong with them. Partly, people who write are not just asking for help; they also want to make a statement about how badly they're being dealt with and how they deserve some sympathy. Perhaps most important, people believe that unless there is an obvious medical reason for a sexual problem, the reason must be someone's faulty behavior—someone else's, that is. The issue of the relationship of medical to psychological causes of sex problems is complex, as I will discuss.

Second, notice that the question-writers want me to tell them things about their partners. For some reason, these women are unable either to get these men to give them straight answers, to get any answers, or maybe they have not been able to express their questions directly to the men at all. You might not believe how much of sexual problem solving is "merely" a matter of improved communication, but if you have any experience in long relationships, you probably will realize how difficult it is to change communication patterns a couple has established. The marital or sexual therapist works hard at enabling a couple to talk and understand each other better. We'll return to sex therapy and sexual problem solving near the end of this chapter.

Finally, note in these letters that the emphasis is not on performance (sexual "function") or pleasure so much as on psychological gratifications related to sex. The first woman wants to maintain her self-esteem, not to feel betrayed. The second woman misses intimacy, closeness, the feeling of being desired. The third woman wants her expectations met, wants to feel respected. Even the fourth writer wants me to join his or her moral vision of sexuality, a matter apparently of great importance to this person. Far more than is popularly realized, sexual acts are the means to gain or maintain important psychological feelings, and a challenge to one's sexuality often means a threat to these personal rewards. Self-esteem, closeness, feelings of competence and well-being—men also seek these benefits from sex, although their conversation rarely dwells on more than the physical side.

But we are getting ahead of ourselves. Let us begin with a long look at what we actually mean by sexual normality, and why people feel so desperate about it.

What Is Normal?

Why do people write letters like the ones above to media sexuality "experts"? Why have they made radio phone-in shows on sexuality so immensely popular, night after night, coast to coast? The conventional answer is that questions on sexuality have always existed in people's minds, but that only recently has there been the opportunity to discuss such matters openly. Dramatic changes in broadcasting and publishing rules about explicit sexual language and imagery, this argument goes, have opened the door to public discussion of issues that have been on people's minds forever.

Another popular hypothesis to explain the explosion of public sex discussion is that people are nowadays more aware of the importance of sexuality and recognize that sexual ignorance is widespread. They refuse any longer to passively endure sexual problems and sexual dreariness, and feel less embarrassed to admit their concerns. Both the openness and impatience, this argument goes, are signs of liberation, of admission that sex is a great human joy and worth working on.

While I agree that as long as there have been human beings there have been questions about sex, I believe that the current deluge reflects less eternal inquisitiveness than an epidemic of insecurity and worry generated by a new emphasis on sexual functioning as a central, if not *the* central, aspect of a modern relationship. Such emphasis naturally leads to tremendous concern about and need for advice, education, support, and a variety of repair services.

The new importance given to sexuality and other nonmaterial sources of reward in a relationship—emotional intimacy, good communication, support, sharing—is due, I believe, to several large social changes, discussion of which would take us far afield from our primary subject. Briefly, though, these social changes include:

- The purpose of marriage has shifted from economic necessity to companionship, bringing a dramatic change in obligations and expectations.
- There has been a shift in how we measure a person's "success" to include physical vitality along with material achievements.
- Divorce and "serial monogamy" have become increasingly acceptable, placing additional stresses on relationships.
- Changes in social attitudes and improvements in contraception have allowed women to view sexuality as separate from reproduction, and as an avenue for self-expression and pleasure.
- People are relying on personal relationships to provide a sense of worth they lack in the public sphere, due to increased technology, mobility, and bureaucracy.

These social changes provide the backdrop for the increasing emphasis on sexuality as a value in modern life. But most people are not prepared for this new emphasis. Sex, for the most part, is still a private and secret matter. The majority of people have never seen any sex acts but their own. Most people do not talk openly about sexual activity, and until recently there was no formal education available on the subject. Imagine how you would feel if playing gin rummy, and playing it well, were considered a major ingredient of happiness, but no one told you how to play, you never saw anyone else play, and everything you ever read implied that normal and healthy people just somehow "knew" how to play the very first time they tried. It is a strange situation!

Norms for sexual activity, such as they were, were set until recently by religious authorities primarily concerned about moral transgressions. Sexuality was governed by a right/wrong mentality, with homosexuality, masturbation, and promiscuity among the wrongs, and marital coitus, greater male drive, and a complete absence of talk on the subject between parents and children among the rights. Aspects of sexuality such as female orgasm, the idea that a couple might negotiate a mutually acceptable frequency of intercourse, and comfort with one's body were not discussed.

During the late nineteenth and twentieth centuries, as the social changes I mentioned earlier were unfolding, religious authority eroded in many spheres, and the authority of science and science-based medicine grew. Numerous forms of disapproved and deviant behavior (e.g., chronic lying, drinking, disobedience, sexual "wrongs" of various sorts) were seen less as violations of God's law and more the products of diseased, sick minds. The authority for interpreting deviations of behavior shifted almost imperceptibly, category by category, from the domain of sin and evil to that of disorder and abnormality. At least the language shifted. It may be that the public has continued to believe that behavioral transgressions represent moral violations, despite the best efforts of medical experts to alter the basic framework of discussion. The rapid resurgence of the religious right wing in the 1970s and 1980s has renewed the language of sexual "sin" and "deviation" that was common decades ago, before the medical takeover.

Five Meanings of Normal

Well, what *is* sexual normalcy? There are at least five approaches to answering the question.

- *Subjective.* According to this definition, *I* am normal, and so is anyone who is the same as I am. Anyone different is deviant, abnormal. Secretly, most of us use this definition a lot of the time. Publicly, few will admit it.
- *Statistical.* According to this definition, whatever behaviors are most common are normal; less frequent ones are deviant. If you list—along a continuum—numbers of lies, drinks, or sexual partners that people report in the past five years, the most frequent numbers will be those in the middle, with extreme highs and lows at the ends. This is true for practically every behavior we can think to measure. Thus the idea of normalcy as something that is not too high and not too low is based on the statistical viewpoint. In the United States today "too little sex" has joined "too much sex" as cause for worry.

- *Idealistic.* Freud once said, "A normal ego is like normality in general— an ideal fiction." From this point of view, "normal" means "perfect," an ideal to be striven for but rarely obtained. Those who model their behavior on Christ or Gandhi, for example, are taking an ideal for their norm, against which they measure all deviations. (In terms of sexuality, those particular models would probably not be too popular!)
- *Cultural.* Without realizing it, this is probably the standard most of us use most of the time, and it explains why our notions of what's normal don't always agree. According to this definition, we tend to accept as normal whatever behaviors our cultural values endorse, and reject everything else as "abnormal." Other cultures, with other rules, evaluate things differently. Bare breasts in public is normal in one place, abnormal in another; men kissing when they meet on the street is wildly abnormal in one place, completely accepted and expected in another. It is common for deviant behavior to be perceived as dangerous and frightening in a culture that rejects it, though it may be as common and harmless as chicken soup a few tribes or national boundaries away. A few years ago I wrote an article about kissing and was amazed to discover that mouth-to-mouth erotic kissing is not only *not* commonly practiced around the world, it is regarded as truly disgusting by many different cultures.
- *Clinical.* All the above definitions seem arbitrary, seem to depend on individual or group *opinion* as to what's normal rather than on "objective" evidence. The clinical standard, by contrast, uses scientific data about health and illness to make judgments. A particular blood pressure or style of walking or diet or behavior pattern is considered clinically abnormal when research shows that it is related to disease, deterioration, or disability.

It is more difficult, you can see, to use the clinical standard with regard to psychology than to physiology, because it is harder to prove psychological disease, deterioration, or disability. Who's to say, for example, that absence of interest in sex is abnormal according to the clinical definition? What sickness befalls the person who avoids sex? What disability? Clearly, such a person misses a life experience that some people value very highly and most value at least somewhat, but who is to say that avoiding sex is "unhealthy" in the way that avoiding protein is? Avoiding sex seems more akin to avoiding countries where you don't speak the language or avoiding investments in anything riskier than savings accounts.

We need to look at the clinical standards that have been established for sexuality and attempt to determine whether they are in fact based on objective (and presumably universal) standards of health and illness, or on cultural and class opinion dressed up in scientific language.

Dysfunction and Deviation

Current "expert" thinking about sexuality divides problems into the categories of "dysfunction" and "deviation." Let's first consider "dysfunction."

The third edition of the *Diagnostic and Statistical Manual of Mental Disorders* (nicknamed DSM-III) of the American Psychiatric Association states that sexual dysfunction exists wherever there is "inhibition in the appetitive or psychophysiological changes that characterize the complete sexual response cycle." The particular dysfunctions listed in this manual are "inhibited sexual desire" (this is the absence of the appetite for sex indicated by "appetitive"), "inhibited sexual arousal" (difficulties in erection or vaginal lubrication, included in the psychophysiological changes mentioned in the definition), "inhibited male and female orgasm . . . premature ejaculation . . . pain during intercourse, vaginismus" (this last is an involuntary spasm of the vaginal opening which prevents intercourse), and "miscellaneous."

Each of these items is described in several pages, but no scientific evidence is presented showing that people with these patterns are actually ill in some way. Dysfunctions do, however, represent deviations from what is implied to be a universal and biological standard, "the complete sexual response cycle." The DSM-III cites as authority for this standard the historic work of William Masters and Virginia Johnson in the 1950s and 1960s, but, as we shall see, merely citing a scientific authority does not necessarily mean that there is scientific proof showing that certain behaviors are clinically abnormal.

Masters and Johnson, as everyone who has picked up a magazine or watched a television talk show in the last fifteen years knows, are the St. Louis husband-and-wife team of researchers who observed hundreds of couples and individuals engage in sexual activities in their laboratory. They collected thousands of physiological measurements pertaining to arousal, orgasm, and postsexual relaxation. In their bestselling 1966 book *Human Sexual Response,* Masters and Johnson coined the concept "sexual response cycle" to describe the sequence of physiological changes that occur during intercourse and masturbation. Every person they observed did in fact become aroused, did display all sorts of physical changes, and did have orgasms during both masturbation and sexual intercourse in the laboratory.

Since 1966 the media, the helping and medical professions, and the lay public have used the concept of "sexual response cycle" to describe "normal" sexual function, and have considered deviations in arousal, excitement, orgasm, or relaxation in either men or women, old or young, to be evidence of, usually proof-by-definition of, "dysfunction." Codification of these dysfunctions by the DSM-III in 1980 represents the final crowning acceptance.

The trouble with adopting these physiological changes as a *clinical* norm is that there is no evidence that people who deviate are not well, are broken, will get sick if they continue deviating, or suffer any other form of ill health. There is no scientific evidence that arousal without orgasm, absence of sexual desire for short or long periods, or any of the other sexual "dysfunctions" is necessarily a sign of mental or physical ill health.

There are, for example, a multitude of women who choose or are forced by circumstance to renounce sexual activities, but no studies show that they suffer ill health as a result. There have been claims that women who become aroused but don't have orgasm develop a syndrome of pelvic congestion involving fatigue, backache, and persistent abdominal pain, but *no scientific research* supports this claim. It certainly is true that sexual interest and enjoyment can be depressed by physical illness, fatigue, worry, pain, and a wide variety of medications, and it is always important to check out medically a significant and lasting change in desire, function, or enjoyment. However, there are many healthy women for whom sex is simply a negligible priority.

Masters and Johnson cannot even claim that the sexual response cycle is a *statistical* norm, because they didn't survey random inhabitants of St. Louis to see what their sexual function was like. No, they actually *selected* as participants only those volunteers who proved themselves able to display arousal and orgasm during masturbation and intercourse under lab conditions. Many people might think that making such a selection is irrelevant, because in order to measure basic biological processes you need people able to exhibit them. But by excluding from their measurement persons who lack desire, or who have no orgasm as part of their sexual activity, or who have ejaculation without erection, or very rapid ejaculation, or lubrication with intercourse but not with masturbation, etc., the physiology of many people was simply never observed and recorded.

Masters and Johnson did not do research *to find out* what is normal, but rather decided ahead of time what constituted normal sexuality and chose appropriate people to observe. This seems to me to disqualify their work from being used as the definition of normal functioning.

Masters and Johnson's work is not the only source of our current *cultural* norms for sexual function, although it is the main source for clinical experts. In addition, there are numerous surveys which count how often people do what and with whom. Because of the publicity given to these statistical surveys, they have had a significant impact on cultural expectations. Among current American norms for sexual function, we would include the intermittent desire to have sexual activity, the ability of women to have orgasm as easily as men, an expectation that sexual function will be limited by aging processes, the expectation that men will be able to have erections without direct physical stimulation if they merely have sexual thoughts, the positive response of women (but not men) to having their breasts stimulated, and so on. These are the sorts of general beliefs that guide our individual expectations and reactions.

Let's turn now from sexual "dysfunction" to sexual "deviation," a catch-all category of behaviors sometimes known as "perversions," that include activities as widely divergent as having sex with animals, having an ambiguous gender identity (not feeling 100 percent positive that "I am a man" or "I am a woman"), committing rape, or being unhappy as a homosexual. Sexual "deviation" is the aspect of sexual behavior that has most involved religion and the law. The Old Testament singled out certain sexual practices as "abominations." Punishment in many cultures for sexual deviation was and is no less than death, and although indulgers through the ages have been more often ignored than hunted down, people who had "loathsome" sexual habits were the victims of regular outbursts of intolerance.

Many critics of the concept of sexual deviation have pointed out the overlap between permissible sexuality and procreative sexuality. Penis-in-vagina sex, that is, between individuals prepared to conceive and rear children, is the most accepted form of sexual activity in all cultures. Deviations from this standard include the use of contraception, the choice of a same-sex or extramarital partner, a preference for oral sex or masturbation or costumed foreplay or painful pleasure or incest over conventional intercourse. Religious and secular codes, designed to protect society from activities that were thought sinful or harmful, have at one time or another considered all these acts forbidden, and have prescribed sanctions ranging from public humiliation (e.g., wearing a scarlet *A* on your clothes) to castration (found in many codes as punishment for rape or extramarital relations) to torture (common centuries ago when many believed the only reason for deviant sexual acts was possession by devils) to, as I said above, death. Sexual deviance is prominent in legal history for its ability to inspire cruel punishment.

Contemporary legal norms for sexual deviance are in flux, to say the least. Every day, it seems, the newspaper brings fresh reports about one city passing an ordinance that protects gay persons from job or housing discrimination and another city that has repealed such an ordinance. The legal status of explicit sexual materials ("obscenity" or "pornography" or sex education literature and film) has been a matter of intense public controversy since the invention of the printing press, and the debate is far from over. Many states currently have removed their penal-code provisions against sodomy (e.g., oral or anal sex) or restricted their prohibitions to adult-child or coerced acts. Because of the recent epidemic of child sexual abuse cases, most state legislatures are considering expanding and making more specific what sorts of physical acts between adults and children constitute "sexual abuse" and are therefore criminal.

I think the changing condition of our laws reflects the uncertainty in our cultural norms regarding sexual deviance. Studies show that there is a broad continuum of opinion ranging from those who value consensuality as a standard—anything goes as long as both partners consent freely (the "liberal" position)—to those who believe that certain acts are wrong regardless of intention (the "conservative" position).

The clinical community is also divided on these issues; more liberal clinicians consider "abnormal" an *exclusive* reliance on sexual acts other than intercourse or with partners other than appropriate intimates, and more conservative clinicians considering abnormal *any* participation in homosexual or sadomasochistic sexual acts, for example, even if they are consensual. There are additional differences of opinion within the clinical community on the acceptability of nudity in the home, masturbation in adulthood by persons who also have regular partners, and participation in "recreational" sexual activities such as visiting pornographic films, prostitutes, or swapping clubs.

The clinical standard for sexual deviation does not, however, derive from assumed biological health norms, as in the case of sexual dysfunction. Rather, the typical clinician evaluates the normalcy of a person's intentions for his or her particular sexual activities. A normal person presumably doesn't have extreme needs for power or rebellion or humiliation or isolation, and so will internalize cultural values and develop conventional interests. The very persistence of unconventional interests is often seen as evidence of immaturity or mental disorder, or, at the very least, as evidence of poor judgment.

Obviously, these are extremely complicated issues, involving individual rights and preferences versus people's need to sometimes be protected from their own lack of self-understanding. In generalizing too broadly from their years of experience with unhappy people, clinicians may err in concluding that certain behaviors are hallmarks of clinical disturbance. On the other hand, nonprofessionals are often unaware of the complexity of human feeling, and take the sexually unconventional person's cheery insistence that "everything is great . . . no problem . . . everyone should do their thing . . . there's no accounting for taste" at face value.

Granting that the experienced clinician brings a valuable perspective to this issue, when we ask for scientific evidence that unconventional sexual patterns are related to mental or emotional disturbance, there is little available. The only way to decide if a person's sexual habits are related to mental illness would be to find evidence other than the sexual habits themselves that the person is disturbed. Women hospitalized for mental illness, however, are sometimes quite typical sexually and sometimes not; there are no consistent patterns. Studies of large nonclinical samples of homosexual men and women do not show differences from heterosexuals in mental health or emotional disorders. People who come to sex therapy clinics for help with sexual dysfunctions are often depressed and anxious, but this may reflect their distress at being dysfunctional rather than any direct connection between sexual patterns and psychological states.

Basically, there are no good studies to back up the clinician's belief that certain preferences and practices are related to mental problems. This suggests that clinicians tend to rely on cultural or statistical norms in making their judgments, and that their expertise is based less on a scientific medical model and more on adjustment to cultural values, like that of earlier religious authorities. In their desperate quest for authoritative assurances of normality, people are blinded to the validity of the answers they are given.

Why People Care About Being Sexually Normal

We don't want abnormal blood pressure because we don't want to feel ill or shorten our lives. But why do people want to be *sexually* normal? I think there are three interesting reasons.

- First, in spite of the limited evidence for the medical-model notion of sexuality, people believe that sexuality is an aspect of health, somewhat like blood pressure. Abnormal sexual desires, actions, or interests are presumed to be signs of physical or mental illness.

• The second reason goes back to our opening discussion of recent broad social changes. I believe an important reason that people are so concerned about sexual normalcy is that they believe sexuality can make or break a relationship. The threat of all too common divorce and breakup puts a lot of pressure on sexual adequacy.

Is it true that sexual complaints, problems, and dissatisfactions lead to divorce? Marriage counselors and therapists say no, that sexual dissatisfaction is often a *consequence* of marital troubles rather than a cause. Indeed, an often-quoted 1978 study (published in the prestigious *New England Journal of Medicine)* of one hundred self-defined "happy" couples found that there was some sort of arousal or orgasm dysfunction in the *majority* of cases, but that the couples considered themselves happy both sexually and nonsexually nonetheless. This is not to suggest that sexual problems or incompatibilities are trivial, but only that they are rarely the linchpin of relationships. (See Chap. 9.)

• The third, and I believe most important, reason that people stress the importance of sexual normality has to do with the human need for social comparisons. The current use of "normal" is code for socially okay, appropriate, customary, "in the ballpark." The average person uses the word in a kind of cultural-statistical way. It is a basic truth about human beings that how we feel about ourselves depends to an enormous degree on whom we compare ourselves to and how we stack up in that comparison. Leon Festinger, a noted social psychologist, formulated this theory in 1954, but as he is the first to admit, this fundamental aspect of human nature has been observed since the beginning of human society.

Social comparison is the process by which people evaluate their own satisfactions and adequacy not in terms of some unique, internal standard, but by looking to see what others get and do. How else to decide "how we're doing"—in work, marriage, tennis, looks, financial success, or any other social behavior? In the area of sexuality, however, social comparison becomes difficult, because people have no way to know *really* what other people are doing (and how they are doing it). Because we cannot just look at others' sexuality in order to make a comparison with our own, we are forced to rely on information provided through books and other media—television, radio, magazines, movies. The public's need for sexual information—for social comparison purposes—is part of the reason sexual topics are so popular in the media.

But the agenda of magazines or programs such as the "Donahue" TV show is not primarily to educate, but rather to attract readers, viewers, and, not least, advertisers, through providing something *new and different*. How often have you seen "latest findings" splashed across the cover of a magazine or a paperback sex book? I think the public assumes that new information is almost continually emerging and that these media are serving a useful function by informing the public. In fact, guests on "Donahue" and articles in magazines are usually part of new book promotion or merely represent the beliefs of individuals who have some personal experience to reveal ("I was an incest victim") or point of view to expound ("I think women have sexual problems because the media tell them they have"). Most books published are based less on scientific validity or accuracy than on their ability to capitalize on a new trend, such as group marriage, bisexuality, or the "G" spot.

The media have also created a class of sex "experts" who write magazine columns, give radio advice, talk to TV viewers, and produce a seemingly endless number of question-and-answer books for the sexually perplexed. These "experts" never go into enough detail to show that their statements or advice are based on sound scientific evidence. Most media people feel that anyone who has "M.D." or "Ph.D." after his or her name is "qualified" to speak about physiology and medicine, normal and abnormal psychology, couple interaction, parent-child problems, or sexual abuse and assault. The audience often has absolutely no idea where the "expert's" information comes from, and, anyway, people have only the faintest idea of what might qualify as valid research in this area. Anything the "expert" says becomes authoritative. In that sense it is clear how contemporary health professionals have directly replaced religious and moral leaders as sexual authorities in the public's pursuit of sexual "normalcy."

If magazines and nonfiction TV exaggerate the "new" in what they communicate about sexuality, soap operas, nighttime TV dramas, and movies exaggerate the sensational and passionate aspects. If the only knowledge of people's looks were gotten from these media, we would all conclude that absolutely everyone in the world had a perfect body, skin, hair, and teeth except ourselves.

The information about sex from these sources suggests that (1) everyone wants a lot; (2) everyone breaks up relationships, families, and lives to get it; (3) everyone's sexual episodes are full of desperately urgent desire; and (4) the best sex is between strangers, especially strangers forbidden or prevented from consummating their desires. Even though we say that we don't take these images seriously, they shape our ideas of what is true, and we end up suspecting that incredibly passionate sex is an immensely important part of many people's lives, and perhaps, therefore, should be of our own. A perpetual nagging disquiet is born, even though most people do not have these experiences in their own lives.

The shock that followed Kinsey's revelations in 1948 and 1953 about the frequency with which various sexual acts occurred in America upset the public belief that people were following in their private lives the official cultural norms pertaining to sex. Prior to these books, most people got their information for social comparison by comparing themselves to the official moral values. People differed in how much discrepancy from the norms they would tolerate for themselves and others, but at least people believed they knew where they stood. With the publication of Kinsey's surveys, that certainty disappeared, and a new era began in which the public seemed insatiable for information upon which to rebuild an answer to the question "Am I normal?"

Sex Therapy—Who Needs It?

I could stop at the end of the paragraph above, satisfied that I had fulfilled my obligation of writing about sexual normalcy, and not a single one of my sociologist or social psychologist friends would fault me. But as a clinical psychologist, I feel an additional obligation, and that is to deal with the real quandary that many people are in precisely because of the social changes in our society. The fact is, for various reasons, many people are distressed about their sexual habits and sexual function, and would like some guidance on where to turn. Without contradicting anything I've already said about how the wise course is to take any advice from a "sex expert" with a large grain of salt, let me speak to that need.

Masters and Johnson are credited with inventing sex therapy with the publication of their second book, *Human Sexual Inadequacy,* in 1970. Starting from a medical model that specified the "sexual response cycle" as healthy and deviations from it as disordered, Masters and Johnson drew on a variety of psychotherapeutic and educational traditions to develop their model of treatment. In the years since, numerous therapists have modified and elaborated the original design, but basically there are five elements:

- Treatment of involved couples is more effective than treatment of symptomatic individuals alone. Therapists view the *couple* as the patient, regardless of whom the couple identifies as "the" patient. In Masters and Johnson's original words, "there is no such thing as an uninvolved partner in any relationship in which there is some form of sexual inadequacy." This is a subtle notion, borrowed from family therapy, but it really does turn out to be true that both members of a couple contribute in some way to their sexual problems. I wondered, for example, what the contributions of both the second letter writer, whose sex life is "nil," *and* her husband have been to their current situation.

Sometimes a person will have had a problem in several relationships and will come in for help though currently without a partner. In these situations sex therapists use educational and behavioral techniques; these are most effective with problems such as premature ejaculation for men and, for women, never having had an orgasm.

• Psychological treatment (individual or couple) begins only after medical possibilities have been eliminated. This rules out inappropriate treatment and removes the excuse that "the problem really is physical, so all this talking and homework won't have any effect."

• The couple is prohibited from having intercourse during the treatment. This element is essential. It probably serves to shake up a couple's sexual routine and establish the therapist's authority to determine what they do together. It also interrupts the familiar cycle of unproductive blame and remorse. Finally, this radical change removes the goal-oriented pressure to perform.

• Homework exercises are assigned to be practiced at home and discussed during the therapy sessions (which usually occur on a weekly schedule). These exercises, tailored to address limitations and deficits the therapist has perceived in the couple's previous sex habits, serve to shape a new physical relationship. The "homework" is a remarkable and underappreciated element.

Most couples think that sex therapy will merely remove some obstacle or other so they can return to their previous level of functioning. But in fact the therapist has a more subversive agenda, to teach a whole new way of being sexual (usually less intercourse-oriented, less goal-oriented, more sensual, more playful, more experimental). Sometimes this lesson meets with tremendous resistance, and all the persuasive abilities of the therapist are mobilized to convince the couple that the new way will be pleasurable, facilitate a closer bond, and reduce the history of negativism, antagonism, and anxiety that usually exists.

• Discussions between couple and therapist focus on the positive and negative experiences and outcomes for each partner of the homework assignments, until, ultimately, with any luck at all, the couple has reestablished mutually pleasurable sexual activities. These discussions often bring up nonsexual issues, are often emotional and intense, allow the therapist to make useful observations about the couple's style of interaction and problem solving, and help create a greater understanding between the sex partners. That is, of course, unless they drop out, which often happens as one or another of them realizes that there is no simple gimmick that will eliminate the sexual problem without their having to deal with it by *talking* together.

How effective is sex therapy? It depends on what you measure. Most couples recontacted months or years after therapy report that it improved their relationship both sexually and nonsexually. Often, however, the specific problem that was their original reason for therapy has changed little, if at all. What seems to happen is that the homework assignments and weekly discussions with the therapist help couples create a new intimacy. This ultimately becomes more important than the frequency of sexual relations, the hardness of his erection, or the ease of her orgasm.

Why don't the symptoms improve as much as the relationship? At this point no one can answer this question with confidence. It may be that we are often dealing with basic biological differences, perhaps in level of drive or ability to respond to various types of stimulation, that are fairly inflexible. My own opinion is that biology gets much more of the credit and the blame than it warrants, because whenever the source of a problem is unknown, people prefer to pin it on something they don't feel responsible for. But if these differences aren't biological, then they seem to involve long-standing habits of feeling and thinking that are not changed in brief, symptom-oriented therapy, which sex therapy usually is.

Often, what seems like a discrete sexual symptom—such as absence of orgasm or difficulty maintaining an erection—turns out, on further examination, to represent the most visible part of a whole syndrome, for example, an aversion to intimacy or an inability to relax in "performance" situations. Because many people insist on viewing sexual desire and function as an isolated issue, they are unwilling to see that their patterns of response are similar in many situations and must be addressed at a more general level. The current biological emphasis in research and writing about sexuality encourages this mechanistic attitude, as if one could tinker with one's sexuality the way a mechanic can tinker with an uncooperative automobile.

Frequently, when a couple reaches the office of a sex therapist, they are suffering more from the consequences of a sexual problem than from the problem itself. Feelings of anger, rejection, and disappointment (in oneself as well as one's partner) are almost universal. These "secondary" problems are often what brings the couple to the point of crisis, and it takes a skilled and empathic therapist to be able to see both points of view (since each member of the couple almost invariably wants you to see it from only one point of view!) and be of help.

How *do* you find a qualified sex therapist? This question is more difficult than it might seem, because anyone can call him- or herself a sex therapist. Unlike the titles "psychologist," "social worker," or "psychiatrist," the title "sex therapist" is not licensed or regulated in any way. In New York City, for example, many "sex clinics" advertise in local newspapers and magazines. I've talked with several men with erectile problems who answered the ads, and none of them was helped by the "therapists" who talked with them or the "surrogate partners" who had sexual relations with them, though, the men said, the women were "nice" and "tried hard to help."

The best route is through a hospital-based clinic. Call the Department of Psychiatry of your local medical school and ask if there is a sex clinic or service available. If you go to someone not so connected, be sure to ask what their specific training has been in dealing with sexual problems. Not every licensed social worker, psychologist, or psychiatrist has studied sexual behavior or learned the methods of sex therapy, so be sure to ask how much experience they have had. I advocate spending the time and money to have preliminary consultations with two or three therapists, so that you can compare what they say and how they say it. You should choose to work with someone who impresses you with his or her warmth and understanding, as well as comfort with and mastery of the subject of sexual problems.

While I clearly have major reservations about the validity and appropriateness of the medical model for sexuality, I am convinced that unhappy people are better off consulting and working with a qualified member of the helping professions than sitting around waiting for larger social values to change and thereby eliminate their distress.

For example, let's consider again those opening sexual "problems." I think a professional consultation (though perhaps a single session would be sufficient) would be in order for the first letter writer, the teenager who is unsure about having sex with her friend, to give her someone to talk with about her conflicting feelings over beginning her sexual life. However, I don't get the feeling that the third letter writer, the divorced woman who has had several affairs, really does want professional advice. Despite her questions to the expert about normalcy, my impression is that she wants merely to air her discomfort with and annoyance about recent dating experiences. She is emphatic that there's "nothing wrong" with her, and so I can't imagine what therapy would have to offer. Were she to have called rather than written, I probably would have directed her to join a weekly discussion group of the sort to be found in many clinics, religious institutions, or schools, where people can voice their opinions and complaints and hear those of others.

The second letter writer, whose husband seems to have lost interest in sex with her, would seem to be the only candidate from the group for whom sex therapy might be indicated. I would want to hear her husband's perspective on what has been happening over the last two years and learn from each of them separately what their sexual goals together might be. It's impossible to say more than that, such as "what she should do to change him." In my experience what people say when you finally sit them down for a long, personal talk bears little if any resemblance to a one-sentence statement of a complaint first encountered in a letter or over the phone.

Some sexual problems are medical, some are psychological, some are specific to a couple, some are the result of social expectations, some are a combination of all these—and some aren't really sexual problems at all. When we talk about "sexual normalcy," unless we take the time to define just *what kind* of normalcy we're discussing, we usually talk without clearly understanding each other. It is best to maintain a skeptical attitude whenever you hear anyone speak about what's "normal"—those of us "in the business" avoid the word whenever possible!

For a person whose Ph.D. dissertation was called "Gonadal Hormones and Mating Behavior in the Golden Hamster," LEONORE TIEFER has progressed rapidly in her studies of human sexuality. She is now a psychologist in the Department of Urology at Beth Israel Medical Center in New York, clinical associate professor of psychiatry at New York University School of Medicine, and also has a private practice in psychotherapy.

Dr. Tiefer was born and raised in New York, where she had an excellent public school education and two years at City College. She then migrated westward to the University of California at Berkeley, where she took her B.A. and Ph.D. She taught introductory psychology, psychology of women, human sexuality, and other courses at Colorado State University from 1969 to 1977; while there she was a cofounder of the local chapter of NOW, the University's Commission on the Status of Women, and the Faculty Women's Caucus. During a sabbatical year spent working at Bellevue Hospital, she became interested in clinical psychology. From 1977 to 1980 she was administrator of the Center for Human Sexuality, Department of Psychiatry, Downstate Medical Center, New York.

Dr. Tiefer is author of *Human Sexuality: Feelings and Functions* (Harper & Row, 1979) and of many articles on the physiology and politics of sexuality for popular magazines and professional journals. She has served on the New York City Advisory Task Force on Rape since 1977. She is currently writing a book to be titled *Sex Is Not a Natural Act.*

Further Reading

Ehrenreich, Barbara, and English, Deirdre. *For Her Own Good: 150 Years of the Experts' Advice to Women.* Garden City, N.Y.: Anchor Press/Doubleday, 1978.

Federation of Feminist Women's Health Centers. *A New View of a Woman's Body.* New York: Touchstone Books, 1981.

Haddon, Celia. *The Sensuous Lie.* New York: Stein & Day, 1982.

Laws, Judith Long, and Schwartz, Pepper. *Sexual Scripts: The Social Construction of Female Sexuality.* Hinsdale, Ill.: Dryden Press, 1977.

Snitow, Ann; Stansell, Christine; and Thompson, Sharon, eds. *Powers of Desire: The Politics of Sexuality.* New York: Monthly Review Press, 1983.

Vance, Carole S., ed. *Pleasure and Danger: Exploring Female Sexuality.* Boston: Routledge & Kegan Paul, 1984.

4

About Love

CARIN RUBENSTEIN

Love is _____. (Fill in the blank.)

Whatever words you use, they have already been spoken, written, or sung about. Love is just about everyone's favorite topic and probably has been ever since women and men found warm caves. It is the source of human beings' greatest joy and also of their greatest anguish.

What is love, exactly? The popular notion is that if it's true love, *you'll know*. In fact, it may be easier to guess the weather from an aching bunion. "Am I in love?" and "Am I loved?" may be the most commonly asked questions of every confidant, from fortune-tellers to hairdressers to psycho-analysts. The reason is that love is an extremely complex emotion; it can be positive and negative, passionate and passive, liberating and constricting. People talk about many different kinds of love: love of a mother for her child, love between best friends, love of cats, love of God, love of a good pizza. But it is romantic, sexual love that causes the most passion and puzzlement, and that is the kind of love I will be discussing in this chapter. To do so I will call on research about love and interviews with people who are in love, and leave philosophy to the poets.

Considering how much people love love, they also have many misconceptions about it. For example, are the following statements true or false?

• Love always feels good.
• Women are the romantic sex.
• Most married couples fell in love with each other at first sight.
• Most people nowadays believe that sex without love is enjoyable.
• It is impossible to be in love with several people at once.

- Love knows no social boundaries.
- True love is risk-free.
- Passionate love should last a lifetime.

If you said "true" for any of these, you may have seen too many movies or read too many romance novels. They are all false.

The Meaning of Love

The best way researchers have of finding out what people mean when they say they love, or are in love, is to ask them. (So far, there is no physiological test that indicates a state of being in love.) Fifteen years ago psychologist Zick Rubin began asking college students to describe the thoughts and expectations they had for love. According to Rubin, love has four components. First is *needing*—if you are in love, you have a strong need to be near the loved one and expect that it would be hard to get along without that person. Need is reflected in statements such as "If I were lonely, my first thought would be to seek _____ out" and "If I could never be with _____, I'd be miserable." *Caring,* the second part of love, is wanting to help the person: "If _____ were feeling badly, my first duty would be to cheer him/her up." Finally, the love scale also includes mutual *trust* through the exchange of secrets and revealing oneself completely ("I feel that I can confide in _____ about virtually everything") and a willingness to *tolerate* the other's faults ("I would forgive _____ for practically anything"). In contrast, liking consists of feelings of respect and evaluating the friend as mature and responsible.

These definitions may seem a bit obvious, or even naïve, but they are a first step in teasing out the threads of the cloth of love. Another researcher asked people to describe the feelings they had while in love. The most common responses: desire to touch, hold, and be close to the other, wanting to give of oneself, wanting to be tender and gentle, sense of trust and appreciation, warm inner glow, feeling optimistic and cheerful, feelings of harmony and unity with the other, an exclusive belonging with the other, total concentration on the other. Yet another study of romantic love found that college students' descriptions of love included, along with feelings of euphoria, painful feelings of depression, difficulty sleeping, agitation and restlessness, and an inability to concentrate. Thus, love has its highs and lows. Indeed, the intensity of feeling that accompanies love means that it can have a dark side—of anger, jealousy, and even hatred. "The opposite of love is not hate," says psychologist Elaine Hatfield, "but indifference."

The meaning of love seems to vary, depending upon who is asked to define it. While young people like to give wild-eyed, dramatic versions of what love is, older adults tend to be more levelheaded. In a study on love and romance that I conducted for *Psychology Today*, twelve thousand adults (on the average, about thirty-three years old) selected friendship, devotion, and intellectual compatibility as the three most important ingredients of love.

Romance and Falling in Love

Americans are in love with romance. They love to read about it in novels, watch it on television, see it in movies. And they want it more and more in real life. In my *Psychology Today* survey 96 percent of men and women said that romance was important to them, although less than half of the couples agreed that they had had a great deal of romance in the beginning of their love affairs. Most said that walking on a moonlit beach, declaring one's love, and kissing in public were romantic. Others described their own personal definition of romance as being in a special place, being given a fabulous gift, or having good sex in exotic settings—the tub, under the stars, or outside during a storm. Couples who agreed about romance and its importance in their lives were happiest about their love lives, had sex most often, and were least likely to have considered divorce.

Although it might seem that women are more romantic than men (they certainly consume romance novels and soap operas at a voracious rate), most research during the past twenty years or so has found that men are actually more romantic than women. For all their grousing about "irrational women in love," men fall in love more readily than women and they are more likely to fall into *unrequited* love—to have passions and crushes, to decide they have found the "woman of their dreams." In studies of dating couples men say they recognize feelings of love sooner than the women do. Until recently, men could afford to be more romantic than women; after all, they aren't dependent on a man for a standard of living and they don't get pregnant if they let their romantic passions lead them to bed. Now that women can earn their own livings and use birth control, they too are succumbing to the luxury of being romantic.

Once women do fall in love, however, they seem to have more emotional symptoms than men—or perhaps they are just more willing to talk about their emotions. They describe feelings of "floating on a cloud," "wanting to run, jump, or scream," having "trouble concentrating," feeling "giddy and carefree," and higher levels of euphoria than men report.

Love at First Sight

The belief in the ability to fall in love at first sight is part of American romanticism. Very often people confuse lust for love. A young man in my survey, though admitting that his first-sight love was based on sexual electricity, pined for a woman he'd met only twice. "My heart yearned to be with her," he said, "and I felt like crying all the time." But he also confessed that had he ever consummated his passion, it would have diminished considerably.

A more mature couple, however, fell in love at first sight and eventually married. "We met at a crowded dinner party," Cindy reports. "I knew he was a good man from mutual friends, but I wasn't especially interested in meeting him. But when he walked into the room, he just looked, well, *darling.* Everything about him seemed great. He seemed too wonderful for merely me, so I didn't set out to charm him. I didn't flirt, I barely spoke to him. I assumed he'd have no interest in a mere mortal like me. I didn't know what he thought of me, if anything at all."

Two months later Cindy saw Russell again at a friend's house. "It was like bringing a starving person to a banquet and telling her the food was off limits," she recalls. "I could see him, but I couldn't touch. I was so nervous that night I was trembling. And I noticed that when he held his coffee cup, his hand was shaking. We both went to the bathroom that night about nineteen times. The minute we were alone, we fell into each other's arms." Cindy says that this wasn't like her, because she usually had to know someone for a while before falling in love. "But this was unusual," she says. "It was just . . . *boinnng!* And after the *boinnng* part we were still in love."

As Russell tells it, he simply "became captivated" that first night. "She was funny, perceptive, witty, bright, and charming. It was love at first sight. But not merely the physical look, because it's silly to fall in love with a woman just because she is beautiful. I fell in love at the whole taking-in of her, realizing that the package was not one-dimensional. It was her sweetness, warmth, vulnerability, all the qualities that entrance. And we just went on from there."

There have always been scientific theories to account for the love-at-first-sight phenomenon. At the turn of the century some believed that love was a chemical or electrical reaction. One theory held that people fell in love because of similar chemical elements in their bodies. A popular French notion of the time was that each person carries in his or her unconscious a special "love type." When the type is matched by finding someone who has the right look, smell, and sound, love blooms at once. More recently, some neurochemists have proposed that preprogrammed nerve circuits control all emotions, including love. These circuits are supposedly programmed by early associations with love; later in life, strangers might fall in love by triggering each other's circuits. And on a more mystical level, psychoanalyst Carl Jung argued that every man is born with an *anima,* or the unconscious representation of his female side. Every woman has her *animus,* the masculine side. When a man meets a woman who resembles his archetype, or vice versa, the result, said Jung, is instant love. All of these theories are very lively and entertaining, but unfortunately there is no evidence for them at all.

What few studies there are, though, indicate that love at first sight is more common in the movies than it is in real life. A 1940s study of engaged couples showed that only 8 percent of the men and 5 percent of the women said they felt an attraction for their partner within the first day of meeting. It isn't much different today. Most married couples report having known each other for several months to several years before they fell in love.

Sex and Love

Woody Allen once distinguished sex from love by saying that "sex alleviates tension and love causes it." The idea that adults could rid themselves of tension *without* being in love was encouraged by the sexual revolution of the 1960s. But that ideology has become less popular during the past several years—perhaps because of the rise of romanticism as well as a new concern about sexually transmitted diseases. By the early 1980s more and more people were beginning to agree that sex without love was unsatisfying. In 1969, for example, less than a third of *Psychology Today* readers—17 percent of the men and 29 percent of the women—said that sex without love was either unenjoyable or unacceptable. By 1983, among a similar group of *Psychology Today* readers, one third of the men and almost half of the women felt that way. Without love, sex holds little appeal to a growing number of people.

Still, men are more able than women to make love without being in love. Among young people men rate sex as more important than love as a goal of dating, and women say that love is more important than sex. In *American Couples,* a nationwide study that included thirty-six hundred married couples, sociologists Philip Blumstein and Pepper Schwartz found that more husbands than wives approved of sex without love (52 percent versus 37 percent). Most men, they reported with academic understatement, "maintain the capacity to distinguish love from lust." As one husband told them: "It's always been my belief that sex and love are two different things. For a man, sex is a physical thing and it can be as impersonal and as casual as shaking somebody's hand or eating a sandwich."

As of today it hasn't occurred to many researchers to investigate the comparable condition—the people who have love without sex. In America, at least, such people seem to be rare.

Unrequited Love

Love unreturned can be one of the most heartrending experiences. In *Love and Limerance* psychologist Dorothy Tennov coined the word "limerance" to define the first stage of passionate love, when the lover is unsure if the love is returned. Limerance consists of obsessive thoughts of the loved one and terrible (often frustrated) longing for reciprocation. Martin, a married business executive, fell passionately in limerance with Emily, who was twenty-five years younger. "I don't direct this thing, this attraction, to Emily," he said. "I try desperately to argue with it, to limit its influence, to channel it, to deny it, to enjoy it and, yes, dammit, to make her respond! Even though I know that Emily and I have absolutely no chance of making a life together, the thought of her is an obsession."

Limerance also means complete dependence on the other's actions for one's emotional state. "Her look when we pass each other in the hallway," Martin admitted, "can send me into an ecstasy of belief that she feels as I do." Another man agonized over a woman with whom he had spoken only a few times. "Our eyes seemed to meet and linger together just a fraction of a second longer than they should," he told Tennov. "I puzzled over it. Was it really happening? And if so, which of us was the initiator?"

Perhaps the most important hallmark of limerance is a fear of rejection, characterized by a sensation of an aching in the heart when uncertain of the lover's feelings. The people Tennov interviewed spoke of their terror in talking to or even writing to the one they loved, in case they would be rejected. Almost all of them expressed a depth and intensity of emotion that was overwhelming and uncontrollable. For example, a woman named Joan told Tennov that "when I was intensely in love with Barry, I was intensely in love. When he seemed rejecting, I was still intensely in love, only miserable beyond words. Later," she added, "when my feelings were less intense, I could still flip-flop depending on how I perceived his feelings for me."

In the *Psychology Today* love survey about 4 percent of the women and men tended to be "love-prone": that is, they had fallen in love often (usually unrequited), they had fallen in love at first sight, and they had been in love with several people at once. Many of these people described themselves as "very susceptible" to falling in love, and indeed, they were most likely to believe that love is ephemeral. Their "first loves" occurred much earlier than those of most people—on the average, at about the age of fourteen (compared to nineteen for others). But these pursuers of love often found their quarry eluding them. Many had had extramarital affairs and believed that their chance of divorce was high, and they were the least happy in love.

One of the most love-prone people I interviewed was an eighty-six-year-old California man, who remembered falling in love for the first time (naturally, "at first sight") with a girl he knew for only two weeks, over seventy years ago. "I'll never forget that mountain girl," he said. All of the other times he had been in love (more than ten) it had been at first sight. "I can give you names and addresses," he told me. "It's all quite delightful to recall." Another love-prone man, only twenty-eight years old, had been in love "131 times—all of them serious emotional relationships." He had kept a record of his love life from the age of six, when he first fell in love. For this man "romance is the motivating force of my life."

People who are prone to falling in love may be entranced with the pursuit but not the capture. They love the initial passion but can't abide the subsequent comfortable companionship. Another possible explanation is that such people may be hungry for love because they lacked it in childhood. In fact, some of the love-prone people I interviewed told stories of disrupted or traumatic childhoods filled with rejection. One had lived with five different families; another was an adopted and battered child. Growing up without enough love and affection may impel some people to spend a lifetime trying to capture what they missed.

Some women seem especially vulnerable to falling into unrequited love. Psychoanalysts often assert that such women are masochists. But the real problem may be that these women mistake good sex for true love. They need to believe that they are in love to legitimize a sexual relationship—an erotic rationale that men rarely need to make.

Barbara, an attractive woman in her forties, had been married to Dennis for almost fifteen years. He was kind and affectionate, but, to her, boring and sexless. She met a man with whom she had a passionate affair that included fantastic sex. With a great deal of guilt and pain, she divorced her husband, took her three children, and began a life on her own, assuming that her lover would marry her. He did not marry her—and never had any intention of doing so. Barbara's train of thought had been: "I am having terrific sex with another man, so I must be in love. Therefore, I don't love my husband anymore. Therefore, the only right thing is to get a divorce." In other cultures, where it is commonly (if not publicly) accepted that a wife or husband will have extramarital sexual affairs, her marriage would not have been destroyed by what she now sees as flawed logic.

Single women who fall in love with married men or with men who refuse to make a commitment are also often accused of being masochistic and of having low self-esteem. Yet such relationships do have benefits, such as the pleasure of the lover's company, regular sex, and attention. For some women, the guarantee of a part-time lover is better than a life with no lover at all. Demographically, this is not an unrealistic issue. Women have always tended to pair off with men who are slightly older, richer, and more educated than they. The longer women wait, and the more success and education they achieve, the fewer traditionally appropriate men are available. The result, according to sociologist Jessie Bernard, is that women who are the "cream-of-the-crop" are left with men who are the "bottom-of-the-barrel." When the demand for available men exceeds the supply, women must make do with what is on hand. These relationships should be considered "self-defeating" only if a woman has a *choice* between available and unavailable men who are equally attractive, and persistently chooses those who are unavailable. But many women of the baby-boom generation and most older women do not have this choice.

Fear of Love

A minority of people (no one can say for sure how many) have never been in love and seem to be afraid of it. They do not, however, fear love itself, but all that love requires. Love involves a great many emotional risks that some people—especially men—are afraid to take. Psychologist Elaine Hatfield has identified a few of what she calls the "dangers of intimacy." These include:

- *The fear of exposure.* Lovers tend to share profound secrets that include information about their weaknesses and idiosyncracies. Some people are afraid of revealing their secrets for fear of shame and embarrassment about their bad qualities. A man who finally shared some of his feelings with his lover learned this lesson when he heard his girlfriend respond that she was disappointed in his lack of "manliness." Likewise, a woman who told her boyfriend that she was queasy about certain sexual activities was afraid that she would lose her image as a sex bomb.

- *The fear of abandonment.* Some people worry that if their lovers know them too well, they will be hated and therefore spurned. Better to present a good face and keep one's lover than reveal the truth and risk his or her loss. A beautiful, apparently self-confident Swedish student of Hatfield's was attractive to many men—until, says Hatfield, she revealed her insecurity to them. They were more interested in her image as a perfect woman than in her reality as a human one.

- *The fear of angry retaliation.* Some people fear that their lovers will use the revelations of intimacy to damage their reputations, so trust is therefore dangerous. A man who was having a love affair with a colleague revealed to her that he was sometimes unsure of himself when involved in important business negotiations. She happened to mention it to a friend, who told someone else, and the story eventually got back to the man's boss. He was convinced that his lover had spread the story so that she would be promoted before he was.

- *The fear of loss of control* is one to which men are especially sensitive. A real man, so the social rules go, hides his feelings and controls his thoughts. Many people believe that men should be and *are* effective doers who are in control, whereas women should be (and are) expressive, "overemotional," and occasionally helpless (see Chap. 7). This stereotype puts many men (and some women) in a double bind: They value being in control above all else, but they are constantly told that the ability to love depends on the ability to "let go."

- *The fear of losing one's individuality,* or being engulfed and over-

whelmed by the lover. A newlywed began to have this feeling only
several months after his marriage to the woman he had thought he
would love forever. "I'm afraid that the old 'me' is disappearing," he
said. "I can't tell where, or if, 'we' stop and I begin. All of a sudden,
we're this new thing, a couple, and I'm finding it harder and harder to
think of myself as just me alone. That scares me."

All of these fears are realistic. In theory, intimacy is the opposite of
independence, a quality that is prized by most Americans. The struggle
between depending on one special person and being answerable to no one is
a difficult one. It is also something that almost everyone who falls in love
must deal with, either consciously or not. Only infants have absolutely no
qualms about total, trusting love, and even they learn to value independence
in a few years. The solution to the dilemma, then, is not to choose either
independence or intimacy, but to accept a compromise that includes them
both.

Who Falls in Love with Whom?

Statistically speaking, the man you are most likely to fall in love with is the
boy next door. Research shows that people tend to love (and marry) those
who live nearby, hold similar attitudes, and come from comparable social,
religious, and economic backgrounds.

A classic 1931 study of five thousand Philadelphia marriages showed that
one out of four couples lived within two blocks of each other at the time of
their application for a marriage license, and another third lived within five
blocks. Many dating and mating habits have changed during the past five
decades, but recent studies also find similar patterns throughout the country. It's simply easier to love someone nearby than someone far away.

Another rule of love is homogamy, which means that people who have
much in common tend to be attracted to each other. No one knows, however, which comes first—whether people are similar and then fall in love, or
whether people who are in love become similar by wanting to agree about
important interests and values. We know that people tend to overestimate
how much the people they like share their attitudes. Studies of husbands
and wives, for example, show that spouses assume that their attitudes are
more similar than they really are: He may love Clint Eastwood movies and
she may hate them, but ask them separately and they will each tell you they

agree almost totally about Clint Eastwood movies. Lovers probably emphasize their similarities and avoid their disagreements (at least in the beginning). In any case, love tends to make people seem to have a lot in common.

Lovers tend to love people from similar religious and social backgrounds, who have similar levels of intelligence and education. And, notwithstanding fairy tales like *Love Story* (in which the poor Italian girl falls in love with the wealthy aristocrat), people tend to fall in love with those in or near their own social class. Finally, lovers tend to hold similar values, everything from views on smoking and drinking to the importance of economic security and premarital sex.

Although we might expect that people also fall in love with those with similar personality or temperament, this does not seem to be the case. Like marries like, but opposite personalities sometimes attract. Lovers tend to be more unlike than alike when it comes to personal traits, which psychologists refer to as "complementary needs in mate selection." People tend to be attracted to those who have qualities that they lack, whose emotional style completes rather than competes with their own. Thus, an outgoing, sociable woman may fall in love with an introspective, shy man; an excitable, energetic man may be attracted to a calm, sedate woman. (Then, of course, they set about trying to change the lover into a carbon copy of themselves.)

Unromantic as it may seem, the fact is that women and men embark upon love in a social marketplace. They enter it equipped with looks, personality, professional status, and potential earning ability. When they fall in love, they expect a fair value for what they have to offer. An attractive woman, for example, tends to fall in love with either an equally attractive man *or* one with relatively high earning ability. Psychologist Bernard Murstein describes this as the process of seeking out the "fairest exchange of interpersonal assets and liabilities." Several psychologists tested this theory by setting up random computer dates for 752 college students whose physical attractiveness had been previously rated by other students. The students also rated their own popularity and expectations of their dates. It turned out that the physically attractive students expected their dates to be good-looking, personable, and considerate. The unattractive students had much lower expectations for their dates.

Why Women Are Better at Love

Some experts believe that women are better at love than men. Anthropologist Ashley Montagu, for example, wrote that women's natural superiority is "precisely in their capacity to love." But what does that mean? Men and women often differ, according to research, in at least three realms of expressing love: intimacy, caretaking, and stroking.

Women are better than men at intimacy, if intimacy is defined as talking about and revealing feelings, being able to confide in the other person about anything. Most family research shows that women tend to be the intimacy experts—they give intimacy and men receive it. No one knows if this is because society encourages women to behave this way, or because they have inherited a maternal knack for it. But perhaps it is only that women and men define intimacy differently. Many men regard "intimacy" in terms of action—*doing* things rather than *talking* about them. To a wife "love" means talking about love. To her husband it means earning a living, taking out the garbage, and simply being there. One woman I know, having never heard her husband say those "three magic words," finally asked him if he loved her. "I vote with my feet," he said. "If I didn't love you, I wouldn't be here."

In studies of friendship, more men report that they had recently done something for a friend; more women say that they had had an intimate talk with a friend (see Chap. 6). Women disclose more than men to their friends and are more likely than men to say that they have an intimate, same-sex confidant. And wives tend to disclose more than husbands do. During rough times, for instance, wives are more likely to tell their husbands that they feel tense and to try to explain their feelings. (Women are generally more likely than men to seek emotional support from others whenever they feel stressed or troubled.) When they do reveal themselves, men tend to talk about their political views and their strengths; women often talk about their feelings about other people and their fears.

Women also outdo men in family caretaking. In 83 percent of all American homes, women make the medical and health care decisions. They are responsible for the care of children, husbands, parents, and friends. They run their households, shop and cook meals, nurture everyone through flu and measles, arrange family dinners, and make sure that relatives receive birthday cards on the right dates.

Finally, women are better than men at what some sociologists call "stroking." This is nonphysical support, such as soothing wounded feelings, providing moral support and praise, giving encouragement when it is needed.

Unfortunately, women stroke a lot more often than they are stroked in return.

Perhaps because they are giving so much more than they are getting, women tend to be less satisfied with love and with marriage than men are. In surveys men of all ages say that they are happier in love than women are; more husbands than wives say that they would marry the same spouse if they could do it again, and fewer believe that they will ever be divorced. In a national survey conducted by researchers at the University of Michigan, more wives than husbands said that they wished their spouse talked more about thoughts and feelings, and more wives felt resentment and irritation with husbands than the other way around. "In marriage," the researchers concluded, "women talk and want verbal responsiveness of the kind they have had with other women, but their men are often silent partners, unable to respond in kind."

Staying in Love

Whatever it is that causes a woman and a man to fall in love with each other —chemistry, biology, similarity, economics, or personality—the longevity of their love will depend on their ability to let love mature, to express their love effectively, and to take care of each other.

It is hard to imagine Romeo and Juliet as a middle-aged married couple, quarreling about their children and criticizing each other's waistline. Theirs was an intensely passionate first love, one that lasted for a brief moment at a tender age. Passionate love, no matter when it occurs, is almost always characterized by an uncontrollable level of arousal. It is most likely to flourish if there are obstacles to its formation and consummation. If Romeo's and Juliet's parents had cheerfully consented to the marriage, the love affair would undoubtedly have withered within several months. Indeed, a study of the "Romeo-and-Juliet effect" showed that parental interference actually inspires rather than discourages their children's love affairs.

Theorists have contrasted passionate love with pragmatic love, which is based on trust and tolerance and is built up over a period of years. The partners have more control over their feelings than do those in passionate love and they develop a sense of mutual caring and dependence over time. By its very nature passionate love tends to be short-lived; to survive, it must be transformed to pragmatic love. The pounding heart and sweaty hands that used to accompany every meeting eventually disappear, as do incessant thoughts of the loved one and the sexual electricity that seemed to crackle in the air. When these symptoms of heightened physiological arousal disappear, a friendly sense of trust and companionship often takes their place. This change does not mean that love is dead, simply that it has matured. It would be difficult for a couple to decide about finances if their hearts were always pounding, and strenuous for them to jump into bed every time they tried to wash the dishes.

Whether passionate or pragmatic, successful long-term lovers learn to express their love in ways that their partner understands. Unfortunately, many people have different styles of love and different ways of expressing that love. Marriage counselors Marcia Lasswell and Norman Lobsenz offer the example of a husband and wife who wanted to revive a marriage that was "spiraling downward into non-caring" (see Chap. 9). The therapist told them to set aside a day when each spouse would do things to please the other. On the wife's day to care for her husband, she brought him breakfast in bed, ran him a hot bath, bought him a new book, and gave him tickets to an afternoon concert. He was not pleased; in fact, he hated everything about the plan. But, quite by accident, he realized that she was doing exactly what *she* would have wanted *him* to do for *her.*

Misunderstandings of how love "should" be expressed are as common as ragweed, and twice as irritating. As Lasswell and Lobsenz observe, every lover sees the problem this way:

> I, like every man and woman, want to be loved. But, like every man and woman, I have my own idea, grounded in my personality and temperament and experience, of what loving and being loved means. Moreover, locked in the prison of my own ways of thinking and feeling, I assume that my definition of love is the only correct one. As a result, I want and expect to be loved in the same way that I love others, with the same responses that I interpret as the evidence of lovingness . . . But I am *not* loved that way. Instead, I am loved the way my *partner* thinks and feels about love, the way he or she understands and expresses it. In my own distress, I do not recognize that my partner is experiencing the same incongruity in reverse. Puzzled, hurt, unable to communicate our confusion to each other, we both unreasonably feel unloved.

Lasswell and Lobsenz propose that there are six styles of loving that guide people's actions when they are in love:

• Those who have the *Best Friends* style regard love as close association, a sharing of interests that develops slowly over time. People who are predominantly best-friend lovers agree that "I did not realize that I was in love until I actually had been for some time" and "the best kind of love grows out of a long friendship."

- Those who view love as a challenge or contest engage in the *Game Playing* style of love. They agree that "sometimes I get so excited about being in love that I can't sleep" and "when my lover doesn't pay attention to me I feel sick all over."
- The *Logical* love style is just that. People with a practical view of love tend to agree, for example, that "it makes good sense to plan your life carefully before you choose a lover" and "I wouldn't date anyone that I wouldn't want to fall in love with."
- *Possessive* lovers tend to be jealous and excitable. They agree that "I can get over love affairs pretty easily and quickly" and "part of the fun of being in love is testing one's skill at keeping it going and getting what one wants from it at the same time."
- The *Romantic* style is characteristic of those who are in love with love, who agree that "we kissed each other soon after we met because we both wanted to" and "at the first touch of his/her hand I knew that love was a real possibility."
- *Unselfish* love is self-sacrificing and unconditional caring. Those who love in this style agree that "I would rather suffer myself than let my love suffer" and "I am usually willing to sacrifice my own wishes to let my lover achieve his/hers."

Lasswell and Lobsenz say that although most people have a combination of love styles, more women than men tend to love in the Best Friends, Logical, and Possessive styles, whereas more men are likely to be Game Players or Romantics. Just as couples must learn to adapt to differences in styles of eating and sleeping, so should they be tolerant of different styles of loving as well.

In order to love, it seems, people need first to learn to accept themselves and their lovers as is, without constant nagging and tugging to change them into someone else. "Most people have the idea," Dr. Hatfield writes, "that everyone is entitled to a perfect partner, or at least one a little bit better than the one available." This false idea is ultimately self-defeating. No one is perfect, and people can't be molded into ideal types according to a lover's specifications.

Second, people need to learn to express their ideas and feelings openly. "To be intimate, people have to push toward a more honest, graceful, complete, and patient communication," Dr. Hatfield says, "to understand that a person's ideas and feelings are necessarily complex, with many nuances, shadings, and inconsistencies." She concludes, "In love, there is time to clear things up."

Ultimately, falling in love and staying there are top priorities for most of us. But if success in love were a simple matter, we would not need pop experts advising us on how to love, vicarious love experiences such as soap operas and romance novels, or such a thriving marriage-counseling business. The love industry reflects an ongoing frustration with and preoccupation about what it takes to sustain love over a lifetime.

The key to having a lasting, happy marriage may have little to do with love. In a recent study of couples who had been married for at least fifteen years, Robert Lauer found that most spouses believed that their marriages had lasted because they viewed their partners as a best friend and liked them "as a person." Love comes and goes even in good marriages, but liking and companionship are constant. In *Married People: Staying Together in the Age of Divorce*, Francine Klagsbrun notes that trust may be more important than love because it "sums up much of the dynamic of a marriage, the back-and-forth interaction from which everything else grows."

Love has been so overpublicized, overromanticized, and overemphasized in American society that many couples are unsure about what love is and if they are still in it. Instead of spending a lifetime looking for the fireworks of passionate love, people might do better to find someone to trust, respect, and depend upon. If they are lucky, they might then find the steady flame of an abiding love.

CARIN RUBENSTEIN holds a Ph.D. in social psychology from New York University and is coauthor with Phillip Shaver of *In Search of Intimacy* (Delacorte Press, 1982), a book about loneliness in America. She has written for *Family Circle, Glamour, Discover, Vogue, Self,* and is a former senior editor of *Psychology Today.* Dr. Rubenstein grew up in Levittown, Pennsylvania, where she fell in love at first sight with Paul McCartney, of the Beatles. A decade later, she fell in love with and eventually married David Glickhouse. She and her husband have a baby daughter, Rachel.

Further Reading

Bernard, Jessie. *The Future of Marriage.* New York, Bantam Books, 1972.

Blumstein, Philip, and Schwartz, Pepper. *American Couples: Money, Work, Sex.* New York: Morrow, 1983.

Guttentag, Marcia, and Secord, Paul. *Too Many Women?* Beverly Hills, Calif.: Sage Publications, 1983.

Hunt, Morton. *The Natural History of Love.* New York: Minerva Press, 1967.

Klagsbrun, Francine. *Married People: Staying Together in the Age of Divorce.* New York: Bantam Books, 1985.

Lasswell, Marcia, and Lobsenz, Norman. *Styles of Loving: Why You Love the Way You Do.* Garden City, N.Y.: Doubleday, 1980.

Murstein, Bernard. *Love, Sex, and Marriage Through the Ages.* New York: Springer, 1974.

Peele, Stanton, and Brodsky, Archie. *Love and Addiction.* New York: Taplinger, 1975.

Rubenstein, Carin, and Shaver, Phillip. *In Search of Intimacy.* New York: Delacorte Press, 1982.

Rubin, Zick. *Liking and Loving.* New York: Holt, Rinehart & Winston, 1973.

Tennov, Dorothy. *Love and Limerance: The Experience of Being in Love.* New York: Stein & Day, 1981.

5

Family and Career: Why Women Can "Have It All"

CYNTHIA FUCHS EPSTEIN

"How to avoid stress" is a topic of primary concern to men and women alike today. Newspapers and magazines are filled with articles on the dangers of stress and how to recognize it and avoid it. Stress is often posed as a uniquely modern ailment, resulting in heart disease, cancer, and a host of other ills, touched off by today's society, with its demands for aggressive and single-minded behavior. Current wisdom tells us that the stress of modern life affects men and women somewhat differently, targeting hard-driving men on the rise and women who are beset by the many demands caused by their multiple jobs as mothers, wives, and homemakers, coupled with their new roles as workers in the labor force.

Advice to men and women also differs. Men are told to relax while climbing the career ladder, but it is suggested that women consider getting off the ladder because the costs to their mental and physical health may be too high.

How reasonable are these recommendations and how sound are the assumptions on which they are based? Is stress a function of modern living? Is it always bad for your health? Is working hard or aspiring hard the root of the trouble? Were women able to avoid the consequences of stress before they entered the marketplace recently in such numbers?

Three Myths of Work Stress and Role Strain

Each season there seem to be new theories attempting to explain what makes people tick, and many of us try them on to see whether they hold the answers to the questions that perplex us about our own behavior and that of our friends. Last year women were warned that the trouble with their relationships may be due to their men falling prey to *The Peter Pan Syndrome;* or if their careers have not been proceeding on target and they are not as enthusiastic as they once were about them, perhaps it's because they have a *Cinderella Complex.* Theories from social science often provide the new "truths" reported in the popular press, and these are enthusiastically received by many people as a new way to explain their situations in life. A few years ago the bestseller *Passages* caused people to think that their lives are characterized by life cycle phases. A year or two later middle-aged men found comfort in explaining depression or career plateaus as the predictable outcome of "mid-life crisis," and recently a physician has maintained that *all* men go through this *Crisis Time.* Still later people learned to explain success as due to the proper role models or adoption by a "mentor." Of course, all of these theories have their validity in certain circumstances. But media hype too often parlays these yet-to-be-proven theories into the final word.

More recently, a book warns women against having *The Superwoman Syndrome*—the dangers of trying to balance too many roles. Today "role strain," another concept from social science, has come to identify a supposedly major source of stress in modern life. This idea rests on three assumptions:

• *Women suffer role strain; men don't.* In the popular view "role strain" has been used to identify distress stemming from women's taking on work roles in addition to their homemaker roles. Men are usually not regarded as having role strain because their roles as husband, father, and son are seen as complementary to their roles as workers; whereas women's roles as wife, mother, and daughter are seen as conflicting with their roles as workers. Thus, role strain has come to mean not only having many or too many roles, but conflicting ones.

• *Career women suffer role strain; traditional women don't.* Today more concern is directed to women who are competing for the *good* jobs that society has to offer. We hear terrible warnings about the mental health of women who do work that leads to power, authority, and money, and only faint murmurings about the conditions of work that are *actually* likely to produce stress—routine, low-paying, traditional "women's work." Yet medical research has established that the women who are most at risk from hypertension and heart disease are those who work in jobs where decision making is out of their hands, where they feel they get no support from their employers, where they have few opportunities for advancement.

• *Role strain is a new phenomenon, a problem suffered by modern "superwomen."* Many people assume today that only in recent history have women taken on so many conflicting roles and suffered sickness, unhappiness, or divorce as a result. Women who combine families and careers—and who manage both well—are considered "superwomen"; ordinary women are believed to be unable to handle such a medley of tasks and responsibilities. But people who use the term "superwomen" have a short-range view of history, and they close their eyes to the fact that tens of millions of working mothers are doing just fine combining work and family.

In the course of my research as a sociologist over the past two decades, I encountered hundreds of women who balance very demanding careers with family life as wives and mothers. Moreover, this ability turns out to be as old as motherhood. A backward glance at family history can provide an example of women's skills at multiple roles in the past. Let me first introduce you to the life and times of my Grandma Davis, so that you may reflect on the experiences of your forebears.

Grandma Davis (we never thought to ask what her first name was) was my great-grandmother. When I was a child and conscious of her as a person, she was already in her eighties. White hair in a bun, she was the picture-book old lady I visited each week together with my grandmother and mother. They would sip coffee (my grandmother would drink hers with a lump of sugar between her teeth, Rumanian style) and we shared the cookies she baked. My grandmother was her eldest child, and Grandma Davis lived with her youngest child, my great-aunt Daisy, a lively and chic red-haired woman just a few years older than my mother. Aunt Daisy seemed exotic to me. I learned from my mother that she was a "business-woman," something that sounded a little disreputable, but she seemed normal in other respects, especially as the mother of two sons (one of whom was the object of my first infatuation).

It wasn't until ten years ago at a family reunion that I had a chance to ask seventy-five-year-old Aunt Daisy (still lively, still chic, and still working) about her youth, and thus also find out about the history of Grandma Davis. It seems that Aunt Daisy's first job was at four years of age. Her father and mother owned a mom-and-pop dry goods store on the Lower East Side of

New York and scraped to make ends meet to support their seven children. Grandpa Davis died prematurely, and thus it fell to Grandma Davis to run the store by herself as well as raise her young children. Aunt Daisy, with her red Shirley Temple curls, sat on the newspaper stand by the door of the store singing popular songs to attract customers, and the other children ran errands after school. It wasn't unusual for women in the neighborhood to run or help run a family business and also take care of their numerous children. Life was tough, families were often fragmented; sometimes husbands and wives were separated by an ocean while one worked to provide passage from the old country for the other. Nobody thought hard work was unusual or regarded these women as superhuman. People were nervous about being able to pay the rent (it took its toll in heart trouble and allergies), or nervous about failed love affairs; but juggling tasks was not regarded as a source of trouble. In fact, the neighborhood was filled with men and women who worked during the day, went to school some nights and union meetings other nights, and ministered to the neighbors in between. Everybody, including the children, had multiple roles, and most of them didn't turn out badly. Of Grandma Davis's brood, Aunt Daisy ran a business and a family like her mom; Uncle Morty became a wealthy accountant whose limousine, parked at our door at festive holidays, caused the neighbors to gape; Uncle Murray had some mysterious job—at the racetrack, I learned later; Uncles Sam and Harry struggled in various small businesses; and my grandmother became a conventional housewife.

The housewife role assumed by my grandmother and mother was the pattern of life that girls of my generation thought was normal. Even then we were aware that taking care of the house and children was only one set of duties a grown woman was expected to perform in our community. My mother never regarded herself as having much energy, but a day didn't go by when she wasn't going to a meeting of the PTA, helping raise money for war relief or for hospitals through several organizations she belonged to, editing a newsletter, writing book reviews, and being a Cub Scout den mother. For my mother stress didn't come from these worthy and interesting tasks, but from her lack of self-confidence, probably caused by her feeling that she was not a truly productive person. (Social science research today confirms this hunch I had about my mother.)

With this perspective today's woman's assumption of many roles in and of itself has not seemed as new nor as stress-producing as modern Cassandras of both sexes would have us believe. In fact, some people seem to thrive on it. What then is really going on?

What Has Changed—and What Has Not

Probably at no time in history have women had the chance to take on so many demanding and disparate tasks—to try their hand at what some people somewhat disparagingly define as "having it all." The notion of women "having it all" refers to their taking on work that brings in a paycheck as well as being wives and having a family. This is the big issue of the 1980s, just as the question of the 1970s was whether women could break down the barriers to the good jobs in society and have real careers. But it is certainly not a new issue, although a lot of people regard it as new. Not only the immigrant women of Grandma Davis's generation had families and "worked," but through the ages women have had to perform a balancing act carrying out their work as wives and mothers *and* doing the multitude of chores historians remind us were typical of the premechanized household. In the past a woman raised chickens as well as children. She might also work in the fields at harvest, make soap, preserve food, and cook for farmhands. All these tasks were simply what a housewife was expected to do. Women worked at many jobs, and worked very hard—woman's work was truly never done. From the beginning of industrialization, there were women who had to negotiate the demands of multiple roles: caring for aging parents and siblings; doing housework; working in the mills and offices of a growing society. Although not many mothers of small children worked outside the home, they did engage in income-producing work by taking in boarders or working in family businesses, although their work often went undocumented by the census takers and the economists.

Today, as many of the traditional tasks of the housewife are done outside the home, women are also moving away from the home to perform them, and in so doing they are adding to their jobs. Women are still housewives, but they are also workers; and society treats these as separate and distinctive roles. What is new is that most women now work *away* from the home as well as *in* the home, and the fastest-growing sector of the labor force is comprised of married women with children under the age of six. Further, a good proportion of these women are assigning high priority to their work, ambitiously looking to excel and reap the rewards expected by men who do such work. The reality of women's lives today, however, as in the past, does not match the cultural image and certainly not the cultural ideal. Many people consider it objectionable, unhealthy, or immoral for women to assume multiple roles; the right wing, including some of our national leaders, implores women to relinquish roles outside the home and focus on the family. These messages have roots in the writings of the old philosophers, who believed women ought not have independent bases of existence but should be identified by their relationship to their fathers and husbands.

Many people are threatened by the vitality and productivity of the women who "do it all." Strong and confident women are regarded as unfeminine in society, even as society depends on women's strength to keep things going! In a nation in which up to very recently people believed that the typical American woman was incapable of balancing a checkbook or driving a van, women's new competence as bank officers and truck drivers creates confusion.

The mythology of role strain limits women's freedom to assume multiple roles and unusual combinations of roles (unusual, that is, for a woman) that offer them independence and confidence. The culture reinforces women's second-class status and their exclusion from top jobs, long regarded as male domains, by creating stress and preventing women from finding solutions. My research on women lawyers, which spans a twenty-year period from the mid-1960s to the early 1980s, provided some insight into these processes.

Let's look first at this role terminology. One of the contributions of sociology has been to conceptualize the behavior of people as organized in "roles." Just as actors play the role of another person—a hero, a salesman, a writer, a thief—sociologists point out that all people learn to "play" the roles required when they acquire the various positions in society they are expected to take on as mother or banker, teacher or politician. Not everyone can play any role—people of a certain age, sex, or race are confined to particular kinds of roles. In addition, there are rules (sociologists call them norms) that specify how people ought to behave, and sometimes even how they ought to think, while playing roles. In modern society the number of roles one person can play is apt to be high—banker, parent, caretaker of aged parent, good neighbor, cook, member of social club, and so on.

Steadily accumulating evidence indicates that whether a person feels stressed or happily busy depends on the combination of roles one has, and whether society makes it easy or hard to meet the rules attached to them. Thus, it is not the *number* of roles that necessarily causes stress but the *combination* of them and whether a person gets help in meeting his or her obligations. Role strain can occur when people take on roles that are regarded as unusual or unsuitable for them. "Good" occupational roles, for example, were saved for white middle-class men and kept from people regarded as being of the wrong sex, color, or age. People whose roles were unusual, such as blacks who became doctors or women who became engineers, were made to feel awkward because patients or clients were confused or annoyed by not "knowing" how to treat them. Blacks were not *supposed* to become doctors, nor women to become engineers. As a result, their patients or clients (their "role partners") often did not accord them the respect or attention their occupation would normally elicit, causing those black people or women considerable stress.

Twenty years ago two sociologists, Robert K. Merton and William J. Goode, studied the techniques people use to reduce the role strain that stems from having "too many" roles. For example, they might delegate some of the tasks to people who had some commitment to helping them (as managers did to secretaries or husbands to wives). Or they might compartmentalize, by not letting the obligations of one role intrude when they were concentrating on another (men do not usually concern themselves with children's activities during the nine-to-five workday; and managers would not interrupt a Sunday family dinner to discuss a work problem). But it turned out that women or minorities could not as easily use these techniques, especially at work.

Further research showed that society helps certain groups of people more than others—depending on their rank and power—in juggling role demands. Women had fewer resources from which to draw and were more apt to suffer from role strain than men in the same situations. Power and social rank were important in handling roles of all kinds—the more you have, the easier it is.

Finally, some strategically placed people, known as "gatekeepers," can help individuals and groups manage their roles, but these people can also put roadblocks in the way. Gatekeepers in school admissions, in "male" occupations and in society at large made the cost of choosing a career high before the 1970s. In my study of women who became lawyers before the 1970s, gatekeepers in the legal profession clearly were the major source of role strain. Partners in firms in charge of assignments often assumed women would have difficulty traveling or working late and would keep them from important assignments they had worked hard to get. Women who sought to become lawyers had to be stronger, more resourceful, and generally more advantaged than men to enter this career. Although most of these women were highly competent (they had high grades on law school entrance exams and excellent grades in law school), the common view was that women lawyers were poor risks and worth little investment either in training or development of careers. They were only permitted to practice in low-prestige, low-paying, and low-responsibility specialties. "Hold back," they were told, "no one can handle roles as wives and mothers *and* as high-powered attorneys." The tone of language used to convey this message was that of concern for the women: "We are going to put you in trusts and estates, because women are not comfortable handling rough cases in the court-room." But the courtroom and corporate practice, another specialty consid-ered too rough for tender women lawyers, often provides the route to part-nership. Most women lawyers could find jobs only in government or legal aid, because there they were kept from dealing in the really "important" realms of finance and policy.

Messages to women said to hold back, to moderate their commitment to career, and not to aim for the rewards of money and power that men ex-pected, for their own good or the good of others. At each crossroad in their career paths, women faced barriers to their move to the next step. Women law students often were told by male fellow classmates that they were taking the place of a man who needed training for a career to be able to support a family. Interviewers for jobs asked them how they would avoid neglecting their husbands and children. At each level, should women not be convinced of the injustice or inappropriateness of their striving, structural barriers were put in their way to raise the cost of their involvement in their careers. Women often faced distrust and suspicion from their colleagues about their "real" commitment to work. They had to work harder to demonstrate com-petence than men of equal or lesser ability.

What did this do to the women lawyers? Were they under stress? Among those I interviewed, a common complaint was that "a woman has to be twice as good as a man"; "we have to work harder . . . and be on the ball . . . because if you make a fool of yourself, you're a damnfool woman instead of just a damn fool." They needed to "prove themselves" just to keep working, let alone to pursue prestige, money, and power. They told me that they wanted to accomplish good things, to help people, to make enough money to support themselves, to help their families, or to provide needed services.

This was clearly the acceptable thing to say, but I came to believe that many of these women were deluding themselves as well as me. Underneath, they were hoping to show that they were faithful to "feminine" roles by using the language of "service and helping" even though this was not the case or only half the story. Studies that have analyzed the motives of women choosing law as a career show that women, like men, vary in their reasons. Wanting to "do good" (an acceptable woman's motivation) does not pre-clude wanting success. Even today women are ambivalent about how "just" it is for them to have aspirations, to have the "right" to assume roles that carry high rank and rewards and demand high commitment. It is the ambiv-alence that takes its toll, not the demanding work.

Women who entered careers in a male-dominated profession before the

1970s had to face disapproval for aiming higher than it was believed they should, and if their role demands created overload, they could not expect sympathy. In fact, people were often appalled that women took on such "inappropriate" careers, especially when the women also gained attention and money.

It is important to point out that the physical and time-pressure overload problems that result from working and maintaining private lives are the same for women *no matter what kind of work they do.* Throughout history there has been little concern for the long hours women have worked in the household and in the arduous employment they have had as factory workers and clerical workers (to say nothing of the hard work of mothering half a dozen children instead of today's average of two). Few people have thought it necessary to put limits on women's working hard at those tasks defined as "woman's work"—in the textile mills of New England or the New South or the sweatshops of a hundred cities. Women were circumscribed in the number of roles, but not in the amount of work those roles might demand.

Thus, when the general view was that women's place is in the home, women who chose careers probably did have a certain amount of role strain to contend with. They could not and did not expect much help from society in sorting out and coping with their role demands. They didn't know how to delegate their duties, and family members usually refused to cut back on their demands on the women despite the evidence of how busy they were. Where there was conflict between work and family roles, women were encouraged to use the ultimate mechanism—cutting off one of the roles causing the conflict. For women, that usually was their paid job. When I looked at the obstacles women faced in becoming professionals two decades ago, I found that women who *left* a career, at any level from training to practice, did so with society's full approval. (Unlike men, who drew society's contempt if they "dropped out," abandoning their professions.) Quitting was a poor solution for the growing numbers of women who were eager to work and needed to, and whose talents were needed by society.

Successful Strategies and Defeatist Ones

As I interviewed women in the 1970s who had not given in to these pressures and who held demanding jobs in law, business, and academia, I gained a new perspective on the problem of role strain. Like other researchers on women and work, I was documenting the many problems that working women faced, but I also encountered an interesting paradox: *The most successful women professionals turned out to be those who had the most to do.* In 1980, of the forty-one women partners then in Wall Street law firms, twenty-seven were married; all but two had children. This was also true of the majority of women judges I interviewed and of women faculty at law schools.

These women simply downplayed the problems of managing a career and a family. Despite the absence of child care programs or flexible work schedules, many of the women in my study reported that they never felt so effective before—a feeling I had experienced myself. Some of the most successful women I spoke to told me they did not feel they had any problems! I asked a woman who had attained early partnership in a large corporate firm about the problems she faced in reconciling her roles as a Wall Street partner and a mother with three children under the age of twelve. She answered, "No problems." "No problems?" I asked incredulously. "Well," she responded, "not no problems, but none I can't deal with." That was a common response for women at the top. It mirrored those of many other women with demanding jobs and children who refused to let problems get in the way of what they wanted. They were problem solvers, not problem seekers, and had become as gifted in handling multiple roles as they were gifted in delegating work responsibility in their jobs.

They also were benefiting from a changing culture. Another lawyer in her early forties expressed the opinion of many professional women looking back only a decade:

> A few years ago both my husband and I thought having a baby would interfere with our careers. . . . Today, I go into court and see a lot of women in their thirties with pregnant bellies out to here. And I think they look just beautiful, handling their cases with confidence and professional skill, and also confident to have the baby, too. And I think, "I can also do my thing in court and have children, too."

The women's movement had a lot to do with the fact that many women felt it was legitimate to work hard at a career. And there was growing awareness in society that it was becoming more normal for women—even those with families—to work for pay rather than only in the household and to work at jobs that could lead somewhere.

I did find considerable differences in individuals' perceptions of demanding situations: Some are defeated by the obligations of multiple roles and some are not. The differences lie in the situations in which women find themselves. Women who feel stress usually deal with husbands, friends, colleagues, and relatives who believe that multiple roles for women—mixing work and home—will create strain, and who believe that no one can do both, or certainly not do both well.

When women believe these assumptions, they often act to reduce anticipated problems by reducing their aspirations in the occupational sphere. They don't try for tenure or promotion. They settle for low-paying work. They don't volunteer for an overtime assignment. Or they reduce their private aspirations. They decide not to marry, or not to have children, or to divorce. When individuals accept the view that time is limited and people can only do a limited number of tasks, such assumptions usually produce a self-fulfilling prophecy. Strains are created by the anticipation of having strain or by the guilt created by people expecting women to feel strain. It is socially induced by a culture still suspicious of and hostile to women's acquisition of important and prestigious roles, and by powerful people who preserve their interests by undermining the competition of women.

I am focusing on some of these issues because I believe that the *actual pressures* of high-demand jobs, and the demands incurred when one must balance them with the obligations of family life, are less of a problem than the symbolic impact of certain demands and the reactions of other people.

In my research I learned many strategies that women create to meet the demands of their multiple obligations. Some were practical: "freezing seven blocks of food each Sunday and thawing one out each night"; hiring caterers and interior decorators; asking a widowed mother to move in; using quality help, often more than one person; or enlisting the aid of their children's teachers to take over in the case of emergencies. But of utmost importance were the psychological strategies—either self-created, or created by sympathetic rather than hostile parents, husbands or lovers, colleagues, friends.

With regard to children, women lawyers who successfully combined work and home life did not feel guilty about using paid help. The higher their level in the profession, the more adequate help they could obtain, and they did not tend to brood about the amount of time they spent with their children. They worked out what they thought was an adequate amount of time, whether it was every evening or primarily weekends, and did not wallow in guilt over someone else's idea of the "ideal" amount of time. Many of those mothers felt comfortable letting their husbands take on mothering responsibilities, whereas some women are jealous of their husbands' encroaching on "their" territory (a real but unacknowledged problem today). There are fads and fashions with regard to what is considered quality care of children (or of husbands or lovers, for that matter) and there are class differences and national differences in these fashions as there have been historical differences.

Ironically, many lawyers who worked in "feminist" firms tended to think ideologically about women's status and carried their ideological stances into their mothering roles. They felt more guilty and torn about being "good mothers" and often put themselves in a no-win situation: If they were working, they felt they ought to be home; if at home, they felt they ought to be working. Women in big firms and powerful corporations, on the other hand, usually were more pragmatic and less ideological, delegating responsibility to trusted caretakers.

Of course, people make different choices. Some wish to work in the highest-demand careers and some prefer less pressured jobs; some want to spend many hours in their mothering role and some feel most comfortable when they devote fewer hours to mothering. Neither choice is necessarily right or wrong; it depends on the woman and on her freedom and ability to choose what is right for her. However, choice was not always available to women who were plagued by the assessment of others that they were not delivering quality office time because they were mothers, or not delivering quality mothering time because they were also lawyers.

Popular assessments of women lawyers' capacities to manage things and the costs of their success have always been prey to stereotypes. Many women are led to believe that being ambitious is itself costly, and, indeed, others make ambition costly for women because they don't approve of it. The stimulating and therapeutic effects of a rich, varied life can be undermined by traditional views that success is not an appropriate goal or condition for a woman. This attitude is at the root of the kind of stress that can destroy women, their careers, and their families if it is not confronted.

Instead of applause for their efforts and achievement, women often are punished for doing too well at work or venturing too far from traditional work roles. Significant others—coworkers, threatened husbands or lovers—conspire to make even small victories pyrrhic. Saddled with such "friends," some women throw in the towel before their careers take off, and deescalate their ambitions; they cannot live with the guilt created by those who find women strivers "too masculine," "too ambitious," and too eager for a place in the "male establishment."

"Only women who have unhappy marriages are active lawyers," said one woman, a bitter, divorced attorney I interviewed in the mid-1960s. This was a common view among many career women, who were judged suspect as females to have traded the joys and responsibilities of the home and motherhood for the harsh world of the professions. This view still turns up today. The lawyer who reviewed my book for the *New York Law Journal* offered his own explanation as to why women didn't become lawyers in great numbers before the 1970s: "They stayed home like a good woman should, like my mom did," he said.

Since the launching of the women's movement, women have fought hard for the right to have both careers and families, yet the issues of integrating public life and private life, of pursuing a full and rewarding career *and* having good relationships with men and happy marriages are constantly posed as problems. Women who do succeed frequently have family obligations similar to those of women who give up. But they are in situations and networks that offer support and encouragement.

The women lawyers I studied who managed their lives best were those married to other lawyers who understood the demands on them and had their own demands to meet. Indeed, most women in top jobs do choose husbands in the same field. The favored marriage pattern for women attorneys, like women doctors or social scientists, is that of "like marrying like." Close to half the lawyers I interviewed were married to other lawyers. Twenty-two lawyer couples (at last count) teach in American law schools on the same faculties. Perhaps the reason is an affinity based of a common mind set—or simple proximity—but couples who do similar work share interests and understand each other's work worlds. Sometimes marrying a man in the same profession can produce problems with competitiveness. But overall, sharing a career with sympathetic husbands greatly helps reduce the role strain problems of lawyer wives.

Regardless of their husbands' work, something about marriage helps working women. Women who achieve unusual success are more likely to be married than single, to have family roles as well as professional roles. Are married women better team players? Does every successful woman have a man behind the throne? Probably, the answer is that married women lawyers are considered more "normal" than single women lawyers. They pose fewer problems socially to coworkers and clients. Further, husband lawyers provide women attorneys with contacts, make it easier for them to be accepted in male networks, and make it easier for the women to act normally because they are less likely to face sexual innuendo or harassment. Debra Kaufman, a sociologist at Northeastern University, has shown, in a study of academic women and men, that married women are more integrated into male networks than their unmarried female colleagues and potentially are more able to use contacts they make through these professional networks.

Thus, marriage can reduce role conflict; marriage can lower the costs of career!

Of course, there are husband-wife problems; of course, single women face problems in finding men who will accept the prospect that a wife may not have the time or inclination to make them the central point of their lives. Our society doesn't make it easy for a woman to admit that work may be more interesting to her at various times than the man she is dating, her husband, or her children. That is not the way the system is supposed to work for women.

Another cause of strain for career women may come from the negative feelings that others have about their success. I found that many women feel uncomfortable about having a higher-ranking job or making more money than their husbands or lovers. Some women make it their business to travel a different track, often a less prestigious one, to avoid any prospect of strain resulting from a possible loss of male esteem. That is, they take measures to reduce their husbands' fear of their success.

The Benefits of Having It All

Hans Selye, a physiologist and stress researcher, wrote some years ago that stress can be of two varieties—negative or positive. Positive stress can produce exhilaration. The women attorneys I interviewed felt confident and good because they were doing jobs that not only were demanding but also had many satisfactions, among them prestige and power. Their confidence came from becoming accomplished in a respected profession and doing work that most people didn't think women had the capacity to do. They had begun to win cases in court, although they had been told in the past that they didn't have "the right stuff" to be courtroom attorneys. They had begun to do good corporate work despite being told that corporate law was a male field and that women weren't good at numbers. They were working for reputable firms that elicited an almost automatic trust from clients; when a woman can say she is "a Cravath lawyer" (Cravath, Swaine & Moore is a prestigious Wall Street firm), the stress of insecurity fades into the past. And they were juggling work and family successfully. As Margaret Richer, a lawyer in her mid-thirties, put it: "I feel successful this year because I did what I set out to do—have a baby and still practice law and make some income out of it. As a bonus to that I succeeded in getting some interesting cases."

High-level jobs are important sources of self-esteem, according to researchers Grace Baruch and Rosalind Barnett, who have been studying women between the ages of thirty-five and fifty-five. Their findings dovetail with a study of stress and psychiatric disorder by Frederic W. Ilfeld, Jr., professor of psychiatry at the University of California at Davis Medical School, who found that women exhibit twice as many stress symptoms as men, unless the men are poor, black, widowed, or single. The only group of women with as few problems as white middle-class men are employed women whose occupational status is very high. This does not mean that these women are under less stress—just that stress does not overwhelm them.

But women at other occupational levels also benefit from doing work they enjoy (see Chap. 11). Brigid O'Farrell and Sharon Harlan found that women doing nontraditional crafts and technical work have a high degree of satisfaction. Barnett and Baruch, looking at employed mothers of preschool-age children, found that the mothers who are committed to their work—in a variety of jobs—rank high in well-being and satisfaction and that their work contributes to a sense of mastery. And when researchers Lerita Coleman and Toni Antonucci analyzed dozens of factors that they thought would affect a woman's well-being, they found that self-esteem rested largely on one important one, employment; not children, not income, and not education. In their national sample of women aged forty to forty-nine, of whom about half worked full- or part-time and half were not employed, employment was one of the most important predictors of physical health and lack of psychological anxiety. This certainly rang true to me when I considered my mother's low self-esteem in spite of her busy schedule as a homemaker.

Those feelings of self-esteem, by the way, are not illusory. Work can offer people the chance to grow and become more competent. Melvin Kohn and his associates at the National Institute of Mental Health in Washington have discovered that women and men who work at jobs that encourage self-direction gain an increased ability to be open, flexible, and intellectually adept.

Nothing succeeds like success. Interviewing women over the years, I was struck by the amount of confidence I saw in the women in business and professional life. For some of them confidence was not a trait established by a good childhood experience (as many think is the case). It emerged this way, as an attorney in private practice, reported:

In college I was unsure of myself and started out thinking I might go into art history or something like that, but I decided on law because that's what my classmates were doing. I wondered whether I would be able to be a good lawyer, but the more I did the more capable I felt and the more I developed a clear sense of career goals. I had a fantasy of becoming a judge in the past, but now that it seems it is something of a possibility I am definitely thinking that is what I probably will be in ten or fifteen years.

Another practical benefit to having many roles is that they may free a person from certain obligations. A recent study by a Columbia University sociologist, Judith Thomas, has shown how parents with joint custody both perform parental roles, but by sharing these roles with ex-spouses they have more time to spend on work and other activities. The notion that more roles create stress is clearly incorrect in this situation. Multiple roles can and do create pressure and carry with them society's permission to compartmentalize. Otherwise, women often are prey to the limitless expectations families seem to produce; their role obligations follow a kind of Parkinson's Law in which activities expand to fill the time available.

These findings contrast strongly with the "stress" model common in our culture, which focuses only on the stress that can incapacitate. A new model offered by University of Maine sociologist Stephen R. Marks builds on Selye's observation that stress also can exhilarate. Marks views human energy as renewable and able to be stimulated, not as a reservoir that can leak or be used up. He points out that some people with multiple roles tend to run out of time and energy, yet others, who have exactly the same number of roles and obligations, are not the apparent victims of "strain" or "overload."

Marks identified the conditions under which people are energized or enervated. It is not number of roles, but commitment that makes the difference. Psychologist Faye Crosby is finding that women have a sense of well-being from accomplishing the tasks of many roles if they are roles they *choose* (see Chap. 11). This is true of the women lawyers I studied and for other women who have top jobs. Individuals seem to have both time and energy for things to which they are highly committed. Commitment may be rooted in personal idiosyncrasy, such as overcoming a weakness caused by childhood illness, or it may be rooted in cultural values, such as the American desire for independent work. Society rewards success in some careers with wealth, power, and prestige, creating high energy in those who perform them. Many men have found that high-demand work gives them more energy and enthusiasm, not less.

Today some women are achieving the same kind of energy because they are in the same kind of stimulating jobs. The strengths provided by reward and recognition enable these women to juggle the roles in their lives. In the process they may enrich aspects of personality and acquire greater capacity to cope well. Having diverse roles may even be essential to mental health, enhancing one's self-conception, providing greater freedom and autonomy, new options, and a new breadth of vision. Recent work by Peggy Thoits of Princeton also shows that multiple identities contribute to well-being. When people's satisfactions are based on the enjoyments from a number of roles, such as spouse, worker, friend, or parent, they do not feel destroyed when one role changes (abruptly or naturally) through retirement, children leaving home, or the death of a partner.

Yet society could make it easier for people to handle multiple roles by providing day care and other services for the family. I have pointed to the costs unnecessarily created for women by making them feel guilty about their choices, judging them inferior as mothers or professionals because they choose to be both. Role strain is induced by ambivalence and stress, and efforts could be made to reduce these conflicts. Women have taken on multiple roles for millenia. They are used to hard work and used to doing many things at the same time. This era is no exception, and today's women are no more "superwomen" than those who preceded them. Today women face other problems, however, and one of them is legitimation.

The essence of successful role management is that it is done in conjunction with others. Friends and relatives have to be amenable to the new rules. The successful women I have studied had in common one crucial element— the goodwill and supportiveness of others in their lives.

With these returns in, the prognosis seems clear. As long as one avoids the naysayers and alarmists who cause guilt and stress, and as long as one chooses life partners and associates who cheer one on, doing challenging work, "having it all," may not only be good for one's health but a necessity for well-being.

CYNTHIA FUCHS EPSTEIN is professor of sociology at the Graduate Center of the City University of New York, and a resident scholar at the Russell Sage Foundation. She has been codirector of a National Institute of Mental Health training grant on the Sociology and Economics of Women and Work at the Graduate Center and was codirector of the Program in Sex Roles and Social Change at Columbia University.

Professor Epstein received her Ph.D. in sociology from Columbia University in 1968. She has held a Guggenheim Fellowship and has been a Fellow of the Center for Advanced Study in the Behavioral Sciences at Stanford, California. Her books include *Women in Law* (Basic Books, 1981; in paperback, Anchor Press, 1983); *Access to Power: Cross-National Studies of Women and Elites* (Allen & Unwin, 1981); *The Other Half: Roads to Women's Equality* (Prentice-Hall, 1971); and *Woman's Place: Options and Limits in Professional Careers* (University of California Press, 1970); and *Deceptive Distinctions: Theory and Research on Sex, Gender, and the Social Order* (Russell Sage Foundation, forthcoming). Professor Epstein has written and lectured extensively on her research on women in professions, business, and politics.

Further Reading

Baruch, Grace; Barnett, Rosalind; and Rivers, Caryl. *Lifeprints*. New York: McGraw-Hill, 1983.

Cowan, Ruth Schwartz. *More Work for Mother*. New York: Basic Books, 1983.

Crosby, Faye J. *Relative Deprivation and Working Women*. New York: Oxford University Press, 1982.

Epstein, Cynthia Fuchs. *Woman's Place: Options and Limits in Professional Careers*. Berkeley: University of California Press, 1970.

———. *Women in Law*. New York: Basic Books, 1981; in paperback, Anchor Press, 1983.

Goode, William J. "Why Men Resist." In *Rethinking the Family: Some Feminist Questions*, edited by Barrie Thorne and Marilyn Yalom. New York: Longman Group, 1982.

Kessler-Harris, Alice. *Out to Work: A History of Wage-Earning Women in the United States*. New York: Oxford University Press, 1982.

Marks, Stephen R. "Multiple Roles and Role Strain: Some Notes on Human Energy, Time, and Commitment." *American Sociological Review* 42 (December 1977):921–36.

O'Farrell, Brigid, and Harlan, Sharon. "Craftworkers and Clerks: The Effect of Male Co-Worker Hostility on Women's Satisfaction with Non-Traditional Blue-Collar Jobs." *Social Problems* 29 (February 1982a):252–64.

Schreiber, Carol T. *Changing Places: Men and Women in Transitional Occupations.* Cambridge: MIT Press, 1979.

Selye, Hans. *The Stress of Life.* New York: McGraw-Hill, 1956.

Strasser, Susan. *Never Done: A History of American Housework.* New York: Pantheon, 1982.

Thoits, Peggy. "Multiple Identities and Psychological Well-Being: A Reformulation and Test of the Social Isolation Hypothesis." *American Sociological Review* 48 (April 1983):174–87.

6

The Pleasures and Problems of Friendship

KAREN ROOK

God gives us our relations, but thank God we can choose our friends.
—English proverb

Friends are God's apology for relations.
—Hugh Kingsmill

Friendship is a simple matter, or so it seems. Friends are important to us because they provide companionship and support. We all want to have friends, and we are inclined to pity or wonder about those who lack them. After all, finding friends is easy. In fact, given the benefits of friendship, it would seem that the more friends we have, the better off we are likely to be. But is friendship really this simple? Consider the following examples:

- Irene M. and her neighbor, Rose G., both lost their husbands just over a year ago. Both women are in their late sixties and both now live alone. Irene is very involved in activities at the senior citizen center and also does volunteer work at the local museum. She describes herself as having "many, many friends." Rose, in contrast, has just "one bosom friend," whom she sees or talks with at least once a week. Rose has fewer friends and spends far more time alone but, ironically, is happier than Irene.

- Jean B. and Ellen S. have worked together in the same office for the past four years and in that time have come to think of each other as good friends. They have lunch together nearly every day, often socialize outside of work, and can count on each other for help when it's needed. Jean's eleven-year-old son has been having serious problems at school, and this has become a frequent topic of discussion at lunch. Last week, as Jean was describing her son's latest difficulties, Ellen interrupted with "What do you expect? He's just a chip off the old block," referring to Jean's husband. Ellen then abruptly changed the subject. Jean was stunned and hurt. She feels that both her husband and her son had been insulted and that Ellen was insensitive to her feelings. She has been very upset since then and can't get this incident off her mind.

- Katherine W. is twenty-eight, single, and considered attractive by most people. After graduating from law school, she moved to a new city to accept a position with a growing law firm and to try living in a different part of the country. She has lived there now for over two years and enjoys her work but feels terribly lonely because she hasn't been able to make close friends. At first, Katherine didn't worry about this since she had just moved. She explored the city on her own and generally enjoyed herself. But in the past year she has begun to wonder if something is wrong with her since she hasn't succeeded in finding friends. She feels depressed much of the time and increasingly stays at home because she is ashamed to go out alone.

- Suzanne R., who is forty-three, has long fantasized about returning to college to finish her degree and possibly pursue a career in graphic arts. She mentioned this idea to several of her friends at a party recently and was surprised by their reactions, which ranged from "At your age?" to "Don't you think it would be better to study something more practical?" Suzanne realizes that her friends may have been trying to be helpful, but she wishes they weren't so conservative and quick to react judgmentally. She worries about how they will respond to her if she goes ahead with plans. She wonders, with some guilt, if it might be better to see less of her old friends and to try to meet other women who seek to make major changes in their lives.

As these examples illustrate, friends can hurt and disappoint as well as help. Some people are content with only a few friends, while others who have many friends are unhappy; the causes of loneliness can be elusive. To understand the puzzling and sometimes paradoxical nature of friendships, and the ways that friendships affect our well-being, scientists have investigated their benefits and costs. In this chapter I will concentrate on friends rather than romantic partners. While many people think of their partners as "best friends," love relationships raise different issues than friendships, and my primary goal is to explore how friendships function in our lives.

How Friendships Help

Most of us would readily agree that people who have friends are better off than people who don't have friends, but what does this mean exactly? Are friendships beneficial primarily because they make us feel happy, or do they help in other ways? What are the things that friends do to enhance our well-being?

EVIDENCE THAT FRIENDSHIPS HELP

Sophocles avowed the importance of friendships as early as 430 B.C.: "To throw away an honest friend is, as it were, to throw your life away." Humans have formed social groups throughout history, and some researchers regard this as evidence in itself that social bonds are essential to our well-being. In prehistoric times tight-knit social groups offered protection against the very real threats of a hostile and unpredictable environment. Although the dangers of attack by saber-toothed tigers and other predators have long since passed, other hazards of modern living continue to make protection, or mutual assistance, an important function of friendship. Phillip Shaver and Cary O'Connor describe in Chapter 15 how contemporary stresses increase the risk of emotional and physical disorders. *Social support* provided by family members and friends makes us less vulnerable to the deleterious effects of crises and stressful events. National surveys indicate that most people turn to close associates rather than to professionals for help with their problems. This fact is reflected in the current popularity of self-help groups and informal support groups.

The idea of social support has captured the imaginations of many researchers as they have tried to learn why some people are so seriously affected by stressful life events while others maintain their equilibrium. Although the findings of some studies conflict, the current best conclusion is that social support does indeed make a difference for a wide variety of stresses. For example, two British researchers, George W. Brown and Tirril Harris, set out to learn what predisposes many women to depression by interviewing 458 women about their daily lives and recent experiences. Women who had experienced a recent life stress *and* who had a confidant with whom they could discuss personal problems were far less likely to suffer from depression than were women who had experienced a recent stress but who lacked a confidant.

Social support from friends and family members may enhance our ability to resist physical illness as well. For example, much interest has focused recently on the health effects of unemployment. Studies of unemployed workers indicate that those who have social support are less prone to health problems than those who lack social support. In a particularly convincing demonstration of the health risks incurred by people who lack supportive social ties, Lisa Berkman and Leonard Syme surveyed nearly seven thousand people about their social relationships and then examined official mortality records nine years later. People with low social support at the start of the study, regardless of their sex or socioeconomic status, had significantly higher mortality rates at the follow-up than people with high initial social support. Of course, it is possible that people with low social support were sicker at the start of the study or engaged in less sound health practices, such as smoking, drinking too much alcohol, eating improperly, or failing to exercise. The researchers examined these factors and found that they did *not* explain why those with low support had higher mortality rates.

Scientists do not yet know what makes those who lack supportive contacts more vulnerable to illness, although some speculate that the immune system is involved. Clues that this may be the case come from recent studies of the bereaved. These studies show that during periods of intense grief, the immune system functions less well than it does normally. Perhaps immune system functioning is similarly suppressed among those with little social support.

Having friends who can be counted on to provide support when it is needed offers protection from the harmful effects of stress, and this protection extends to our physical health as well as our emotional health. But might lacking friends be considered a form of stress in its own right? People who are lonely also tend to be depressed and to have low self-esteem. This is particularly true of people who have been lonely for a long time. Letitia Anne Peplau and her colleagues, who have conducted many studies of loneliness at UCLA, argue that a vicious cycle often occurs among people whose loneliness persists: As time passes, people come to blame themselves for their loneliness, to assume (like Katherine W. in my opening example) that something must be wrong with them. Once they make this assumption, they are likely to curtail efforts to meet new people, thus ensuring continued loneliness and further self-blame. Given such a vicious cycle, it is easy to see why loneliness can lead to depression. Of course, some people are depressed or suffer from low self-esteem to start with and only then become lonely, rather than the other way around (see Chap. 19).

To observe that loneliness and depression are associated does not tell us *why* they are associated. What do lonely people miss by not having friendships that makes them vulnerable to emotional distress? What, exactly, do friends do to help us cope more effectively with life stresses? What do we mean by social support? Are there different kinds of support? Before reading the next section, you might take a moment to think about how you would describe the different benefits you derive from your own friendships.

BENEFITS OF FRIENDSHIP

To identify the key benefits of friendship, some researchers have drawn upon their own experiences and intuitions. Others interview people about what their friends mean to them and how their friends help them. For example, Benjamin Gottlieb took this approach to learn how friends help in times of trouble. He asked a group of women to think about the three most severe life stresses they had faced recently and to explain what, if anything, others had done to help them deal with the stresses. The women identified many specific kinds of help. Some friends communicated concern—"She took the time to be there with me so I didn't have to face [the problem] alone"—or bolstered the woman's self-concept—"He seems to have faith in me." Other friends helped the woman clarify her understanding of the problem she faced—"Made me more aware of what I was actually saying [rather] than just having words come out"—or helped her focus on how to overcome the problem—"He offered suggestions about what I could do." Still others helped by taking some direct action on behalf of the woman— "She helped by talking to the owners and convincing them to wait for the money"—or by simply indicating their readiness to take action when needed —"He'll do all he can do."

A number of researchers, including Gottlieb, have attempted to classify such reactions into categories, which apparently have different effects on our well-being. For example, a friend may simply empathize with us about a problem when we really need concrete advice about how to handle the problem, or vice versa. Most researchers agree that three types of social support are common: emotional support, cognitive guidance, and tangible support.

- *Emotional support* refers to the ways that friends show us that they care about us, respect us, and value their association with us. This kind of support is important because some life stresses directly threaten our sense of self-worth. Losing a job or suffering a serious financial loss, for example, may cause us to feel incompetent even if these problems are not actually our fault. Friends help to restore our self-esteem by communicating concern and affection.

- *Cognitive guidance* refers to the ways that friends help us evaluate problems and plan coping responses. Some traumatic experiences—developing a serious illness, giving birth to a handicapped child—not only involve wrenching emotional adjustments but also the need for information about how to appraise and respond to the problem. How serious is the condition? What treatment alternatives, if any, exist? What can the future be expected to bring? How have others with this problem coped? Sometimes those who have personally experienced the problem are best equipped to provide the information we seek. Psychologists Camille Wortman and Christine Dunkel-Schetter studied the social support offered to people with cancer. The cancer victims reported that their healthy friends and family members frequently offered well-meaning but glib reassurances that were not helpful and, in fact, were often upsetting.

Many would-be helpers feel at a loss about how to aid friends facing problems that they have never personally confronted. Mark Chesler and Oscar Barbarin interviewed the close friends of ninety-five parents who had a child who developed cancer. On learning of the diagnosis, the friends experienced shock and pain akin to that experienced by the parents themselves. Many also reported considerable uncertainty about how to be helpful. One friend commented, "When it first occurred I didn't know what to do. I wasn't sure whether to approach them or not, but decided I would call and offer to help and let them make the decision." We should try to remember that sometimes when friends fail to offer help, it is because they are afraid of being intrusive or inadequate and not because they are callous or indifferent. In Chesler and Barbarin's study, when the parents provided feedback and suggestions about the kind of help they needed, their friends were able to be more effective, and the friendship itself suffered less strain.

- *Tangible support* refers to material resources and services provided by friends in times of need: such as financial help, the loan of a car, food, or shelter; taking care of a friend's children when an emergency arises or dealing with an agency or bureaucracy (e.g., Social Security, the court system) on a friend's behalf. Tangible support is particularly important when life stresses accumulate and deplete one's strength and savings. Most of us can probably recall times when we suffered simultaneous stresses—illness, a lost paycheck, car trouble, backed-up plumbing— that required us to lean on friends. A single calamity, such as a devastating house fire, can also make us heavily dependent upon friends for tangible support.

Tangible support sometimes has a psychological meaning that goes beyond replenishing resources; it also communicates a friend's concern and esteem. After all, if friends did not care for us, they would not come to our aid. Thus, tangible support may at times operate like emotional support in sustaining our feelings of self-worth. People who find it awkward to express their feelings verbally may, in fact, prefer to show their caring by doing something constructive. Many men feel less comfortable than women expressing emotional support directly and so, on learning of a friend's problems, are more inclined to offer tangible support or advice.

Of course, most of the time when friends get together, it is simply to have fun—to exchange stories, cook a gourmet meal, go to a movie or museum, make a weekend excursion or share other good times. Life would be rather bleak without these shared activities. Peter Lewinsohn and his colleagues at the University of Oregon believe that having too few pleasurable experiences of this sort increases the risk of depression. In fact, one form of therapy for depression urges clients gradually to increase the number of pleasurable activities. Persistent loneliness may lead to depression because lacking companions to do things with eliminates a major source of enjoyment. This does not mean that one *must* have friends in order to enjoy oneself; many satisfying activities can be done alone. But some of life's pleasures are lost without friends.

Beyond sharing leisure activities with us and providing support, friends help to *affirm our identities and self-concepts.* Old friends know us well— they have a sense of our history; they recognize our diverse selves—mother, wife, worker, neighbor, organization member; they understand our values and personalities; they tolerate our flaws. Even without saying or doing anything explicit, friends reassure us that we have a place in the world. To lack friends who know us this well can arouse anxiety, as we learn from stories of people who have been uprooted and forced to leave their friends behind. Women who leave their communities because of their husbands' job transfers often experience a period of emotional strain and self-doubt before recovering their confidence in the unfamiliar setting. Such losses are particularly devastating for unemployed women because, unlike their husbands, they cannot rely on their work to affirm their identities.

Friends also provide *status* in a status-conscious world. People who lack friends are likely to be seen as failures in the social marketplace. Even if a woman is basically content being alone, she may elicit puzzled or disapproving reactions from others. Cultural values regarding romantic relationships may also make those who have satisfying friendships but who lack a romantic partner feel inadequate. In her book *Lonely in America,* Suzanne Gordon argues that we live in a "couple culture" where success is measured not only in terms of material possessions but also in terms of achieving certain types of relationships. For the young adolescent this means having a "best friend"; for the teenage girl it means having a "boyfriend." For adult Americans social status has traditionally been attached to marriage. Unfortunately, such cultural pressures drive some lonely people to devote their energies exclusively to the often elusive quest for a romantic partner, when making friends might equally alleviate the pain of loneliness.

Friends enhance our psychological well-being by sharing our joys and pleasures, offering several kinds of support in times of trouble, validating our identities, and providing status in the eyes of others. Given this wide range of important functions that friends perform, it is natural to wonder how many friends a person ideally should have. Is it possible to have one good friend who does it all, or is it necessary to have lots of friends who do different things? Which situation is true for you?

HOW MANY FRIENDS DO YOU NEED?

Robert Weiss, a pioneer in the study of loneliness, believes that each person needs to have several different kinds of relationships, because relationships tend to be *specialized*—we turn to some people primarily for companionship, to others primarily for advice, to still others for tangible aid. According to Weiss, no one friend or lover alone can perform all of the social functions that are essential to well-being.

Weiss also believes that we need specific kinds of relationships. In his view everyone should have both "an attachment figure," such as a spouse or romantic partner, and ties to a social group of some sort, such as a network of friends or a neighborhood organization. An attachment figure provides emotional intimacy and closeness, and belonging to a social group provides a sense of community. People who lack an attachment figure are vulnerable to *emotional loneliness,* which is characterized by pervasive feelings of apprehension and a sense of desolate aloneness. People who lack group ties are vulnerable to *social loneliness,* which is characterized by feelings of social marginality and boredom. Moreover, according to Weiss, having an attachment figure cannot compensate for lacking group ties and, conversely, having group ties cannot compensate for lacking an attachment figure.

Thus, a woman might have a very satisfying marriage but still feel lonely if she lacked group ties to provide a sense of community. Social loneliness can add pressures to a marriage or can lead women to infer that their marriage must have faults. Myrna Weissman and Eugene Paykel, for example, described the experiences of one woman who moved with her family from the city to the suburbs. "She missed her neighbors and friends," they reported, "and as a result had more expectations and desire of companionship from her husband than he was able to supply. Her nagging was beginning to drive him away and she feared that he was unfaithful." According to Weiss, the only way she can alleviate such social loneliness is to join new groups and make new friends.

Weiss's analysis is provocative, but not all researchers agree with it. Some believe that one close, reliable friend is enough, that the risk of emotional and physical problems stemming from life stresses can be greatly reduced by having one trusted ally to whom problems can be confided and who can be relied upon for help. Having additional allies does not necessarily offer additional benefits. Of course, one's sole trusted ally could become seriously ill or move away, leaving no one to provide support. Also, some unforeseen life crises are so overwhelming that our friends' resources are drained as well as our own. In such circumstances it may be valuable to have several friends who can share the burden of providing support. Under ordinary circumstances, however, we can question the common assumption that "more is always better" and relieve some of the pressure felt by people who believe that they *should* have many friends. Indeed, as the opening example of Irene M. illustrates, having many friends is no guarantee of happiness.

Whether one friend is sufficient or whether many are needed, the discussion thus far gives us little reason to doubt that friendship enhances psychological well-being. Yet we can all remember times when our friends were frustrating or infuriating, when they made unreasonable demands, when they hurt our feelings or otherwise disappointed us. Occasionally, friends seem to cause more problems than they solve—and then spending time alone doesn't seem so bad.

How Friendships Hinder

Friends more often help than hinder, but when those close to us do let us down, we can land with a painful thump. Spanish writer Baltasar Gracián commented in the seventeenth century on the poignant pain of friendships gone sour: "Friends provoked become the bitterest of enemies."

EVIDENCE THAT FRIENDSHIPS HINDER

Recently, I interviewed 120 elderly women and asked them to tell me, first, about the people who helped them in various ways—people who would help them if they became ill, who could help cheer them up if they felt blue, who provided companionship, and so forth. Then I asked the women to tell me about the people who caused them problems—people who failed to follow through on offers of help, who sometimes intruded on their privacy, who made them angry, and so forth. Some women reported that no one in their social networks caused any problems; this may reflect their good fortune in having a trouble-free social life or may simply reflect their unwillingness to admit that difficulties existed. Most of the women, however, reported knowing one or more people who occasionally caused them grief—family members, neighbors or casual acquaintances, and, often, their good friends. One woman, for example, was upset by a friend who periodically seemed to be competitive—"She sometimes puts on airs, bragging about things her children have done and how much money they've made. I feel like I have to defend my children just because they don't take expensive trips and drive fancy cars." Another woman complained that she couldn't trust one of her friends to be discreet about self-disclosures—"I like to spend time with her, but you have to watch what you say around her if you don't want everyone to know about it right away. She likes to gossip too much."

I conducted analyses to evaluate how these helpful and unhelpful actions by others affected the women's psychological well-being. I wanted to know, for example, whether helpful and unhelpful actions would simply cancel each other out, with no net effect on well-being. Alternatively, I speculated that people would be most affected by the helpful things friends do and would simply try to overlook their negative side. The results supported neither of these hunches, however. I found instead that the elderly women's emotional well-being was affected more by others' problematic actions than by others' helpful actions. That is, others' misdeeds may *lower* our well-being more than their good deeds *elevate* our well-being!

Similar findings have emerged in several other studies, showing that this special sensitivity to irritating or unhelpful friends is not limited to elderly women. Why should the effects of problematic relationships loom so much larger than the effects of pleasant ones? After all, the former are probably much rarer than the latter.

Actually, the very fact that misdeeds by friends are relatively rare may help to explain why they are so painful. If most of our dealings with friends are pleasant, we develop expectations that this is how it will always be. We relax our guard and, in a sense, come to take for granted our easy, pleasant times with friends. When friends hurt us or let us down, it catches us by surprise and may even stun us. We remain upset for a long time because such events puzzle us. We turn them over and over in our minds looking for an explanation and trying to reconcile them with our previous beliefs about our friends, as Jean B. did in my opening example. Perhaps this is why the "sting" we feel when a friend lets us down is often more potent, or at least lasts longer, than the "glow" we feel when a friend comes through for us.

COSTS OF FRIENDSHIP

Recognition of the fragile nature of friendships is implicit in French novelist Colette's advice that "it is prudent to pour the oil of delicate politeness on the machinery of friendship." Indeed, philosopher Bertrand Russell suggested that "if we were all given by magic the power to read each other's thoughts, I suppose the first effect would be to dissolve all friendships."

Whether intentionally or unintentionally, our friends occasionally criticize us, reject us, ignore our needs, mock our beliefs, and violate our privacy. Most of us can remember times when we felt hurt or angry as a result of such actions by someone we felt close to. Sometimes friends' very efforts to be helpful can backfire. For example, friends may offer us gifts or help that we know we cannot repay and cause us to feel uncomfortable and indebted. Or, in an effort to mobilize support for us, they may disclose our difficulties to people with whom we prefer not to share personal matters. Mark Chesler and Oscar Barbarin's study (of support provided to parents of children with cancer) illustrates how friends may unintentionally blunder in trying to be helpful. Comments such as "Maybe you'll get pregnant again and replace her" were intended to offer hope but actually angered and upset the parents.

Of course, we usually forgive our friends' clumsiness in trying to offer help for threatening problems with which they have no personal experience. But sometimes we simply want to make changes in our lives, and friends appear to throw up roadblocks. Suzanne R., whom I described at the beginning of this chapter, encountered friends' resistance when she contemplated returning to college at the age of forty-three. Her friends did little more than challenge her plans. Sometimes friends wisely deter us from a foolish course of action, perhaps foreseeing pitfalls that we cannot see ourselves. In such cases we are appropriately grateful (though often belatedly) for their challenges. At other times, however, friends merely seem to oppose our trying something new. One of the factors that binds friends together is similarity—sharing similar backgrounds, values, and lifestyles. When we contemplate a major change, it may threaten our friends because the pact of similarity is broken.

Our efforts to grow and make changes may meet the greatest resistance when our friends are also friends with each other. A social network in which most people know each other is referred to as high in *density*. In contrast, a network in which few of our friends are friends with each other is low in density. Barton Hirsch studied the social networks of women who were reorganizing their lives, including a group of mature women who had recently returned to college. He found that women with high-density networks reported less adequate social support and poorer mental health than women with low-density networks. He concluded that high-density networks provided fewer opportunities for the women to establish new social identities and to explore their new interests. Women may adapt more easily to new and varied roles if their friendship networks themselves contain people with diverse backgrounds.

Thus far, I have focused only on what friends provide to us and have said little about the support that we provide to friends. Obviously, support is usually exchanged on a reciprocal basis: You offer help to me, and in return I will offer help to you. Most people unhesitatingly help their friends when it is needed, and providing care to others is apt to enhance their self-esteem by making them feel needed. Yet such care giving can at times be quite exhausting. Some friends seem to have one problem after another, making their needs for support unending. Some may have poor coping skills, limited income, or no transportation, forcing them to rely heavily on others. Even our most capable friends who rarely have problems can be hit with a catastrophe that doesn't go away and that creates needs for indefinite support. We can pitch in and rather quickly help a friend sort out the mess from a kitchen fire, but we cannot so readily help a friend "recover" from a disabling accident, interminable divorce, or loss of a child. As a participant in the Chesler and Barbarin study commented, "I felt drained. You can only hear so much. I love them dearly but I can't deal with the child's illness for seven days a week for a long time, because we have a life too."

Women traditionally have been the caregivers in our society, and this makes women most vulnerable to being drained by the needs of others. Indeed, some women get involved in such extensive and strenuous caregiving, on behalf of their friends and family members, that their own physical and emotional health is jeopardized.

We all have a limit on how much of other peoples' anguish we can absorb. Sometimes we wish our friends would tell us *less* about their troubles. Perhaps Jean B.'s friend (in the opening examples) became frustrated at repeatedly hearing about the difficulties Jean's son was experiencing, prompting her to respond harshly rather than sympathetically.

In her book *Anger: The Misunderstood Emotion*, psychologist Carol Tavris challenged the popular belief that it is always best to "ventilate" one's negative feelings and grievances. Many people think that keeping feelings private is unhealthy, and that emotions inevitably erupt in an unfortunate form if not released. While it is often valuable to disclose one's feelings to others, occasional circumspection also has virtues. Tavris reviewed many studies that indicate that expressing one's feelings of anger (in an angry way) often does not help the anger to dissipate. Indeed, rather than having the expected cathartic effect, expressing anger often serves to intensify and "rehearse" the emotion. Tavris recommends neither that people suppress their feelings nor that they reflexively give vent to their feelings but, rather, that they try to be judicious in deciding when and to whom to disclose feelings. Friendships require some self-disclosure to achieve intimacy, but inappropriate, constant, angry complaints can strain the closest bond. As one woman told Tavris: "I listened to a friend ventilate her various rages for years—she was angry at everyone. Finally I suggested that perhaps she could let go of some of her peeves. She was furious—at *me*. 'I have a *right* to express my anger!' she shouted. 'And I have a right not to listen,' I said."

Friends occasionally insult us or disappoint us, extend support that is clumsy and ineffective, resist our efforts to grow and change, and have needs of their own that drain us. Friendships are not cost-free.

Improving Friendships

Being assertive with a friend can be far more difficult than being assertive with a stranger, but it is sometimes necessary to let a friend know that something he or she did upset you. Friends are often completely unaware that they have disturbed us, and sometimes it is enough just to call the problem to their attention. At other times friends knowingly behave in a way that conflicts with our needs or wishes; in such cases it may be important to discuss the differences and try to negotiate a compromise. When working with clients who have been angered or hurt by another person's actions and who want to make their complaints known, therapists sometimes advise their clients to distinguish between emotion-focused discussion and problem-solving discussion. Sometimes we simply want the other person to understand and acknowledge our feelings. In other instances we may not particularly care if the person understands how the problem affected us emotionally, but we may be eager to discuss possible solutions. Feelings of distress are apt to be compounded if the other person does not grasp what we want from the discussion. We may feel annoyed, for example, if the person ignores our feelings and focuses only on practical solutions. Or we may be frustrated if the person repeatedly addresses our emotional state and does not offer problem-solving ideas.

To avoid such confusion you can convey directly how you would like to discuss the problem—for example, by saying that you want the person to try to understand your feelings. Indeed, if the other person's actions aroused intense anger or hurt, it may be best initially just to make these feelings known and, after a "cooling-off period," to explore solutions in a subsequent meeting. Further, don't expect friends to read your mind. Friends often feel uncertain about what kind of support we need, particularly when we face major stresses such as serious illness or bereavement. They are likely to appreciate information about how to be most helpful and are less likely to make matters worse by offering clumsy or unwanted support. On the other hand, if you want to help a friend who cannot articulate her need, remember what writer E. W. Howe said in 1911: "When a friend is in trouble, don't annoy him by asking if there is anything you can do. Think up something appropriate and do it."

Being assertive with friends and offering guidance about how they can be supportive may strike many people as somewhat risky. Yet taking risks with friends sometimes strengthens the relationship. Revealing parts of ourselves that we tend to keep private is one such risk. Self-disclosure entails the possibility of disapproval but also entails the possibility of increased intimacy. Some lonely people have many social relationships but complain that others do not really know them, that their relationships are superficial. One way to deepen a relationship over time is to share one's true beliefs, interests, and values—gradually, without making others feel uncomfortable or compelled to reveal more than they care to.

Making Friends

Friends enhance health and emotional well-being; friends sometimes detract from well-being. Perhaps we can reconcile these two different perspectives if we think about how we choose friends.

Social psychologists argue that we choose friends who will maximize our benefits and minimize our costs. We try to pick as friends people who are fun to be with, who can provide help if we need it, who afford us a certain amount of status, and so forth. We will not select as friends people whose behaviors disturb us in some way or even people whom we like a great deal but whom it is "costly" to get together with, such as people who live far away or who are available at inconvenient times because of odd work schedules. To the extent that we exercise control over the people we deal with, we can construct networks composed of compatible people. Many of us are able to exercise a good deal of control over our social lives and therefore insure ourselves of primarily positive experiences with others. But we rarely have perfect control.

Many factors influence the chances of forming friendships that are satisfying and lasting. Some factors have to do with the social environments we find ourselves in—how many people around us have similar interests, whom we live close to, whether our workplaces are competitive or cooperative. Other factors have to do with our personal characteristics—how much social skill we have, how pessimistic or optimistic we are, how anxious we become in social situations.

THE ROLE OF THE SOCIAL ENVIRONMENT

Why are we drawn to some people as potential friends more than to others? When people meet for the first time, what determines whether or not they like each other enough to want to meet again? Roman historian Sallust offered an answer to this question in the first century B.C.: "To like and dislike the same things, this is what makes a solid friendship." Research indeed indicates that people gravitate to others who share their values, interests, and backgrounds. Similarity makes socializing comfortable and predictable. It allows people to relax with each other, relatively secure that disagreements about important issues are unlikely. People who are similar to us enhance our self-esteem by affirming the wisdom of our beliefs and preferences.

Because similarity is such an important determinant of friendship, people who differ from those around them—the only black family in a neighborhood, the one elderly woman in an apartment building—may have few opportunities to form friendships. Sociologist Zena Blau found, for example, that widows who lived in an area in which most people were married had fewer friends generally than widows who lived in an area in which many other people were also widowed. Her study illustrates very clearly that people sometimes lack friends not because of personality problems or limited social skills, but because the social environment affords few opportunities to meet compatible people.

Another obvious but underestimated feature of the environment that affects friendship is proximity. It takes relatively little effort to see someone who lives nearby, which may make that person more attractive as a friend than someone who is equally pleasant but who lives farther away. And "farther away" needn't be very far. Studies find that next-door neighbors are more likely to be friends than neighbors separated by a few houses. Even within a single dormitory or apartment building, proximity is still important —people who live in adjacent units are more likely to become friends than people who live only a few units apart. People who live next to staircases have been found to have more friends than people who live at the end of a hall, apparently because it is easy for others to stop in or say hello on their way in and out of the building. Thus, your popularity may be partly a matter of proximity—how accessible you are to others.

Considering how much similarity and proximity influence friendships, it is easy to understand why many people look back nostalgically on college as a time of easy and abundant friendships. School life, along with such experiences as summer camp, theater groups, and professional training programs, guarantee proximity to people with similar backgrounds, goals, and needs— people in the same boat—so friendships are easily initiated. Once we move out of such settings, the opportunities to meet similar people become more haphazard and unpredictable.

Consider Katherine W., in our opening examples, who moved to a large city to accept an attractive job offer after graduating from law school. Many people would assume that because she is in a large city, she has access to a virtually unlimited pool of potential companions. This assumption may be correct in some technical sense, but it overlooks the difficulties of finding suitable contexts for meeting similar people who are open to new friendships. One's place of work could be a very convenient context for meeting others, but some jobs encourage competition and wariness rather than friendliness among workers. Even if the setting is friendly, one's fellow workers may have dissimilar interests or social needs. Many professional women who, like Katherine, defer marriage to launch a career find that they feel "out of synch" with their peers who married at a more typical age and are now engrossed in child rearing. Women who divorce and must reenter the marriage marketplace often feel a similar sense of despair at being out of step with married peers and not knowing how to go about meeting potential mates and friends.

To deny the role of the environment in making friends adds to the stigma felt by people who have fewer friends than they would like. Such basic constraints as lack of money or time also make a difference: An impoverished student who carries a heavy course load and works full-time may have little time for sleep, let alone making friends. A single parent on a tight budget may not be able to afford the baby-sitters who would give her time to get out and about.

Although Americans are allegedly free in their choice of companions, these constraints affect our ability to form the kinds of friendships we would like. People sometimes lack friends for reasons largely beyond their control.

THE ROLE OF PERSONALITY

In some cases, however, personal characteristics predispose people to be lonely. Psychologist Warren Jones and his colleagues at the University of Tulsa brought students into a room on campus and asked them to have a "get acquainted" conversation with another student whom they did not know. These conversations were videotaped and later scrutinized. It turned out that lonely students were less likely to make statements that focused on their partners, asked fewer questions, changed the topic more frequently, and responded more slowly to previous statements by their partners. Jones reasoned that lonely people tend to focus their attention inward in social situations, causing them to miss other people's words and body language. Lonely students have greater difficulty than nonlonely students in introducing themselves to others, talking on the phone, initiating social contact, matching the intimacy level of others' self-disclosures, enjoying themselves at parties, and asserting themselves.

Much of the awkwardness that lonely people reveal in these studies may be traced to social anxiety. Many lonely people are also shy, and shyness often causes them to feel distracting physiological arousal in social situations. Their hearts pound, they get butterflies in their stomachs, and they develop sweaty palms. Instead of being able to concentrate on the people they are with, they find themselves concentrating on their physiological reactions. A middle-aged salesman interviewed by shyness researcher Philip Zimbardo described this problem: "I find myself developing a habit of turning red in the face in certain situations. This is *most* distressing to me as it hinders my involvement in many activities . . . even face-to-face communication is difficult without showing signs of embarrassment." Zimbardo suggests that if shy people approach new social situations with a specific agenda, such as learning as much as possible about another person, they would be less likely to be distracted by their symptoms of anxiety. This suggestion is reasonable, although people should not be so rigid about their "agendas" that they miss what others are telling them!

Social skills can be taught in relatively short-term training programs that make use of role modeling, practice exercises, and extensive feedback. Many university and community clinics now offer social skills programs. A recent book, *Intimate Connections* by David Burns, also contains practical suggestions for improving one's social effectiveness.

Not surprisingly, given the objective difficulties they sometimes have, lonely people evaluate their own social skills harshly. In the "get acquainted" study described above, the participants were asked at the end of the conversation to rate their own skill level and personality appeal, to rate their partner on these same dimensions, and to guess how their partners had rated them. Lonely students evaluated themselves negatively and also guessed that their partners had rejected them; in fact, the partners were not particularly critical of them. The lonely students not only rated themselves negatively but also rated their partners negatively. They were critical of their partners' personalities and expressed less interest in getting to know their partners better. In other studies as well, lonely individuals turn out to be more cynical and distrustful of others than nonlonely individuals.

In extensive interviews with lonely and nonlonely people, psychologists Carin Rubenstein and Phillip Shaver encountered some very lonely individuals who "tended to be humorless complainers who made us feel tense and defensive." Such individuals tended to be reluctant or negative during the interview, often soliciting "support for their opinion of the world as a lousy place." After spending time with these people, the interviewers were apt to feel emotionally drained.

These findings point to a pattern of "rejecting others first"—lonely people expect to be rejected by others, and to avoid the pain of rejection, they focus on others' inadequacies and deny a desire for further contact. Of course, this defense against anticipated rejection leads some lonely people to avoid meeting new people altogether and leads others to search for perfection in mates and friends. Both strategies are costly because the lonely person misses out on realistic opportunities to develop friendships. One woman who had been miserably lonely for years told Rubenstein and Shaver that most of the men she met "just don't meet my standards." She habitually belittled people who tried to get close to her. As a result, most of her relationships were short-lived.

Thus, even people who have enviable social talents can suffer from loneliness because of their self-defeating ways of thinking about themselves and others. Unfortunately, maladaptive thought patterns can be tenacious. People tend to regard their automatic thoughts and assumptions—such as "I'll make a fool of myself at that party" or "He doesn't want to go out with me because I'm unattractive and boring"—as facts. If they carefully examine such automatic thoughts and the evidence that supports them, they often discover that the evidence is flimsy. A shy woman may be unable to produce convincing evidence, for example, that she always acts foolishly at parties; she may discover perfectly reasonable explanations for events that she construed as social rejections ("He didn't reject me by ignoring my wave; he didn't see me."). Mental health professionals have developed therapies to help people correct self-defeating thought patterns. These are usually called cognitive therapies or cognitive-behavioral therapies (see Chaps. 19 and 20).

Another personal characteristic that affects the ability to make friends is, paradoxically, the ability to spend time alone. Jeff Young, a psychologist at the University of Pennsylvania who has developed a form of therapy specifically for loneliness, argues that many lonely people are afraid to spend time alone. Since they do not know how to enjoy themselves on their own, he says, they are desperately dependent on other people and may overwhelm potential friends with their neediness. Young suggests that once they overcome their fears of spending time alone, they often can initiate friendships more easily. In his work with lonely clients, he first helps them identify activities that they can enjoy by themselves, such as a hobby or evening class. After they have become comfortable doing this and have learned that they can take steps independently to improve their morale, the focus of therapy shifts to how they can meet people.

Carin Rubenstein and Phillip Shaver offer similar advice. "When you are alone, give solitude a chance," they say. "Think of yourself as *with yourself,* not *without* someone else." They suggest that when we are by ourselves, we experience our most genuine needs, thoughts, and feelings—"We listen to our deepest selves." Intimacy involves disclosing our private selves to others and, in turn, listening to their private needs, thoughts, and feelings. Learning to be intimate with oneself—for example, by learning to spend enjoyable time alone—may increase one's capacity to be intimate with others.

Both environmental factors and personal characteristics determine how much success people have in establishing satisfying friendships. Unfortunately, many people whose loneliness can be traced to environmental constraints come to believe that they have major personality deficiencies simply because their loneliness persists. Such people may become cynical about themselves and others and spiral downward into self-defeating thought patterns like those described above. The general public and even many mental health professionals tend to share the bias that if someone is lonely it is because of personal failings. People who suffer from loneliness over a period of time should be urged not to underestimate the role of environmental factors.

Sometimes the best antidote to loneliness, therefore, is to change your environment rather than yourself, to immerse yourself in settings in which you can join other people doing things that you enjoy—music, watercolors, photography, camping, sports. You might sign up for an evening class or join a group such as the Sierra Club. By finding activities that you enjoy, you increase the likelihood of meeting people who are similar to you in one or more ways. In addition, if you genuinely enjoy these activities, you are less likely to be disappointed if you do not make new friends right away—at least you will enjoy yourself in the meantime. If you venture into activities that are of little interest to you personally, solely with the expectation of meeting people, you risk the double disappointment of not meeting anyone *and* of feeling that you wasted your time on something you didn't enjoy.

People whose loneliness persists over time must struggle against the tendency to become highly self-critical, since loneliness is so often at least partly due to external factors. Most lonely people eventually develop the kinds of relationships they would like to have. To avoid becoming depressed and hopeless, lonely people should not overlook the potential benefits of finding pleasurable activities that they can do alone. This is not a recommendation of last resort, because having solo satisfactions contributes to feelings of personal control and competence, and it protects against the downward spiral into self-defeating thoughts and depression.

I do not mean to endorse an ethic of excessive sociability, or to imply that dozens of acquaintances are better than one close friend. Many Americans exaggerate the benefits of friendship and overlook its very real conflicts and difficulties, even as they exaggerate the hazards of loneliness. Sometimes loneliness is unavoidable, a natural reaction to transitions in life (such as going to college or taking a new job) or to the inevitability of loss; understanding this fact can lead to greater self-acceptance and growth.

But human beings are a social species, and we depend on, we need, other people throughout our lives. Good friendships, like love, cannot be manufactured overnight. "Old friends are the great blessing of one's later years," wrote Horace Walpole, "—half a word conveys one's meaning." Perhaps the realization that friendships require the same tolerance, perspective, and humor that marriage does will encourage people to value the bonds that have taken years to develop—and not to take friends for granted.

KAREN ROOK is a psychologist on the faculty in the Program in Social Ecology at the University of California, Irvine. She studied social and clinical psychology at the University of California, Los Angeles, where she received her Ph.D. in 1980. She has written widely on the topics of social support, loneliness, and social isolation. These interests developed at an early age, when she observed what happened to elderly women when they moved to nursing homes. Her current research focuses on how the beneficial and detrimental aspects of social networks affect mental health, particularly older adults' mental health. A central goal of her work is to learn how people can be helped to have satisfying social relationships.

Further Reading

Brain, Robert. *Friends and Lovers.* New York: Basic Books, 1976.

Brehm, Sharon. *Intimate Relationships.* New York: Random House, 1985.

Burns, David D. *Intimate Connections.* New York: Morrow, 1985.

Gordon, Suzanne. *Lonely in America.* New York: Simon & Schuster, 1976.

Gottlieb, Benjamin H. *Social Support Strategies: Guidelines for Mental Health Practice.* Beverly Hills, Calif.: Sage Publications, 1983.

Hartog, Joseph, et al., eds. *The Anatomy of Loneliness.* New York: International Universities Press, 1980.

House, James S. *Work, Stress and Social Support.* Reading, Mass.: Addison-Wesley, 1981.

Lederer, William J., and Jackson, D. D. *The Mirages of Marriage.* New York: Norton, 1968.

Lynch, James J. *The Broken Heart: The Medical Consequences of Loneliness.* New York: Basic Books, 1977.

Peplau, Letitia Anne, and Perlman, Daniel, eds. *Loneliness: A Sourcebook of Theory, Research, and Therapy.* New York: Wiley-Interscience, 1982.

Rubenstein, Carin and Shaver, Phillip. *In Search of Intimacy.* New York: Delacorte Press, 1982.

Weiss, Robert S., ed. *Loneliness: The Experience of Emotional and Social Isolation.* Cambridge: MIT Press, 1973.

7

Are Women "Emotional"?

STEPHANIE A. SHIELDS

Last year the San Francisco *Chronicle* published a survey of their male readers' opinions about women. The questions were aimed at finding out what men want and don't want from women. When asked what they disliked most about women, what was the men's major complaint? Was it that women are too rational? That women aren't social enough? That women don't share enough? It should come as no surprise that heading the list of men's complaints was women's emotional behavior. Women's nagging was first, with 44 percent of the respondents naming it as their major irritation. The second most common problem (39 percent) was simply that women "get too emotional when I argue." Of course, the poll wasn't conducted in any sort of scientific, or even systematic, fashion, but still there is a bit of truth that's immediately recognized by any woman who ever disagreed with a man. Why is it "arguing" when *he* does it, but "getting emotional" when *she* does it? Why does the word "nagging" immediately bring to mind the picture of a petulant, emotional tirade? And why is the individual doing the nagging almost invariably portrayed as a female?

The popular stereotype is easily recognized. He is coolly rational, even in the face of danger. His emotional displays are limited to righteous anger and gosh-shucks tongue-tied in love. She, on the other hand, swoons with emotion at the slightest provocation. Emotions, of all qualities and quantities, are her trademark. Of course, the most exaggerated instances of the stereotypes only show up on the late, late movie. And, of course, we all know of many exceptions to the stereotype—you may even be one of the coolly rational types yourself. Nevertheless, why does the stereotype persist?

In this chapter I want to explore some of the questions raised by the persistent link between femaleness and emotion. Is there something about women's behavior that signals emotion? Should we try to stop acting emotional? How do we use "acting emotional" to get what we want? And how is the accusation that we are "acting emotional" often used to mean being *too* emotional and to prevent us from getting what we want?

What Is "Emotional," Anyway?

As the first woman to run on the presidential ticket of a major party, Geraldine Ferraro had to be mindful of the thin line that separates the expression of enthusiasm from the appearance of emotionalism. Many remember her performance in the nationally televised vice-presidential candidates' debate as especially impressive. With women so often and so easily portrayed as overly emotional, Ferraro's professional demeanor dented the stereotype. What the audience saw, however, was in no small way influenced by political allegiances. When asked for comments after the debate, Maureen Reagan, activist Republican and daughter of the Republican President, said, "I think the Vice President did an excellent job. I felt very comfortable with his positions and with the way he expressed himself. And I like a little emotion in my vice presidential debates. I get real bored real easy with people who just sort of lounge along. . . ." When queried as to whether Representative Ferraro was lounging, Reagan replied, "Well, if the shoe fits . . ." In contrast, liberal feminist Gloria Steinem concluded that Ferraro had won the debate "because she was calm and presidential and in command of the facts, and Bush was shrill and hysterical." Both Steinem and Reagan were interviewed on network television immediately after the debate and so both, well aware of the potential impact of their words, chose those words carefully. In each case the presence or absence of emotion was the factor selected to justify an opinion.

Even though emotion and emotionality are part of our everyday experience, we rarely are either specific or unambiguous about exactly what we are referring to as emotion. Even social scientists who have made it their business to investigate the causes and consequences of emotion rarely spell out how they are using their terms.

What exactly do we mean when we say that someone—or maybe even ourselves—is being "emotional"? We use the word to refer to what a person is doing in a particular situation—"Stop being so emotional!"—and we also use it to describe an enduring personality trait—"She's the emotional type." What is it about the person or situation that says "emotion"? And who is an emotional person? Is it something about the intensity of the response, the quickness of the response, the magnitude of the response, the frequency of the response, the "appropriateness" of the response, or something else? At least some of the time, as in the Ferraro-Bush debate, the observation that someone is emotional depends on who is being observed and who is doing the labeling.

For the most part, the label "emotional" is one to be shunned; emotion is believed antithetical to reasoned, mature behavior. But there is a positive side to the image of emotionality: A person who "speaks from the heart" is far more credible than someone who merely speaks. When, then, is emotion a valuable quality and when is it a defect?

A History of the Stereotype

The study of emotions posed fewer problems a hundred years ago. Scientists of the late 1800s accepted the fact of female emotionality without question: It was all simply a matter of reproductive capacity. According to one theory, development of the female brain was arrested at puberty, when blood that would ordinarily nourish the brain was diverted to the reproductive system to support fertility. As a result, the female brain was unable to develop to the point of exercising rational thought to the same degree as the male brain. Hence, there was a handy sexual division of mental labor: The "lower mental processes" (emotion and perception) were more prominent in women; the "higher mental processes" (reason and creativity) were more prominent in men.

Female emotionality seemed, to the Victorian scientist, to provide elegant validation of the structure of middle- and upper-class everyday life. In 1894 one British scientist summed up the accepted facts of psychological sex differences with the observation that "there is nowhere, perhaps, a more beautiful instance of complementary adjustment between the Male and Female character, than that which consists in the predominance of the Intellect and Will, which is required to make a man successful in the 'battle of life,' and of the lively Sensibility, the quick Sympathy, the unselfish Kindliness, which give to women the power of making the happiness of the home, and of promoting the purest pleasures of social existence."

In other words, man thinks, woman feels. This belief still lives. Whether one peruses newspaper comic strips, college textbooks, or television, the consensus is still that to be female is to be "emotional." This stereotype of female emotionality even carries over into how we view ourselves and our personal relationships. Whether the responses are collected through anonymous surveys or individual interviews, women are willing to report that they express their emotions more than men. Like other gender stereotypes, ideas about sex-related differences in emotional expression and emotionality are learned early in life.

Not all emotions are associated with being a woman. Some emotion-related qualities, such as creativity, sense of humor, and charisma, are much more likely to be attributed to men than women. Nor is the emotional female an angry one; anger and aggressiveness are commonly viewed as male traits. Some of the respondents in the *Chronicle* newspaper survey, in fact, complained that women were not aggressive enough! One group of research psychologists found that even preschoolers know which emotion is associated with which sex. Children, like adults, associate anger with men but happiness, sadness, and fear with women.

Although women today are better educated and better employed than ever, the image of women in the media has not progressed much beyond Betty Boop. Even though some sex stereotypes are less prevalent than they were twenty years ago, emotion is still portrayed as a female quality. A recent study found that while few sex-stereotypic behaviors characterize male and female characters on prime-time television, women reveal more emotional distress than men do. Further, even though girls and women are greatly outnumbered by boys and men on TV, female characters are more likely to deal with the problems of others or require assistance from others to deal with their own problems. Children's programming is even worse. Not only is the proportion of female characters even smaller, but those few females are far more likely to be portrayed as silly, overemotional, and dependent on husbands and boyfriends.

The link between femaleness and emotion may be strong in the public mind, but the link between emotion and irrationality is even stronger. The continuing popularity of "self-improvement programs" has been accompanied by increased popular attention directed toward emotion research. Experts and pseudoexperts hold forth in newspaper interviews and television talk shows. Popular books give us advice on how to understand and use emotion, especially interpreting others' and controlling our own. Some books even encourage us to get in touch with and express our feelings. Although these exhortations purport to celebrate emotion, their real message is to get potentially unruly feelings under control. The well-understood emotion, the one we're "in touch" with, is the emotion that won't get in the way. The message is to regularize emotion, to express it ("appropriately," of course), but to prevent it from interrupting "normal" rational thought.

Everywhere we turn the message is the same: Women are ruled by emotion, and too much emotion or the wrong kind of emotion is bad indeed. Is it any wonder that we begin to believe this stereotype about ourselves? To worry that maybe we are too frequently being just another emotional—read *over*emotional"—female?

The Stereotype Up Close: Are Women "More Emotional"?

Some of the most exciting contemporary work about the way that women express and experience emotion can be found in four areas of research: nonverbal expression of emotion, emotion talk, emotion in relationships, and emotion and cognitive complexity.

NONVERBAL EXPRESSION OF EMOTION

Have you ever been aware that the person you are talking to, someone who might well seem to be bubbling over with effusive honesty and sincerity, was, nevertheless, lying to you? How could you tell? What was it about the expression on that individual's face, the body posture, the small hand gestures, the direction of gaze, that told you something was amiss? It wasn't in the person's words, which conveyed a quite different message, but in the nonverbal qualities of behavior. We rely on these cues for much of the information we use to understand and manage our interactions with others. The only way we really have of understanding other people's emotions, if they do not choose to tell us, is through the silent signals they give.

The study of nonverbal cues has produced consistent differences in women's and men's production and interpretation of facial expression. Most of what we know comes from the study of emotional expressiveness, which, of course, doesn't necessarily correspond to what the person experiences. Women's faces tend to be more expressive than men's, and women's expressiveness is more easily interpreted by others. Most of these studies of expressiveness are done in controlled laboratory situations, and so participants are aware of the fact that *something* about their behavior is being observed and measured. Women and men might, therefore, be influenced by how they believe they ought to be acting. Nevertheless, the greater expressiveness of women is a fairly consistent finding. Whether the researcher asks women to complete a mock interview as themselves or asks them to role-play a character, women's behavior has more of an "emotional," expressive quality than men's. Similarly, adult men and women differ in their ability to "read" and understand others' nonverbal expressions of emotion. Think of the emotional dynamics apparent at the simplest dinner party. How often does a woman find herself explaining that covert emotional text to her male companion on the way home?

But no one really knows why women are more expressive than men (in the United States). Most often the writer whose job it is to make sense of these findings explains the difference as probably a bit of nature and a bit of nurture, without going into any detail about exactly how biology and learning might interact. One problem is that, even though much of our nonverbal behavior is spontaneously expressed and involves no conscious effort, we are very adept at intentionally overriding spontaneous displays. We suppress giggles on sad occasions, we playact rage to get a child's attention, we smile when we're inwardly miserable. As adults we not only monitor our expressions, we are highly practiced at exaggerating, neutralizing, attenuating, or substituting expressions. The first-grade teacher learns early on that success or failure as a teacher depends in no small way on the ability to control expressions: A too subtle communication of approval or a too angry reprimand can interfere with the product of weeks of establishing rapport with the child.

Research psychologists Carol Malatesta and Jeannette Haviland have proposed a way of understanding where these sex-related differences in expressiveness might come from. Each has done extensive research on the development of infant's expressiveness, and the expressiveness that characterizes the way that babies and mothers relate to one another. They suggest that sex-related differences in expressiveness have their roots in the earliest social interactions of infancy. They hypothesize that innate sex-related differences in infant temperament interact in an important way with caregivers' expectations for boys' and girls' behavior. In their research they have found that boy babies, who, in general, begin life as more emotionally changeable than girls, evoke a different pattern of expressiveness from their mothers than girls do. Adults—both men and women—seem to expect more negativism from boy babies and appear to make more of an effort to placate them. Early in life, boys and girls learn to expect different consequences for expressiveness, whether it be smiling, laughing, or crying.

Girls also apply their knowledge about the meaning of expressiveness to social situations differently than boys do. In an ingenious series of research studies, Carolyn Saarni investigated children's knowledge about when and when not to show one's feelings. In research with six-to-ten-year-olds, she has found that children show a steady and significant increase with age in their knowledge of when and how a person should try to disguise his or her feelings. The complexity of the reasons that children give for the desirability of controlling emotional expressions also increases with age. In one particularly interesting study, Saarni turned her attention to children's spontaneous management of their expressions. After all, just because children say that smiling through one's tears is a good idea, they may not follow their own advice when the time comes. One of the most important social occasions for controlling expression is receiving a gift. In our culture you are expected to look pleased, even if you don't like it. So Saarni interviewed children individually, having them complete an assignment from a typical school workbook while being videotaped. The children had been led to expect a nice gift in appreciation of their work, but when they picked a gift out of the grab bag, it turned out to be a drab baby toy. Each child's reaction to this disappointing turn of events was videotaped, and Saarni looked at the frequency of positive, negative, and mixed expressions. Once again, performance was strongly related to age. The older children were much better at putting on a polite smile. But girls showed more positive expressions to the undesirable toy at all ages, and even older boys revealed more mixed expressions than positive ones. Saarni suggests that not only have the ten-year-old girls learned what it means to be "nice," but the ten-year-old boys have learned that they don't need to make the same degree of effort.

EMOTION TALK

Some research suggests that women, at least in the United States, like to talk more about emotions than do men. Women say that talking about emotion helps to sort out their feelings and to express closeness in relationships. These conclusions, though, are based on what people *say* they prefer to do, but not what they might actually *do* in real-life conversations. The main reason that we know so little about ordinary talk is that it's very difficult to collect samples of it. You have to persuade people to carry around and use a tape recorder in their personal conversations. Then they have to be responsible enough to remember to turn the recorder on and off! If those aren't problems enough, you then have pages and pages of transcription to do, including all those "uhs" and "umms," to yield enough emotion talk for systematic examination. Given these difficulties, very little research using actual conversation outside of "set-up" laboratory situations has been done.

A researcher at the University of California at Davis, Susan Shimanoff, has undertaken this formidable task, and, given the stereotype of the emotional female, the results she has obtained so far are surprising. First of all, the amount of talk in which emotions are named—as in "I'm really furious" —represents a very small proportion of everyday conversation. In the pages and pages of transcription of conversations, only a very small percentage of the talk actually named emotions. Second, women and men use about the same number of emotion words in conversation. The only sex difference that she found was in the greater number of references to emotion men made when they talked to women than when they talked to other men. It looks like men talk to women about their feelings, but women talk to men and women equally.

EMOTION IN RELATIONSHIPS

Gushing emotionality is perhaps the most fundamental, and most damaging, component of the emotional female stereotype. Whether as Blanche DuBois oozing emotional vulnerability or as Scarlett O'Hara willfully manipulating emotional display, the preoccupation of women with the emotional qualities of a relationship is presumed to be essential to their satisfaction with it.

In the few naturalistic studies that have investigated how frequently people actually experience different feelings, men and women do not differ much, even when the prototypically "masculine" emotion of anger is considered. Although women report that they feel emotion more frequently than men, when people keep diaries of actual emotion episodes, the difference in reported frequency and intensity disappears.

The *value* the sexes place on emotion is another matter, however. And although more women than men again report that emotional sharing is important to them, unexpected findings emerge if we consider romance and falling in love. If we leave aside the question of who really *feels* more love, and focus on people's beliefs about the nature of love and its importance, men are more romantic than women. According to Letitia Anne Peplau and Steven Gordon, a psychologist-sociologist team, men (as a group) are more likely than women to believe in love at first sight, to value flirting, to endorse romantic values, to consider love as the most important basis for marriage, and to fall in love more easily. And they are less likely than women to think of a romantic partner as a best friend! (See Chap. 4.)

Once the honeymoon is over, however, the division of labor in household tasks—i.e., she does them—seems to have a counterpart in the division of responsibilities for communication—i.e., she has them. Women of all classes report that they expect to share feelings, and they spend a good deal of effort drawing their partners out. Working-class men are more likely to disdain efforts to share feelings and middle-class men are more willing to place a positive value on emotional sharing. The kinds of expectations that spouses have about one another's emotional expressiveness is played out in roles they assume when talking to each other. One researcher at the University of Illinois, John Gottman, found that in self-described happy marriages, it is the husband who deescalates minor conflicts by meeting his wife's negative remark in a positive way. At higher levels of conflict it is the wife who takes over the role of emotion moderator. In unhappy marriages, he found, neither member of the couple could successfully defuse the buildup of tension.

The weeping Scarlett image—of the woman who turns on the tears to get her own way—must also be questioned. A group of psychologists at Peabody College, intrigued by the discrepancy between the manipulative image and the worries that women report having about breaking down and crying, decided to look at some of the causes and experiences connected with "public tears." In their study of a group of professionals, they found that women were about four times as likely as men to report having cried in a professional situation. These women said that they felt a special sense of helplessness, a desire to remain in control that somehow totally eluded them in the situation. They often reported anger as a component of their feelings, but felt incapable of acting on that anger. Those in the presence of the crying woman felt that they were being called upon to console her or do something about the situation, but, far from trying to manipulate anyone, she simply wanted the whole incident to be ignored.

EMOTION AND COGNITIVE COMPLEXITY OF THOUGHT

The "emotional" person is supposed to be primitive, irrational, and immature, but Psychologist Shula Sommers wondered about what the "emotional" person is really like. Someone who tends to let emotion win out over reason? Someone who is less socially mature and responsible than others? Or are there some qualities possessed by the emotional person that, contrary to the stereotype, are positive and constructive? To find out, Sommers asked people who varied in emotional range (defined as the reported capacity to feel a variety of emotions within and across situations) to complete an empathy test—a measure of the ability to take another person's perspective. Those who had the greater emotional range were more easily able to understand a situation from another perspective and also produced more complex descriptions of other people. Sommers interpreted the capacity for applying a broad understanding of emotion to situations as indicating a highly organized appreciation of factors that influence one's own and others' behavior, an awareness that suggests a highly developed personal value system.

Up close, the stereotype of the emotional female is clearly a gross oversimplification. Both women and men are likely to believe that the stereotype is true, but if we take an unbiased look, we find that men and women differ little in how much they talk about emotion or in how much "emotional" behavior they reveal. Further, the ability to appreciate the complexity of one's own and others' emotions—rather than being nonrational—appears to be linked to other very sophisticated cognitive skills. But women and men do differ in their *expectations* about emotion and the *meaning* that emotion has for them. The differences in grown women's and men's ideas about emotion begin in the earliest social exchanges of infancy.

The breadth and power of early socialization is especially powerful in influencing emotional development, instructing us to become effective members of our culture, to hold the values and attitudes considered appropriate for a person of our ethnic group, family background, and sex. Internal qualities, such as ideas about right and wrong, and visible qualities, such as "ladylike" behavior, are products of our early learning. From the time we are young children, we watch others and model our behavior and our attitudes on respected and powerful others. Our "appropriate" emotional behavior is rewarded, as when Mom comes to our aid when we cry after falling off the bicycle. "Inappropriate" behavior is not rewarded and may even be punished, as when our high school girlfriends tell us that we'll never get dates if we insist on appearing too smart in front of boys. Much of what is popularly considered the emotional "nature" of women is more likely the outcome of early and abiding learning.

Constructing Emotions: How They Are Identified, Labeled, and Used

If you were to ask a cross section of American adults where emotion "comes from," most would explain emotion as a natural capacity, an inescapable biological fact of being human. Many would also mention the existence of "basic" emotions, such as happiness, fear, and anger, as the fundamental building blocks from which all more complex emotional states are formed. This idea—that all people are born with the capacity to experience specific, fundamental emotions—is not only the prevailing layperson's view, but it is also the oldest scientific explanation of emotion.

Yet another, more recently developed approach looks at emotion in terms of its social, rather than biological, foundations. In this view emotion isn't an outpouring of a biologically based impulse, but a well-learned social response. Psychologist James Averill at the University of Massachusetts asserts that human emotion is fundamentally a deeply acted social role. That is, without any intent to be manipulative (in fact, without any real conscious strategy), we behave emotionally as part of a role; we experience the emotion when we are in a conflict or in situations that threaten conflict.

But if emotion is just a social role, why don't we think of our emotions as a charade? Why do we believe so deeply that they are uncontrollable and unplanned reactions? This belief runs throughout the language: "I couldn't help myself, it just came pouring out of me, it just couldn't stay bottled up any longer." These and other common references to emotion, Averill says, point to how strongly we believe, and need to believe, in emotion as something that just happens to us. How exactly does emotion reduce conflict if we believe that emotion itself is uncontrollable? According to Averill, it is precisely that belief that makes emotion effective—"If I don't have control over something, I can't be responsible for it." Emotion is a way of relinquishing responsibility for one's words and actions.

For example, think of the last time you were angry with a friend. Perhaps it had some of the features of the following scenario. Kim and Jill have plans for a tennis game Tuesday afternoon, but when Kim drives over to pick Jill up, Jill isn't ready; she's just come in and hasn't even changed her clothes yet. It seems that Jill met a terrific guy that afternoon, had coffee with him, and let time get away from her. Kim will just have to wait a few minutes. Jill's been late before—in fact, she's late more often than she is on time. But now Kim feels she has had to cool her heels at Jill's house once too often. What does she do? Of course, there are drastic measures—coolly terminate the friendship; do something to harm Jill as a way of evening the score. Kim could also just ignore the problem, but that would solve nothing. What does Kim do? She gets angry. She doesn't plan to, mind you, nor does she particularly like what is happening. The situation "gets the best of her" and the next thing anyone knows, she has let Jill know exactly how she feels, how unfairly she believes Jill is treating her, how selfishly Jill is acting, and maybe even more. In short, Kim's anger does the talking. The next day when she makes up with Jill, she is free to do so because, after all, it was just another case of emotion getting the upper hand. As for Jill, her happiness with a new romantic prospect also helps to maintain her friendship with Kim. Of course, she wasn't rejecting Kim with her tardiness—she was just so carried away by being happy that she temporarily forgot her responsibilities to her friend. She was so happy that she just "couldn't help herself." The air is cleared, and the friendship is saved. Score another victory for emotion—Jill's joy and Kim's anger.

What about your own experiences? Chances are you have said some things that hurt a friend's feelings, some things that, though honestly felt and honestly believed, could only have come out in the heat of anger. If that angry episode has been resolved and you've made up with your friend, you might be a bit more inclined to believe how important emotion is in making some kinds of revelations possible. Would you still be friends if you had said and done those things believing that you were being coldly rational and "in control"? Would your friend accept an apology without being able to forgive your momentary lapse in rationality—without believing that there was something almost "accidental" about it? This is precisely the function of emotion that Averill and others have focused on. For emotion to serve its social purpose, it is essential that we believe ourselves helplessly in its thrall. Human beings, after all, are social beings. So it makes sense to ask what's social about the very private experience of emotion.

Chances are very good that if you took a small poll your friends would agree that feeling happy, sad, angry, or scared is feeling an emotion, but feeling hungry, sleepy, nauseated, or alert isn't. Even though we are never really sure whether others' experience of some emotion is the same as our own, even though people may express this emotion very differently, we agree that it is an emotion. We learn other things about emotion as well, for example, that emotions are irrational, difficult or impossible to control, and that they can't really be trusted under most circumstances. Not only do we learn what we should feel and when we should show what we feel, we also learn the importance of labels for those feelings. In the example of Kim and Jill, what would you have thought of Kim's behavior toward Jill's irresponsibility if I'd called her reaction "pouty"? Would it be different if I'd called it "exasperated"? Or what about "upset"? There's a lot in a name, especially when it says so much about how rational and how much in control, in other words, how "reasonable," the behavior is.

For example, Debbie and Rebekah own a small business together, and because the business is new, they have to share responsibility for many of the mundane tasks that keep an office in order. Things are going well for them and they know that soon they'll have the money to hire permanent help to manage the office. This morning Debbie arrived for the day's work and found that once again she had to finish up some filing and make some telephone calls that Rebekah was supposed to have taken care of yesterday. Rebekah's irresponsible behavior is beginning to cost their new business money, and Debbie is concerned that lack of attention to details could make the difference between survival and bankruptcy. So when Rebekah comes in for the day, Debbie says that they need to talk over these problems. Rebekah immediately counters with, "You sound upset. You don't have to get angry, you know." At this, Debbie, who a moment ago neither looked angry, sounded angry, nor felt angry, loudly announces, "I am NOT upset. I am NOT angry." And yet it is clear to Rebekah, to any other bystander, and even to Debbie herself that, yes, she is indeed upset.

What has just happened? "Upset" and "angry" are both emotion labels. By suggesting that Debbie was acting under the influence of emotion, Rebekah has effectively undermined Debbie's reasoned position. If Debbie were simply under the sway of emotion, then she obviously couldn't help what she was doing, was not being completely rational, and was not in complete control of herself. In short, she wasn't being responsible and so we should not place great value on the content of what she has said. Then why did Debbie respond angrily? Debbie knows as well as we do that emotion, when it is a replacement for reason, is to be devalued and even disbelieved. When Rebekah labeled her behavior emotional, Debbie responded as does anyone who believes he or she is the victim of injustice. She responded with anger. She had been speaking from the vantage point of reason and rightness, and so when she was treated as being *merely* emotional, she was provoked to anger.

Think back to the *Chronicle* newspaper poll I mentioned at the beginning of this chapter. A substantial proportion of the male respondents felt that women's emotions get in the way during an argument. If we consider what the statement says about the relative value of one's own and another's position, the men's real message is clear: "I believe what I'm saying—therefore, I am arguing rationally; I don't like what she's saying, so she's just being emotional."

Applying emotion labels to ourselves and to others is typically not a deliberate strategy, but neither is it an accidental or random process. Sociologist Arlie Hochschild suggests that there are implicit rules that govern what we should feel and when we should feel it, just as there are other social rules that dictate when to shake hands or leave a party or smile. On some occasions it feels "right" to feel sad, but on others it seems inappropriate. Hochschild contends that rules for *feeling* are as rigid and as stringently enforced as rules for *behavior.* And like the rules for behavior, others let us know when we fail to follow them; we actively attempt to alter our feelings to conform. If I'm a guest at a wedding, there are strict social conventions that specify my behavior. During the ceremony I should be quiet, attentive, and generally on my best behavior. During the reception festivities, I should be enthusiastic and, depending on the wedding's formality, I might even be expected to let go altogether. Likewise, there are rules to guide my feelings. If I'm not happy, I wonder why and attempt to get into the proper emotional state. If others notice that I'm not happy, they will question me, encourage me, and even goad me into feeling as I ought to. And they won't be satisfied by my simply *acting* happy; I must *be* happy. We also apply these emotion rules to ourselves and we work to make our emotional state conform to what we believe it "ought" to be. Have you ever, for example, found yourself *trying* to make yourself happy for a friend's success? Have you ever worked at staying in love after the romance was clearly over? This is what Hochschild calls "emotion work."

Hochschild has investigated who has to spend the most effort managing emotions as well as the circumstances when emotion work is expected. It shouldn't surprise us that women are often called on to monitor their feelings, both in the role of the nurturant mother and at work outside the home. In fact, in many traditionally female occupations, showing correct feelings is an essential part of the job. The waitress, the worker in a home for the elderly, the bank teller, the teacher—all are expected to be *feeling* a certain way as much as each is expected to perform other tasks on the job. Hochschild estimates that having appropriate feelings is an essential part of the job for fully one half of all female workers. The emotion work that we do— to make sure that we have those correct feelings, and to display them to clients and customers—is seldom recognized as significant. And it may—sooner for some than for others—contribute to a sense of alienation from one's real self and real feelings, a central feature of burnout.

The Pros and Cons of Emotionality

Although most people think of emotion in negative terms, as the opposite of reason, emotion is a natural and valuable process. It is a powerful and constructive factor in everyday life. It has great power to motivate, whether we are fleeing in fear to reach safety or reaching out to be closer to someone we love. Moreover, "to speak from the heart" is to speak not only with the voice of reason, but with the conviction of emotion. Would you rather vote for a political candidate who is invariably cool and rational or one who speaks reasonably, yet with passionate involvement? At the movies do you want the leading lady to choose the lover who says "I love you" flatly, in a voice devoid of energy, or the one whose voice trembles with desire?

As women we have had years of learning to value our emotional feelings and expression. We enjoy the benefits of shared confidences, social support, and a sense of belonging that grow out of the emotional dimension of relationships. We are well aware, too, of the expectations that are placed on us to be emotional at particular times in particular ways, whether in doing emotion work on the job or through assuming the arbiter-of-emotion role in relationships with men. What should we then do—if anything—about being "emotional"?

First, we have to remember that emotionality, to some extent, is in the eye of the beholder. Whether they are judging Geraldine Ferraro in a vice presidential debate, or Debbie trying to make it through another day at the office, people put labels on "emotional" behavior whether it corresponds to true feelings or not. In this sense a woman's emotional well-being depends on her being able to convince others of the seriousness of her words, her wishes, and her intentions—whether she is expressing them calmly or with passion. The reason that "You're beautiful when you're mad" is so infuriating to women is that the man who thinks he is offering a compliment is not listening to the *content* of her anger.

Second, emotional well-being depends on understanding and identifying our inner emotional experience (the emotion we feel, instead of the emotion we use or display). Feeling depressed and displaying misery have very different consequences—for a woman and the people around her—than feeling angry and displaying irritability. The particular emotions we feel can have long-term consequences for health and psychological well-being. One especially telling example of the relationship between emotion and health has come out of a long-term study of women's reactions to and recovery from sexual assault. The probability that a sexual assault would result in rape was correlated with the immediate experience of fear in the situation: Women who avoided potential rapes were more likely to report that their immediate emotion was anger rather than fear. Further, the fear persisted in those who continued to suffer from feelings of victimization in the weeks and months following the attack. At Temple University another group found that self-defense training or assertiveness training can in fact help women to reinterpret fear-evoking situations as situations that violate their rights and so to develop the capacity for self-protective anger.

These findings suggest that improving the quality of our lives is not just a matter of learning self-control or becoming "nonemotional." Self-control, after all, was a very important component in learning to be "good girls" as children. In the end, we may discover that the question of emotional well-being depends not simply on *whether* to be "emotional," but *which* emotion to feel, where to express it, and to whom.

STEPHANIE SHIELDS did her graduate work in psychology at Pennsylvania State University. She received her Ph.D. in 1976 and is currently associate professor of psychology and director of the Women's Studies Program at the University of California, Davis. She first became interested in the social meaning of emotion as a Head Start Program college-student intern while watching the children's use of humor on the playground. Her research is directed toward explaining how the process of socialization affects emotional experience and how the concept of emotion is used as a social construct. She is especially happy when the results of her scientific research can be applied to understanding everyday life.

Further Reading

Averill, James R. "Studies on Anger and Aggression." *American Psychologist* 38, no.11(1983):1145–60.

Hochschild, Arlie R. *The Managed Heart.* Berkeley: University of California Press, 1983.

Mayo, Clara, and Henley, Nancy M., eds. *Gender and Nonverbal Behavior.* New York: Springer-Verlag, 1981. See especially Jeannette Haviland and Carol Malatesta, "A Description of the Development of Sex Differences in Nonverbal Signals: Fallacies, Facts, and Fantasies."

Peplau, Letitia Anne, and Gordon, Steven L. "Women and Men in Love: Sex Differences in Close Heterosexual Relationships." In *Women, Gender, and Social Psychology,* edited by Virginia O'Leary, Rhoda K. Unger, and Barbara Strudler Wallston. Hillsdale, N.J.: Erlbaum, 1985.

Rubin, Lillian B. *Intimate Strangers.* New York: Harper & Row, 1983.

Saarni, Carolyn. "An Observational Study of Children's Attempts to Monitor their Expressive Behavior." *Child Development* 55 (1984):1504–13.

Shields, Stephanie A. "To Pet, Coddle, and 'Do For': Caretaking and the Concept of Maternal Instinct." In *In the Shadow of the Past: Psychology Portrays the Sexes,* edited by Miriam Lewin. New York: Columbia University Press, 1984.

Shimanoff, Susan B. "The Role of Gender in Linguistic References of Emotive States." *Communication Quarterly* 31 (1983):174–79.

Tavris, Carol. *Anger: The Misunderstood Emotion.* New York: Simon & Schuster/Touchstone, 1984.

TRANSITIONS

8

Adolescence

ELIZABETH DOUVAN

Adolescence, a transitional stage between childhood and adulthood, is often compared to a bridge: The child starts at one end of the bridge, travels over a deep, mysterious chasm, and arrives at the other side transformed into an adult. The bridge image serves pretty well but leaves out certain complexities of the situation. Sometimes the adolescent herself is the bridge; that is, sometimes she will span the chasm with her own self, with one foot firmly in adulthood but certain other aspects still clearly childlike. If we think of the bridge as the path that society offers the young person on which to make her way to adult status, then it is clear that different societies and different parts of our own society provide very different paths.

In some parts of the world girls are transformed into women by the stroke of a ritual: The day the young girl menstruates, she is taken to a ritual bath or a special women's hut where she is introduced to the mysteries of adulthood and the society of adult women. She has been preparing for this ritual all her life, learning the skills and ways of doing things that she will need in her adult life. But the transformation itself is short, clear, and decisive.

In our own complex society the beginning and end of the passage are less decisive. Beginning to menstruate may be the start of the process of becoming adult, but what would we say is the end? In traditional parts of our culture (in some small towns and in rural areas; among some religious groups) marriage makes the girl a woman. Or if not marriage, then certainly the birth of her first child marks her as an adult. In very traditional cultures the time period between a girl's first menstruation and the birth of her first child is short.

But in our society, particularly in more educated groups, the transition period has grown and the young woman's development through adolescence to adulthood has come to share characteristics with boys' development: She is now expected to continue her schooling and to develop an adult identity anchored at least in part in her individual talents and skills. Her identity is no longer to be completely or largely based on her family roles of wife and mother. Now the young woman will reach adulthood when she assumes a work role *or* the role of wife. Her journey from childhood to adulthood now looks more like her brother's.

Adolescence, then, has become more a process of self-exploration and choices. When girls had just one possible route to adulthood, they may have had a hard time fitting into the path, but they did not have to worry about choosing among many possible routes. Expanded opportunities bring increased freedom, and an increased demand for making choices and developing a complex and aware self. The increased complexity makes the process more ambiguous and open-ended. When adulthood meant marrying and/or having a baby, it was clear and easy to pinpoint. When adulthood has more aspects (economic independence, achievement of an individual identity based on work as well as marriage and parenthood), then it also becomes possible to be an adult in one arena but not in another. The whole question of the end of adolescence becomes more ambiguous.

In our society the entire period of adolescence is one of enormous ambiguity. You are no longer a child yet not quite adult. You look adult, but you are not accepted into adult society. You are expected to behave responsibly in many areas and with all the self-control and skill of an adult, yet you are often not treated as though you were responsible and you are not given many of the privileges adults enjoy and expect. You can at any moment be told what to do and expected to obey without question, just as a child is expected to do. At the next moment you are expected to think for yourself and be responsible for yourself. At the same time that the world is changing in the way it looks at you and the demands it puts on you, your body and your experience of it are also changing dramatically. The most familiar of all realities—your own body, your own self—is changing rapidly.

Lest this begin to sound as though adolescence is overwhelmingly difficult, I should note right away that many of the changes in body and self are pleasurable, the source of new powers and new delights. You are growing taller and stronger. Though you may not be aware of it, you are also getting smarter: You can think about the future and the possible as well as the present and actual. You are capable of highly abstract thought. You can pose the largest and most profound questions that human beings are capable of. You don't have as much experience as adults have, but you have as much brainpower and are capable of as hard and complex thought as adults are.

Besides changing in height and strength, your body is changing in shape and in other ways related to your sexual identity. During adolescence you develop breasts and other distinguishing sexual characteristics. Your sexual and reproductive organs develop and produce great hormonal changes in your body. You become capable of conceiving and bearing children and your sex drive increases in strength.

Hormonal changes can create puzzling changes in your moods and your feelings about yourself. You may experience mood swings that seem entirely mysterious, for which you can discover no reason or outside cause. In the past when you felt sad or angry, it was because of some real, definable event that happened to you. Now your feelings sometimes seem completely detached from reality, neither understandable nor manageable, and not entirely welcome.

So adolescence is complicated, a mixture of great, expanding, exciting developments and plenty of puzzles and problems. Sometimes the only comforting thought is that it *is* a stage, that you will not always feel like this, and that whatever pain and confusion you're feeling, it's probably par for the course. Remember, too, that while this may be one of the hardest stages of life, nature arranged things so that just when you face this hard time, you are also developing new strengths and abilities with which to handle problems. You will discover your own powers as you deal with the hurts and challenges, the ambiguities and confusions of adolescence.

In the rest of this chapter I will look at the major tasks that adolescent women confront and outline various resources that can be useful in handling them. I will discuss body and health issues; relationships with parents and other family members; relationships with friends and boyfriends; developing values, your own ideas, standards, and personal responsibility; and finally, making choices and building a vision of your future. At the end of this discussion there is a small section intended for mothers of adolescent daughters, offering some thoughts about living with adolescents and helping them to grow.

Your Body, Your Physical Health

Because of the extremely rapid growth and change you are going through, your body is operating under stress. It is especially important that you pay attention to good nutrition and to your need for regular exercise and sufficient rest. You are on the go most of the time, and it's not easy to eat properly when you're out with friends and stopping at fast-food places, or running from home to school to work and back to school for play rehearsal or band or other activities. But you *do* need nutritious meals and a balanced diet to give you the energy for all your activities and to protect your body against illness and strain. Some of you will grow as much as four to six inches in a year. To fuel all this growth and activity without becoming vulnerable to illness, you need the natural vitamins and minerals and other nutrients that only a balanced diet can provide.

In recent years psychologists have become more and more aware of disturbances in young women's patterns of eating. Eating disorders are more common and more extreme now than they were in previous generations. Anorexia, bulimia, and uncontrolled binge eating are signs of serious problems that need to be understood in relation to many other developments in adolescence.

For example, the changes in metabolism that are natural during adolescence may cause some young women to gain weight; others, as they grow taller, lose their "baby fat." A certain amount of fat is *necessary* for the onset of menstruation, but nowadays many teenagers have an unrealistic "fear of fatness." Crash diets, fasting, and "yo-yo" binges or diets are not only unhealthy; they don't teach you how to eat to maintain the best body weight—and they may even prime your body to be fatter. Eventually, the metabolic swings will settle down, and so will your weight (see Chap. 16 for more information on diets and weight).

If you worry about your eating habits or find that you are developing new and strange attitudes toward food and eating, don't let fear or embarrassment keep you from turning to your family or friends for advice and help. You can try to handle the problem on your own, but if it continues to worry you, talk to someone about it. If for some reason you can't talk to your parents, go to a sympathetic teacher or the school nurse, your family doctor or your friend's mother. But do talk to someone. Maybe your worry is unfounded and you have just gotten frightened by some of the things you've read about eating disorders (we all tend at times to be influenced by things we read and come to feel that we have whatever is being described). But if there is a real base for your worry, you should get some help before you get sick or develop a serious health problem.

Despite the fact that your body is changing and at times seems to be playing tricks on you, and despite the fact that we all find things about our bodies that we might wish were different, your body is, nonetheless, the source of your strength and health and pleasure in life. Treat it with respect and it will repay you with years of good feeling and health. When you are young, it is hard to imagine that something you are doing now could have permanent ill effects. Who can imagine that the junk food, bad diet, or heavy smoking you enjoy now could lead to high blood pressure or heart problems at the age of forty? Some facts we have to take on faith or on the experience of other people. The consequences of learning through trial and error are too grave to risk experimenting.

Your Changing Body: Sex Drive, Sexual Feelings, and Sexual Behavior

Aside from your body's growth spurt, the most startling changes you have experienced since puberty are those that involve sex and your sexual identity. Your body is not just larger now than it was before puberty. It has changed in ways that are specifically associated with being female. Changes in the sex organs and in the production of hormones prepare you for adult sexual love and reproductive functioning. Biologically, you are now (or will soon be) ready to have babies. This does not mean that you are socially ready to take on the responsibilities of motherhood. But your *body* is now capable of reproducing.

Sex is nature's way of insuring that a species will reproduce itself. Falling in love, feelings of sexual attraction, sexual excitement, and romance are all forces that help insure that babies will be born and the species will continue.

The sex drive is part of our animal nature, an aspect of life that human beings have in common with species throughout the animal kingdom. But human sex is neither as controlled by instinct nor as restricted to reproduction as it is in lower animals. It is freer of biological constraints and more malleable. Of all the species, only we humans write romantic poetry, or change our standards of "sexy" clothes every year. We can even choose to live a celibate life in a convent, thereby radically denying expression to an important aspect of our nature.

Accepting one's sexual nature and integrating it into a new, grown-up sense of one's self is a central task of the adolescent years. Learning about the nature of one's sexual feelings, coming to understand them and test out one's sex drive and one's ability to control it: These are all part of the work of becoming adult that you will accomplish during adolescence.

Integrating sexual feelings and behavior into one's developing self—making this element of life part of one's self without either rejecting or being overwhelmed by it—is among the most subtle and profound aspects of development. Changes in our society's attitudes toward sex—the greater openness in discussion, the inclusion of sex education in schools, the reduction of fear and superstition that treated sex as somehow shameful or "bad," and the acceptance of sex as both natural and one of life's special pleasures—have eased the task of integration for young people. Yet it is still tricky to come to understand one's sexual nature and to find ways to express it that are satisfying and acceptable to oneself and the people one loves. Sex is special and it merits respect. It can be one of life's profound experiences, but it can also be misused and painful if it is not respected.

In some ways the changes in society's sexual attitudes and norms have also complicated adolescents' task of coming to terms with sex. Norms are changing; there is no single way of behaving and thinking that everyone agrees on in our society. There are now many ways of defining what it means to be a sexual being and what it means to be a woman. Although this means greater tolerance for a variety of definitions, it also puts a greater burden on each individual to choose her own definition and construct a way of being that fits her own sense of self. Today it is possible for a woman to express her sexual nature through a monogamous marriage or a series of relatively long-lasting relationships. She may have children in a legal marriage or as a single parent or she may decide not to have children at all. She may put her career at the center of her life rather than the family roles of wife and mother. The options are much broader than they were even twenty-five years ago.

The availability of many options has made our society a better and more reasonable place for more different kinds of people. Fewer people get punished for not meeting society's standards when more than one standard is available. But when there are many acceptable ways to live, each of us has the responsibility for choosing the one that fits best with her own taste and preference. In this sense freedom brings greater responsibility.

Let me give an example. Until the 1960s colleges used to have parietal rules that governed most aspects of students' lives, particularly women students' lives. It was often the rule that women had to be in their dormitories by 10 or 11 P.M. on week nights. If a young woman was out with a date and he pressed her to stay out a little later, she could point out that if she didn't get in by ten, she would be grounded for the next week (or two weekends, or whatever). Once parietal rules are abandoned, she has to take the responsibility for her choice more directly. If she wants to go home, she has to say "I don't want to stay out any longer—I'm tired" or "I have too much studying to do." She can no longer rely on the rules to cover her preferences.

The same kind of self-responsibility is required in more explicitly sexual behavior. You are the one who must decide what your own standards will be. You will be influenced by your family and friends, but in the last analysis you are the only one who will decide how to behave in specific situations. You must know your own mind and heart. You don't want to give in to peer pressure and do things because "everyone else" is doing them. On the other hand, most young people don't want to be governed completely by "obedience" to what their parents want or think is right. In fact, for most adolescents, learning to distinguish between their own opinions, ideas, and standards and those of their parents is a central concern. In the process of becoming adult and taking full responsibility for her own self, the adolescent feels that she must develop her own beliefs and ideals—ones that she builds up through her own experience, out of her own thoughts and feelings—beliefs that are truly her own and not just adopted or swallowed whole from her parents.

If you don't want to be too influenced by peers or parents, and you haven't had a lot of experience on which to base your own ideas, where do you find guidelines for behavior until you know for sure what your own ideas and ideals are? Clearly, you borrow from here and there, try to assess the consequences of certain choices your friends have made, try out a particular style of behavior and see how it fits with your own sense of your self. You try to learn from the experience of others while you experiment with various ways of being until you find the way that "fits," that pleases you and meets your inner sense of your self and your personal values.

Sometime during adolescence some of you will become sexually active. In studies conducted during the 1970s, between 25 and 50 percent of young women reported that they had experienced sexual intercourse by the age of seventeen. We do not have exact information on adolescents in the eighties, but there is no reason to think that the numbers declined over the last ten years.

Our society's attitude toward premarital sex has changed dramatically over the last fifty years. The standard of conduct endorsed now by college students holds that sex should be judged on the basis of the relationship in which it occurs and that it is all right for young people to have sex if they feel love and affection for each other. Earlier generations tended to hold different standards for males and females: For a woman sex was only permissible within a strong permanent relationship; for a man it was all right to have sex on a more casual basis.

The important things in sex, as in most other areas of personal conduct, are: (1) to choose on the basis of one's own values and standards—not to be pushed into doing what you do not want to do, or feel obliged to go against your own standards to meet someone else's wishes or because "everyone else" does it—and (2) to take responsibility for one's choice. Sexual intercourse can have consequences. Taking responsibility for your behavior means considering these consequences and controlling them. Specifically, you have access to birth control and should use effective birth control if you do not want to have a baby.

The number of babies born to adolescent women who are not married, and the number of adolescent marriages that occur because of unplanned pregnancy, are *very* large and startling in this era of effective birth control. And the stories behind the numbers do not always have happy endings. Adolescent marriages are highly unstable and adolescent unmarried mothers often have hard and unhappy lives. People who work with adolescent single parents are convinced that often the young woman gets pregnant because using birth control would require her to admit to herself (and perhaps even more frightening, to admit to her partner) that she is sexually active and plans ahead for sex. She needs to act as though she had been "swept away" at the moment rather than deliberately sexual—perhaps to convince her partner (and herself) that she is not promiscuous or "sex-mad." The consequences of this romantic illusion, this fantasy, are often very sad. For one small deception a young woman may lose control of her life for a long time. Self-knowledge and honesty can be hard, too, but in the long run they allow you to hold on to your own choices and your own life.

Becoming Independent: Relationships with Parents

At adolescence you begin the task of becoming your own person, of taking the reins of control and choice into your own hands. Your sexual development demands that you assume control. So does your size and the fact that you spend most of your time away from home. You need to develop your own system of controls, your own ideas and values about how you want to behave and how you want to be seen by the world.

You may *feel* capable of managing your own life and behavior, and you begin to press for greater freedom from your parents' rules. Your parents, on the other hand, may want you to grow in independence yet recognize that you have not had all the experience you need to be prepared for independence. Or sometimes they may resist your pressure for greater freedom just because all of us tend to resist change, to hold on to what we have gotten used to and feel comfortable with. It takes time to get used to the idea of change.

In any event, you and your parents are likely to differ about how far and how fast your independence should grow. They will for the most part want you to achieve greater freedom, but you will not always agree on when or where. The freedoms you are seeking and the behaviors they involve— driving cars, staying out late or traveling to a distant city with a young man you love—are serious. Though they trust you, your parents also know the potential dangers on the highway and the danger of strong but inexperienced love. They want to save you from harm. So they try to protect you.

The differences you have with your parents won't all be about freedom. You are developing your own ideas and opinions about many things, and some of these will differ from the way they think or feel. The most obvious differences will be about taste. Your mother will object to your bikini because "it's too skimpy, as though you took your little sister's by mistake." Or she will not let you go to school with your hair in turquoise spikes ("like everyone else") or with chains around your waist for a belt.

And, speaking of taste, you sometimes create a storm when you point out to your mother that her winter coat is about ten years out of style. It's hard to see why she should be so touchy about *your* opinions when she's so free to give *hers*. Sometimes it seems that you can't agree on anything. You *are*, after all, from different generations!

The fact is, when you are just constructing your own ideas and values, sometimes the thing that makes your own idea clear to you is its difference from someone else's idea. You might go along for years not having any particular opinion about miniskirts or punk hairstyles until someone you know says she thinks miniskirts are ugly. Then, all of a sudden, you think about your opinion and realize that *you* sort of *like* them. Sometimes it is the strong opinion your mother states that leads you to define your own views. Some psychologists have questioned the "storm and stress" idea of adolescence. Most large surveys of adolescents do *not* find that the majority of youth experience turmoil or feel at odds with their parents. Yet we cannot ignore the fact that this age is one of enormous ambiguity and new tasks to master, and that many teenagers *do* struggle to gain independence and work out their own identities.

It also seems sometimes that your parents don't understand you or that they treat you as though you were still a child. When you're in a bad mood and your mother tries to joke with you or suggest things to do "to take your mind off it," it seems to you that she is not taking you seriously and thinks that you're just like a little kid who can be distracted by a lollipop. It's almost insulting. If you could change your mood, you wouldn't be sitting around in a blue funk in the first place! It certainly isn't that you like to feel this way!

Time will resolve some of these conflicts. Changing from a child to an adult takes time. You are trying on and trying out your own ideas, opinions, and values. When you can see with greater clarity what they are, you will feel less defensive about them. Until you know what they are, you feel pushed to accept your parents' ideas whenever they say how they feel or what they think. They may or may not mean to influence your beliefs on a particular issue, but until you know for sure what your beliefs are, it feels as though they are always trying to push you to think or believe what they do.

With a little time and help from your friends (including your parents), you will be clearer and more certain about your own beliefs, less confused about yourself, and less moody. Your parents will also have greater faith in your judgment and your ability to think for yourself and take care of yourself, and your relations with them will become easier and less touchy. Most of us discover near the end of adolescence that our beliefs and values are quite similar to those of our parents. As one old joke has it, the eighteen-year-old is surprised to discover how much her parents have learned in just three or four years! The point is, in the end, your values may be very much like those of your parents, but you have to distinguish them from your parents' values (read "fight" or "argue") first, make them truly your own, before you can discover or accept the similarity.

Some of you have had your relationships with your parents complicated by separation or divorce. You may be having to work through your new independence needs with more than one family. You may have to come to terms with your own developing sexuality at a time when one or both of your parents are dating, falling in love, and behaving in ways that emphasize their sexual nature and needs. Unlike your friends who can concentrate all of their energies on their own development, their own struggles to become independent and know themselves, you may be having to tend to the needs and conflicts of one or both of your parents and of your younger brothers and sisters as well as your own.

Coping with the divorce of one's parents is hard at any age, and it may be especially hard for adolescents. It is often claimed that adolescents are narcissistic or self-centered, because so much is going on *inside* at this stage. When your body is changing fast and sending you all kinds of new signals (moods and desires and feelings) just when you're trying to clarify who you are, a lot of your energy and thought naturally turns inward to these struggles. If, then, problems in your family also get laid on you at this stage, they either distract you from your adolescent tasks or add that final straw to the things you're trying to figure out.

Robert Weiss, who has spent years studying families in divorce, has said that the children in divorced families "grow up a little sooner." He means by this that youngsters growing up in the midst of parents' struggles *are* likely to be distracted from working on their own struggles, that they assume responsibilities and tasks in their families that other young people do not assume until much later. For adolescents this often means developing an idea of themselves based on their competence to manage responsibilities. They may miss some part of the internal struggle to develop a clear sense of self, but they nonetheless gain a sense of self almost without attending to the problem. Assuming responsibility is one way of coming to know who you are.

Other problems in families can also change the experience of young people going through adolescence. A significant number of students entering college have lost a parent to death. Other young people grow up in a family where one parent is alcoholic or has other serious problems. In all of these situations, the adolescent may be called on to assume responsibilities that would in most families be handled by parents. Sometimes adolescents in troubled families have to handle problems that are too complex for their stage of life and their experience. Although they may actually manage, adolescents in such situations should have some adult—an uncle or aunt, grandmother, teacher, a church youth leader—to whom they can turn for help and advice or at least a sympathetic hearing. When you are in *any* situation that seems too big to handle or worries you a lot, find someone who has had more experience and talk over the situation with that person. It's remarkable how much more clearly we see things sometimes just by saying them out loud. And the more experienced person may have ideas that you would never have thought of, or may know of possible sources of help that you don't know about. Sharing troubles is a human and also a most effective way to begin to find solutions to them.

Friendship

Problems often arise between adolescents and their parents because the parents don't like some of the young person's friends or feel that their daughter is spending too much time with her friends or that the friends are a bad influence. Often adolescents will feel pulled between what their parents want and expect from them and what their friends expect. These are important problems because they raise basic questions about loyalty and about maintaining one's own integrity.

Friendship changes in many ways and to a significant degree during adolescence. It changes for young females more than for males, and this seems to be related to female socialization, the fact that girls and women are expected and taught in our culture to be experts in relationships of all kinds. We are beginning now to insist that we have a right to be experts in other areas too—areas such as law and medicine and mechanics that are associated with the male world of work and were for a long time barred to women. But no one has seriously suggested that girls and women give up being experts on friendship, love, and other relationships. While it is to be hoped that boys and men will have more chances to develop close relationships in the future, girls and women will probably have the advantage in this area for a long time.

At the beginning of adolescence (at eleven, twelve, or thirteen) young girls think of friendship in very much the same way that boys of this age do: A friend is someone with whom you share activities, who is pleasant and easy to get along with, and who has enough self-control not to have temper tantrums or in other ways disrupt ongoing activities. The focus is on *activity* rather than the relationship itself. Demands on the friend as a person or personality are minimal: She should not impose herself on you and she should do favors for you when you need or want her to.

Around the age of fourteen or fifteen, adolescent friendship in girls takes on a more vivid mutual character (and begins to diverge from boys' friendship, which continues to focus on shared activity). The emphasis becomes mutual disclosure and exploring the relationship itself. Girls talk to each other about their deepest and most important thoughts. They talk a lot about boys and their feelings about particular boys; they explore together the nature and meaning of their own sexual feelings. They spend endless hours discussing their looks, their bodies, their opinions, their dreams and aspirations. Through all this talk, comparison, and exploration, girls express and come to know themselves. By identifying with the style or opinions of the friend—even sometimes imitating them perfectly—a girl will have a chance to sort out those admired traits that fit her own integration and those that are *not* for her.

This is also the stage in adolescence when most girls start to go out with boys, when boyfriends begin to take center stage. And friendship with girls is affected by these developing relationships with boys. The boyfriend becomes the topic of shared conversations among girlfriends. From sharing your thoughts and feelings about dating, you sort out and come to terms with what you feel. But the boys' entrance onto the scene can also raise issues of loyalty between girlfriends if popularity with boys is framed as a competitive game. (Some of these attitudes may have changed in recent decades, as women have developed more self-confidence and greater opportunities for creating satisfying lives on their own.) If you had planned to go to the movies with your girlfriend and at the last minute a boy called to invite you out, what is the right thing to do? Is popularity with boys somehow a value that overrides issues of loyalty and friendship? These are conflicts and concerns that girls share with each other, and because they are real issues at this stage of development, girls stress the importance of loyalty and security in friendship. Your girlfriend is someone who will not desert you or be disloyal. A friend is someone you can count on.

Later in adolescence, when friendship with boys is less of a mystery, easier and more comfortable, the stress on security in friendship also eases. And friendship takes on a more diverse and stimulating character. It's not that loyalty isn't still valued, but that loyalty can be taken more for granted. And the girlfriend, rather than being someone "just like me," now comes to be appreciated and valued for her individuality, precisely for those unique qualities that represent difference, variety, and stimulation in the friendship.

Friends are especially important during adolescence. When you're in the process of figuring out who you are and what you think and how you're going to live your life, it's crucial to have a sounding board and a point of comparison. And because they are *too* close, your parents won't do for this purpose. It's your parents you are trying to distinguish yourself from. You need breathing room to explore various ways of being, to try on a variety of opinions and styles. Among your friends you find an alternative to your family's ways. It feels good to find a group of like-minded people to be with. Since you need an anchor for yourself that is outside your family—to allow you the space to find your own internal anchors—your friends and their acceptance of you can become powerful forces in your life. Sometimes that very importance of adolescent friendship worries parents. It may seem to your parents that your friends have too great an influence on you.

An interesting reverse twist on this pattern sometimes occurs between best friends at adolescence. If two young women have been best friends throughout childhood, it may become necessary for one or both of them to break away from the friendship in adolescence, just as they will break away from their families. Adolescence is a time for differentiating the self, for exploring one's own views and forming one's own life plan. Just as one must, above all, get outside the family to do this, even push the family away temporarily in order not to get pulled back into the childlike stance of accepting one's family's views without question, so also the closest friend may endanger one's autonomy. Often best friendships that have lasted through all of childhood will break up temporarily or for good at adolescence. While it may be a necessary step toward autonomy, it is often very painful for the friend who is left or rejected. Understanding the reasons and knowing that it probably has nothing to do with oneself can ease the pain a little but not eliminate it.

Dating

Between the ages of fourteen and sixteen most girls in the United States begin to date, to spend time alone with boys. Dating is another challenge, another new set of things to learn. Getting to know boys as people takes a while. At first in this new game, the boy is not really a person. He's the "other," an alien or even an "opponent" in a game you are trying to play with skill and grace (to look "cool" and win popularity) when in fact you don't understand the rules or the plays.

With time and experience you will discover that boys *are* people, that you like some of them and not others, that they have feelings, personalities, fears, and vulnerabilities just as girls do. You will learn this in part by spending time with a boy or several boys. And you will learn a lot about boys from your talk and sharing with your girlfriends who are also beginning this adventurous game.

The Peer Group

The "peer group" is a popular topic in discussions of adolescent development. Little children and adults have friends and friendship circles, but adolescents have "peer groups." As I mentioned earlier, parents fear the adolescent peer group, attributing to it mythic powers to control and mislead their own adolescent children.

This view is not without some foundation. In adolescence you *are* starting to develop your own standards, but you don't have them yet; you haven't had the experience that would allow you to test and temper a completely independent set of values. Yet at least for now, while you are forming your own view, you can't rely on your parents' values. You can't because then you will *never* know what your own values are. In addition, you can't because your parents grew up in a different time and do *not* know what it's like to be a teenager today.

This means that you are likely to look to your friends for guidance, at least in some areas. And that's what makes parents nervous, the idea of the inexperienced leading the inexperienced. They see you wearing the latest teenage fashion, looking very much like all of your friends in your jeans and down jackets or preppy blazers, and it makes your parents think that you are following your peers in more important internal attitudes and values as well. It may be a case of parents' overgeneralizing. Or it may not.

We all like to be accepted by our friends; having other people you like and admire accept and approve of you is important. You want to be popular, to be "one of the crowd." What friends do often does come to seem very attractive to us. This is true at any age, and especially in adolescence when you're just beginning to know yourself.

In taste issues—even dying your hair turquoise or purple, and using safety pins for earrings—the long-run effects of doing what your friends do are not going to be important. But other choices—for example, smoking tobacco or marijuana, drinking, using drugs, having sex, or racing cars or motorcycles—can have consequences that are very important in the long run. And it's these behaviors that parents worry about. Will you, they wonder, have the strength to resist these choices if your friends make them and press you to choose them, too?

No one likes to be rejected, to be the "odd person out." It can be hard to resist pressure from your friends if they "are all doing it." Adolescents can be hard on one of their group who stands out or holds out or is different. Here's what one father wrote to his adolescent son who was being teased by his peers for being different:

> You are beginning to realize that your independence is not just
> because you are a freak, but because you are a person. The same
> idea is occurring to your contemporaries. Go on being the same,

only with a smile on your lips. They may tease you about it, but at the bottom of their hearts they respect you. Being "odd," being "different," is a sign of individuality. It exposes you, when a young boy among other young boys, to the jeers of the herd. But the herd is growing older even as you are growing older. You may find that the stand you have taken, which seemed so odd to them at first, seems to them now a rather courageous thing—a thing far finer than their own subservience to the course of the stream.

Although Harold Nicolson, an English diplomat and author, wrote this letter more than fifty years ago, the advice is still sound. It recognizes how hard it is to hold out for one's own way when everyone else takes a different position and gives you a hard time for being different. But it also recognizes that in the long run the adolescent who holds out for her own way, who does not give up her own standards just to "go along with the crowd," will be the one who leads the group later, the one whom the others will come to admire. Even if you never come to be a leader, you will at least gain respect for yourself because you have done what *you* think is right. Being "odd" is sometimes just a matter of timing (as Harold Nicolson's remarks to Ben make clear). Each pattern of timing—being ahead of the group or later than the "crowd" or in the mainstream—has its costs and benefits. Recent research has shown, for example, that girls who begin dating early often reduce their options for later periods of life. The girl who begins dating later than average may explore aspects of herself that in the long run will allow her more choice and more interesting options.

Sometimes you're not sure what feels right for you, and then it's especially easy to "go along." But think first. Sometimes it makes things clearer when someone suggests a course of action. You're not always sure what it is you *want* to do but you may be clearer about what you *don't* want to do. Opposition is one of the ways we learn about ourselves.

In these choices that confront you during adolescence and have consequences that you can see are important, the hard part is that now you have to take responsibility for your choices. A few years ago you could say "my parents won't let me" when you didn't want to do something that your friends were doing. Now it's the last thing you can say as a self-respecting, independent teenager. If you don't want to smoke or take a drink or have sex because you don't think it's right, or right for you, you have to hold out for your own view without any immediate help from your parents or anyone else. And that can be hard. You will want to find a friend—a peer or some loving adult you can trust—to share some of these struggles with. Talking things over can help us (at any age) to clarify our own thoughts and strengthen our resolve and ability to resist pressure.

Identity

A lot of this discussion about friendship, dating, and the peer group (as well as relations with parents) has centered on the problem or task of knowing yourself, clarifying your own opinions, values, and standards, coming to a concept of who you are and how you intend to live your life. Part of the task of forming a personal identity is deciding on certain future directions you want to take and beginning to prepare for the roles you will fill in your adult life.

This vision of your future will include some idea about the work you will do, whether you will marry and have children, how central a role friendship will be in your life and what kind of a friend you will be, how you will share your life with your parents and other kin, what kind of a citizen you will be, and how important religious beliefs and practice will be. You are practicing some of these future choices now, with your family and friends. You practice citizenship in school activities and perhaps in organizations at church and in the community.

A very important concept regarding the future—because it organizes a lot of adolescent life—has to do with the kind of work you think you want to do as an adult. If you think that you want to be a teacher, mechanic, commercial artist, or computer programmer, that choice will inform your plans and activities between now and the time when you actually take a full-time job. You will spend time in college or art school or in other kinds of training or apprenticeship. And that choice will, in turn, require that you take certain courses in high school. Especially in the sphere of occupation it is easy to see that the shape of the future begins to determine aspects of your present life.

But the same thing is true in family roles, even though it's sometimes harder to see or describe them clearly. If you have a vision of your future as a young professional woman married to a successful man who shares with you the responsibilities and pleasures of child raising and creating a warm and happy family life, then clearly that vision requires that you take college preparatory courses, attend college, and move into circles where you will meet people (including a particular young man) who have similar visions.

You can't stay on a farm or in a village in Montana and expect to realize this particular dream.

Fitting various aspects of your self together is the task of identity—integrating your adult sexuality and new sense of yourself as a woman; finding continuity between the past, present, and future; and meshing your own view of yourself with how others (especially those others who are important to you) see you. Early in adolescence, when young people are beginning to work on these tasks, their self-esteem suffers. Young adolescents do not have as good an opinion of themselves or feel as comfortable with themselves as they did in childhood or as they will later in adolescence. The process of adolescence is hard on everyone. But as you begin to master various aspects of your new identity, your feelings about yourself become more and more positive.

Part of the reason for this dip and rise in self-esteem may be that with newly developed powers of abstract thought, adolescents are able to distance themselves and look at themselves objectively. You can now separate the self as observer from the self as object, and you can criticize and attempt to change yourself. It is this ability to think about what might be that supports the active work of identity formation. You decide how you want to be and then go about adjusting your behavior to that ideal.

Adolescents' capacity for abstract, powerful thought can sometimes lead them to ask questions for which there are no easy answers and for which the only possible solution lies in living a little longer, experiencing life a little more fully, discovering its important gifts, and becoming more solidly committed and enmeshed in its flow. You may ask about life's meaning and purpose, why we are born and why we must die. You have all the ability to probe the mysteries, to ask the same important questions that philosophers have asked since the first philosopher began asking "Why?" But it is not easy for you to find the answers because in many cases the answer requires you to put the question in a different form. Or in other cases the answer may not be one that can be reduced to words at all. It can only be experienced, and the particular experience that will give an answer to an individual cannot be produced on command. It often seems unique and chancy, almost a random occurrence: the sun dappling a lawn through lacy spring foliage one day when your little brother comes running across it. Or, in the future, the answers you seek may occur when you fall in love or see a pyramid for the first time or meet a saintly person.

When you can't find the answer right away, it is easy to get discouraged or frightened. So much is opening before you and so few answers seem available, either inside or outside your own being. In another part of the letter I quoted above, Harold Nicolson gave his son Ben another bit of advice. "My darling," he said, "I am so glad that you are less bored at Eton and less unhappy. Seek out the things you enjoy and forget the things you hate." When you feel discouraged because you can't find the meaning of things, try if you can to remember what you passionately enjoy: a particular song; a scene from a ballet; a movie or a friend or a place. *That* at least has unquestionable meaning. And remember, more of the answers—about yourself and your feelings and your life as well as about deeper meanings—will be yours next year and in the future. Adolescence is one of the hardest periods of life for most people, but it doesn't last very long.

Here again I would stress the helpfulness of sharing your fears, problems, worries with someone who has had a little more experience. An older friend in school or a favorite teacher, club leader, or relative can often help with some of your questions. If they can't, they may know someone who can. Don't carry the burden all alone when there are others who can share it and perhaps show you how to unload at least some of it.

As adolescence draws to a close, many of you will be leaving home to go to college or to join a service or take a job in another city. Many of the problems that you faced early on in adolescence will not seem as important or as frightening as they once did. Now you will be taking important steps toward independence and facing new tasks and challenges in the world.

For Mothers of Adolescent Daughters

Most of us would not want to go back to adolescence if we had the magic capsule for time travel. Of all periods in life it is the one we are glad to be done with. It is true that it brought new excitement and power; and that in a youth-centered culture it is designed to be carefree, to allow more time for leisure and for self exploration and friendship than any other life stage. But most of us, when we're honest with ourselves, also remember the pain of feeling awkward, self-conscious, rejected, left out. And we remember the mistakes we made, some very dangerous, from which we escaped only by the skin of our teeth. No, for most of us, the ideal time of life is somewhere past adolescence when we have gotten ourselves together and feel more sure of ourselves and life.

This exercise in memory can make us much more tolerant and compassionate in dealing with our adolescent children. If we remember how painful it was to go to a school party when we were self-conscious and nervous, we are less likely to get angry with an adolescent who decides at the last minute not to go. We can encourage her to go, remind her that half of the teenagers are probably just as nervous about it as she is. But we will be less likely to be frightened or upset and keep pushing her if we can step back in memory to that difficult time. We will be less likely to continually lean on an adolescent for her clumsiness if we remember that she hates being awkward at least as much as we do.

By remembering the pain and anxiety of adolescence, we paradoxically can gain some distance from our children's adolescent struggles. We can advise and support them, with compassion, but we need to remember that the struggles are *theirs* and in the last analysis they must handle them. We can take some comfort in the fact that for all our own narrow escapes, we made it through adolescence without permanent damage. The chances are good that our children will, too. Adolescence is difficult, but not infinite.

The hardest time, it turns out, is the same for parents as for the youngsters themselves, the early part of adolescence. It is the time when the youngster is most self-conscious and self-doubting and also the period when parent-child conflict peaks. In the earliest stage of self-exploration and self-discovery, the young person has only the vaguest ideas about what is happening and where she is going. She will play out her anxieties—often taking a defensive, oppositional, rebellious stance—with the people who are closest to her. She will follow this path to test her independent ideas and thoughts; she will do it also because just now her childhood relationship to you—its closeness and tenderness—is dangerous.

Several prominent psychologists, who have spent years talking to adolescents and their parents, think that conflict is crucial to adolescent development and particularly to girls' development. Diana Baumrind thinks that if young women are to develop independent values and an independent identity, they must be allowed and encouraged to stand up for their own views. When parents legitimize conflict, they allow the adolescent to take this route to self-discovery. If parents avoid or forbid conflict, they make it hard for the young woman to become independent, active, and assertive. Norms in the larger world will push her to accept a traditional, passive stance. To develop the stamina to resist these conventional pressures, she will need permission and some experience with conflict. She needs to learn that disagreeing, even fighting, will not cause her to disappear or blow away. Nor will it destroy you, her opponent. Her anger is like anyone else's. She needs to know it is controllable, and with control it can be an important and useful asset to her throughout her life.

Parents worry about adolescents' ability to handle their new and intense sexual impulses, and we worry about their needs for extraordinary—out of the ordinary—experience. These latter needs are part of the human condition, part of our search for the transcendant. Those of us who find satisfaction of these needs—in religious experience, nature, love, or art—are lucky. But many young people struggle to find that numinous, luminous reality that confers immediate and compelling meaningfulness to life and releases them from painful self-consciousness and alienation. Each generation finds troubling paths to transcendance. Recent generations have used marijuana and other drugs in place of the alcohol that was the choice of their parents. Drugs, dependence on drugs, the clouding of judgment produced by drugs are all sources of parent concern.

Most youngsters do not become dependent on drugs, but many of them do experiment with marijuana and alcohol. As parents we have the responsibility to advise them about the hazards of any chemical substance. We have the responsibility to provide reasonable models of restraint in our own use of alcohol or other substances. We can teach them the social use of alcohol, which, if one's religion permits, begins with not forbidding it. Families who teach their adolescents to drink moderately, with meals, neither create an attractive taboo nor encourage abuse of one forbidden substance.

Helping adolescents to find sources of meaning in themselves and in the world, to find a personal system of values and controls so that they can trust themselves and resist external pressure, is ultimately the greatest contribution we can make to their welfare—and to their ability, and ours, to weather this difficult developmental stage.

ELIZABETH DOUVAN holds the Catharine Neafie Kellogg chair in psychology at the University of Michigan. She has done national surveys of adolescents and adults and has written extensively about the American family; her books include *The Adolescent Experience* (Wiley, 1966) and *The Inner American* (Basic Books, 1981). She has a grown son and daughter who share her wonder and pleasure at the fact that they all (including the husband/father of their family) survived the younger generation's adolescence and emerged loving and admiring friends.

Further Reading

Bloom, Michael V. *Adolescent-Parental Separation.* New York: Gardner Press, 1980.

Blos, Peter. *The Adolescent Passage.* New York: International Universities Press, 1979.

Coles, Robert, and Stokes, Geoffrey. *Sex and the American Teenager.* New York: Harper & Row, 1985.

Guardo, Carol. *The Adolescent as Individual: Issues and Insight.* New York: Harper & Row, 1975.

Konopka, Gisela. *Adolescent Girls in Conflict.* Englewood Cliffs, N.J.: Prentice-Hall, 1966.

———. *Young Girls.* Englewood Cliffs, N.J.: Prentice-Hall, 1976.

Matteson, David R. *Adolescence Today: Sex Roles and the Search for Identity.* Homewood, Ill.: Dorsey Press, 1975.

Offer, David, and Offer, Judith. *From Teenage to Young Manhood.* New York: Basic Books, 1975.

Sorenson, Robert C. *Adolescent Sexuality in Contemporary America: Personal Values and Sexual Behavior Ages Thirteen to Nineteen.* New York: World Publishing Co., 1973.

9

Marriage

AYALA M. PINES

Donna, an attractive woman and a successful architect in her early forties, feels "burned out" after fourteen years of marriage. She describes the experience:

> I feel hollow in this relationship. There is nothing between us: no bond, no communication, no sharing, no contact, no feelings, nothing. We have no plans together, no interests together. The tensions are making me tired and sad. There is no hope for us. There is nothing that he does to enhance my life in any way, either emotionally, intellectually, or physically. I don't feel like part of a couple, I feel emotionally deprived. I feel resentful and irritated. I have to close myself off emotionally to stop feeling that way. I can't give myself sexually or emotionally anymore. I don't believe life has anything to give me. I would do anything to be free of him. I have no feelings for him except irritation and sometimes pity. When I come home and he is there, I get all uptight. I wouldn't stay with him for anything.

Ellen, a counselor, is in her late thirties, and after five and a half years still feels very happy in her marriage. She describes the experience:

> I have never felt so close to another person in my whole life. It's as if we were made from the same primal material. We think the same way, we respond the same way to people and events, we have the same tastes. And it gives me this wonderful feeling of togetherness. No matter what happens during the day, I know we are going to

talk about it when we get together at night. We talk all the time, about absolutely everything. There is no subject that is taboo. And issues of conflict we come back to over and over and over again, each time from a new angle, until we resolve them. But what is as important to me as the verbal communication is the physical communication between us. I have never had better sex with anyone, never felt more beautiful and desirable. Our sex life gives everything a pink glow.

What is the difference between Donna and Ellen? They are both attractive, bright, warm, and successful professionally. And since they both married their husbands for love (for both it was the second marriage), we can assume that the difference is not a result of Ellen's having a nicer husband or better luck. As we shall see, the difference lies in what I call "marriage burnout."

Donna's emotional depletion, helplessness, and hopelessness are the hallmarks of burnout, a painful experience shared by many married women. Why does it happen? How? And what, if anything, can be done to prevent it? In an effort to answer these questions I have, for several years, been studying the dynamics of marriage burnout. I collected and analyzed several thousand questionnaires and interviewed in depth hundreds of individuals and couples. The couples included both those who experienced burnout as well as those couples who had managed to keep the spark alive even after many years together. I interviewed couples in traditional marriages, couples in companionship marriages, and couples in a variety of unconventional marriages. I interviewed straight and homosexual couples. I conducted workshops on burnout both in this country and abroad, and have worked with individuals and couples in my private practice. Although the research involved both men and women, I am going to focus here on the women's perspective.

One of the most important findings in this entire body of research was the fact that there is *no correlation between length of marriage and burnout.* This means that there are women who have been married for many years whose marriages are still exciting and alive, and other women, who have been married very briefly, whose marriages are already burned out. It also means, of course, that there are women who have been married for many years whose marriages are burned out, and other women, married briefly, whose marriages are exciting and alive. The fact that the passage of time, in and of itself, does not cause burnout answers the most frequent question asked about it, namely, is it inevitable? The answer is—no!

The other good news I learned from the years of studying burnout, both on the job and in marriage, is that it can be conquered. As with most difficult emotional experiences, burnout, if properly dealt with, can provide a trigger for personal and marital growth. Often women (or, more accurately, couples) who have experienced burnout and have learned to cope with it effectively end up with a better, fuller, more exciting marriage than if they had not experienced burnout at all.

With this in mind, let us examine what this phenomenon is: its symptoms and danger signs (how can we recognize it in ourselves and in our husbands?); what causes it in women; and what are some of the techniques for coping with it after it happens, or, better still, how to prevent it altogether.

From Bliss to Burnout

Burnout is best defined as a state of physical, emotional, and mental exhaustion caused by long-term involvement with people in emotionally demanding situations. Let me break this formal definition into its components and describe each component in some detail.

PHYSICAL EXHAUSTION

The physical exhaustion of burnout typically appears as chronic fatigue that is not relieved by sleep. You drag your feet all through the day, longing to get to bed. And yet when night finally arrives, you are so annoyed with your husband that you cannot fall asleep. Your stomach churns. Each unkind word, each inconsiderate act, is magnified. You are furious. You toss and turn. When you finally manage to fall asleep, you are haunted by nightmares: a volcano erupting; your home struck by an earthquake, caving in. To get some peace of mind you reach for the bottle of sleeping pills or alcohol. A drug helps to calm you down; maybe you even fall asleep. But the drug's effect is evident the next morning when you wake up groggy, with a splitting headache, exhausted again.

You grow increasingly weary and weak. You have frequent headaches, stomachaches, or back pains. You become susceptible to illness, catching every cold and flu around. You eat too much ("At least I can get this enjoyment out of life") or too little ("I have a gigantic lump in my throat") and seeing the results in the mirror, you hate your body.

EMOTIONAL EXHAUSTION

You feel emotionally drained, depleted of affection. You still remember how you fell in love with your husband; you may even remember how wonderful it was to love and be loved. But now nothing is left of these wonderful feelings. You feel that there is no hope for the two of you, and not much hope that you will ever find someone else you could, or would, want to marry. "Besides," you reason, "what's the point anyway, since this is how it always ends?" You are depressed and unhappy. Every day seems worse than the last. You feel like a helpless, trapped rabbit. In extreme cases the feelings of futility and despair can lead to an emotional breakdown or to thoughts of suicide.

MENTAL EXHAUSTION

The mental exhaustion of burnout manifests itself in a low self-concept and negative attitudes toward your husband. When you were in love, you didn't only adore your husband, you also felt pretty good about yourself. Now you are painfully aware of the endless little things your husband does that make you want to jump out of your skin ("the way he coughs," "the way he drives," "the sight of his back," "his smell"). In addition, you discover some cold and nasty streaks in your own personality you never even knew existed. The sense of disappointment, like the love before it, transcends the two of you. It affects the way you feel about your hopes, your life, and your ability to love. Burnout, you discover, is the overwhelming sense of distress and failure in the quest for romantic ideals.

LONG-TERM INVOLVEMENT IN EMOTIONALLY DEMANDING SITUATIONS

Living with another person always requires adaptation and compromise. One has to accommodate the other person in one's emotional—as well as in one's physical—space, and that accommodation is never easy, especially when one cares deeply about the other person. A long visit by a close relative can be much more stressful than a long visit by a casual acquaintance with whom one is not emotionally involved.

Contrary to the romantic notions popular in our culture, burnout in marriage is more likely to occur to women who start out "starry-eyed" and infatuated than to those who enter marriage feeling practical or even cynical, or those who marry for reasons other than love (such as for economic need, or because they share a particular ideological or religious worldview and lifestyle).

In order to burn out one must, by definition, once have been "on fire." That is why it happens faster to women who, at the beginning of the relationship, were "madly in love," idealized their husbands, and were sure they had found the Prince Charming with whom they were going to live happily ever after. The stresses that these women find most unbearable are, on the one hand, their frustrated hopes and dreams (and the inevitable discovery that their husbands are not quite what they seemed at the infatuation stage), and, on the other hand, the daily drudgery and hassles typical of any long-term intimate relationship.

Often the very thing that initially attracts a woman to her husband is what becomes a major source of stress in her marriage. When Donna first met her husband, she was attracted to him because he was "the romantic, strong, and silent type." He knew what he wanted and did not always wait for her to decide about everything the way her ex-husband used to do. Now, talking about the most stressful aspects of her marriage, she complains that her husband is a closed, uncommunicative person who never shares his feelings with her. She complains that he always has to have his way and is unwilling to accommodate to her wishes or plans. Another woman who was attracted to her husband's "energy" now says he drives her crazy with his "nervousness." A woman who was attracted to the "boyish" quality in her husband now laments his "childishness and immaturity."

Similarly, I almost always found that frustrated hopes and expectations were among the most stressful aspects of these women's marriages. In Donna's case the hope was to have a relationship of "total sharing" and intimacy, and the greatest source of stress was the fact that there was "no bonding," "no sharing," "no intimate friendship." Another woman had hoped to escape her low-status family background. She married a highly successful businessman whose busy social life involved encounters with a large number of business acquaintances. Her greatest source of stress was the feeling that her social life was "phony and artificial."

Many times seeing stresses as frustrated hopes makes them seem less overwhelming and insurmountable, and seeing the most stressful aspect of a husband's personality as what was initially the most exciting aspect clarifies the role our own preferences play in the kind of man we chose to marry. Both of these insights can reduce feelings of hopelessness and entrapment. The task is no longer to overcome an insurmountable situation, but to find a way to realize those hopes and dreams. The goal is not to try to change an unchangeable and unbearable aspect of a husband's personality, which is futile, but to find a way to regain the positive perceptions of that very aspect of his personality.

Before we proceed to a discussion of the causes and prevention of burnout, you may be interested in finding out just how burned out you are. You can find your burnout score by answering the questions in the accompanying box, whether you are madly in love, totally burned out, or somewhere in between. A brief discussion of the scoring system at the bottom of the questionnaire will help you interpret your score. Filling out the questionnaire should serve as an occasion for you (or even better, for the two of you) to think about your marriage. (After completing the questionnaire, you can compare your responses.) Responding to the questions preceding the Burnout Measure will help sensitize you to the issues involved, and if done jointly, may bring about an exciting dialogue between you and your husband.

Marriage Burnout

BACKGROUND ISSUES

What attracted you to your spouse when you first met?

What were your hopes and expectations when you decided to get married?

What is your image of the ideal marriage?

What are the three most stressful aspects of your marriage?
1.

2.

3.

How do you usually cope with these stresses?
1.

2.

3.

How successful are you in your coping?

If you found someone else you could love, would you leave your spouse?

1	2	3	4	5	6	7
Definitely Not			Not Sure		Definitely Yes	

The Burnout Measure

You can compute your marriage burnout score by completing the following questionnaire. How often do you have any of the following experiences? Please use this scale:

1	2	3	4	5	6	7
NEVER	ONCE IN A GREAT WHILE	RARELY	SOMETIMES	OFTEN	USUALLY	ALWAYS

_____ 1. Being tired.

_____ 2. Feeling depressed.

_____ 3. Having a good day.

_____ 4. Being physically exhausted.

_____ 5. Being emotionally exhausted.

_____ 6. Being happy.

_____ 7. Being "wiped out," whole body hurts.

_____ 8. Feeling burned out, "can't take it any more."

_____ 9. Feeling unhappy.

_____ 10. Feeling rundown, susceptible to illness.

_____ 11. Feeling trapped.

_____ 12. Feeling worthless.

_____ 13. Being weary, "nothing left to give."

_____ 14. Being troubled.

_____ 15. Feeling disillusioned and resentful about husband.

_____ 16. Feeling weak as a result of sleep problems.

_____ 17. Feeling hopeless.

_____ 18. Feeling rejecting of husband.

_____ 19. Feeling optimistic.

_____ 20. Feeling energetic.

_____ 21. Feeling anxious.

Computation of score:

Add the values you wrote next to the following items:
1, 2, 4, 5, 7, 8, 9, 10, 11, 12, 13, 14, 15, 16, 17, 18, 21 (A) _____.

Add the values you wrote next to the following items:
3, 6, 19, 20 (B) _____. Subtract B from 32 (C) _____.

Add A and C (D) _____.

Divide D by 21: _____. This is your marriage burnout score.

A score of 4 defines a state of burnout; a score of 3, danger signs; a score above 5, crisis; above 5, need for immediate help.

Disillusion and Misconceptions

Marriage burnout is almost never sudden. It tends to be slow and insidious. Seldom does it result from a single traumatic event or even several traumas. Rather it starts with a growing awareness that things aren't quite as good as they used to be, or that one's husband is not quite as exciting as he used to be. There is an irritating conviction that one is pouring more into the marriage than one is getting back from it, that some of one's most important needs are not being met.

If nothing is done at this stage to stop the process, things go from bad to worse. The infrequent periods of discontent become more and more frequent. The mild feelings of dissatisfaction grow into a smoldering fury. When it reaches a crisis point, burnout may lead to a dead, listless marriage, to extramarital affairs, or to divorce.

When we think about a marriage breaking up, it is tempting to seize upon concrete traumatic events. The husband starts seeing other women. He gets drunk, beats the wife, and screams at the children. Or else the wife has a lover and no longer cares to stay in the marriage. Occasionally, such events do constitute the cause of the breakup of a marriage, but these are not the most common causes of marital burnout. Marriages dissolve most commonly by gradual erosion, by a gradual increase in boredom, by the accumulated weight of small daily hassles and pressures. The gradual erosion of caring is exacerbated by trivial incidents: "He would leave full ashtrays everywhere." "He would squeeze the toothpaste tube in the middle." "He would throw his clothes all over the house." "He would spend too much money on his records." Donna describes some of the causes of her burnout:

> There were many incidents. Every morning something would happen. Like, he'd bang a door shut that I hadn't shut. I often leave doors open. Instead of thinking "What a charming thing—here's a person with an open personality" (I think it's very symbolic), he'd bang this thing shut. And it immediately caused tension. And my immediate thought was: "Another nail in your coffin." That's what I kept thinking everytime he'd do something. Every day is cementing that thing. . . . I like things around and Andrew doesn't like things. He was always clearing things out and putting them in the garage. He wouldn't even ask me. Like he'd take all Gail's mugs, and leave her with one, putting them in the garage, and that's it. It would just infuriate me. . . . His smoking cigars

drove me up the wall. Every night he would smoke one cigar. [I hated] the smell, and the sort of staleness of the thing.

Donna's complaints have not always been a good enough reason to break up a marriage. Not so long ago problems were regarded by both the wife and her mother (to whom she was most likely to go with a marital problem) as natural and normal. ("I had the same trouble with your father. That's the way men are.") Unhappiness alone was rarely justification for leaving a marriage. ("He doesn't drink, he doesn't beat you up, and he brings home all the money he makes. What else could you want?")

Most modern women, on the other hand, regard happiness as the principal goal of marriage. If they cannot find happiness with a particular man, they regard divorce as a reasonable alternative. This change in attitude, which is a part of the more general change in the sex role definition of modern women, had a profound impact on the traditional marriage. James and Janice Prochaska, who surveyed twentieth-century trends in marriage and marital therapy, reported that "the most common reason for couples coming into marital therapy is that the marriage is being shaken by the wife's struggle for equality." Similarly, Philip Blumstein and Pepper Schwartz, in their 1983 survey of twelve thousand American couples, reported that some "wives stay in marriages because they cannot support themselves outside them. . . . Women who can support themselves can afford to have higher expectations for their marriages beyond financial security, and because they are more self-sufficient, they can leave if these are not met."

These findings, on the surface at least, contradict the proposition that traditional marriages are breaking up because of *men's* dissatisfactions. In her book *The Hearts of Men* Barbara Ehrenreich argued, for example, that the women's liberation movement is actually a result of men's rebellion against their traditional role as breadwinners. If it were not for the men's rebellion, runs this view, women would have stayed happily in their traditional roles and marriages. Whatever the original reason, my research indicates that at present wives are more burned out in their marriages than are husbands.

Of course, a burned-out wife rarely thinks about the cultural trends that could have influenced her feelings. Even more important is the fact that she is usually unaware of the effect of situational stresses that are far more concrete and evident causes of her burnout, such as financial difficulties, a work-home conflict, or the wearying stress of caring for young children. What she is all too aware of is her husband's apparent failings: "He is a total narcissist." "He is not in touch with his feelings." "He is controlling and manipulative." "He is a spendthrift, wasting money like there is no tomorrow." The result is what psychologists call an "attribution error"—a common tendency to overattribute problems to dispositional (personality or character related) causes, and underattribute them to situational causes.

When we see a woman slipping during a dance we can attribute the cause of her fall to the slipperiness of the dance floor, to the slipperiness of her new shoes, to her clumsiness, absentmindedness, physical exhaustion, or intention (she fell on purpose to amuse her little boy). When the focus of the explanation is on the environment, the attribution is called "situational" (e.g., the woman slipped because of the slippery floor, or because of her slippery shoes); when the focus of the explanation is on something in the person, the attribution is called "dispositional" (e.g., the woman slipped because she is clumsy).

The difference between dispositional attributions and situational attributions is not semantic. It has far-reaching implications for the person making the attribution and about whom the attribution is made. People making dispositional attributions explain their own and other people's actions by saying that that is "the kind of person" they are. This explanation puts them in what social psychologist Philip Zimbardo calls "a prison of their own mind." A woman who marries someone whose only redeeming feature is faithfulness because she is "a jealous person" has created such a self-made prison. Similarly, the woman who experiences marital problems and is convinced that they are caused by her husband's inherent personality deficiencies is also creating such a mental prison. For both women there is no point in trying to bring about change in their lives because they assume that even if the situation changes, they (or their husbands) will remain the same.

People who make situational attributions, on the other hand, explain their own and other people's actions by saying that they are "reacting to a particular situation," which means that in another situation they may react differently. For example, a woman may note that she feels excluded and jealous when her husband is flirting with a good-looking stranger, or that she has felt differently about her marriage since the three children came along. Such women are much more likely to recognize that their emotions result from a particular, stressful situation, and consequently focus their efforts on changing that situation.

Situational stresses that have little to do with a couple's love for each other can erode a marriage more quickly than any character deficiency. Women pay a high price for this attributional error, blaming their husbands, or themselves, or both for marital problems that are the result of situational stresses. An essential step in preventing or treating burnout, therefore, is to make the transition from dispositional to situational attributions. The pressures and stresses that are built into sharing a life with another person are enormous; it is almost inevitable that these stresses will become intense and at times even unbearable. For many women, merely identifying their feelings as "burnout" has therapeutic value. A typical reaction is, "So it's burnout! And I thought it was us [or "me" or "him"]! I thought there was something seriously wrong with us as a couple!" Guilt, blame, and confusion are replaced by relief and renewed motivation for active coping.

Why Some Women Burn Out—and Others Don't

I conducted several studies to answer this question. As the findings in all of them were rather similar, I chose, for the purpose of this chapter, to discuss only one of those studies and to do it in some depth. The study included one hundred middle-class suburban married couples. For all but six of the couples this was their first marriage. Most had two or three children living at home. The average length of marriage was 15.1 years and ranged from several months to over 34 years.

I asked participants in the study to describe their marriages and their feelings about those marriages, in both a questionnaire and an in-depth interview. All the data I will present are based on self reports and consequently may be influenced by such factors as the honesty of the respondents, or conversely, the respondents' desire to say certain things in order to put themselves in a favorable light. My best guess is that these factors account for only a small part of the findings. This "best guess" is an informed judgment based upon corroborating evidence from the interviews.

As I said, the difference between a burned-out marriage and a marriage that is alive, even after many years, does not lie in the personalities involved, in some characterological deficiency in the couple. The difference lies in the situational circumstances of the couple's lives, in the environment. In emphasizing the role of the environment I do not mean to deny the importance of personality characteristics. I assume that personality plays an important role in the initial stages of mutual selection in which two people fall in love. But following the initial stages of infatuation and courtship, all couples, no matter how compatible or incompatible, no matter how many or how few unresolved conflicts they carry with them into the marriage, have to deal with the realities imposed by the environment in which they live. These realities include other people (such as extended family, friends, colleagues, neighbors). They include involvements in other spheres of life (such as child rearing, work, politics, religion). The effect of these other people and these other activities on the marriage can be positive, supportive, and growth-producing, or they can be negative and stressful.

The one hundred wives who participated in the study filled out the Burnout Measure and then described various aspects of their daily circumstances, the most stressful aspects of their marriages, the most rewarding aspects, their styles for coping with stress, and their original hopes and expectations of the marriage. Here are ten negative features in the women's marriages, of which all but housework were significantly related to burnout:

Conflicting Demands	Work-Home Conflict
Commitment Pressure	Stressful Environment
Overload	Boredom
Guilt and Anxiety	Demand to Prove Self
Exploitation	Housework

CONFLICTING DEMANDS

How often do you feel caught between conflicting demands caused, at least in part, by demands imposed on you by your husband? Conflicting demands had the highest correlation with marriage burnout for women. The more frequent the experience of conflict, the more burned out a wife was likely to be.

The wife who feels caught in a conflict between the demands for attention and nurturing of her children and those of her husband; the career woman who feels caught in a conflict between the demands of her family for financial security and a comfortable lifestyle (which requires putting in extra hours at work) and her family's demand for her time and attention, are both experiencing a similar conflict. The demands of people in a woman's life, whether legitimate or not, whether real or imagined, can seem impossible to satisfy, and are thus extremely stressful. These include the demands of her husband, children, parents, friends, relatives, colleagues, and bosses.

There are two major ways to alleviate this kind of conflict. First, confront the possibility that some of the demands you think are imposed on you by people or tasks are actually demands you impose on yourself. If you are working, for example, is it your husband or you who imposes high standards for the housework? Second, if the demands are indeed imposed by others, you must make a list of priorities of the various demands and let some go. For example, if you have an important deadline at work, the family wash will have to wait.

PRESSURE OF FAMILY COMMITMENTS

How often do you feel pressured by family commitments and obligations (the kinds of things you, as well as your husband and the rest of your family, feel they can demand of you because you are their wife, mother, sister, daughter, or daughter-in-law)? The more frequent and the more intense the pressure of such family commitments, the higher the level of burnout.

As in the case of conflicting demands, it is important to scrutinize family commitments in order to clarify any ambiguity that may exist between an actual stress emanating from the environment, in this case a demand imposed by a particular family member, and our own self-demand. For example, a wife's mother might like her to call her occasionally, but the wife puts the demand on herself to call her mother every day. After a while she may act as if the "every day" dictum came from the mother. Only after close scrutiny will she realize that it is self-imposed.

In order to avoid the stress caused by excessive family obligations, we must separate actual demands and commitments from our interpretation of them and from the demands and obligations we impose on ourselves. Occasionally, we can even test this. Thus, the wife in the example above could try to cut back the number of calls to her mother from seven to two a week, then wait for the repercussions. Once the distinction between real and imagined obligations has been made, the task of ranking obligations in order of importance becomes much easier.

OVERLOAD

How often do you experience overload, a feeling that you have gone beyond the point of endurance, because the tasks imposed on you are either too many or too hard? The higher the frequency of experiencing overload, the greater the burnout in marriage. This factor, which was the third environmental pressure to correlate with burnout for women, was the most highly correlated with burnout for the complete sample of both men and women combined.

When you feel harassed, hassled, and pressured, you are not exactly in the mood for attending to your marriage or your love for your husband. This is especially true for lovemaking, an activity that involves experiencing your body rather than thinking; a present, rather than a future orientation; and feeling relaxed, playful, and sensual—the exact opposite of feeling overloaded.

What can be done about it? Sometimes nothing. Sometimes you really do have to cope with a sick parent, a cranky boss, and a child with reading problems. But something can almost always be done about the focus of the blame for the fact that the spark has gone out of the marriage. Rather than blame yourself or your husband, you may want to consider blaming the overload in your life. Just doing that may free enough energy for a constructive look at the causes of the overload and may even result in some brilliant ideas about reducing it.

GUILT AND ANXIETY

Conflicting demands, commitment pressures, and overload have many things in common, most obviously that they drain energy. When caught in conflicting demands, we feel that no matter what we do, we would not be able to satisfy all the demands imposed on us. When we feel burdened by family commitments, we feel that those obligations exceed our emotional or physical resources, and when overloaded, we feel that the demands on us are more than we can bear. In all three cases we believe that we don't have the energy to respond to the demands imposed on us. This feeling, especially for women, is the cause of tremendous guilt, anxiety, and hopelessness.

How often do you feel guilty that you will never be able to fully accomplish your marital obligations, your personal goals for your family, and the things you consider your responsibilities? For the one hundred women who participated in the study, the frequency of these feelings was very highly correlated with burnout. (It was far less correlated with burnout for men.) In my clinical experience, likewise, I often have to help women overcome debilitating feelings of guilt and anxiety over not doing things quite the way they think they ought to be done. One of the most effective methods for dealing with this unreasonable emotion is to have groups of women discuss each other's self-imposed demands and guilt over not fulfilling them. Often, as women see how obviously unreasonable the other women's self-imposed demands and guilt are, they become free from their own.

Other negative environmental features that are related to marriage burnout in women included:

- feeling emotionally exploited by a husband ("I give, give, give, but it's never enough, and I never get anything in return");
- being torn by a work-home conflict ("When I am at work, it is difficult for me to concentrate because I can still hear the baby's screams when I left in the morning, but when I am at home, it is difficult for me to be fully there because I keep thinking about all the things I didn't do at work");
- suffering from such environmental pressures as crowded living conditions ("There is no space I can call my own, no place to retreat to when I need to be alone");
- noise ("With the children and endless phone calls inside, and the cars and trucks outside, there is not a moment of peace and quiet");
- boredom ("There is no excitement left in the marriage, no spark. I find his conversation dull, and most times we are together I am bored to tears");
- the constant demand to prove oneself ("I feel like I am constantly on trial and have to prove myself. But what is worse is the feeling that I am not managing to do it, that I am always failing the test").

Curiously, household chores, one of the most popular complaints of married women, was not at all correlated with burnout! What this finding shows, again, is that it is the *emotional* pressures in the marriage that are most stressful and the likely causes of burnout. These emotional pressures are to a large extent the result of the discrepancy between the way we think things "should" be and the way they are. What can alleviate these emotional pressures?

Positive Aspects of Marriage That Prevent Burnout

It may seem obvious that stresses, pressures, and hassles can erode a marriage, but many women tend to forget that the lack of positive features can erode a marriage just as easily. The feelings associated with the absence of positive features are disappointment and regret, a sense that some important needs are not being met. These same positive features, when present in a marriage, can prevent burnout:

Positive Overall Attitude	Success
Communication	Compatible Personality
Variety	Emotional Attraction
Feedback	Input into Decisions
Similar Goals	Support
Appreciation	Intellectual Attraction
Security	Independence
Self-actualization	Things in Common
Good Sex Life	Significance
Physical Attraction	Self-expression

The more of these twenty features a woman has, any of them, the less burned out she is likely to feel. But remember that they represent only a small part of all the positive features possible in marriage. I chose them because they have the highest effect on reducing burnout. (The list is rank-ordered in terms of correlations with burnout, so that the features that were the most correlated with low burnout scores are placed at the top.) Because of space limitations, I will discuss only the top three in detail.

A POSITIVE OVERALL ATTITUDE TOWARD THE MARRIAGE

Women who had a positive overall attitude toward their marriages were significantly less burned out than women who were not able to look at their marriages positively. Sounds like a tautology, doesn't it? But what exactly does "a positive overall attitude" mean? Consider the testimony of Patricia, a woman who had a very low burnout score and a very positive overall attitude toward her marriage. She says:

> . . . He burns pots. Not once, or twice, or even three times, but regularly, weekly . . . He puts the kettle on the stove, or a pot of soup, and then starts reading something, and when he reads he is totally gone . . . He usually remembers that he left something on the flame when the whole house is full of smoke. But every time I get furious with him, I stop short of saying "that's it, I've had it" when I remember what a good thing we have going between us; how lucky I feel to have a husband I can talk to about anything, who is loving and supportive even after all these years to-gether . . .

In comparison, here is Jane, a woman who had a very high burnout score and a very low overall attitude toward her marriage:

> What really gets to me are the things he does repeatedly, which seem to be motivated by nothing else but a desire to drive me crazy. Like putting bottles of soft drink in the freezer, and leaving them there till they explode. And each time this happens and I tell him he is going to forget to take the bottles out in time he insists that he knows what he is doing. Another example is when I come home from work (and this is after leaving the house in perfect order in the morning) and the place looks like a pig sty, clothes and food leftovers everywhere, and my papers hidden under piles of junk. This is especially infuriating when I wake up early and spend hours putting things in order, before I leave for work. Every time this happens, and believe me it happens very often, I am ready to kill him.

Both women have, in their minds, "legitimate grievances" about their husbands, but only one of them is able to keep his positive qualities in mind. This ability is highly (and negatively) correlated with burnout. Of course, we don't know whether it is the positive overall attitude that prevents burnout, or conversely whether it is burnout that causes the focus on particular annoyances. But knowing that the two are related has far-reaching implications for coping. Donna provides an example of a negative overall outlook on marriage and in doing so actually suggests a very powerful technique for reversing it:

> What happened is that a lot of things took place on symbolic occasions, which made it easy to remember . . . One of the things that actually cemented my decision to divorce was my birthday, which is a symbolic day for me. I got a phone call at six o'clock in the morning from Europe, from a cousin, to wish me a happy birthday. Here is someone miles away who's taken the trouble. And he was sitting there listening, and didn't wish me a happy birthday. So I got home from work that night. I'd given him a lot of opportunities to get me a present because it is also symbolic. And I said I'd like a book, maybe a book certificate. This is what he said to me: "I went to look for a book, and then I decided that a book, or a gift certificate, isn't a good idea. Why don't you just go there and choose what you want." Which I haven't done. Obviously. And I suddenly realized, you know, that here are all these

people who do love me, and here's a person who doesn't appreciate me. He doesn't value me, he doesn't love me. If he did he
wouldn't treat me the way he did. He would want to do something
special for me. And it being such a symbolic day . . . I must also
tell you I kept a hate book all these years. Because whenever I've
been terribly depressed and upset I've written it down. And I've
got a book, and I can look back for twelve years . . .

Keeping the "hate book" helped Donna focus on the negative aspects of
the relationship, remembering all the traumas she experienced in her fourteen years of marriage. Couldn't we assume, following the same line of
reasoning, that keeping a "love book" would have helped her to remember
the good times, and the positive aspects of the marriage? Whenever something bad happened, reading through the book could have helped her to put
it in a more positive perspective.

As you may recall, Ellen has been married five and a half years and, like
Donna, for the second time. Unlike Donna, Ellen is very happy with her
marriage. She has a very low burnout score and a very positive overall
attitude. Ellen describes a situation very similar to the one described by
Donna, but with a very different resolution:

I don't like to carry grudges. I sometimes imagine myself standing
on a bridge, and throwing whatever troubles me down to the water, visualizing it going with the 'water under the bridge.' I remember, for example, the birthday present incident. My family
and friends made a big party for me, which was very touching, and
made me feel loved and cared for. He was the only one who did
not give me a present. I was very upset with him, and after every
one was gone asked him why I didn't get a present from him. He
said he was thinking about it for weeks but couldn't come up with
something that he was sure would make me happy, and was in a
panic on the day of the birthday . . . I can't tell you it really
made it all right. Birthdays, anniversaries, New Year's Eves and
such are very important to me, and I wish he would have given me
something—anything—I told him that, like I am telling him all of
my thoughts and feelings. And as I was doing that I was thinking
to myself how wonderful it is that I can express openly all of my
feelings, even the negative ones, something I was never quite able
to do with my former husband. The left over negative feelings I
just sent down with the water under the bridge . . .

COMMUNICATION

In recent years "communication" has become a buzz-word, so much so that when hearing that one of the most important features in preventing marriage burnout is good communication it sounds like a cliché. But what does communication *mean?* Women who are not at all burned out describe themselves as being able to talk to their husbands about everything. Women who are burned out describe communication that is curt, mechanical, and kept to the bare minimum. Again we don't know whether it is open communication that prevents burnout, or whether it is burnout that causes the communication to dwindle. In either case, however, burnout can be avoided only when the communication lines are open. The difference between communication in a burned-out marriage and in a close one is described by the prominent social psychologist Elliot Aronson, in his book *The Social Animal:*

> In a closed relationship, people tend to suppress their annoyances and to keep their negative feelings to themselves. This results in a fragile plateau that appears stable and positive but that can be devastated by a sudden shift in sentiment. Unfortunately, this may be a common kind of relationship in this country.
>
> In an open, honest, authentic relationship, one in which people are able to share their true feelings and impressions (even their negative ones), no such plateau is reached. Rather, there is a continuous zigzagging of sentiment around a point of relatively high esteem.

Ellen has had both kinds, and describes the difference:

> One of the most difficult things for me in my relationship to my ex-husband was that we were not really honest with each other. There were so many subjects that were taboo, that towards the end of our marriage communication was reduced to such things as who picks the kids up from piano lesson . . . We would never talk, for example, about being attracted to somebody else. It was simply unacceptable. But of course in the fifteen years of our marriage it did happen. So we had to deny it, which made us lie to ourselves and to each other. After doing it for so long I didn't know whether it was even possible to untangle this gigantic tangle of lies, half truths, and things unspoken. This is why I value so much my new marriage. We share absolutely everything with each

other. And it is such a relief not to have to worry about what can be said and what not. To be able to share every thought and every feeling. Of course part of it also means feeling a pang of jealousy when he is attracted to another woman. But experiences like that also add spice to our life.

Many books have been written in recent years detailing the "how to" of communication—how to express your feelings without hurting your husband and making him defensive (e.g., imagine yourself hearing the same statement; could your husband say to you the thing you are about to say to him without hurting your feelings and making you defensive?); how to fight fair in a way that will enable you both to vent frustrations, will provide resolution, and will not close off channels. One good way to improve the quality of the communication is to improve its quantity, which is to say— spend more time talking. Ilana, a career woman who has been married twenty-two years, told me that her marriage had improved tremendously since they got a dog; walking the dog at night together dramatically increased their time for talking.

VARIETY

The third factor in the list of positive marriage features can be found somewhere on the happy ground between overload and boredom. People function at their best at an optimal level of stimulation (variety). Extremely high levels of stimulation (overload) create anxiety and strain, while extremely low levels (underload) create boredom and anger. The optimal level is different for different people, and it requires a constant and continuous stimulation from the environment. This is why no matter how initially exciting a marriage can be, in the absence of variety, boredom and monotony can wear it down.

The ways women introduce variety into their marriages are as different as the women themselves. For some variety involves travel. Every so often they get "antsy" and just have to go somewhere—hiking in the woods, traveling in Europe, or driving to a sea resort. For some, variety involves study. They regularly attend classes and weekend courses in subjects they find interesting, of some practical value, or just fun. (Sometimes they do it with their husbands, other times without.) For many women variety involves making certain times or dates special: a lunch out every Wednesday, each time at a different restaurant; Sunday mornings reserved for a luxurious breakfast in bed with the newspapers; creating a special evening atmosphere by cooking a gourmet meal served with candlelight and soft music; or making love during different times of the day or in different rooms of the house.

Other Positive Environmental Features included:

• feedback from husband about performance (such as a "honey, that was one of the best meals I have ever had" after a gourmet meal);

• similarity to husband in terms of goals and expectations from life (such as the goal of "living a simple and honest life close to God and the land");

• receiving appreciation and respect from your husband for your contribution to the marriage (such as "raising five delightful children");

• security in the marriage (feeling "loved unconditionally," feeling that your home is your nest, a place from which you can spring out, and to which you can always return for comfort);

• feeling supported in your personal growth and ambitions;

• last but not least, a good sex life. It is interesting that with all the publicity given to this aspect of marital life, sex came out only ninth in its rank ordering as a burnout correlate for women! For women, the kind of intercourse most related to a happy marriage seems to be verbal, not sexual.

If unhappily married women tend to attribute their difficulties to their husbands' personality deficiencies or else to some character incompatibility, happily married women also tend to overattribute the success of the marriage to personalities—their own. "The reason why we have such a wonderful marriage," they say, "is that we are both such wonderful people." This attributional error, for obvious reasons, causes less pain than the former.

Subjective Realities

In all the preceding pages the discussion assumed that environments are objective entities out there in the real world—overload, conflict, obligations, variety, being "appreciated," having the chance for growth. But the study did not measure the objective features of these women's marriages, only the wives' subjective *perceptions* of their marriages. The same marriage can be perceived as full of variety by one woman, as too overloaded by a second woman, and as boring by a third.

This fact can be seen as a criticism of the study, since we don't know whether "real" overload, "real" conflict, and "real" variety have the same effect on burnout as does their subjective experience. The answer is that for purposes of coping with marriage burnout, a woman's perceptions are more important—because burnout itself is a subjective experience and because we know that perceptions of the world affect our feelings and actions. It is not necessarily the objective conditions that cause misery or even happiness, but how we interpret and explain those conditions. Crowding, for example, is less stressful to families that take four-in-a-room for granted, or who are so pleased to be safely in a new homeland at all that crowding is a relief. An old rabbinical story makes this point very well.

A man came to the rabbi in great distress asking for help. "Rabbi," he said, "I am going out of my mind. With me, my wife, and the six children all living in one little room, there is no space for breathing. The noise and the crowding are making all of us crazy. I don't know what to do." "Do you have a goat?" asked the rabbi. "Yes," the man answered. "Bring the goat into the house," said the rabbi. "What do you mean, bring the goat in?" the man asked in alarm. "I just told you, we don't have enough air to breathe as it is." "Do you want my advice, or don't you?" the rabbi asked sternly. "I do, I do," replied the man meekly. "Well, in that case, my advice is that you bring the goat into the house."

So the man did as he was told. A week later he came to the rabbi, in even greater distress. "Rabbi," he said, "Life is not worth living. Now in addition to the noise and the crowding of the children, we have to deal with the filth of the goat. I can't take it any more." "In that case," said the rabbi, "Get the goat out." The next day the man came back to the rabbi, kissed his hand and said, "Rabbi, thank you! What a pleasure it is to have the goat out of the house! So much air, so much space, no goat filth. We can breathe!"

What does this mean for women (and men) who would like to avoid burnout in their marriages? It means that burnout is not inevitable and that people actually have more power than they realize to actively avoid it. Couples can take three steps:

- stop blaming each other and look instead to stresses in the environment, such as job worries, children, lack of stimulating new activities.
- change the stresses to make the marital environment as positive and romantic as possible, rather than trying to change the spouse.
- realize the impact our own perceptions have on the way we understand reality and the way we respond to it. Since the reality of our lives is our own subjective version of that reality, we have the power to change it.

In other words, get the goat out of the house.

AYALA M. PINES is a social psychologist at the University of California at Berkeley, and a psychotherapist in private practice specializing in issues relating to burnout on the job and in marriage. She is internationally known as an author, speaker, and organizational consultant on the subject of burnout. Dr. Pines's pioneering research involved more than five thousand people (Americans, Israelis, Canadians, Australians, and Japanese) and hundreds of workshops all over the United States and abroad. She is coauthor (with Elliot Aronson) of *Burnout: From Tedium to Personal Growth* (Free Press, 1981) and author of *The Psychology of the Sexes* (Tel Aviv Open University Press, 1985). Her latest book, *Burnout in Marriage: Keeping the Spark Alive,* will be published soon.

Further Reading

Aronson, Elliot. "Attraction: Why Do People Like Each Other?" Chap. 7 in *The Social Animal.* San Francisco: W. H. Freeman, 1983.

Blumstein, Philip, and Schwartz, Pepper. *American Couples.* New York: Morrow, 1983.

Ehrenreich, Barbara. *The Hearts of Men: American Dreams and the Flight from Commitment.* Garden City, N.Y.: Anchor Press/Doubleday, 1983.

Paolino, Thomas J., and McCrady, Barbara S. *Marriage and Marital Therapy: Psychoanalytic, Behavioral, and Systems Therapy Perspectives.* New York: Brunner/Mazel, Publishers, 1978. See especially the Introduction by James and Janice Prochaska.

Pines, Ayala. *Marriage Burnout: Keeping the Spark Alive.* [in press]

———, and Aronson, Elliot. *Burnout: From Tedium to Personal Growth.* New York: Free Press, 1981.

———, "Sex Differences in Marriage Burnout." Paper presented at the annual convention of the American Psychological Association, Los Angeles, CA, August, 1985.

10

Motherhood

ELIZABETH HALL

When I first bathed my infant daughter, I was convinced that she was as fragile as a blown crystal goblet and would shatter if I grasped her slippery limbs too tightly. Two years later when I first bathed her baby brother, I was amazed at how sturdy human infants had become in such a short time. My experience is probably typical, and if babies were as delicate as most new parents fear, our species would have vanished long ago. The human infant is not only physically sturdy, but psychologically sturdy as well. Yet intelligent people continue to approach parenthood with apprehension.

No matter how delighted they are to become parents, most first-time mothers are beset with fears and uncertainty. The real concern, of course, is not the baby's physical care. Although a new mother feels an awesome responsibility for the immediate well-being of the seven pounds of wriggling baby in her lap, her major worry is the nearly two decades of opportunities to make grievous mistakes in the enterprise of child rearing that stretch before her.

Today's first-time mother may be better educated and better equipped to earn a living than her own mother and grandmother were, but when a baby cries at three in the morning, a Harvard M.B.A. does not seem terribly relevant and the knowledge that a substantial deposit has just been made in an IRA account does nothing to end a baby's distress. And so mothers turn to experts, to psychologists, psychiatrists, and pediatricians, reading their books and articles, looking for the magic words that will enable them to survive motherhood and steer their infant along the path toward a confident, capable adulthood.

For centuries experts have advised women on how to go about the business of motherhood, but the advice has varied so wildly as to make skeptics of us all. In the early nineteenth century, a mother's primary job was to instill obedience, breaking the "will" of unruly toddlers. Toward the end of that century mothers were told to avoid authoritarianism and become loving, sympathetic guides and friends. By the time the twentieth century was a decade old, mothers were advised never to pick up their babies between feedings, to play with them, or to evoke squeals of infant laughter. And to indulge young children's fancies in food or drink was to set them on the path to degradation: Accustomed to sensual enjoyment, children—or at least the sons—would wallow in sexual pleasures as soon as they passsed the brink of adolescence.

Before many more years had passed, psychologists had turned child rearing into child training and mothers into conditioners. Through rewards and punishment, mothers were to instill correct habits. John B. Watson, who unleashed radical behaviorism on an unsuspecting world, believed that only stoic, independent, and highly disciplined children could fit into American society. And so he urged mothers to purge all irrational emotion from the parental relationship. "Let your behavior always be objective and kindly firm," he wrote. "Never hug and kiss them, never let them sit on your lap. If you must, kiss them once on the forehead when they say good night. Shake hands with them in the morning."

Within a few decades infant control was out and permissiveness was in. Mother was to be a gushing fountain of love, who cleared away all obstacles and encouraged her child to explore the self and the world. The natural impulses of a child were good, and so were the natural instincts of the mother. But by now the psychoanalysts had also jumped in, warning mothers that they might damage their children. Without knowing it, a mother could reject a child, making the youngster withdrawn and neurotic. The possibility raised specters of guilt in each mother who let her baby wail for ten minutes, stifled angry impulses as she mopped up the third glass of spilled milk, or told a youngster she was "too busy" to play a game or read a story. But indulging childish whims and hovering anxiously over a youngster put her in danger of becoming that other monster of the nursery, the overprotective mother, whose damaged children were legion.

When one generation of mothers is ordered to avoid overstimulating an infant with childish play and another is urged to step up the intellectual stimulation of the nursery with mobiles, games, and songs; when one generation is warned against letting babies suck their thumbs or masturbate and another is instructed that such exploration is normal and healthy; when one generation is admonished that showing love is dangerous and another is cautioned that the failure to show love is disastrous, women have good reason to be wary of experts and their advice.

Today most psychologists are less dogmatic and more tentative than they once were. There are fewer pat answers and more flexibility for the struggling parent. If psychologists now know what the typical course of child development looks like, they are still not sure exactly which childhood experiences have which effects. It is now generally recognized that there are many ways to bring up a child. Each child comes into the world with a particular biological organization that continually interacts with experiences in the home and the wider world. The effects of any particular experience—good or bad—are no longer seen as permanent. A child is not like a fragile crystal goblet, but more like a soft plastic tumbler. You can change its shape by squeezing it, but when you relax your grip, it returns to the original form. It takes great heat to push it permanently out of shape.

All that changing advice about child rearing should have told us this was so. No matter which experts mothers followed, most children seemed to emerge from their ministrations unscathed. Consider the barbarous custom of forty years ago, when across the country tiny three-month-olds who could not sit alone were held on a warmed potty each morning. Or the practice of cowing a colicky baby into silence with a midnight enema. Horrible as they sound, these practices apparently had little effect on the health, personality, intelligence, or sexual habits of the millions of babies who endured them.

One of the most important things we have learned in the past few years is that there is no "right" or "wrong" way to be a mother. It has become clear that children are not only resilient but that parents are not the all-powerful gods they once seemed. Many things happen to a child that are outside a mother's control. Children have their own genes, their own temperaments, their own personalities, perceptions, and memories. There's little you can do about this fact, no matter how carefully you try to manage a child's environment. All those dark analyses of the nursery—as well as all the rosy pictures of a mother's guiding hand—ignored the tremendous influence exerted by the rest of the world. Peers, social forces, experiences outside the home, and that great nonstop influence, television, are going to affect your child's future and help determine what sort of adult he or she becomes.

Psychologists discovered that a child's future is not necessarily shaped in the nursery when they began pulling together case histories of children who had been isolated or abused in infancy or early childhood and then rescued and placed in a foster home. When these children were given loving care, the scars of their early experience gradually faded and they differed little from their more fortunate peers. War orphans brought to this country from all over the world, youngsters who had not only suffered extreme disruption and deprivation but who also had to adjust to a new culture and a new language, became physically healthy, socially competent children with above-average IQs.

Does this mean that what happens in the family has no effect on the child? Of course not. It means that mistakes along the way are not indelibly engraved on your child's psyche and that unless a bad situation becomes permanent, most children will surmount its effects.

This is a liberating concept for mothers, because until recently we have been warned that the experiences of the first few years invariably set the course of a child's development. And since mothers have been given the responsibility for the care of infants and young children, many women worried about the harm caused by their mistakes as they strove mightily to provide a perfect environment for their child. In the late 1950s, when the influence of Freud was strong, some of us ran scared. A college-educated friend, pregnant with her second child, told me she hoped she would have another girl, because she was certain if she gave birth to a boy she would be such a smothering, overprotective mother that the baby was certain to grow up homosexual.

The Care of Children

Before you smile at those fears, think about your own. The guilt that stalks today's nursery arises out of decisions about whether or how soon a mother returns to paid employment. Those who decide to go back to work harbor secret fears that placing an infant or a toddler in child care robs their offspring of a mother's tender nurturance and sets her or him on the path to (a) school failure; (b) emotional disturbance; (c) juvenile delinquency; (d) all of the above. Those who decide to stay at home have their own brand of guilt. Although they are uninterested in climbing up the corporate ladder, teaching other people's children, or building houses, they feel as if they should apologize for their contentment in the role of mother and home-maker.

Women worry because society's view of motherhood has not changed as fast as the culture has changed. As the twentieth century draws to a close, the view of woman as primarily guardian of hearth, rearer of children, and comforter of husband has become a faded picture of Victorian society—a picture that omits all the Victorian women who left their own families to cook, clean, and care for those middle-class households. The idealized portrait of the American family, in which the father is the sole breadwinner and the mother stays at home, appears in fewer and fewer American families.

In fact, most of the profamily rhetoric we hear today describes a situation that has not existed in this country for some time. Smaller families, rising divorce rates, economic demands that a single salary can't meet, and the change to a service economy have combined to put women back into the labor force. By 1981 a majority of mothers worked outside the home. Married mothers of preschoolers are least likely to be employed: "only" 47 percent of them hold jobs, a figure that rises to 63 percent among those with older children. But one child in five lives in a one-parent home, and that parent is usually the mother; 65 percent of divorced mothers with preschoolers and 83 percent of divorced mothers with older children work. In fact, it is the mother who has never worked who is especially vulnerable to the stress that follows divorce. Unprepared to support herself, she has a difficult time finding a decent job, and because her children are accustomed to a full-time mother, their lives are disrupted more by divorce than the lives of employed mothers' children.

Most mothers eventually go back to work, but the time of their return varies. Some psychologists continue to insist that mothers belong at home for the child's first three years, but their number is shrinking. The most vocal champion of the homebound mother is developmental psychologist Burton L. White, who has carried his worries about the dangers of "full-time substitute care for baby" into radio campaigns prepared by his Center for Parent Education. White's concerns are not shared by the majority of developmental psychologists.

Some suggest that babies can start in child care at three months; others believe that it is a good idea to wait until they are six months old. Developmental psychologist Sandra Scarr, of the University of Virginia, believes that mothers can start work as soon as they like. After all, she points out, until babies are two months old they don't even know who is taking care of them. By the time babies are about six months old, they not only know who is caring for them, but become distressed when left with strangers, a development that makes the adjustment to child care more difficult. Even so, says Scarr, who has brought four babies into adolescence while continuing her work at universities, most babies adapt to their new situation within a few weeks. However, T. Berry Brazelton of Harvard University's Medical

School believes that a baby should either be placed in child care at four months or else kept at home until about eighteen months, when the protests at being separated from parents begin to subside.

Why have most developmental psychologists stopped urging mothers to stay home during those first years? For one thing, homebound mothers don't seem to spend any more time playing with their children, reading to them, or directly interacting with them than employed mothers do. The homebound mother is simply "there," but even if her child is in the same room with her, she is likely to be cleaning, cooking, eating, or watching television. It has been estimated that typical children spend about 5 percent of their waking hours interacting with mothers who are home all day. They spend nearly that much time—4 percent of their waking hours—interacting with their fathers, who spend the day away from them.

Another reason fewer psychologists are insisting that mothers stay home is evidence that a baby's mother is not a child's only source of love, comfort, and security. When psychologists first began doing research on the bond between infant and care giver, they concentrated on the mother and baby. Babies without this emotional bond, known as attachment, were believed to be in serious psychological difficulty. And indeed, that seems to be the case. But when psychologists' angle of vision widened, they discovered that babies become attached to both parents—and at about the same time. What is more, researchers who studied eighteen-month-old babies at an Israeli kibbutz discovered that the infants were attached to mother, father, and the care giver in the nursery. Someone once suggested that babies from large, extended families were especially lucky because they had so many people to love them—brothers, sisters, grandparents, aunts, uncles, and cousins. If that is so, babies whose lives are wrapped up with only one person will be the most vulnerable children. A child whose only close bond is with mother may be devastated if Mommy gets angry; one who has close bonds with several people will feel less threatened. It is the children with only one close relationship whose lives are most disrupted should their mothers have to go to work.

Finally, psychologists who have studied the children of employed mothers have found that youngsters do not seem to suffer any ill-effects. A more important influence on children than whether their mothers are employed appears to be how their mothers feel about working. If a mother feels guilty or resentful, her employment may well have negative effects on her child; but the boredom, dissatisfaction, and resentment of a mother who is cooped up at home against her will is likely to be just as harmful. When Anita M. Farel studied kindergarten children in North Carolina, she found that the youngsters who scored lowest on tests of intellectual development, showed the least consideration for others, and had the most trouble sticking to a task were those whose mothers were not employed but thought that working was a good idea.

Working does not necessarily mean putting a baby in a day care center. In our grandmothers' generation, a mother who had to work left her children with her own mother or mother-in-law, but that situation is on its way to extinction in this country. The grandmother of today's infant is likely to be going off to work each day herself and is probably at the peak of her earning powers. There is no perfect way to handle substitute care, but then there is no perfect solution to any of the problems of being a mother.

No matter what you decide to do, you give up something. If there were a way to be with your children through all their waking hours and still follow the typical male career path, life would be beautiful. But life is full of trade-offs. The major choices faced by today's mother are child care or home care; working or not working; and early or late parenthood. The reason these choices don't press in on husbands is that society has effectively taken the critical decisions away from them. Some fathers might like to stay home and enjoy their children, but until recently the idea was unthinkable. Paternity leave is beginning to creep into the workplace, and a few fathers are electing to spend their days at home while their wives go off to work. But such fathers are generally concentrated in a handful of professions with flexible hours, and they often find themselves the butt of jokes.

Some families handle the responsibility with shift work: The father usually works nights and the mother works days. More than a million American families have chosen this path because they don't want strangers to rear their children. Not much is known about the effect of shift work on families, but it appears that children of shift workers tend to take responsibilities early; some of these couples say that their own relationship improves because their time together becomes more precious. As you might imagine, there are definite drawbacks to shift work. Time together may be more precious, but many couples find that their sex life suffers. When one parent goes to work twenty minutes after the other comes home, sex gets shoved to the weekend—providing both have the same days off. As for the children, once they pass babyhood, they may have so little opportunity to see their parents together that they never discover how men and women relate on a daily, intimate basis.

A well-trodden path for infant care is the sitter who comes into your home while you work. The advantage of bringing someone into your own home is that your infant or toddler is in familiar surroundings and may be more comfortable than in a stranger's house. However, this is probably the most expensive way to care for a child and it gives you no way to check up on the sort of attention—or lack of it—your child receives. Nobody but your child knows what happens while you are gone, and your child may either be too young to tell you or believe that the sitter's methods were approved by you. A day care home may be a better solution for an infant or very young child, since most homes care for several children, and parents can compare notes. The disadvantage to the day care home is that nothing in it belongs to your child and the rules it establishes may not be the same as yours.

Once your child is about three, however, he or she will probably be happier in a day care center or nursery school, where there is a wonderful variety of toys and opportunities to do the sort of messy things (easel and finger painting, water play) that most homes don't permit. Three-year-olds are ready for the company of other children and most thrive on it.

Some of the best evidence on the effects of day care has come from studies in Bermuda, where 90 percent of the children are in some kind of day care arrangement by the time they are two years old. Researchers from the United States have been studying these children for several years, and they report that using sitters or day care homes seems best for babies. Placing youngsters in day care centers before their second birthdays may hamper their emotional development. As eight-year-olds, such children were less cooperative, more aggressive, and more active than the rest. But eight-year-olds who had spent their first two years with sitters or in day care homes were no different from those who had spent the first two years at home with Mommy. The best explanation for this difference seems to be the ratio of staff to children. Babies may not get enough attention when the care of one staff member is spread over eight infants.

The mountain of studies examining the development of youngsters who grow up in good day care indicates that they seem to get a head start on children who stay at home. Perhaps because of educational programs, interaction with other children, and because they have learned to get along during the day without their mothers, children in day care are more advanced intellectually and socially, and they are more assertive. But as we said, nothing's perfect. Along with that assertiveness goes less compliance with their parents' wishes and sometimes more aggression. Children in day care also are exposed to the viruses brought in by other youngsters, so that the series of colds and minor illnesses that kindergartners usually encounter begins a few years sooner.

Choosing a sitter, a day care home, or a day care center for your child requires some research. Not all day care centers are good and some are decidedly inferior. Much of the research has been done in centers near colleges and universities, and experts are uneasy about inferior day care centers where children are unsupervised or unchallenged. It's important to visit the center yourself before handing over your youngster. The best guide to this important decision is Sandra Scarr's book, *Mother Care/Other Care,* which tells you exactly how to go about checking out the staff and facilities.

Recent headlines about sex abuse in nursery schools has made some parents uneasy about leaving their children, awakening all the old guilt that first accompanied a mother's decision to go back to work. Despite the lurid television and newspaper coverage, such incidents are rare and would be even rarer if standards for day care were established. There are no federal standards, and state standards often focus on the physical layout of facilities, ignoring the workers. Perhaps because society has not yet accepted the new family situation, government has been more interested in making sure your barber is qualified than your day care worker. Even so, children run a much higher risk of being sexually abused at home than in a day care center —ask any social worker.

Society is much more tolerant of the mother who goes back to work after her children start elementary school. Even so, for years there were deep suspicions about the effect of a mother's employment. Psychologists simply assumed that working mothers were bad for children and designed studies to look for the ills that developed. Despite the search, most of the news was good. Children of employed mothers had more responsibility for household chores, a factor that appears to increase a child's self-esteem in a society where most children feel they contribute nothing. Children of employed mothers were more independent and less bound by sex role stereotypes than children of homebound mothers. Their daughters were more likely to look forward to having careers. Their sons, though, seemed to have troubles; their psychological adjustment, especially in the sons of lower-class mothers, was somewhat poorer than that of their counterparts whose mothers stayed at home. Psychologist Michael Lamb has suggested that lower-class boys, brought up in homes with traditional expectations about men's and women's roles, may regard their mother's employment as proof that their father is unable to provide for the family. But no matter what their social class, mothers who were doing what they wanted to do—whether going out to work or staying home—had well-adjusted children.

The Stress of Children

Everybody worried about the effects of mothers on children, but for a long time nobody worried about the effects of children on mothers. Couples needed no expert to tell them that parenthood was not a condition of unalloyed bliss. Children are wonderful, and they generally increase our sense of self-esteem and personal worth. Who else could produce such a beautiful child? And few pleasures can match that of watching babies and children discover the world; their delight and wonder are infectious.

Yet hidden among each bouquet of childish rosebuds are a good many sharp thorns. Couples find that children disrupt the lives they have so carefully arranged. Their personal and economic freedom is suddenly controlled by the needs of their offspring. The whole tenor of family life changes: Most couples find that serious—or even playful—conversation becomes scarce, and the spontaneity that characterized their relationship dries up. Babies have a way of screaming for attention at the most inopportune times— almost invariably as an orgasm nears—and older children are the eternal spectators of any sexual or emotional exchange. The problem becomes so serious for some couples that sex therapists often recommend that a baby-sitter be hired and the couple flee to a local motel for relaxed, sensuous weekends. It is either that or a deadbolt on the bedroom door.

The disruption goes beyond a couple's private life, and some researchers maintain that a couple's level of marital satisfaction is determined by the presence, number, and age of the children. The daily stresses of parenthood seemed to concentrate around the mother. Of course, psychologists had long been familiar with postpartum depression, that emotional letdown that sometimes follows the euphoria of childbirth. Some said postpartum depression was the result of a dramatic drop in hormone levels, but others pointed to the stress of adapting to the role of mother. As the demands of infant care closed in, many women reported feeling trapped and isolated, especially those who had been strongly committed to their jobs. The final straw was picked up by psychologists Judith Laws and Pepper Schwartz: Such feelings were probably intensified by the new mother's major complaint—lack of sleep.

Once through the postpartum period, mothers were supposed to bounce back, creating the idyllic families of situation comedies, where everyone is charming, money is never a problem, and all crises are solved in thirty minutes. In 1975 a national survey revealed that life did not imitate television. Among more than two thousand adults, parents of young children were less satisfied than childless couples, and young mothers were more likely than any other group to say they were unhappy, dissatisfied, doubtful about their marriages, and at times wished they were free of any parental responsibilities. A few years later a pair of researchers reported, with some amazement, that one fourth of mothers with preschoolers went through at least one period when physicians prescribed tranquilizers for depression or some related disorder.

At last psychologists began to take the plight of the young mother seriously. It was not major crises that were responsible for the unhappiness of so many mothers, but chronic stress, the piling up of those familiar, small annoyances such as broken-down washing machines, babysitters who fail to appear, bowls of cereal smashed on freshly waxed floors, squabbles between siblings, toys strewn across the carpet, disagreements over discipline. Any mother can fill out the list herself.

After studying young mothers in the United States and Israel, psychologist Norma Feshbach of the University of California at Los Angeles discovered that children were not the only source of maternal stress, but contributed more to a mother's stress than any other single category of life, including her personal problems, men, time, housework, finances, and disruptions. The level of stress felt by any mother appeared to stay steady; weekends were no more nor less stressful than other days. Employed mothers were under additional stress from job-related difficulties and conflicts between work and home schedules, but homebound mothers complained of being bored and lonely. Mothers who felt the least stress had friends in whom they could confide their problems, and those who could confide in their husbands reported less stress and unhappiness in their marriages.

Not all mothers are equally stressed, and those with good marriages report the least aggravation. Women who are satisfied with their marriages seem to be less bothered than other women by their toddlers' impact on their leisure, their daily activities, and their marriages. These mothers also had warmer attitudes toward their children and encouraged their independence.

When women are under chronic stress, their relationship with their children may suffer. Among the women studied by Feshbach, when stress came in the door, reasoning went out the window. When their stress levels were high, mothers turned to direct disciplinary measures—commands, physically moving the child, or resorting to physical punishment. Beleaguered mothers were less likely than others to express warmth and affection when interacting with their children and more likely to talk to their children in a negative or rejecting way. Feshbach is quick to point out that mother, child, and situation affect one another. Some of the stress that makes mothers punitive may come from having to cope with a difficult child who persists in misbehaving. And when the washing machine has broken down, the dog has just tracked mud onto the carpet, and it's clear that she will be at least twenty minutes late to work, only the most heroic mother can remain warm, affectionate, and reasonable.

Why aren't fathers under the same kind of stress felt by mothers? Probably because society has few expectations for the father role. If a mother feels she is doing a poor job at her maternal responsibilities, her self-esteem plummets. If a father can't diaper a baby properly, he stays serene—it's really not his job. A mother who is employed outside the home loses none of her responsibility for child care; she handles it all—home, child, and job—with little assistance from her husband. Today an increasing number of husbands are beginning to take over some of the housework or child care chores, but the biggest share remains with the mother. If the system doesn't run smoothly, it's her fault, and her attempts to get things back on track may bump into angry resistance from her children.

Sometimes unhappiness develops because the birth of a baby pushes couples into traditional sex roles. Researchers have found that no matter how egalitarian a couple's working arrangement, household chores tend to get divided along traditional lines after a child is born. He may keep carrying out the garbage and cleaning the garage, but suddenly the dishes and vacuuming are all yours. It seems to happen without any conscious intent, and it may make women resentful.

Many women handle their overload by cutting back on jobs they used to consider essential. It was a day of liberation for me when I discovered that every room did not have to be cleaned every week, as my mother had maintained. Unless you live in a city where soot sifts over every surface, you learn to clear out the debris, and fudge a few days on the dusting and vacuuming. You buy permanent-press clothes and put away the iron. You put Julia Child on the shelf and fall back on simple, quickly prepared food, and you learn to bring home a bucket of fried chicken or a pizza without apology.

Each woman finds her own solutions to the impossible overlap of schedules, and each family adjusts in its own way to changes over the years. When the second child comes along, for example, there's another shift in family roles. Researchers who followed families for two years after a second child was born found three major ways of accommodating the additional responsibilities. In some families the father took over a good deal of the older child's care, giving the mother more time to spend with the baby. In other families the father assumed additional household chores while the mother concentrated on child care. In yet other families both parents passed the responsibility for any aspect of family life back and forth, depending on the situation.

The Timing of Children

One of the major changes in women's lives during this century has been in the diminishing portion of life they devote to rearing children. Most of us now have our babies later than our mothers did, but we have fewer of them, so that we can look forward to a long stretch of life after the children are grown.

Because child rearing has been compressed into two decades or less of their lives, women have new choices to make—choices of timing. You can have a baby while you are in your twenties or postpone motherhood until you have established yourself in a career. This last option is gaining in popularity—the birth rate among women between thirty and thirty-five years old rose 15 percent between 1980 and 1983. No matter which choice you make, there are trade-offs.

Couples who have children early usually have a tough time economically. They have had no chance to save any money, neither spouse is established at work (one or both may be in school), and the early years of child rearing are a time of scrimping and making do. Many fall back on financial assistance from parents; some young fathers take a second job. Couples who wait until both are in their thirties are likely to have savings, perhaps own their own home, and one or both are established in their careers. They are likely to have money for the extras that make life smoother—meals out, vacations, and the like.

Emotional issues are also involved in the timing of parenthood. Psychologists Pamela Daniels and Kathy Weingarten interviewed couples in their thirties, forties, and fifties, asking them how they decided (if they did decide) when to have their children and what effect it had on the experience and on their marriages. Couples whose first child came early tended to be involved with their own extended families—a grandmother often was as much of a care giver as the father. Perhaps because parenthood arrived before adulthood had been firmly entered, the women in these families tended to mother their husbands as well as their children.

Late-timing couples tended to be solicitous of each other's emotional needs, and if one did a lion's share of the nurturing, it was as likely to be the father as the mother. Fathers in late-timing families tended to be involved in household duties and the daily care of their children to a degree not found among early-timing fathers. This probably came about because most late-timing mothers had established themselves in careers, an accomplishment that gave them more power within the family, and had husbands who were accustomed to helping with the chores.

When early- and late-timing are weighed in the balance, early-timing becomes advantageous in the last half of the life cycle and late-timing has the advantage during the early years. More than half of the early-timing couples in this study said that if they could do it over they would postpone the timing of their first child's birth by at least a few years. Yet they were delighted with the big advantage of early timing: Those who were then in their thirties were happy to have their last child in school; those who were in their forties were looking forward to an empty nest and a second honeymoon or a new career; those who were in their fifties were carefree—no more college tuitions and only themselves to worry about.

Late-timing couples were more enthusiastic about their choices; only about a quarter wished their children had been born sooner. They felt that they had completed their growing up and were ready to become parents by the time their first child was born. This readiness for parenthood among older women has appeared in other studies. Among homebound mothers between the ages of sixteen and thirty-eight, the older the woman, the more pleasure she derives from motherhood—even though she has more caretaking responsibilities and less social time away from her baby than younger mothers do. Late-timing parents did find some distinct disadvantages in late parenthood: They had often felt they lacked the energy required to keep up with boisterous children. Those who had postponed parenthood until they were forty wondered whether they would be a burden to their children and whether they would live to see their grandchildren. And they were aware that they would have fewer years to themselves after the nest had emptied.

Social scientists used to warn of the "empty nest syndrome," when women—but not so much men—grieved for their departed fledglings. Men were supposed to be too wrapped up in their careers to suffer much, but women were regarded as trembling on the verge of depression. Then researchers began to study mid-life women and discovered that most were happier than they'd been in years. Even women who had not worked outside the home, and so might have been wrapped up in their children, were happier. Perhaps it was because, for a change, they could think about themselves. For most women it is a rewarding period. Money goes further, time seems to expand, school schedules no longer dictate vacations, and intimacy and spontaneity between husband and wife can flourish anew.

Some women *are* miserable when the children depart, but the empty nest syndrome may be limited to women with a history of emotional problems. When psychologists Grace Baruch and Rosalind Barnett interviewed a group of women between the ages of thirty-five and fifty-five, they ran into a style of mothering that could lead to problems when there is nobody left to mother. These women, whom the researchers called "coupled" mothers, believed that children gave meaning to their lives, that they provided the women with a sense of being needed, and that being the best caretaker for their child gave them a sense of being special and irreplaceable. Their self-esteem, indeed their very identity, depended on their children. And so when their children left home, these mothers had low self-esteem, felt they lacked control over their lives, and often had symptoms of anxiety or depression.

Women who showed another style of mothering seemed to be much better off. These "autonomous" mothers enjoyed mothering but saw their children as separate people instead of as extensions of themselves. They liked the kind of people their children were, enjoyed doing things with them, and got pleasure out of seeing them mature and change. Autonomous mothers tended to have high self-esteem and a sense of control over their lives. They also were optimistic about the future, fairly satisfied with their present lives, and often expressed feelings of joy and delight. It is not hard to guess which mother is going to have a more satisfying life when the nest is empty.

An Encouraging Word

The two decades of tears and kisses, pouts and praise, that precede the empty nest are best navigated with help. You need friends and family who support you in your choices, no matter what they are. You need companionship. You need a sense of immunity against advice from experts, whose generalizations never fit all cases and who would be the first to admit it. And you need to be easy on yourself. If you make a choice, don't feel guilty about it. If your reaction to a childish misfortune is "I wasn't there when he needed me because I was being promoted to vice president," you're kidding yourself. If you had been there, your dimpled darling probably would have ignored you or told you to buzz off.

Most important of all, you need a sense of humor. Whatever you do, it will be wrong—and your kids will tell you so. Murphy's Law operates in the nursery as surely as it operates in the boardroom. Whatever can go wrong, will. No matter what you do, your child will blame you for something. Let me tell you about a couple of my friends, both mothers of writers. Both mothers read every word their charming sons wrote, from the first, laboriously printed, childish stories to the professional productions of their maturity. One of my friends was completely accepting and lavish with her praise. Believing that budding talent was a tender plant that could be nipped by the frosts of criticism, she never uttered a word that implied her son was of less than Nobel quality. And what did her successful son say about his mother's encouragement? "Why couldn't she have given me a little constructive criticism? I needed it badly, and instead she kept telling me how great I was."

The other friend complimented her son's writing, but always tried to give him a little critical assistance, pointing out places where his noble efforts could be improved. Her successful son plays the flip side of the complaint record: "Why couldn't she have given me the uncritical praise I needed? Instead, she always kept pointing out what was wrong with my work. I thought I'd never make it as a writer." Neither boy was so discouraged that he turned to another career, but both are certain their mothers planted obstacles on their path. In this imperfect world, there are no perfect mothers.

ELIZABETH HALL's experience with motherhood is both personal and professional. The mother of two children born during the 1950s, she stayed home during their preschool years, like nine out of ten other women in her situation. After her children entered school, she combined motherhood with full-time employment as a librarian. Later she worked as managing editor of *Psychology Today* and editor in chief of *Human Nature* magazine. She is the coauthor of five college textbooks in psychology, child and adult development, and sexuality. She has also written novels and nonfiction books for children, including books explaining psychology to children *(Why Do We Do What We Do: A Look at Psychology* [Houghton Mifflin, 1973] and *From Pigeons to People: A Look at Behavior Shaping* [Houghton Mifflin, 1975]).

Further Reading

Daniels, Pamela, and Weingarten, Kathy. *Sooner or Later: The Timing of Parenthood in Adult Lives.* New York: Norton, 1982.

Hall, Elizabeth; Lamb, Michael; and Perlmutter, Marion. *Child Psychology Today.* 2nd ed. New York: Random House, 1986.

Kagan, Jerome. *The Nature of the Child.* New York: Basic Books, 1984.

Scarr, Sandra. *Mother Care/Other Care.* New York: Basic Books, 1984.

11

Work

FAYE CROSBY

Living out there in rural Colorado, she thought somehow a job might help. They could sure use the money. Who couldn't? But it was more than just the money. A job might help to ease the loneliness. And so Martha made the elaborate babysitting arrangements and took a part-time job as a salesperson in a local shop. She enjoyed interacting with the customers and being responsible for ordering supplies, and she liked the boss. The pay was not superb, but anything seemed better than nothing. For a while life proceeded with more of a lilt. Fourteen months into the job Martha and her family had the opportunity to return East to visit her parents and her childhood friends. She quit her job—with no regrets and with no hard feelings. That was in 1976.

The year 1977 saw Martha return to school and take classes in early childhood education. She had a choice of attending the local community college or driving two hours each way to attend the state school. She chose to attend school locally, but the classes proved so boring that Martha did not continue her education straight through to the certificate. She sampled different courses, liked art and psychology, and began to accept jobs as a substitute teacher. Again, the pay was not superb, but the children provided pleasure. The job demanded no sacrifices in Martha's domestic routine.

The education classes came to an end. The year 1977 yielded to 1978; 1978 and 1979 slipped by in turn, a substitute job here, a substitute job there. In between jobs, Martha exercised horses for her husband and for some other ranch managers in the area. Occasionally, she did a few book-keeping jobs. Once she took the children back East to visit again; and two or three times Martha and her husband traveled around the great Southwest.

So life went along, with the usual number of moments of heel-kicking joy and the usual number of moments of unrest and discord. But as slowly and unobtrusively as the gray began to streak Martha's hair, the ground shifted. Forty hove into close view, and Martha began to think of putting an end to her occupational meanderings and of settling into a career. In the summer of 1984—the frightening forty still at bay—Martha visited the East again. This time she stopped off at her alma mater to discuss career possibilities with the impressive-sounding Career Guidance and Advisory Office.

It was not long after her visit to the Career Guidance and Advisory Office that I saw my old friend. Martha and I spent a day talking and hugging, and hugging and talking in the manner of friends who continue, year after year, to cherish a fundamental sense of sameness as their lives take very different turnings. Our talk returned often to Martha's experiences at the Career Office, and although my career had solidified years ago, I recognized my own dilemma and questions in the experiences of my friend.

What had happened to Martha in the advisory session? Essentially, after an informal chat with the counselor, Martha was placed in front of a computer terminal and instructed to rank the importance of five separate factors, shifting and reshifting the weights so as to meet a specified total ranking. The roster of job titles numbered in the hundreds, but based on Martha's responses and ratings, the computer deemed only three jobs suitable to my friend's background, interests, and needs. How depressing, and how wrong!

Fortunately, Martha had engaged in a little clever detective work at the terminal. She found that when she shifted the importance of one factor, the program listed not three but thirty jobs as appropriate for her needs and talents. The one factor that had such a large impact was scheduling—something the computer (programmed no doubt by an unmarried person) called "leisure time" but something that Martha, as the mother of two school-age children, thought of as essential to family survival.

We extracted several lessons, Martha and I, from her conversation with the computer. First, we concluded that the paid labor market is not as attuned to women's lives as much as it is to men's lives. We saw, further, that for women today the real and important benefits and rewards of having a paid job or a career can come at a cost, and that there is no single set of answers to the raft of questions, which Martha and thousands of other women ask themselves daily, about the role of paid employment in their lives.

Uniting all the specific questions is, of course, the larger uncertainty about whether paid work helps or hurts a woman's mental health. In the 1950s a woman's employment outside the home was thought to cause harm, often irreparable harm, to her children and thereby indirectly to herself. Scholars, revealing the assumptions and presumptions of their own moment in history, studied how "father absence" could impair the cognitive functioning of children and how "maternal deprivation" could warp emotional functioning. (Back then, no one ever published papers about "paternal deprivation" or "mother absence.") Times changed, researchers exploded the myth of maternal deprivation (see Chap. 10), and the psychological homilies of one era yielded to the great questions of the next: What is the association between paid employment and a woman's mental health? In particular, should you or should you not work? Would part-time employment assure better psychological functioning than full-time? What sort of job or career will enhance your happiness and sense of well-being? What can you do to keep the stress level low while reaping the emotional benefits of paid employment?

There is only one simple answer to all these and related questions. The answer is: It depends. Without knowing the particular circumstances of your life, no one—no matter how well versed in psychological theory and research, no matter how clever at computer programming—can offer definite answers.

Although the psychologist cannot make pronouncements, sight unseen, about what any particular woman ought to do, an impressive amount of research documents certain observations about the benefits and costs of paid employment for most women in today's world. The purpose of this chapter is to present what researchers know about the connections between paid employment and mental health in women. First comes the good news: the psychological benefits of paid employment. Second, I give the bad news: some of the costs of paid employment. I do so with the hope that knowing what the costs are can help a woman keep them low. While this chapter could no more dictate what you ought to do than could an article in *Consumer Reports* dictate what you ought to buy, the chapter aims to provide you with solid and useful data with which to make informed decisions.

Benefits of Employment

"Paid employment" is a broad term, and as everybody knows, one job is not just like another. Recently, researchers have documented how certain aspects of life at work have special impact for workers. Several studies show, for instance, that the attitudes of one's supervisor loom large in a woman's work life. The problems that come from working for a hostile boss can outweigh the many benefits which derive from working.

Despite the variety of ways in which jobs differ from each other, however, most jobs share some similarities. All forms of paid employment, for example, involve an exchange of money for labor or services rendered. One very important conclusion from a number of studies is that employed women tend to enjoy good psychological health. The benefits of paid employment include the money it brings, the friendships it allows, the structure it gives to daily life, the healthy separation of self from home it provides, and the sense of competence it fosters.

MONEY

The first obvious benefit of paid employment would appear to be the pay itself. Yet, while common sense and Tallulah Bankhead tell us that one is better off rich than poor, research shows that money benefits working women indirectly rather than directly. Money benefits us psychologically when it empowers us to do what we want to do.

Note the verb. I do not say that money benefits us when it empowers us to *have* what we want to have. To be sure, what we can do often depends on what we have; it's no fun to go skiing without skis. But we must remember that our ability to do what we want does not relate in a one-to-one fashion with what we have. When you want to travel frequently, having responsibility for a big house can in fact prevent you from doing what you want.

Another reason to stress the indirect rather than the direct benefits of money is that satisfaction with possessions per se can be rather fleeting. The quest for possessions puts us on what Donald Campbell and Philip Brickman have called "the hedonic treadmill." The acquisition of one object only whets our appetite for another. Then, if our hopes and expectations outstrip our ability to acquire, or if those around us acquire more than we, we feel deprived. As long as we ask ourselves "Do I have what I want?" rather than asking "Can I do what I want?" we run the risk of feeling less satisfied with more pay.

Survey researchers who study job satisfaction find that money is impor-

tant primarily when it is absent. A few years ago I conducted a complex
survey of over three hundred randomly selected working men and women in
the town of Newton, Massachusetts. When asked what aspects of their jobs
they found gratifying or rewarding, 45 percent of my sample answered "a
sense of accomplishment." The other sources of job gratification included:

social relations	43 percent
learning and challenge	31 percent
helping other people	28 percent
advancement	23 percent
independence and control	20 percent

Only 17 percent of the sample mentioned pay and fringe benefits as an
important benefit of working. Interestingly, the group who cited pay most
often were the men in low-status, low-paying jobs. About one third of the
men in low-prestige jobs mentioned pay as a reward of working; 13 percent
of the men in high-prestige jobs did, as did 14 percent of the women in low-
status jobs and 7 percent of the women in high-status jobs. Apparently, it is
the shortage of money that makes pay important to us.

Should women become more concerned with money? Some feminists argue that women will never attain their rightful power until they learn to
value money and until they acquire money. Others go further and argue that
women fear money as they fear success. I know of no research that substan-
tiates the claim that women fear money and precious little that shows that
women fear success. What women do fear—and who can blame us?—is the
social consequences that may accompany some types of success: the loss of
relationships, the accusations of being "unfeminine," the threats to men of
female achievement. As to valuing and acquiring money, the massive laboratory research on bargaining and power shows that caring too much about
money prevents one from using money as a resource! We should be sure to
remember that money is a means to our own desired ends and not an end in
itself.

FRIENDSHIP

Social interactions are one aspect of work life that has a more direct and
powerful effect than money. Most jobs in an advanced economy involve an
enormous amount of structured and rather superficial contact with other
people. One study found, for example, that managers in large corporations
tend to spend more than three quarters of their work time in meetings.

People working in the medical, legal, and teaching professions must spend at least three quarters of their time at work in contact with others.

Being with other people is enjoyable for most women. Whether women and men differ in this regard is hard to say. Some surveys show that women rank social contact as a more important part of an enjoyable working situation than do men, but men tend to value (indeed, even perhaps to overvalue) prestige and recognition more than women do. Thus, while social interaction may appeal to women more than men, men may be more dependent on social approval than are women.

However, men *and* women tend to emphasize the benefits of social relations at work when they lack opportunities of advancement. Sociologist Rosabeth Kanter finds that both sexes scale down their achievement dreams and concentrate on other benefits of work when they assume their dreams are in vain. It is hard to know right now how persistent the gender differences will prove, given the enormous changes in sex role norms and employment patterns.

Certainly both women and men rely heavily on friendships at work in times of crisis, as I found in my study of work life during divorce. My colleagues and I interviewed twenty-two male managers and eighteen female managers of a large corporation. All of the managers were between thirty and fifty years old, all had been divorced one to five years prior to the interview, and all had children from the dissolved marriage. We interviewed each manager four times, for a total of four to ten hours of interviewing.

Most of the managers who participated in our study spoke with warmth of the friends at work who had seen them through their divorces. Sometimes close bonds developed as people confided their domestic troubles to workmates. One woman told how she spent her lunch hours during her stress-filled separation from an alcoholic husband. "I would go to lunch with those two girls I told you about," she said to the interviewer, "and we would talk about all crazy things, you know. They were going through some stressful periods too . . . both of them with boyfriends, neither one was married, and we would just laugh and joke about it. After lunch we would more or less hold one another up until four-thirty."

While deep and confidential friendships do develop at work, most of the important social interactions involve less sharing of private information. In fact, for the managers participating in our study of divorce, counting on one's coworkers and feeling well supported by them usually did *not* mean opening one's heart to them. Another woman in our study, Ms. J., described how she worked in a cohesive training group at the time she left her husband. The group spent eight hours a day working together and then sometimes went sailing together or went for a drink together after hours. The woman never discussed her domestic crisis with her friends at work, and no one in the training group learned of the separation until long after the divorce had taken place. Yet Ms. J. felt at the time, and continued later to believe, that it was the social support of the training group that more than almost anything else helped her survive the upheaval.

One might be tempted to think that Ms. J. was deluding herself about the support she received, but the same pattern occurred again and again in the interviews. In truth, it seems that the lack of confirmation given Ms. J. at home made her glad simply to be accepted, liked, and respected for the competent woman that she was at work. One aspect of the respect given Ms. J. was, of course, the way in which her coworkers honored her privacy.

Friendships at work do not have to be intimate in order to constitute an important means of insuring your mental health. Especially in times of crisis, a bit of pedestrian conversation, a bit of unemotional chitchat, can provide a needed escape from intense emotionality. Such was a finding of our divorce study.

Even under normal circumstances, we sometimes need to confide, vent, or explode to our friends (at work or elsewhere), and sometimes we benefit just as much from minor diversions. Psychologist Rena Repetti interviewed clerical workers in several branches of two different banks. Not surprisingly, Repetti found that women who worked in pleasant, friendly offices reported less depression and anxiety than did women in unpleasant offices. But what mattered was not so much the presence of close friends in whom one could confide as the presence of a general atmosphere of cooperation and trust.

THE STRUCTURE OF DAILY LIFE

Another benefit of paid employment is structure. Work structures our days and helps us to establish a rhythm of living. Although it is usually overlooked, the importance of structure is great.

A total absence of structure, at one end of the continuum, leads to bizarre behavior and disturbed feelings. Twenty years ago psychologists in Canada performed a classic experiment of sensory deprivation, showing how much people depend on stimulation. The experimental volunteers were college students. Following a set of exams, the students reported to separate experimental cells that contained only a comfortable couch. White noise filtered into the room, and the walls were all white. The students were paid on a daily basis to remain in the room. At first most of the students enjoyed the lack of sensory stimulation and did what students like to do best after exams: They slept. Within a few days, however, most of them begged to be released from the experiment. Lacking external stimuli, the typical subject began to manufacture his or her own internal stimuli—in short, to hallucinate. Not only was the lack of stimuli disturbing, so too was the lack of structure—of required things to do, of activities, of scheduled events.

Of course, unless you are in prison or you are a hermit, you are unlikely to encounter days as bland as those encountered by the students in the experiment on sensory deprivation. But many people do lead lives with little daily structure. Retired men and women, housewives, and unemployed teenagers represent three groups in our society whose daily lives tend to be less structured than the daily lives of members of the paid work force. Many of the problems of retirement and adolescence clearly spring from boredom. Many of the problems of housewives do, too.

The importance of structure in creating a sense of well-being is indicated by several studies of depression. Myrna Weissman and her associates in the Depression Unit of the School of Medicine at Yale University have been investigating depression in women for more than a decade. Like journalist Maggie Scarf, Weissman feels that depression is primarily a woman's issue. Women, says Weissman, are more often depressed and more severely depressed than are men. Part of the problem is the depressing nature of the housewife role. Part of the problem with the housewife role, further, is its unstructured nature. The housewife can sit in bed all day, feeling sadder and sadder. The working person may start out the day in a very low mood; but by force of having to put one foot in front of the other, the working person has a better chance than the housewife of escaping from the grip of blue feelings and of inertia that keeps her feeling blue. Even when she is depressed, a worker can engage in activities that may help lift her out of the depression.

SEPARATE SELVES

When you feel good, when you feel alive and invigorated, you generally have a sense of wholeness and integration. When you feel upset or bad, you feel as if you are coming apart or disintegrating. Given these commonplace observations, it would seem logical that people who invest themselves in multiple roles—who have several identities—drive along the road to psychological perdition and that those who throw themselves single-mindedly into one identity may travel more rapidly to some sort of lasting happiness.

As it turns out, however, the connection between the playing of many roles on the one hand and a sense of disintegration on the other is neither necessary nor logical (see Chap. 5). Monoliths can and do crack. A geodesic dome, with its many little triangles, proves stronger than an unsegmented one. So, too, with personality structure: It is when you act in several different plays, with different supporting casts, that you usually have the strongest sense of a unified sense of self. It is the woman whose life includes only one or two major roles, and not the one whose life includes several, who usually experiences a vague sense of disorganization. People who confine their central life activities to only one stage with one cast and forever play out one role in a never changing script are usually people who feel trapped by life. Indeed, as Erving Goffman has pointed out in his brilliant collection of essays, *Asylums,* a devastating characteristic of life in a "total institution" is the sense of fragmentation that seems to come so invariably from the circumstances of a monochromatic life.

The value of having a self that exists in the context of work and is separate from the self or selves outside work becomes most evident in times of crisis. When the outside-of-work self is buffeted by troubles and sadnesses, a woman can keep some psychological balance at work. One of the managers in the study of work life and divorce was adamant on the issue of separate selves. Going to work proved the woman's salvation because, as she put it, "I had my work life. I had my social life. I had my home life. They were all separate. When I got to the door at work, that was it: No more home life to bother me."

Two points deserve a moment of reflection with respect to how work may or may not foster a sense of personal integration. First, women today need to be careful not to abandon their lives outside of work in their quest for professional advance. Thirty years ago American men and women appeared to be held captive by the feminine mystique. Many a self-respecting woman proudly considered her one occupation in life to be that of housewife. The ideal of housebound womanhood has, over the last few years, been exposed for the bankrupt notion that it is; but some observers fear that the pendulum has swung too far in the other direction. Many psychologists, including Rena Repetti and myself, wonder if the housebound female has not simply yielded her place on the pedestal to the office-bound female. Trading in one prison for another may be no improvement, and the career woman who does not wish a family life should be certain to develop interests in the community or to cultivate those parts of her being that are separate and different from her work self.

The second observation also relates to changes in sex role stereotyping.

There was a time when women and men led rather different social lives. The English pubs with their male bars and mixed bars, and American men's clubs with their "ladies' auxiliaries," remind us of the extent to which most societies have honored the division between women's worlds and men's worlds. What the traditional divisions meant was that a woman could be married to a man and could work with him (say, in a mom-and-pop establishment), and she could still have an identity in other circles quite separate from the man. Now most of the gender divisions have melted away. This means that the woman who works in the same establishment as her husband probably has very little identity separate from his. If Goffman is right—and I think he is—the value of multiple selves for a feeling of psychological integration depends not only on having a variety of different activities to do, but also on having a variety of different people with whom to do them.

COMPETENCE

The last, and perhaps the most important, benefit of paid employment for women and men is the opportunity that most jobs afford a person to accomplish something of value. Accomplishments promote a sense of psychological vigor. Twenty-five years ago one of the founders of contemporary American psychology, Robert White, wrote a seminal paper on what he called "the competence motive." White noted that people have a drive to behave in a competent fashion, that is, to encounter problems and solve them, in much the same way that people have a drive for sex. White claimed that to thwart the drive for competence would result in unhappiness, bitterness, frustration, and self-defeating behavior.

White's views on the competence motive have gained wide acceptance. Modern educators, for example, now take it as axiomatic that teachers should inspire children to feel confident in their own abilities and should devote as much time to fostering a sense of positive striving in the child as to pumping the child full of facts and figures. Few today doubt the importance of feelings of competence for good mental health.

Over the last two decades many studies have shown that paid employment is associated with feelings of competence among women. Women who work outside the home have higher self-esteem than other women, and they evaluate their abilities more positively. The association between high self-esteem and participation in the paid labor force does not appear to be an artifact of self-selection. It does not seem, in other words, that only the healthiest and most self-possessed women seek and keep employment. Some longitudinal studies have found that women's self-confidence rises after they obtain a job and that it drops again if they quit working.

The question is why. If feelings of competence come from meeting and solving problems, why does working for pay enhance feelings of competence? Housework and child care certainly require a person to solve problems. Do women have more opportunity to solve problems at work than elsewhere because work problems are more solvable than others, or is it simply that at work there are more problems to be solved?

I know of no research in psychology that bears directly on these questions, but a lot of research has indirect relevance. Paid labor enhances feelings of competence because it sustains a sense of progress. Most organizations in the economy involve products, even if it is the case, for some, that "service is our only product." Further, one's own efforts within the organization often can be and are evaluated in terms of how well one meets certain specified objectives. And the evaluations produce tangible or explicit rewards. You *know* how you are doing.

In contrast to the *product* orientation of paid labor is the *process* orientation of home life. Raising a child is a more intangible process than raising a crop of soybeans. When the process matters more than the product, actions gain importance not as means to specified ends but as ends in themselves. At work one may seek to please the boss in order to obtain approval, praise, or increased pay; but at home, one may more often seek to please the husband or the children (not to mention parents, siblings, neighbors, or houseguests) not for any extrinsic reward but just for the sheer pleasure of making them happy. A process orientation can, of course, bring great feelings of warmth and well-being, but it does little to engender feelings of competence.

One type of work that combines product and process orientation and does bring feelings of competence, however, is volunteering. Some women, at certain times in their lives, find unpaid work valuable. A woman with no need for an income but who does need a sense of her own achievement and maybe even her nurturing ability can get a feeling of accomplishment from volunteer activities. As long as a woman has a firm sense of her goals, and the volunteer work she is doing provides clear markers of her progress, the satisfaction and heightened self-esteem she derives can be every bit as great as in a paying job. Moreover, the skills she learns and the people she meets may give her the experience needed for paid employment.

Costs of Employment

Numerous though its benefits are, paid employment represents no earthly Nirvana. Two problems face most women in the paid labor force. First, sex discrimination has long been a feature of the American economy. Second, the woman who stakes out a career for herself must deal with certain domestic repercussions of her occupational success. Neither problem admits of an easy solution, but scholars and feminists (and certainly feminist scholars) observe that the problems will not simply fade away if we ignore them.

DISCRIMINATION

Twenty years ago the industrial psychologist J. Stacey Adams formalized his observations about grievances experienced in the workplace. Working people, said Adams, feel upset if they think that rewards are being distributed unfairly. They usually decide whether the distribution is fair or unfair by using (without necessarily being aware of what they are doing) the so-called equity formula. Adams's equity formula includes two critical terms: "inputs" and "outcomes." Inputs are a person's qualifications and behavior, within a social structure, that ought to entitle her or him to certain rewards. Those rewards Adams calls outcomes. Education, training, years on the job, and level of responsibility represent typical inputs; salary and power are typical outcomes.

Fairness or equity exists, according to Adams, when the ratio between outcomes and inputs for one person equals the ratio between outcomes and inputs for another person. Imagine a company in which one person receives a high salary and has had a lot of education, while the other person, with little education, receives a lower salary. In such a situation, although pay is unequal, equity obtains. To pay the two individuals equal salaries, if their inputs were unequal, would, on the other hand, be unfair or inequitable.

While the logic is clear, practical difficulties make it harder than one might expect actually to measure sex discrimination. What attributes ought to count as inputs? Scholars have spilt more than a little ink over this question. Also what, in particular, is one to do about level in a job hierarchy? It is sometimes the case that women and men are paid equally at every job level in a given organizational hierarchy, but that the women are not promoted at the same rate as the men. In such a situation, if one considers job level as an input and salary as an outcome, one might conclude that the organization does not discriminate against women; but if one treats job level as an outcome and, say, education and experience as relevant inputs, then sex discrimination would become apparent.

Even if one can decide what factors to count as inputs and what factors to count as outcomes, there remains a measurement problem. Imagine an organization in which everyone agrees to the principle that salary is the only outcome and education the only input of relevance. Salary is easy to measure, but what measure of education should one use? Does a master's degree in English equal a bachelor's degree in science? Should each year of additional education beyond high school be worth a certain number of dollars or should the years in which one earns a degree count more? Or maybe the organization should not count education in years but rather in credit hours.

If two or more inputs are considered relevant to the outcome of salary, the measurement problems multiply. Suppose that education, years on the job, and scope of responsibility all constitute the relevant inputs in a given organization. Each input has its own scale, and you must decide how to make the scales comparable. How many years of education are equivalent to how many years on the job and to how much responsibility?

The issue of rendering judgments across different inputs rests at the center of the great contemporary debate about comparable worth. Conservatives argue that discrimination exists only if a woman and a man are not paid equally for equal work. Feminists argue that the persistent exclusion of women from certain types of jobs makes it inappropriately restrictive to compare gender differences within any one job classification. Rather, say the feminists, one ought to look across the spectrum of jobs and, standardizing all the relevant inputs and outcomes, determine whether men and women are rewarded equally for work of equivalent worth.

An example may illustrate the difference in viewpoints. The conservative would conclude that discrimination exists if, for example, female truck drivers (or librarians) were paid less than male truck drivers (or librarians) with matched backgrounds. The feminist would carry the argument further and say that discrimination exists because there are so few female truck drivers and male librarians to begin with, and because librarians are generally paid less than truck drivers.

Some critics of the feminist point of view suggest that we cannot, in fact, standardize inputs across jobs. They are wrong. The problem of standardization across different job classifications does not differ in principle from the problem of standardizing inputs within any one job classification. If one can decide *within* a job category how to render equivalent the factors of, say, education, years on the job, and scope of responsibility, one can do so *across* job categories, too.

Employers regularly make judgments about how many years of education should be considered equivalent to how many years of experience or to how much responsibility for any given job classification. Because they usually remain unchallenged, the judgments appear easy or self-evident. Yet a formula equating education and experience within one job classification is no more self-evident than a formula equating educational levels across job categories. Once people become accustomed to the concept of comparable worth, judgments about the qualifications of individuals in different jobs will appear more natural.

Given the problems of defining sex discrimination, one can hardly be surprised that scholars have used a variety of techniques to document discrimination (or to prove the lack of discrimination) in various sectors of the economy. Three major techniques have been used. All three show persistent sex discrimination.

The first method is to conduct an experiment. You select a group whom you wish to study. Typically, psychologists have chosen to study managers or employers, although they sometimes use future managers and employers (i.e., business students) as subjects. Then you randomly sample, say, thirty people from the group and, again randomly, split the group into two parts. The first fifteen people receive a set of materials (for example, a curriculum vitae or a number of letters of recommendation) describing a man; the other fifteen people receive the exact same set of materials describing a woman. Both groups make evaluations. If the male evaluations surpass the female evaluations by a reliable margin, you can infer that the group under study holds a promale bias. The promale bias means that they value a male's achievements more highly than they value the exact same achievements by a female.

Psychologists who have experimentally studied sex discrimination have found a weak promale bias among students but a strong promale bias among various samples of managers, department heads, and other employers. Some researchers have even shown a promale bias to be as strong in women as in men.

A quite different technique has been used to measure discrimination throughout the labor force; it goes by the imposing name of "multiple regression analyses." This method allows us to look at the association between, for example, salary and a specified number of other factors such as education, years on the job, and number of hours of work per week. Imagine that in a given group of workers the salary for men increased with more education and training, but for women the salary did not increase with more education and training. Would you conclude that there is sex discrimination? Not if the females worked fewer hours than the males or had fewer years on the job. So you now ask the computer to plot, simultaneously, the association between salary and education, training, hours, and gender. If gender helps to "explain" some of the variation in salary, even after the computer takes education, training, and hours worked into account, you can conclude that there is sex discrimination.

That conclusion has been the unhappy finding of many social scientists. One famous study was published a decade ago by Larry Suter and Herman Miller. Using census data on young males and females, Suter and Miller found that males earned approximately three thousand dollars a year more than females, *after* one adjusted statistically for education, job level, amount worked in a year, and years of experience. This meant that females earned 62 percent of what males earned when males and females had equal qualifications.

Studies published recently have shown remarkable stability in the level of sex discrimination. Discrimination persists despite measurable shifts in the attitudes of Americans toward women in the paid labor force. Although Americans in public opinion polls now endorse egalitarianism (and I do not think they are lying), recent multiple regression analyses demonstrate that women still earn about 60 percent of what comparably qualified males earn. Attitudes have shifted, but the realities remain much as they were in Suter and Miller's study.

The final technique for demonstrating sex discrimination is to sample among highly select groups of males and females so that the group of working males matches exactly the group of working females in education, training, skills, and experience. This technique involves costly sampling methods and so it is used less than the other two techniques. Whenever the technique is used—as it was in a study I conducted five years ago in a Boston suburb— the results show discrimination. In my own survey I included women and men with high-prestige jobs (such as lawyers and doctors) and women and men with low-prestige jobs (such as sales clerks). I did not include people such as schoolteachers and nurses, whose jobs could be rated as professional by some standards but as low-status by others. The 182 employed men in my sample matched exactly the 163 employed women in terms of the prestige rating of their jobs and in terms of all the relevant background characteristics (education, years on job, age, hours worked, and so on) I measured. Given the enormous pains I had gone through to select exactly equal males and females, it came as a shock to me to discover, while poring over my computer print-outs, that the women in the sample earned significantly less money than the men. In fact, with salaries ranging mostly between ten thousand and thirty-five thousand dollars per year, the discrepancy between the male and female salaries was on the order of eight thousand dollars a year. That's some discrepancy.

DEALING WITH DISCRIMINATION

Being discriminated against is not good for a woman's mental or physical health. What do women do to deal with discrimination? And what can we or should we do?

The first way that women deal with discrimination to themselves, I have found, is to ignore it. We no longer ignore, as our mothers may have done, the discrimination that exists for others around us. Neither women nor men continue to believe that America offers equal opportunities and equal rewards to male and female workers. Opinion polls currently reveal that most American women and men would like the labor place to be more egalitarian than it is.

But while most women recognize that sex discrimination is a societal problem, it seems as if almost every woman imagines that she is the great exception to it. In my own survey outside Boston, where the women were discriminated against and where they knew about and felt upset about the position of women in the paid labor force, the employed women were as satisfied with their jobs as were the employed men. Hardly any of the women in the study cited sex discrimination as a problem in her own life.

I believe that there are many reasons why a woman may deny how much she is affected by sex discrimination. For one thing, we do not like to think of ourselves as being at a disadvantage of any sort or of being in any kind of danger. Just as we know that other drivers need to buckle up without imagining that we, too, should fasten our seat belts, so we imagine that other women are placed at a disadvantage without realizing that we personally are subject to the same impersonal forces that affect all women. Each of us can then feel "special," privileged, an exception to the rule. In addition, some women are so pleased with the benefits of working, or with the chance to break into a "male world," that they overlook discrimination and prejudice. One woman I know was among the first to be allowed to take classes at Johns Hopkins University. She was so "honored" that she didn't object to the conditions of this opportunity—she had to sit *in the hallway*, taking notes outside the classroom door, so that she would not "distract" the male students (or the professor).

Not only do we resist the impersonal aspect of applying statistics to our own lives, we may also wish to avoid the anger that usually accompanies the perception of unfairness. When denial becomes impossible, the second response to discrimination is anger.

In her new book *Women in Science* Vivian Gornick recounts in case after case how complacency and denial gave way to anger among women who felt a passionate devotion to their scientific careers and who had, sometimes sooner, sometimes later, to confront the realities of a world that made it hard for them to practice their science. When a woman opens her eyes to the ways in which she is hemmed in and underrewarded, she tends to personalize the situation and to assume that someone has intentionally wounded her.

Like many psychologists, I think that with respect to the perception of sex discrimination anger is healthier than denial, especially when it motivates women to take action. But I also think that the best solution of all is to move beyond anger. By moving beyond anger, I mean that each working woman needs to realize the extent to which sex discrimination touches her life personally without falling into the convenient trap of thinking that someone intended the discrimination.

How can you be put at a disadvantage without someone intending you harm? You can be put at a disadvantage simply as a consequence of all your peers being put at an advantage. Current antifemale behavior, I believe, results more readily from a tradition of promale bias than from any hostility, conscious or unconscious, toward women.

Here is a concrete example from my experience. Every professor in graduate school naturally wants to put forward his or her own student for the plum teaching job of the year. Good students, furthermore, tend to work with and to flourish with mentors of their own gender. That is, female students tend to work best with female professors and male students tend to work best with male professors. There's nothing wrong here. But remember that because of the sexism of the bad old days, the most illustrious professors today are male. Generally, the more illustrious your professor, the better are your chances of landing the plum job. So because of past conditions, because of current honorable standards (it is honorable to lobby on behalf of one's students) and because of old habits (hiring committees are used to listening to the illustrious professor's recommendations), the female graduate student in my little scenario stands less chance than her male counterpart of obtaining the job.

These small and hidden injuries of gender will of course be repeated in many blatant missteps; but the accumulation of small instances can have a more deadly effect. Certainly, small injuries are harder to prove as they occur and are thus more insidious than the large, unmistakable ones.

Realizing that most of the harm women in the workforce suffer, individually and collectively, is unintended can free us to analyze in a dispassionate way some of the causes and the consequences of sex discrimination. Each woman should ask herself, and many should also ask their bosses, What are the factors in my situation that may put me at a subtle disadvantage and that can be corrected? Ask yourself questions like these: How are people in my organization evaluated? What are the standards of judgment? Might the criteria be applied differently to me than to a man in my job category? Are there alternative criteria that might allow the organization to predict my future performance?

Pretend for a moment that when you asked such questions you found that dedication to the organization is much valued and that working on weekends is taken as a sign of dedication. Imagine that you do some work on weekends but that you do it at home in order to supervise your children. Imagine that your male colleague does his weekend work in the office and that the boss makes occasional trips into the office on Saturday and Sunday. Such an analysis, in my opinion, calls more for action than for anger. Don't waste your anger on the male colleague who has the luxury of coming into the office on weekends (if that is a luxury). Don't become angry at the boss; he shows no signs of prejudice or hostility. What should you do? Put yourself in the boss's shoes and think how hard it would be to know of all your weekend work and how easy it would be, in a world of goodwill but limited time and limited imagination, to form the impression that your male colleague feels greater dedication to the organization than do you. Then talk to your boss.

You can see my bias toward pacifism here and away from blame finding. I think that it works well for us to assume that much of the sexism we see all around us is, in fact, unintended. I also think that we need to distinguish between those who are responsible for the problem in the sense of having *caused* it, and those who are responsible for the problem in the sense of *correcting* it. Your organization did not cause sex discrimination. Nor did you. But it is up to you and your organization and to me and mine to do what we can to remedy matters.

HOME LIFE

Social scientists have long suspected that the rewards women reap from working outside the home are somehow debited psychologically to domestic accounts. For a great while psychologists and sociologists thought children were the ones to foot the bill for maternal employment. Anna Freud, the unmarried daughter of the great Sigmund, watched children—many of them refugees—in her London nursery during World War II and inferred that separation from the mother wreaked emotional havoc in those of tender years. Other English analysts, such as John Bowlby, author of a famous two-volume work on attachment and separation, concurred with Anna Freud. An essential part of Bowlby's argument rested on the negative reactions and poor recovery patterns of children who were separated from their parents to go into the hospital.

It may well be true that separation from one's parents, and especially from one's mother, can be psychologically detrimental to children if the separation occurs during traumatic conditions. That is when we all cling to our teddy bears, real or metaphorical. Being separated from one's mother at a time when one needs emotional security could constitute a real psychological deprivation. But what is true of traumatic times may be untrue about other times. In fact, four decades of research have shown, again and again, that young children do not need the constant company and supervision of their mothers. Lois and Martin Hoffman, two psychologists at the University of Michigan, reviewed dozens of studies and concluded that maternal employment has little negative emotional impact on children and can, if handled well, have important positive psychological effects. One positive effect of maternal employment for preadolescent and adolescent girls, for example, is their increased independence, and one positive effect for preadolescent and adolescent boys is their increased ability to be nurturant.

Cognitive development can also be accelerated for children whose mothers work and who are in good-quality day care. In her book *Mother Care/Other Care,* psychologist Sandra Scarr of the University of Virginia explains how children gain cognitively from their interactions with other children. Kathleen McCartney of Harvard University and Yale University's distinguished researcher Edward Zigler agree that good day care can prove essential to promoting intellectual development in children from all types of domestic backgrounds.

If the children of working women do not suffer, who does? The answer is the husband, or more precisely the husband and wife interaction. When the wife starts bringing home an income, her power rises—and his total power drops. This tends to be good news for her, and sometimes a problem for him.

Sociologists Philip Blumstein and Pepper Schwartz of the University of Washington in Seattle studied the distribution of power in couples. They mailed thousands of questionnaires to couples around the country and conducted in-depth interviews with hundreds of couples in a few cities. In one measure of power, they asked couples how joint financial decisions were made. Blumstein and Schwartz discovered that in two-earner households the woman and the man tend to have roughly equal input into financial decisions—large and small. While Blumstein and Schwartz relied in part on self-reports to measure domestic power, other investigators have examined marital power relations under laboratory conditions. One favorite technique is to give a couple a problem to solve and see whose will prevails when they disagree. No matter what the method used to study power, investigators find that employment outside the home enhances a woman's power within the home.

Men may suffer somewhat from this threat to their hegemony. In my study of work life and divorce I often heard that men felt sorry to lose the ability "to call all the shots." When one has been raised to have all the authority in a family, it can hurt to have to share the power.

More hurtful, confusing, and threatening than power sharing for men today are the jealousies and fears that many men feel as their wives achieve occupational success. Robert S. Weiss, of Harvard Medical School and the University of Massachusetts, has been studying successful middle-aged men in four suburbs of Boston. These men are very involved in their jobs and in their families. Their marriages are generally traditional in the division of chores and responsibilities. Although the men spend more time working than they spend in family activities, it is the family that gives meaning to the men's work. Psychologically invested in the breadwinner role, the men believe that they are working hard *for their families*.

What do the men feel about their wives' jobs? Many men in Weiss's study actually encouraged their wives to enter the paid labor force. Typically, as the children grew older and the wife found less satisfaction in the traditional wife-and-mother role, the men would counsel their wives to find employment. These men were genuinely motivated to help their wives feel enhanced and enriched psychologically. Without realizing the implications of their ideas, however, the men considered the wife's employment as something that she did for herself. In the men's minds having a job served for the wife the same function as playing bridge or taking a night course at the local high school. The typical middle-aged man in Weiss's study never considered his wife's job as contributing to the family welfare in the way that his job did.

As long as the wife was able to subordinate all of her occupational duties to family demands, her employment posed no problem for the men. But once a woman attained any position of responsibility, conflicts arose. The men feel confused and betrayed if their wives make demands on them for increased participation in the home, "demands" such as occasionally asking the man to prepare his own dinner if a business meeting interferes with the family dinner time. The men are also hurt by the wife's resentment of their lack of participation in household duties after they had done something so nice as to suggest the wife enhance her life by having a job. Sometimes it seems to them that they just can't figure out what has gone wrong.

Whether or not younger men share the old assumptions about male-as-breadwinner and female-as-homemaker is hard to say. A lot of young men today say that they do not hold such assumptions, but some evidence suggests the opposite. In her doctoral dissertation study of recent graduates of two prestigious business schools, Claire Sokoloff found that the meaning of work in the lives of young women graduates seems more problematic than the meaning of work in the lives of young men graduates. The women worry about how they will combine the roles of professional and of family person, and worry about how the men in their lives will be able to handle their wives' occupational commitments. They do not speak with the same worry about how they will feel about the professional accomplishments of their husbands. For the men the opposite is true. Most men see work and family as complementary activities, each giving zest and meaning to the other. But the men worry about who will raise their children if their wives are committed to their careers. Sokoloff's informants are a generation younger than the men who spoke with Robert Weiss, but the conflicts in values still loom large. It seems that the business magnates of tomorrow are finding themselves caught in an ideological crunch today.

If men support their wives' employment but only to the extent that they themselves are not inconvenienced, someone has to pick up the domestic slack. The someone is usually the woman. A dozen or more surveys show that women's employment outside the home causes only a small reduction in their labor within the home and, in most of the studies, only a tiny increase in the husband's labor within the home.

Employed women have notoriously little leisure time. Of course, some groups are beyond fretting about the niceties. Employed mothers of preschoolers, a group that is increasing yearly, do not often worry about leisure time. They more often find themselves grabbing for the minutes to complete basic household requirements. (It's amazing how much the basic requirements can change—the weekly changing of bed linen now becomes a semiannual event—without any increase in leisure time.)

What is the solution? Easy solutions are nowhere to be found, but a couple of thoughts may help ease some pain. These have been times of enormous ideological change. In any revolution we may find ourselves trying to shoehorn the bright new concepts into old preconceptions. Many a pinch and many a hurt occur in the process. In the home as in the workplace, what we must avoid if we can is the natural tendency to wallow in blame. We must not assume that all other women somehow manage better than we; and we must not blame our husbands, lovers, or other life partners for the ways in which they, like the men in Weiss's study, put us in double binds. We must not doubt their good intentions and our own. Nor must we think that good intentions suffice for good results.

Balancing the Scales

What's the verdict? Do the benefits of paid employment outweigh the costs? Should my friend Martha find a job, any job, even if it does not suit her life in every detail? Knowing that she will face sex discrimination, knowing that she is more likely to be unemployed or underemployed than a comparably qualified man, knowing that she is likely to be underpaid and to have less chance of advancement than a man, should Martha join the swelling numbers of women in the paid labor force? And then if she does overcome the discrimination in the paid labor force to the extent of carving out a career and advancing in it, my friend will have to readjust her relationship with her husband. There will be all those mixed messages to deal with. The price tag seems high.

So, too, does the value. If she found paid employment, Martha might experience the enhanced sense of well-being and the heightened self-esteem which we find in study after study on women, work, and mental health. She could use the money. Money buys the items that would help to empower Martha to do what she wants, and money earned would reassure Martha of her value in the world at large. She would make friends at work. These friends might not know the intimate details of Martha's life, but intimate friends are not the only ones who help to stabilize us. Martha would benefit no doubt from the structured day, and it would help her to have a sense of herself separate from her family. Most of all, my friend in Colorado would exercise her competence.

Freud identified two great signs of psychological health: the ability to work and the ability to love. Neither should monopolize one's energies. This much we have known for a long time. Domestic work is work sure enough, and women who stay at home can have as much work in their lives as women who join the paid labor force (or even more). But there is a critical difference between working for one's family and working for others. For employed women, work and love are less intermingled.

My personal vote goes for employment outside the home. I think we women boost our sanity and increase our well-being if we do not work only for those whom we love nor love only those for whom we work.

FAYE CROSBY, a social psychologist, received her Ph.D. from Boston University in 1976. She taught at Yale University as an associate professor. She is now professor of psychology at Smith College. In 1982 Oxford University Press published her book *Relative Deprivation and Working Women.* The book centers about the paradox of the typical female worker who ignores the extent to which sex discrimination touches her own life and who feels satisfied with her job despite objective handicaps. She is editing a new book, *Modern Woman: Managing the Dual Roles,* to be published by Yale University Press.

Dr. Crosby's interest in women's issues is also evident in her many articles and book chapters. When she is not writing or teaching, Crosby is usually tending to her two children and her husband, with whom she lives in Northampton, Massachusetts.

Further Reading

Baruch, Grace; Barnett, Rosalind; and Rivers, Caryl. *Lifeprints: New Patterns of Love and Work for Today's Women.* New York: McGraw-Hill, 1982; in paperback, New American Library, 1983.

Blumstein, Philip, and Schwartz, Pepper. *American Couples.* New York: Morrow, 1983.

Crocker, Jennifer, ed. "After Affirmative Action." *American Behavioral Scientist* 42 (January/February 1984):285–86.

Crosby, Faye. *Relative Deprivation and Working Women.* New York: Oxford University Press, 1982.

Gornick, Vivian. *Women in Science.* New York: Simon & Schuster, 1983.

Kanter, Rosabeth Moss. *Men and Women of the Corporation.* New York: Basic Books, 1977.

Scarf, Maggie. *Unfinished Business.* Garden City, N.Y.: Doubleday, 1980; in paperback, Ballantine Books, 1981.

Scarr, Sandra. *Mother Care/Other Care.* New York: Basic Books, 1984.

Weissman, Myrna, and Paykel, Eugene S. *The Depressed Woman.* Chicago: University of Chicago Press, 1974.

Further Guidance

If you would like career guidance or other career information, contact Catalyst, 14 East 60th Street, New York, New York 10022. Tel: (212) 759-9700.

12

Mid-Life

NANCY SCHLOSSBERG

Carol's story was written up in the "Style Plus" section of the Washington *Post*. She had raised three children and then returned to get her B.A. She found she loved being a student, so at forty she continued on for her Ph.D. By the time she completed her degree, her husband had taken a job as the top executive of his organization. She started working as a psychologist in the prison system, and by the time she was fifty-five, she had worked her way up to the top and became one of the few women wardens, of a male state penitentiary. She left her husband—much to the dismay and shock of family and friends—married a colleague at the prison, moved from a large house to a house on the prison grounds, bought a small condominium on the Eastern Shore where she and her new husband go on his motorcycle each weekend. She loves hanging onto the motorcycle; she loved being filmed for "60 Minutes"; she loves her new life of excitement and challenge.

Ann started a nonprofit business with a college friend. After fifteen years the two owners began to disagree over problems. The board voted and gave their confidence to Ann's partner. Ann was fired. She had great trouble comprehending why the fight had assumed such proportions and why the board had not supported her. As she was trying to sort this all out, her husband died. She was devastated by the two major losses—one she felt she could have prevented and one that was out of her hands. At sixty she was fearful that she would never get an executive job again. She saw no hope of having a new relationship because of the scarcity of men.

Silvie was shocked to learn that her husband had been having an affair. When she found out, she felt caught in a dilemma. Should she leave him?

Then who would support her and the two children? Should she stay and swallow her pride? Then how would she live with herself? She stayed for two years trying to work out a situation where she would not feel humiliated. What happened is that she became, in her words, "a shrew." She screamed all the time at her husband and at her children. At work she assumed a sickly sweet attitude. She was so afraid of offending anyone that she became almost docile. She finally decided that a divorce would be better than her miserable life. Unfortunately, the aftermath has been even worse than she expected. Her former husband reopened the case in order to obtain custody of the daughters. Despite the problems, she returned to school and obtained a professional degree. She met a wonderful man and felt things were going to work out. He moved in with her and the children. Not long afterward he told her he loved her but needed "space" so was moving out again. Although it has now been five years since the breakup of her marriage, she often thinks back to the early, happy years of the marriage and questions what happened. She has lost confidence.

The thrill for Jane and Stan when their children left home was obvious. Jane had loved being home as a mother to young children but was now ready for school, work, and fun. After six months of a joyful empty nest, their oldest son returned home. He had been living in another city, became severely disturbed—so much so that he finally had to come home, where he sits, watches TV, and eats. He is not violent, so there is no way to commit him. He refuses help; in fact, they have tried all the innovative outreach strategies to no avail. Some well-meaning friends have suggested forcing him out on the street if he will not comply with treatment. Jane and Stan remember John Hinckley and cannot respond that way.

Alice had raised three children, all of whom were in college. She had landed a professional job. It only paid ten thousand dollars but it was hers and it was a beginning. Her mother-in-law broke her hip. Her husband Tom insisted that they bring his mother into the house. They could not afford help with three children in college. The only alternative for care would be for Alice to give up her job and stay home. She refused. She and Tom had terrible fights; he became very angry at her and very depressed. One afternoon they found him in his car. He had committed suicide.

Joan was the head of the Junior League, on the hospital board, at parties all the time. Of course, she agreed with her husband's decision to move for a better job. When they got to the new community, she felt marginal, unhappy, alone, depressed. She was angry at herself for feeling this way. She loved her husband. Why couldn't she adjust?

My secretary remarked as she was typing these vignettes, "You must have made these up." Actually, all are true; in fact, I personally know each of these women (though I have changed their names). And probably most of us know even more complicated stories, some positive, some negative. These stories are only the tip of the iceberg: There are stories of cancer and mastectomies, of heart attacks and heart surgery, of Alzheimer's disease. There are stories of new loves, new beginnings in work, love, and play. Since all of these narratives involve women past youth, we might ask if they are examples of "mid-life crisis." The question is, *Is* there a mid-life story? Is there a scenario that can clearly be labeled "middle-age woman"?

Does Middle Age Have a Corner on the Crisis Market?

Americans are barraged from all sides—television talk shows, Sunday supplements, radio call-in programs—about the mid-life crisis. We are presented with two contrasting stereotypes. On the one hand, we hear that middle age is the peak period. Middle-agers are seen as the command generation, as powerful, in charge of themselves and others. Carol's story, the first woman warden riding on the back of a motorcycle, captures the essence of that view. In contrast are stories of unhappy men bored with their jobs, their wives, their lives. We read that such men find true happiness by leaving their wives of fifteen, twenty, or thirty years to live with much younger women. This reinvigorates them and makes life seem worthwhile. We hear of women, bored with their workaholic husbands, who leave to find true happiness with someone else, who have a face-lift (or at least their eyes tucked), who start new projects, all of which are designed to reinvigorate them after their apparent mid-life crisis.

Most of these stories are based on assumptions about mid-life, assumptions that influence how we look at others and ourselves. Before answering the question "Who is the mid-life woman?" let's look at five major assumptions many of us hold about mid-life.

Assumption 1. Many people define mid-life as a chronological period marked by magic birthdays, funny gifts about sex, and wrinkles. We give and go to birthday parties marking the beginning, middle, and end of middle age. Even though no one agrees about the exact age at which mid-life begins (for some it is thirty, for others forty, for others fifty, and for others sixty), we mark it as if it were ordained by the calendar. In fact, study after study shows that men and women label women middle-aged before they define men as middle-aged; gray hair for men is distinguished, but for women it is a sign of aging. The chronological age that marks "middle age" keeps changing as people live longer and healthier lives.

Assumption 2. Many people connect mid-life with hormonal and other biological changes. The common phrase "It's all patchwork after forty" captures the essence of this position. New data, however, show that biology is not necessarily a negative destiny. Consider the preoccupation of physicians with the menopause. In a survey of physicians and mid-life women, Catherine DeLorey of the Women's Health Research Institute found that over half of the women felt that menopause was not a major or even minor health issue; yet more than three quarters of the physicians defined menopause as a major health concern for women.

The fact is that most women go through menopause with no particular psychological difficulties and very few physical ones. In a large survey of more than eight thousand randomly chosen women, Sonja and John McKinlay found that the majority viewed menopause positively (with relief—no more worry about pregnancy or periods) or neutrally (no particular feelings at all). The vast majority did not feel regret at reaching menopause; only 3 percent said they did. Apart from some "temporarily bothersome symptoms," such as flashes, sweating, and menstrual irregularity, menopause is simply no big deal for most women.

Then where do doctors get the idea that it is? Primarily from their patients, who are by definition an unrepresentative group. Moreover, most of the women whom physicians see for treatment have undergone an artificial menopause because of surgery (for example, the uterus was removed). Naturally, such women report having worries, symptoms, and problems. Because most studies of menopausal women have been done on such atypical patients, many health care workers concluded that menopause is always a troubling "crisis." Fortunately, most menopausal women don't believe them.

On the other hand, most mid-life women work, and yet there is practically no information on occupational health issues. Research on occupational health hazards has apparently been reserved for younger workers and men.

Assumption 3. The mythology abounds with stories about mid-life women and depression, especially for women confronted with the empty nest. What depresses women is not the empty nest but the return of young adult children to the nest; most research demonstrates that depression is more common for women whose children are very young. When the children leave home, most parents report renewed energy and happiness and a decrease in stress. Grace Baruch and Rosalind Barnett find that many thirty-five to fifty-five-year-old women, especially those with multiple roles, have high scores on mastery and pleasure. The degree to which women are satisfied depends not on their age but on what is happening in their lives.

Assumption 4. Another index for marking women as middle-aged is their parental and family status. Women are thought to be middle-aged when their children are teens or young adults, when the parents move from the family home to smaller quarters. Today, however, there is no standard age at which most women have teenaged children. The increasing number of teenage births, designated as "children of children," means that women could be in their early thirties when their children are teenagers; by the same token, there are increasing numbers of women who delay child rearing until they are in their late thirties or early forties, meaning they are in their mid-sixties when their children are teenagers. Finally, an increasing number of women remain childless by choice. Thus, we have no single age at which women are involved in similar family tasks. Note that even though most women work, their lives are still analyzed in terms of family events—children's graduations, husbands' leaving, their parents becoming ill. Men's lives are marked by occupational events—getting promoted or demoted.

Assumption 5. Supposedly, you can tell a mid-life woman because she is harassed by multiple transitions. In fact, some observers, including myself, have labeled this group as those "caught in between"—between the needs of husbands, children, and aging parents. It is only now that I realize how biased I have been, how my assumptions rather than the facts have influenced my vision of women. The facts, however, contradict this view. Leonard Pearlin and Morton Lieberman, in a large research study of stress, found that young *adults,* both men *and* women, experience more transitions in a more concentrated period of time than any other age group. Young adults are moving away from their parents; establishing careers, intimate relationships, families; and moving into their own homes. We have been seduced into believing that crises and multiple transitions are located in one age group and one sex group. We need to free ourselves from barriers that hem us in to age, sex, or any other stereotype.

What is the truth? Give me a roomful of forty-year-old women and you have told me nothing. Give me a case story about what each has experienced and then I can tell if one is going to have a crisis and another a tranquil period. What matters is what transitions she has experienced. Has she been "dumped" by a husband, fired from her job, had a breast removed, gone back to school, remarried, had her first book published? It is what has happened or not happened to her, not how old she is, that counts.

If there were one word I could use to designate mid-life women, it would be "variability." There are grandmothers at forty and eighty; first-time mothers at twenty and forty; newly divorced women at twenty and sixty. There are new loves and increased sexual activity at forty, sixty, and eighty. There are nearly as many patterns as people. In a recent class I asked my students for personal examples of variability. As they eagerly reported their unusual situations, we began to think we could produce an issue of *True Story*. Among the milder stories were the following:

- One woman reported that when she was twenty and her mother forty, they both had new babies. It felt strange to her to have her mother in the same boat as she was.
- A woman student of thirty reported that her father of fifty-five married an eighteen-year-old high school graduate. Her attitude toward her father's new wife was very confused; she was more like a stepdaughter than a stepmother.
- A male student reported that his father eloped with a woman the same week that his fiancée's daughter (his stepdaughter-to-be) eloped.

We can probably all agree that though it is tempting to try to categorize mid-life women, it is not really possible. The differences—the rest of the story—are too great. The fluidity of life, the variability of experiences, and the heterogenity among women make it impossible.

While one can't lump all women together, it is true that not many mid-life women will escape the experience of crisis and change. What, then, can we say about crisis and change for mid-life women? We can say the obvious: that most people face transitions all through life, that no period is "naturally" more traumatic than others, and that understanding what change is and what to expect can help. Let's start with some definitions.

Crisis. Most writers agree that a crisis is a sudden, severely upsetting situation in which individuals are forced to mobilize their resources:

> The phone call comes to the office telling you your husband has been rushed to the hospital for open-heart surgery. You have no time to think. You rush to the hospital. The drive seems endless. You feel suspended, numbed. You are able to think of one thing— making a phone call to the babysitter *telling, not asking* her to stay late that night.

To restate, it is not mid-life that is the crisis. When a woman is divorced —whether at twenty, thirty, forty, fifty, sixty, seventy—it is a crisis, financially, socially, psychologically. When a woman's husband dies from heart surgery—whether she is twenty, thirty, forty, fifty, sixty, seventy—it is a crisis. When a woman gets breast cancer—whether at twenty, thirty, forty, fifty, sixty, seventy—it is a crisis. The awareness of mortality can be a crisis if a person fears aging, whether that happens at fifty or because of the loss of a loved one at twenty-five. As we look at the census figures, we see that though there is more likelihood of certain events occurring at certain ages, there is enough variability throughout life to force us to define "crisis" in terms of what happens rather than the age of the person.

Transition. A transition is an event or nonevent that changes our lives— our *relationships,* our daily *routines,* our *assumptions* about ourselves, and our *roles.* The more the transition changes our lives, the more stressful it will be. Let's look at two women getting divorced. Clearly, divorce is an upheaval for both, but for one it changed only her marital status; for the other it changed every aspect of her life.

One woman had a job she loved, grown children, and lived in a community with many friends. When she and her husband of thirty years decided to divorce, she was sad and depressed. However, the decision was a long time in the making and was mutual. Both had agreed to wait until the children left home, and both agreed that they would be better off living alone, because the relationship was unsatisfactory. Her *role* of wife was changed, her daily *routines* at home were changed, but basically she was staying in their familiar apartment, staying in her same community, retaining all of her supports. A contrasting scenario is the woman with three children, aged ten and twenty. She had never finished her B.A. and worked occasionally at part-time low-level jobs. When her husband announced he was leaving, she was faced with having to move to a less expensive neighborhood, a difficult transition for the children and her. She also was forced to take a full-time low-level job rather than return to school, something she had always wanted to do.

We can begin to see that a transition that on the surface looks the same— divorce—in fact is very different in the extent to which it changes one's life. We can refine transitions even further by differentiating types:

Anticipated Transitions. These are the transitions that you plan. You go to college; you start a first job; you get married; your first child is born; your child leaves home. You plan these changes; you rehearse for them; you expect them.

Unanticipated Transitions. These are the transitions that you did not plan. Your closest friend is in a serious car accident; you are fired; your spouse leaves you; you discover you have arthritis and must give up a favorite sport.

Nonevents. These are the transitions that result from something that *doesn't* happen. You always planned to get married but did not; you always planned to get pregnant but did not; you and your husband always planned to leave the small town and move to a big city, but you did not.

Chronic Hassles. These are the daily aggravations that keep you from making a change or transition. You stay in a job that is degrading because you need the money and see no way out; you stay in a marriage that is demoralizing because you need the support and see no way out.

Bear in mind that what is an anticipated change for one person (retirement) might be unanticipated for another (the company closes unexpectedly). A nonevent for one person (not getting married) can be a planned decision for another and not a transition at all. Then, too, different transition events—widowhood, job loss, a new baby, a slipped disk, retirement—have different impacts on your routines, relationships, assumptions, and roles. It is, however, safe to assume that the more the transition alters your life, the more coping resources it requires, the more crisislike it feels, and the longer it will take for assimilation to occur.

Of course, all women experience transitions all through life—some anticipated, some unanticipated, some nonevents, and some chronic hassles. What can women expect when these inevitable changes occur? We have found that at time of change, either wanted or not, people do what an eminent development and aging expert, Bernice Neugarten, labeled "stocktaking." You take inventory and begin to relook at yourself. You reassess your dreams, your goals, your resources; you rethink your life. We all have periods when everything seems to be going along fine; we work, we play, we love and don't think too much about it. Then something happens—either we bring it about or it happens to us—and we start thinking about ourselves again. I remember a period right after I made a big geographical and professional move. To my surprise and discomfort, I became very self-centered, thinking about myself, my competence, my identity. I began to feel like an adolescent. As I look back at that period, I wish someone had told me that it was perfectly normal to soul-search, to feel insecure at times of major transitions. I have learned to expect stocktaking and soul-searching whenever change occurs. And that is what I want to discuss next—the psychological themes that will recur through life as we face transitions. By identifying and understanding these themes, we will gain some understanding and control of the continuity and change that occurs during the course of our lives. In particular, I believe there are seven themes that connect us with our past and future.

• *Belonging.* Are we part of things or marginal?

- *Mattering.* Do we make a difference? Do others care about us and make us feel we count?
- *Autonomy.* Do we have a reasonable amount of control over our lives, in work, love, and play, without endangering our relationships with others?
- *Competence.* Are we mastering something new? Do we feel skilled at what we are doing?
- *Intimacy.* Do we have meaningful attachments?
- *Identity.* Do we have a sense of who we are?
- *Renewal.* Do we feel rejuvenated? Do we feel our lives have meaning?

Belonging

I have been teaching at a university for ten years. There I feel central, important—I belong. However, when I go to my son's school for parents' night, I feel very marginal. Other parents don't smile or talk to me. It's the same for my husband. We have talked about it frequently. Why are we so marginal in one place and why can't we seem to change that experience of marginality?

There are many instances of feeling marginal. Young people report feeling "out of things" when they enter junior or senior high school. For some, going to college at first makes them feel marginal. People moving from one city to another often feel marginal. In the movie *The Karate Kid,* the teenager who has just moved from Newark, New Jersey, to California and continually is attacked by other teenagers, says to his mother, "I hate it here; I don't know the rules."

Every time an individual moves from one role to another, or experiences a transition, the balance of the seesaw tips. The larger the difference in roles and the less knowledge beforehand about the new role, the more marginal that individual will feel. For example, women faced with divorce or caring for an aging parent are often confused about how to behave. They don't know the rules. According to anthropologist Victor Turner, individuals moving from one role to another experience three phases:

- Being identified in the new role as the new spouse, graduate, grandparent, mover, divorced person.
- Feeling marginal, betwixt and between the old role and the new role.
- Being reincorporated into full membership; no longer seeing oneself as

the new widow or divorced wife or the person who just moved, but seeing oneself as someone who is many things, including a widow, a divorcee, or a resident of a new town.

This process of moving from one role to another, from one transition to another, takes time. Many widows or widowers still feel married to their deceased spouses and cannot feel part of a world of singlehood. What helps move people out of this marginal state? Anthropologist Barbara Myerhoff observed the importance of rituals in helping people understand the paradoxical nature of many transitions. They are especially helpful at times of uncertainty. We have rituals and rites of passage for some transitions, such as the fiftieth wedding anniversary, retirement, marriage, special birthdays, graduation. However, for many transitions we have no rituals, no way of helping people make sense out of the apparent contradictions and senselessness of the new situation. There is no symbolic rite for giving up the family home, getting divorced, completing menopause, relinquishing one's driver's license.

Other examples come to mind. How would we ritualize, signify, dignify the event of an adult going back to school? Of parents of adult children losing their access to grandchildren when their son divorces? Think about the grandparents for a minute. When they first become grandparents, there are rituals—the child is christened or the child has a bris (ritual circumcision). Eventually, they incorporate the view and behavior of themselves as grandparents. But if their son divorces his wife, the children most probably will go to her; if the wife remarries, the grandchildren are further removed. The grandparents are still biological grandparents, but they have moved into a marginal status. They are and they are not grandparents. They have the emotional attachment but they cannot often enact the role as defined by society. They are in a marginal state, with no custom or rules to help them deal with the paradoxical and sad situation.

People should, as Myerhoff maintained, develop their own rituals. Some ministers and rabbis are beginning to develop divorce rituals. Some young women are having "I'm *not* married" parties to announce to the world that they are adults even though they lack husbands. The development of secular rituals helps us deal with the unpredictability of our futures.

It seems certain that we will keep on being and feeling marginal as we or our loved ones enter new transitions. In some instances we might remain marginal for a long period of time. Since we cannot avoid marginality, we need to learn to live with it. We can stand being peripheral if we understand the feeling, control it, and know that it will pass.

Mattering

All of us need to matter to someone. Sociologist Morris Rosenberg says that mattering is:

- The feeling that we are the object of another person's interest, attention, or notice; the feeling that we are important to the other person.
- The feeling of being missed.
- The feeling that we are someone's ego extension in that we reflect on or constitute a part of his or her life.
- The belief that the other person depends on us.

Rosenberg and his colleague Claire McCullough have demonstrated the relationship between mattering and delinquency: The more that adolescents feel they matter to parents, teachers, and schoolmates, the less probability exists for delinquent behavior. Although their original work focused on adolescents, they apply their ideas to people in retirement. This would be an interesting study. Do retirees who feel they matter adjust more easily to this transition?

Mattering affects people differently at different points in life. It is axiomatic that adolescents and older persons need to feel they matter. Paradoxically, for some women the relationship between mattering and satisfaction might be quite different. That is, the more a woman matters to her older parents, to her young adult children, to her colleagues, the *less* satisfied and more pressured she becomes. The research shows that women consider themselves to be, and behave as, the "kin keepers." They care for the various generations, keep in touch on family matters. As sociologist Gunhild Hagestad writes, women are the "ministers of the interior" while men serve as the bridge to the outside world. This raises the question of when mattering becomes a burden and when it is essential to well-being. A divorced woman with four small children, an ill, aging parent, and limited financial resources is at the "end of her rope"; she matters too much to too many people. Sociologists Alfred Fengler and Nancy Goodrich documented the effects of exhausting caretaking responsibilities by interviewing women who were caring for husbands disabled by heart disease, diabetes, arthritis, and other chronic conditions. One woman whose husband had suffered a stroke complained about how suddenly her life and her relationship to her husband had changed: "I didn't expect this—mopping up the bathroom, changing him, and doing the laundry." One wife who tried to work the night shift in a nursing home to earn money for her family while simultaneously caring for her husband succumbed to the overwhelming pressure and was forced to seek psychiatric help. Because their caretaking responsibilities severely restricted their own activities, many women reported feeling isolated. One woman commented, "I feel penned in. I miss not being able to hop in the car and leave when I want to. We were always so free. I used to think because your family is grown you can do as you please, but it hasn't turned out that way for me." For some women the only relief came when a home health aide took over the caretaking for a few hours each week.

With further research I think we will find that mattering matters all through life, but it is played out very differently for men and women at different times.

Autonomy

Autonomous people are thought to control their lives. Many women's lives have been contingent on their husband's jobs, their husband's moves, their children's achievements. As a wife of a football hero said to me: "It just doesn't seem fair. For years I have been on hold while he has become a national hero. When will it be my turn?" By the time her turn came, he had left her for someone else. As consciousness for both sexes has been raised, adults have had to rethink the questions of control over who cooks, cleans, mends; over who moves for a better job; over whose life counts.

Let's look at how divorce affects autonomy. If I were to interview the cast of characters involved in a particular divorce, I would have as many different stories as individuals. From the point of view of the children, they might wish to control and stop the divorce but realize they are powerless to do so. From the point of view of the parents of the divorcing couple, they too might feel out of control; this is a transition they did not initiate, but one which will affect them greatly. From the point of view of the spouse who made the decision to divorce, he or she might feel in control of that decision; the other would not.

But whether or not events happen to you or you initiate them, there is yet another aspect to autonomy: the way you cope with the transitions. Some divorcing couples and their extended families try to change the situation by negotiating, counseling, cajoling, or instituting legislation (as grandparents are doing regarding grandparents' rights). Others try to change the meaning of the divorce with comments such as "This will really be better for the kids." Still others try to accept the difficult situation and relax tension by jogging, meditating, relaxing.

Thus we have two kinds of control: the degree to which an individual controls life circumstances, and the degree to which an individual controls how he or she copes with life circumstances. My teenage son, who lives for football, is having a tough time with his tough coach. I say to him, "I can not eliminate your single-minded coach, but I can help you learn how to cope more effectively. You can change the situation—get out of football. You can change the meaning of the situation—see football as just one activity and the coach's putdown of you whenever you don't score as irrelevant. Or you can try to relax, breathe deeply, and imagine yourself as you want to be on the field. You have the choice." (See Chap. 15.)

Many of those who write about the adult experience see autonomy as a sign of maturity. Carol Gilligan, a developmental psychologist, criticizes these models of adult development as being based on men's lives, which do focus on autonomy. She argues for listening to a different voice, the voice of women. If we did, she says, we would hear concerns about caring for others and concerns about relationships. Instead of seeing this as a sign of weakness, Gilligan suggests we revise our notions of maturity to include interdependence as well as autonomy.

We are left with a paradoxical situation, a situation with no single truth but with two great contradictory truths: It is healthy to have control over one's life, not always to be the one whose plans and goals are dependent on others. It is also healthy to care, to be committed to others and to value interdependence. This "back and forth" process between autonomy and dependence is one that recurs all through life.

Competence

Competence is defined as the constant striving to expand boundaries, investigate the world, and achieve mastery. As Grace Baruch and Rosalind Barnett find in their study of three hundred women, there are two primary sources of well-being for women: pleasure (through intimacy with others) and mastery (through competence in one's work). Indeed, they find that the best preventive medicine against depression is mastery, the sense of competence.

But again, competence is not something achieved once and for all at some critical period. It can be gained, lost, renewed. In a recent study of the learning habits of 126 million adults above the age of twenty-five, Carol

Aslanian and Henry Brickell found that life changes or transitions trigger new learning, new skills. Many more men than women mentioned career transitions (such as job changes or promotions) as the trigger for learning, and twice as many women as men mentioned family transitions (such as divorce or the children leaving home) as the trigger for new competencies. We all know of women who return to school in order to gain new abilities after a divorce that has shaken the very foundations of their self-confidence.

The point is that men and women need to feel capable, competent, skillful at what they do; and this sense of competence may be shattered, and then restored, with the transitions of life.

Intimacy

The term "intimacy" covers a wide range of close human ties: spouses, lovers, parents, children, friends. The mutuality of give-and-take in relationships and the feelings of attachment we have are always in flux. Just when we think we have it together, our lovers leave or die; just when we are pleased with our network of friends, we move for a better job for ourselves or, more frequently, for our husbands.

The importance of close relationships can hardly be exaggerated. Not only do they constitute a strong source of support in times of stress, but they also add color and warmth to our lives. People with no attachments are identified as "at risk" populations; those with attachments and intimacy can cope more effectively with transitions and change (see Chap. 6).

Men and women are said to differ markedly in their ability to form such relationships. American men are stereotyped as tending to shy away from intimacy. In fact, according to a newly released study by the National Academy of Science, the death of a spouse is more traumatic for men than for women because men are presumed to have fewer close ties beyond the wife.

Whether these differences between men and women are accurate, what is true is that both men and women have needs for intimacy, affection, affirmation, and feedback. As the population changes, we are beginning to see that these needs are no longer met by a family living in one household. The number of unrelated people living in the same household will probably increase. The presence or absence of intimacy throughout a person's life is more important than the specific form the relationship takes. When loss of an intimate relationship occurs—through death, divorce, a change in commitment—the crucial issue is whether an individual can become reattached. Because of the lopsided sex ratio (statistically, there are more women than men in every age group over thirty), mid-life men will marry and remarry, and divorced or widowed women in mid-life will socialize primarily with other women. The increase in the studies of friendship in adulthood attests to the importance of intimacy through nonsexual relationships.

The need for attachment and the increase in loneliness are sad commentaries on today's society. Loneliness is not the province of one age; it comes when people's attachments are broken. The feelings of loneliness when people move, when people divorce, when loved ones die, are troubling for all ages.

Identity

Underlying all the other recurrent themes is that of identity. According to Erik Erikson, the "crisis" of identity occurs in late adolescence; young people must establish a sense of self and find a place as individuals in the adult world. If they fail to achieve identity, they are left with "role diffusion" and cannot develop further. But identity is not solidified once and for all at any age. In a broad sense we can say that the crisis of identity is reawakened whenever the individual experiences a major transition. To give an example: A man whose sense of identity is grounded in his career, who defines himself in terms of his work role, will be severely stressed if he suffers a setback in his career or does not progress as rapidly as he had initially expected. For such a man retirement from the world of work will be traumatic. Similarly, the woman whose sense of identity derives from her role as wife will find the very foundations of her life shaken if she faces divorce or widowhood. Formerly, identity for men was couched in occupational terms, for women in family terms. Today, as Gloria Steinem reports in her review of the ten years of *Ms.* magazine, women have become the men they formerly married. Instead of marrying a doctor or a carpenter, they now become the doctor or carpenter.

Our identities are often related to the dreams we have of ourselves. Our dreams, our imagined possibilities of what may be, are a key to identity. The reevaluation of the dream occurs at marker times, such as retirement or the death of a loved one. As an individual pursues one line of work, one set of life choices, other options, other jobs, other lovers are ruled out. As time goes on, there is a creeping consciousness, a grieving over lost opportunities, and a process of disillusionment sets in, complete with "what if's" and "if only's": "What if I had taken that job in Oshkosh?" "If only I had gone to college . . ." "What if I had followed that advice and done such-and-such?" Changes usually provoke a time of questioning and of regrets, a time of thinking almost obsessively about what might have been, how parents or spouses influenced or hindered the course of our dreams.

An Australian movie, *My Brilliant Career*, portrays a heroine who refuses to marry the man she passionately loves for fear of losing her dream, which is to become a great writer. She is afraid he would unwittingly sabotage her dream. If women submerge their own dreams by supporting those of their husbands, deep resentment can creep in.

Many married women not only reappraise their own dreams but the dreams they had for their husbands. If their own lives are not everything they thought they would be, they suffer. But they also suffer in terms of their husbands' lives. Many women have a dream for their husbands: He should be the biggest and best contractor, doctor, lawyer, policeman. As these women are reappraising their own dreams, they are also looking again at their dreams for their mates and wondering, Is this what it is all about?

Many also discover that there is a gap between where they are and where they secretly dreamed of being. Whether they are at the top of their fields or the "best" parents, they often feel they have fallen short. Often these thoughts are induced by a "marker event," an outside happening. For example, one woman I know, who opted happily to make motherhood her full-time career, faced great agony when her twenty-six-year-old son committed suicide. She said, "I am fifty-two and don't know who I am. Has my life been in vain?" In another case a man, recently fired at fifty-eight, said, "I can't believe that this could happen to me. I've been loyal to the organization and now what do I have left?" The aspiration-achievement gap may not result from an external event, but from a dawning awareness: A man suddenly realizes he will never be promoted to vice president; a woman is passed over by a man younger than she and suddenly realizes that she is not going to the top.

Renewal

Stagnation and renewal—two sides of a coin. Erikson believes that stagnation results from the crisis of generativity in mid-life. Generativity includes renewal, which is more than the biological process that assures survival of the species and grants individuals a kind of immortality through the existence of their children. Generativity also refers to the contribution to future generations through creativity and productivity in areas such as the arts and science. Such achievements give life meaning, and enable the individual to feel that he or she has done something worthwhile that will leave a lasting mark in the world. Indeed, generativity relates to the theme of identity; it constitutes an affirmation of the self.

Stagnation, a kind of death in life, occurs at irregular intervals over the life course. One feels boxed in, frightened, bored. Usually, boredom is temporary. But at various points in life the sense of boredom and stagnation lasts longer than an hour or a day. It can become an emotional trough.

Many factors may contribute to a feeling of stagnation. Perhaps one is being passed over frequently for job promotions. Someone in a boring, repetitive situation at home or at work will feel stagnated. Consider a forty-two-year-old male associate professor who has assumed responsibility for his mother-in-law; she now lives with his family in small quarters. He sees no fun or privacy for the foreseeable future; he feels like the "enemy and outsider"; he knows he is doing the right thing but nevertheless feels angry and trapped. He has no time to write, no time for pleasure. Or consider the fifty-two-year-old female secretary who is working hard at a job she dislikes. Her husband is moderately successful, but they have three children in college and a mother to support. She has lost the joy in life and feels she has no fun anymore.

Psychiatrist Daniel Levinson suggests by the very title of his work *The Seasons of a Man's Life* his orientation to the themes of stagnation and renewal. "To become generative," he wrote, "a man must know how it feels to stagnate—to have the sense of not growing, of being static, stuck, drying up, bogged down in a life full of obligations and devoid of self-fulfillment . . . The capacity to experience, endure, and fight against stagnation is an intrinsic aspect of the struggle toward generativity in middle adulthood."

Psychologist Marjorie Fiske suggests that another way to understand stagnation and renewal is to examine changing commitments over the life course. Have you ever known anyone who seems to be living life with little energy, who seems to find no meaning in life, nothing that excites and grabs hold? Such people, she argues, have no commitments. Commitment is that which gives meaning to one's life—football now for my son, work for many of us, relationships with family, learning a new skill. There are two aspects to be considered: the individual (does he or she have a history of low or high commitment and involvement over time?) and the group (in general, do commitments change over the course of life for men and women, young and old?). Fiske has studied commitments over time, rather than the usual dichotomies of work and leisure. She categorized commitments into four major areas: commitments to others, altruistic commitments (including ethical, philosophical, and religious values and goals), commitments to mastery of individual work or creativity, and commitments to oneself (including comfortable survival, self-protection, self-advancement).

What is important, Fiske found, is not what you are committed to, but the fact that you *are* committed: that you *care* about something and work for it. Second, it is generally better to have several commitments than only one, on the fragility of eggs-in-one-basket principle. But third, it is necessary to keep in mind that *commitments require opportunities to express them.* It doesn't matter if you have one major interest or thirty if your life changes in such a way as to make it impossible for you to act on those commitments. Indeed, people who have many activities in mid-life seem especially vulnerable to adjusting to retirement, which often seems to offer much less than they were used to.

Finally, Fiske found that for most people, commitments change over the life span. This means that many people will get stuck and stagnated when a commitment ends and they have no replacement for it, and that most will find the excitement of renewal in new interests and passions.

Considerations: What Does It All Mean?

Recently, a local television reporter interviewed me about the mid-life crisis. "It's an artifact of the media," I said. "Crisis, transition, and change occur all through life." The interviewer was shocked and crestfallen. I had wrecked a story.

But by taking a life span approach, rather than expecting disasters at regular intervals, we can begin to understand what is continuous and what changes over life. There are many consistent aspects of our personalities, for example, that allow us to recognize ourselves as we move to new communities, to new loves, to new jobs. There are many consistent themes in life:

Young and old, rich and poor, male and female are concerned about identity, intimacy, autonomy, competence, renewal, belonging, and mattering. I have presented these issues as if they are discrete and separate. Clearly, there is overlap between commitment and renewal, between mattering and marginality, between identity and autonomy. But I have tried to offer a way of looking at the themes that plague us, challenge us, excite us all during life. And despite these common issues, there is great individuality in how we play them out over time.

The life span approach gives us a greater perspective on change. If you feel marginal today, you know that it will pass, that some day you will be central again, and that if you enter a new role, you may well feel marginal yet again. Well-being is rarely a permanent condition, like brown eyes. It must be renegotiated and reattained through all the events that life brings.

Is there a mid-life crisis? Is there a category called "mid-life woman"? No. The mid-life woman is full of contradictions, complexities, and surprises. We are not one. We are many.

From childhood to adulthood, we are both afraid of and challenged by change. Yet we know that change is inevitable. That it will occur and recur. And that if we do not fight to remain the same, we have the chance to grow.

NANCY SCHLOSSBERG received a B.A. in sociology from Barnard College and an Ed.D. in counseling from Teachers College, Columbia University. Since 1974 she has been a full professor at the University of Maryland. Previously, she was on the faculties of Wayne State University, Howard University, and Pratt Institute. She was the first woman executive at the American Council on Education, where she established the Office of Women in Higher Education.

Dr. Schlossberg's major interests and expertise are in the field of adult development, adult psychology, and career development. Her most recent text, *Counseling Adults in Transition,* is an alternate selection of the Behavioral Science Book Service. Dr. Schlossberg was elected by the American Psychological Association to the status of fellow in 1978. She was the 1983 APA G. Stanley Hall Lecturer on Adult Development and was selected as a Distinguished Scholar at the University of Maryland for 1983.

Dr. Schlossberg's study of transitions began with her move from Detroit to Washington. She and her husband agreed to relocate; they each had excellent jobs. Both had friends, colleagues, children, and each other as stabilizing elements. Yet she was sad and felt lost for well over a year. This experience led to a series of studies of people in transition that resulted in her development of a transition model which can help people deal with the joys and sorrows of change.

Further Reading

Baruch, Grace K., and Barnett, Rosalind C. "On the Well-Being of Adult Women." In *Competence and Coping During Adulthood,* edited by Lynn A. Bond and James C. Rosen. Hanover, N.H.: University Press of New England, 1980.

———, and Rivers, Caryl. *Lifeprints: New Patterns of Love and Work for Today's Women.* New York: McGraw-Hill, 1982; in paperback, New American Library, 1983.

Fiske, Marjorie. "Changing Hierarchies of Commitment in Adulthood." In *Themes of Work and Love in Adulthood,* edited by Neil J. Smelser and Erik H. Erikson. Cambridge: Harvard University Press, 1980.

Gilligan, Carol. *In a Different Voice.* Cambridge: Harvard University Press, 1982.

Schlossberg, Nancy K. *Counseling Adults in Transition.* New York: Springer Publishing Co., 1984.

13

Old Age

LILLIAN E. TROLL

Several years ago I found myself part of a discussion group that consisted exclusively of older women. My first reaction was that somehow I had been demoted: that my individuality had been removed, that I had become a cipher. I was sure that whatever that group did would be boring. I was wrong on both counts.

Last summer, on a train trip down the West Coast, the dining car major-domo seated me in a booth opposite two obvious "old ladies." Before I slid over to my seat, I looked longingly at the booth across the aisle that contained three young people and wondered whether I would have the courage to ask him to seat me there. But I meekly submitted to fate. My two old ladies smiled at me with guarded politeness and every sign of supreme dullness. To make matters worse, a fourth old lady—because of senior citizen discounts, there were lots of us on the train—was placed beside me.

Here, then, were the four of us, close to glowering at each other in disappointment. Then we exchanged introductions—and came alive! The guarded, polite smiles gave way to genuine expressions, to real smiles, even to twinkles. The original two old ladies turned out to be members of a Swedish-American choral group on their way to a national convention in Portland, and the fourth lady was returning from a month on a primitive ranch commune in Montana. Our discussion ranged widely: the history of national choral organizations, agriculture and gardening, back-to-the-land movements in the East and the West, revivals of antique clothing—as satisfactory a conversation as one could hope for anywhere, particularly in a dining car. I remembered my previous experiences of eventually finding groups of old women as fascinating as other groups and, with a sigh of relief, concluded that old ladies are indeed people.

But why do I start each such experience with bias? Why do I, who have studied age bias and should know better, so often assume that old women are polite stuffed shirts who have little to intrigue me?

Perhaps one reason for my difficulty in removing bias was illustrated one week later, when I found myself the slowest member of our nine-person family backpacking trip in the high Sierras. My children and grandchildren all slowed down politely when I struggled for breath in the rarefied air and when my out-of-condition thigh muscles refused to perform on the mile-long upgrades. After we had camped, my eight-year-old grandson Joshua's interest and solicitude did not help. "Your hands are so wrinkled, Grandma! How old are you? I wish I could see a picture of you when you were my daddy's age so I could see what you looked like." To cap it all, he announced the next day, "I'll stay with you wherever you go in case you get into any trouble."

Life has its odd, unexpected compensations, however. The following day, when I had been left with the two youngest while the capable ones went off on an ambitious day hike, I took Joshua and Terry on a short trip into the snow. As California children, they couldn't get enough snow and had to be kept from eating it. Suddenly, the two of them, like mountain goats, climbed up a sheer rock cliff and called to me from the top, "Come on, Grandma, more snow!" and disappeared. They didn't respond to my calls, obviously couldn't hear me. Just as obviously, they were in danger, I was sure, of getting lost. So, propelled by the superenergy of maternal nurturance, I actually climbed that cliff, approximately four times my own height. I shinnied up using hands and knees as I had never been able to do at any point in my life before. Inferiority turned to triumph!

Joshua's protective/patronizing attitude had reinforced the effects of comments I had been getting all year from my younger academic colleagues, alluding to my upcoming retirement in ways that showed my growing irrelevance to the world of adults. My private triumph on the cliff restored a sense of mastery. The future expanded again. The blank wall labeled "The End" changed to an open door labeled "New Careers." I had begun my current career of university professor when I was fifty years old, and compulsory retirement hit me, as it does many women "returnees" of my generation, with a heavy blow. I felt I was just getting into my stride and was ready to follow my mother's path. She had retired at the age of eighty, having returned to college in her late thirties and started her first professional job at forty.

Stereotyping

Bias comes in different modes. It assumes different disguises. One is stereotyping, applying restricted definitions to the subject. The stereotypes for old
women are that we are poor, dumb, ugly, and irrelevant to the mainstream
of life. Nobody notices that some of us may be wise, supportive, independent, even important. With restrictiveness generally goes distortion. People
see poverty, lack of intelligence, and unattractiveness in old women who
might really be rich geniuses with enormous charm. Stereotyping often includes negative attitudes, too. It certainly does for old women, who are not
only seen as poor, dumb, and ugly, but are the objects of hostile or contemp-
tuous feelings.

The worst aspect of such bias is that its objects share the attitudes of the
other members of their society and stereotype, distort, and look down upon
themselves—as I did in my initial reaction on the train. For example, an
eighty-one-year-old woman in my three-generation research sample said,
"It's bad for me to say, but for a person my age I don't like older people. I
like to be around younger people more. I hate old-fashioned things; I like to
be up-to-date. Older people should listen to younger people to learn."

One of my gerontology students, whose fieldwork was in a nutrition project for older people, reported that she had heard one old woman say to
another, "Reagan! He's too old; he's too dumb to be President." (Whatever
you think of his politics, his age hasn't affected them.)

Self-stereotyping like this is startling. It reminds me of those women in
the 1950s and 1960s who said they preferred the company of men because
women were so uninteresting and so bitchy. Such deep-seated negation of
one's own identity and value as a woman can amount to pathological distortion and denial.

Anyway, being an old woman is not generally considered a desirable
state. The determined efforts of organizations such as the Gray Panthers
and the Older Women's League attest, in fact, to its stereotypical undesir-
ability—why else would these organizations feel it necessary to fight for
change? Declaring one's age if one is past sixty-five, or even past fifty, or, in
fact, even past thirty, is an act of courage and bravado and can be considered newsworthy. Gloria Steinem's apparent glee at reaching fifty merited a
flood of feature articles and a full-page photograph showing that she really
did not look fifty.

POOR

Just how true are these stereotypes of poor, dumb, and ugly? First, let us consider poverty. Are older women poorer than older men? Are they poorer than younger women? One way poverty is measured is against what is called the "poverty line," not to be confused with a breadline or a picket line. This is an arbitrary figure, occasionally readjusted to take account of matters like inflation or political expediency. In the last government population report, the poverty of older men and women was compared over a number of years. For those who live with family members (usually a wife for men and a daughter for women), women over sixty-five years of age are consistently more likely to be below the poverty line than are men. In 1970 the relative figures were 20 percent of women, 16 percent of men. In 1975, 13 percent of women compared with 8 percent of men. And in their latest figures, for 1981, 15 percent of women, almost double the 8 percent of men.

Among persons over sixty-five who live with people they are not related to, the percentage who live below the poverty line is much higher. Matters have improved since 1970, when *half* of such women over sixty-five were below the poverty line, but the comparable 1981 figures are 31 percent of women and 23 percent of men. An article in the November 1984 *AARP* (American Association of Retired Persons) *News Bulletin* reports that "the poverty rate for people age 65 and older remains one of the highest for any adult group, with poverty rates among older women and minorities remaining particularly high."

Of course, we all know, if only from reading what used to be called society columns (now called "Family Living"), that there are many older women who are very rich. Occasionally, I meet one of these fortunate beings on an airplane, where they are on their way to expensive mountain-climbing expeditions (Annapurna was the destination of one recent seat companion) or round-the-world cruises. Last January I drove down the Florida coast past Palm Beach and saw the stacked palaces, which, I've read, are inhabited primarily by dowagers. We rarely call the old ladies who frequent senior centers or nutrition sites "dowagers." To be called that you need at least one palace in Palm Beach.

To make matters worse, older women who are not entirely below the poverty line hover just above it, according to a 1983 report of the Senate Special Committee on Aging. The figures they cite do not distinguish by sex, but think what a median per capita income of $6600 for Americans sixty-five and over means! This includes the income of dowagers. It also includes men. The report adds, "There persist clear groups of older persons who bear a very high risk of being poor: widows, minorities, those who are sick, and those who have lived into their eighties. For these groups, poverty remains at crisis levels." Remember that most older women, particularly those beyond their eighties, are widows, and subject to "disproportionately high expenditures for health care, supportive services, and energy costs" at a time when they have used up their savings. From the experiences of my mother, and now myself, I can testify that doctor bills of $150 are rarely reduced more than $10 to $15, even though we both have access to Medicare and Blue Cross. Medicare has been getting progressively more stingy.

In an address to the American Psychological Association in 1982, Bernice Neugarten, one of our most eminent gerontologists, observed that there are wide differences in economic levels among older Americans. She said, "About as many older men have cash incomes over $20,000 per year as the number who fall under the poverty line. The distribution is different for women, many of whom are living in poverty. This is because so many women are widowed and so many have been only intermittently in the labor force, so that their public or private pensions are meager."

So, yes, old women are poor. This part of the stereotype is accurate, at least for many of us.

DUMB

Second, are we really dumb? Well, that depends on how one defines smartness. If we refer to years of schooling, it is true that over the past century in the Western world, each succeeding generation of women—even more than of men, perhaps—has had more years of schooling than its parents and grandparents. Among the three generations of women I have been studying over the past fifteen years, for example, less than 5 percent of the members of the oldest generation—the grandmothers—had any college education. In fact, many had no more than a year or so of formal schooling. One fourth of their daughters, though, had gone to college for at least a year, and one-half of their granddaughters had either gone to college, or, if they were still in their early teens, planned to do so. Because the way we traditionally assess smartness is highly correlated with years of schooling, it is no surprise that old women seem less smart than young women.

If you define smartness in terms of IQ, intellectual changes during adulthood seem to be very different for men and women in our country. All test findings agree in this respect. Girls are more advanced than boys in the preschool years, although boys start edging up during the elementary school years, and boys score higher starting with high school. Longitudinal data—where the same people are followed along over a period of time—show that men tend to increase in IQ during the years of early and middle adulthood, while women decline slightly. It is as if women use their intelligence to grow dumber. Perhaps this is an adaptive strategy to seem less competent than the men they seek to marry, and do marry, in a society that encourages men to "marry down" and to feel good about themselves if they are smarter than their wives. Longitudinal studies show that women who are most "feminine" in a stereotypical fashion are more likely to decline in IQ during their adult years than less stereotypically feminine women, those who are more productive, complex, self-doubting, and independent. In fact, two major longitudinal studies in California, the Terman and Berkeley studies, suggest a release from dumbness in women who return to intellectual rather than nurturant activities in their middle years.

As for the later years of life, most longitudinal data on intellectual performance suggest stability in IQ until the period of general bodily and functional deterioration closely preceding death. That is, distance from death is a better indicator of change in intelligence than is distance from birth. Unfortunately, most of these studies are of men. When Warner Schaie and his associates administered the Primary Mental Abilities Test to three independent samples of adults of all ages, they found very stable and significant sex differences. Although women were superior in verbal meaning, reasoning, and word fluency, men were better in space perception, number processing, and overall intellectual ability. This finding might suggest that the practice of looking dumber than men, which begins in adolescence, is not altogether discarded in old age. Older women continue to seem dumber than their husbands. At least women don't continue to get dumber in old age; they just stay where they were earlier. (But as so many jokes say, they are better with words.)

We could also define smartness in terms of accomplishment. In my own research I have tried to estimate age and generational differences in women's motivation to achieve, using a definition of achievement motivation attuned to the lives of women. Most research on achievement motivation is based on traditionally masculine modes, approaches, and arenas, such as bureaucratic status, money, and interest in jobs labeled "masculine."

Briefly, I consider four kinds of achievement:

1. Achievement through task mastery—doing whatever you do as well as you can, whether it be keeping your house clean or solving a chemistry problem.

2. Achievement through recognition or status.

3. Achievement through influence over others.

4. Achievement through creativity—contributing something new to the world.

I have also considered three arenas of achievement: home and community; traditional "feminine" jobs, such as nursing; and innovative, more traditionally "masculine" jobs, such as law. Finally, I have considered whether women try to achieve through their own efforts or accomplishments, or through the accomplishments of others, like their husband or sons.

Recently, Linda Schwartz, a graduate student of mine, helped me analyze the responses of 75 three-generation lineages of women and 20 three-generation lineages of men: grandparents, their children, and their young-adult grandchildren. It is harder to find three-generational lines of men because of longevity differences and men's later ages of marriage. We found sex differences in both generational and age patterns of women and men. While the levels of achievement motivation of the men increased regularly from the grandfather to his grandson, those of the women showed an irregular pattern. That is, each succeeding generation of men in the sample had a higher interest in achieving—somehow or other—than did earlier generations. The grandsons had higher achievement motivation than their fathers, and their fathers were higher than their grandfathers. But it was the middle generation of women—the middle-aged—who were more motivated to achieve than either their mothers or their daughters.

When we looked at chronological age instead of family generation, we found that three quarters of the male teenagers wanted high achievement, but only one third of the female teenagers did. Women in their twenties were much more likely to want to achieve than female teenagers: four fifths of them as compared with one third of the teenagers. In fact, women in their twenties almost reached the level of the men in their twenties: 79 percent compared with 90 percent.

Even more women than men in their thirties and forties wanted high achievement. Consistent with longitudinal data from the Terman and Berkeley studies, the thirties and forties are the ages when women who have earlier had children now turn back to the other interests they had put aside in the pursuit of continuing the species.

My three-generational data are intriguing because they fit neither the women's movement hypothesis of the "new woman" nor David Gutmann's hypothesis of the "parental imperative." If we assume that today's women are blooming as a consequence of the women's revolution and new options for expression outside traditional feminine modes, why are the teenagers in my sample such duds? This is also true, incidentally, of today's high school and college students in other studies. And if women turn back to nonstereotypical behavior after their childbearing period, why are not the women in their fifties and sixties as desirous of achieving as those in their twenties and thirties?

Generational comparisons of *approach* (whether you want to achieve through your own efforts or those of others) and in *arena* (traditional versus innovative) are clearer than those of ratings of level of achievement motivation. Grandparents are the most traditional in the way they want to achieve, and young-adult grandchildren the least traditional. And this is true for both men and women. Grandmothers are most likely to want to achieve in traditional "feminine" ways: home and community activities, and if in any other arena, they want to do so through the accomplishments of their husbands or sons. In parallel fashion, grandfathers want to achieve in traditional "masculine" ways, for example, by making money, constructing roads and houses, or making and repairing automobiles, and they are mainly concerned with their own efforts. Their grandsons, though, are inclined to turn to less "masculine" or perhaps more "feminine" arenas such as teaching, social work, or art, and they speak not only about their own work but also about the achievements of their wives or mothers or daughters.

Here are some excerpts from the interviews of three women in one high-achievement-oriented family to illustrate this point. The grandmother, a sixty-five-year-old housewife from a rural background, said, "I like working out of doors, gardening, and getting the place in shape. I like to crochet rugs and I enjoy reading and doing crossword puzzles. I like to read to find out things. I read all kinds of things. Just see something or hear about something and want to find out about it. I like to do things that you can see what you've got done."

Her daughter, who was then forty years old, a college graduate and a nurse, said, "When I was a child we enjoyed outdoor activities—hiking, camping, picnicking. So I've always had an interest in natural science. At different times in my life it took different forms: as a child it was collecting things; when older, how they fit into different systems. And now it's more or less focused in the interest of protecting the environment." *Her* seventeen-year-old daughter, still a high school student, said, "I like to dance and sing . . . artwork . . . something, anything unusual . . . just because it's different. I like to be around people, to talk a lot with people who want to relate to you and not those who sit back and say, 'See this little mouse!' "

In spite of many family similarities among these three women—a general finding through all the generational data—there are generational differences in tune with the different eras in which they grew up and in which they were living at the time of the interview in 1969. The grandmother, for instance, had never been employed outside her home and apparently never wanted to be. But maybe if she had been sixty-five in 1984 instead of in 1969, and thus had been in her forties about the time the women's movement started, she would have considered going back to school or seeking employment. Her daughter, in 1969, is not only a nurse, but a nurse-executive, devoted to her job life, as well as to her home. Again, if she were forty today and therefore had been twenty-five in 1969, she might have looked for a higher-level job, one with a more stretchable ceiling than nursing offers—or did at that time. Her interest in science might have guided her toward a research career, for instance. The granddaughter was tuned into the relationship theme of the youth generation of the 1960s, and besides, as a teenager her mind was turned to other things, such as forming *one* serious relationship. She may never take work as seriously as her mother does or household management as seriously as her grandmother does. But now, in 1984, at the age of thirty-two, she might be considering a career in science, too, expanding from her early preoccupations of marriage and child rearing. In short, aging—how people age and whether they change—depends considerably on cohort and period effects, on the influence of the era in which they are born and raised.

What can we conclude from these achievement motivation data about old women and their dumbness? On the one hand, more younger women than older have high achievement desires (with the exception of the teenagers). But when we looked only at highly motivated grandmothers and their descendants, three fourths of their daughters and granddaughters also had high achievement motivation. This is not too different from the men in the sample; 90 percent of grandfathers who were highly motivated to achieve passed this attitude on to their descendants. The tide of high achievement, one of the themes of today's young women, swept up many whose families were not so oriented. But it came in on the wave of women whose grandmothers had led the way.

Different historical periods promote different expressions and different yearnings. The women's movement has had an effect, more on those women who are younger—that is, in their twenties, thirties, and forties today—than on those who may have adapted irrevocably to the conditions prevailing when they were young. The young women of the 1970s had as a "generation theme" the attitude that employment outside the home is more rewarding than occupation in home and community affairs. And those who came from families that believed that high achievement is important for both men *and* women were most likely to adopt that prevailing cohort theme. The transmission of values and personality characteristics interact with the historical spirit of the age.

Aside from transmission of achievement goals, though, there is the issue of arrogance. For a number of reasons, women who chose "masculine" careers with marriage, or who emphasized the realm of employment over the realm of home, tend to feel that they are superior to those who didn't—and for "superior" read "smarter." This attitude fuels age and sex bias, and creates an unwarranted smugness. Diane Alington and I, in a paper on women and change, recently argued that we women are so hungry for progress that we go along with many myths promoted by the media. One of these myths is that the recent changes in employment have been caused by the efforts of women themselves. This myth ignores the importance of the economic needs of the nation as a major source of change, and the reason it is dangerous is that we are blind to the possibility that doors of opportunity opened in response to economic conditions can easily close again when those economic conditions change. We have seen women's opportunities wax and wane in earlier periods of history, and there is no reason to suppose they cannot do so again. In my reading of history, each "women's movement" is but one generation deep.

To assume that the "new woman" has sprung full-blown from the head of Zeus and is, therefore, more godly than previous women denies the vulnerability and tenuousness of women's opportunities in the career world. To assume that old women who were not "new women" are inferior or dumber is to make a dangerous error.

I return to my question about why I react with bias to other old women. I was one of those "new women" of the short-lived breed of World War II, and like more recent "new women," felt superior to my contemporaries who remained focused on their homes. I am continually caught by surprise that they too can be interesting, vital people. And I have particular trouble facing the need to redefine myself in the light of my coming retirement; so did, incidentally, my mother, who came from the brief cohort of "new women" of the post-World War I era. Perhaps if we so-called "new women" would be less snooty and consider the role played by our opportunities, we would be more tolerant of nonnew women.

It is clearly tricky to draw firm conclusions about how dumb or how smart old women as a class really are. Those women with lots of schooling who were able to enter occupations and live lives of intellectual complexity are now coming of age—I mean they are becoming old, and maybe they are going to change (for a while anyway) some of our present conclusions about the smartness of old ladies. In fact, based upon the resurgence of anti-intellectualism and apathy among present-day college students, as well as the prospect of decreasing options for achievement for women altogether, we may find that the old ladies of the near future are *smarter* than their daughters and granddaughters.

UGLY

Now for the third term in the epithet: Are old women ugly? A dozen years ago, before there were any data, I had no doubt that this was true. I believed that few people then would have rated older women as attractive and few old women would be rated as attractive. This view was, of course, shared by old women themselves. A few years later, Carol Nowak, at that time one of my graduate students at Wayne State University, provided some systematic data that supported this hunch. Older men, she found in her doctoral research, are often considered attractive, particularly by young women, but older women are not, particularly not by younger men, *Harold and Maude* notwithstanding. The reverse-sex May-December marriage is still a curiosity, reserved for unusual people, and not a common occurrence, although two days ago I noticed two ads in the "Personals" section of *Psychology Today* for a service providing cross-age combinations—a service that cleverly calls itself Anachron.

What Carol Nowak found was that there is a difference between youthfulness and attractiveness when men (of any age) are judging others. But middle-aged women get youthfulness and attractiveness inextricably confused. If they think the woman in a picture is attractive, they distort her age downward. If they think she is older, they consider her less attractive. Because middle age is the time our appearance starts to change—if we use an age-linked definition of middle age, around the age of fifty—it is not surprising that middle-aged women were hypersensitive not only to their own appearance but to appearance in general. Her middle-aged subjects said they did not like themselves much when their skin began to sag.

When Is "Old"?

What I haven't mentioned so far is what age is old. For many researchers, particularly those geared to demography or social policy, sixty-five is the dividing line. Biologically oriented people divide earlier, at the menopause, which means about the age of fifty. In 1977, when I put together the book *Looking Ahead* with Joan and Kenneth Israel, our editor said we should target it to women over thirty, an age she was then approaching and dreading.

Like most life span terms, "old" depends on what you are talking about. I became a mother for the first time at thirty, and felt equivalent in age to women of eighteen or twenty in most aspects of my life. I went back to work at forty, and felt equivalent to women in their twenties who were also in the early stages of their careers. I finished my Ph.D. and entered academia at fifty, and felt equivalent to women in their late twenties and thirties.

A growing body of research on what Bernice Neugarten calls "social clocks" and Ray Bortner called "expected life history" points to the importance of our ideas about when different life events should occur. Most people in America agree remarkably well on what *should* happen as we go through life. Most of us also agree on *when* these events should happen. If we marry too early or too late, we are "age deviants" and we tend to feel there is something wrong with us. If we don't marry at all, we also feel there is something wrong with us. Obviously, I have always been an age deviant. The only reason I didn't feel worse than I did was that my mother was also an age deviant.

The Canadian sociologist Victor Marshall found that we get a lot of our ideas about when things "should" happen from when they happened to our parents. Probably, when they happened to the parent of our own sex is even more significant. My mother had her first child at twenty-four, so I felt "off time," to use another of Neugarten's terms, for six years. My mother went back to work about the same time I did, so that helped. The other thing that helped was that there were many women in my "birth cohort"—born about the same time I was and therefore influenced by the same historical events that I was—who moved along more or less at my pace. The Depression of the 1930s followed by World War II kept us from having children at twenty. The power of the postwar "feminine mystique," so eloquently described by Betty Friedan, kept us absorbed in child rearing through the 1950s and most of the 1960s, so that we returned to finish interrupted educations and move into careers only when this era was winding down. Perhaps this is why having to redefine myself as an old woman comes more unexpectedly than if I had had a series of transitions in age appropriateness along the way. As most research shows, age appropriateness (or its opposite, age deviance) differs by age, sex, ethnicity, and national origin, among other things. I leave it to you to use whatever definition of old age you wish. I think most of what I have said will fit a wide range of chronological ages.

Aside from our social clocks, there is the biological imperative, which becomes particularly noticeable in old age. Some of us get old fast and some of us get old slowly. Perhaps the fact that aging is to a large part determined by hereditary factors makes for the feasibility of modeling our social clocks on our parents. Again, I refer to Bernice Neugarten, who developed the classification of "young old," those who have their health and mental capacities, and the "old old," those who are ailing and infirm. Too many people who quote her have assumed that we can put age markers on these categories. The big point of diversity is that we can't do that. The "young old" can range anywhere from forty to eighty, and the "old old" likewise, depending on the onset of feebleness and the need for lots of help. Most of what I am talking about here, clearly, refers to those of us who are still "young old," whatever our chronological age may be.

The Diversities of Aging

The opposite of stereotyping is recognizing diversity. The uniform polite smiles of the old ladies in the dining car became nonstereotypical when they dissolved into varieties of expression. To illustrate this diversity, let me quote some more from my three-generation files, responses to the questions "What are some of the kinds of things you like to do (or not do)?" "What kinds of people do you admire (or not admire)?" "If money were no object, where and how would you like to live?" I pulled these excerpts randomly out of the file drawers. It should also be noted that these women are not highly educated. Only a handful had any college experience and many only a few years of grade school. There are no "stars" among them.

A sixty-seven-year-old woman: "I like to create things: sew, crochet. And I like cooking and housework. I don't like snobs, that's for sure. I admire my children and grandchildren and I have very good neighbors. If money were no object, I'd live right where I am. Right in my own home where I've been for the last twenty-eight years."

A seventy-six-year-old woman: "Well, I like to go to dances and for passing the time away I like to putter in the backyard to plant a garden with flowers. I like company, I like to play cards and spend my time that way. I like people that are not too forward, I would say courteous, and those who talk about different things in life, and a good disposition. Well, I think I would probably like to live in Michigan, where I could leave it anytime I wanted to, to go to live in the warmer climate. I'd like to do some traveling, too."

A seventy-four-year-old woman: "What do I like to do? Nothing since I retired. I'm just retired, that's it. I don't take any part in things that are going on today. I like good law-abiding citizens. Don't get into any trouble with the law. They are right and that is the way it should be."

An eighty-year-old-woman: "I like to play bingo, watch TV, cook, and visit churches and funeral homes because I meet friends and make new ones. I admire priests and nuns because of their dedication and education, and religiousness. I would like to live in a large house that was close to a church."

An eighty-five-year-old woman: "I like nursing, working in the contagion wards. It was interesting to see people get better, like typhoids. You could watch them get better. Now I like watching the news. I'd like a nice apartment in New York City."

A seventy-year-old woman: "I am a self-made person. The highlight of my life is opening my business. I like to work, see people, go out. I like to give money to feel that I am giving and people are receiving from me. I feel important. I like to have fun—theater, ballet, etc. Things that I don't like to do I don't do. Describe a man? My married boyfriend. For the last thirty years he cannot make up his mind. Keeps his wife and loving me at the same time."

A ninety-one-year-old black woman: "I'm too old to do much of anything. Times was when I used to get up [in the morning] and not see a chair till bedtime. Now I can just set and look out the window and read all day. You know I ain't the woman I used to be. I thought a mighty lot of President Kennedy and Martin Luther King. They done a lot for the poor Negro and they was killed for it. You know, there's so many mean, low-down people in this world who don't want the poor colored people to get good jobs and good education. But God sees them and they gonna pay for it Judgment Day. I'd like to go back to the South to visit some of my folks for a while if my health could stand it, but I'd like to live right here with my daughter."

Finally, an eighty-seven-year-old woman: "I had a very comfortable life. The last fifteen or sixteen years I have been very independent and happy. I have been caring for many children and have also enjoyed my ten grandchildren. I like everything, listening to ball games, crossword puzzles. Anything I do, I just like to do. Even dishwashing isn't so bad anymore."

There are many ways to be an old woman. There is certainly no right way, either for "successful aging," self esteem, or zestful living. So long as health (and, of course, finances) remain good and people can continue to do what has given them contentment before, they can be happy. Happiness can accompany being "young old" but is diminished when health deteriorates, and people become "old old." Maybe if we could do more to alleviate the helplessness of the "old old," all old people would be as cheerful as the last eighty-seven-year-old woman is.

Power and Age—the Invisible Older Woman

The stereotype of poor, dumb, and ugly does not touch the issue of power or what I referred to earlier as old women's irrelevance, and it seems to me wrong to omit any reference to this issue from a discussion of the psychology of older women. It does not do to talk about the power of old women without comparing their powers or relevance with that of young women on the one hand and with that of older men on the other. Bernice Neugarten stated this point almost two decades ago: that sex differences have to include age differences, that we need to think of age/sex categories.

The point of the double comparison was made, I think, most poignantly by the California psychologist Jacqueline Goodchilds. In a discussion of women and power she noted that women psychologists of our older generation were socialized to assume that they would always be second to men psychologists, that if they stumbled into a room full of men at an APA (American Psychological Association) meeting, for example, they should beat a hasty retreat because it would undoubtedly be a high-level meeting in which women would not belong. Serious and vital issues of APA policy were not the purview of women psychologists then. It is true that today's APA governing bodies do include women, as do many other higher-level policy groups, but how often are these women as old as the men in the groups? Whatever the reasons—socialized expectations, preferences for style, or simple considerations of whom it is pleasant to work with—Goodchilds' words may be as applicable today as they were a decade ago: "Ah, but do you see it? The old men and the young women together as our ruling elite. It has a familiar stereotypical ring about it."

Beliefs about women and power have fluctuated dramatically over the past few years. But one general tenet is constant. If there are changes in power relative to men, it is young women who are experiencing them. This fact counters some anthropologists' observations that old women (generally defined as postmenopausal) gain power beyond what they had before. They are comparing old women to young women, however; they rarely claim that the power older women may gain is an ascendance over men.

Only in one respect can that be claimed—within the family in the modern world. Because women now can expect to live almost eight years longer than men; because women generally are married to men several years older than they; and because health is related to distance from death, many old women are in better health and have more vigor than the men to whom they are married. There is some kind of power that accrues to a healthy person taking care of a less healthy one, to a vigorous person yoked to a less vigorous one. As Barbara Turner and I have argued, though, this kind of power often brings with it virtual imprisonment in the home, not to mention anxiety and drudgery, and is not a major kind of power in the larger world.

Sexual activity is a tangential illustration of these points. Almost all data show that the frequency of old women's sexual activity is contingent upon the presence of a man and decreases as a function of her partner's activity. Far fewer older women who lack a partner look elsewhere for sex than do men in the same position.

One of the places I went last summer was to Banff National Park, to fulfill a dream I had had since I was eight years old, when my father showed me a postcard of Lake Louise looking remote and incredibly beautiful. He had never taken me there on his trips through the Canadian West, and I had never found the occasion to do so since. Great disappointment! Lake Louise and Banff both turned out to be overtouristed, shoddy, and uninspiring, at least against the expectations of my dreams. But I did observe with fascination the phenomena of tour bus composition and behavior.

The day trip I had signed up for consisted largely of older couples who were excessively polite, like the women on the train. The women were even more subdued than their husbands, and I and one young German woman seemed to be the only people on our bus who hiked the trails and did anything but stay near the bus and take pictures of each other. At one stopping place, however, our bus parked near another tour that seemed to consist mostly of older women, no couples. These women were loud and boisterous, full of chatter and laughter. Their dress was colorful and they wore vivid jewelry. They reminded me of the "merry widows" described by Helena Lopata in her book on widows, those women who were widowed late in life, as opposed to those widowed early. It occurred to me that widowed and divorced older women have, in a way, more effective power than those who are still married. They at least can make decisions for and about themselves—unless, of course, their children take over.

Like most others who have taught courses in aging, I have been told by many of the students that they want to learn about aging so they can help their parents. Often these parents are in their early forties! Along with the scorn of daughters who see their mothers as poor, dumb, and ugly goes the conviction that they, the daughters, must do something about taking care of their mothers, who won't know how to take care of themselves. Remember my grandson, who at eight is all primed to take over supervising me. (It is not too surprising that national survey data analyzed by Norval Glenn and Sara McLanahan found no difference in happiness between those women over fifty who were mothers and those who had no children.)

While I am on the subject of family power, I will add the power embodied in the grandparental or even parental role. In both of these roles, older women generally prefer to keep out of direct power transactions. I call grandparents "the family watchdogs," because their active intervention and influence over younger generations result from trying to help with problems rather than desires to intervene. Grandparents step in when there is trouble or need in the family. Otherwise, they would rather go on about their own affairs, or at least are happier when they are able to do so. They do not find many grandparental activities rewarding, except in the sense of helping their families continue to carry the torch instead of dropping it by the wayside.

Many old women compensate for their lack of societal power through power in more personal relationships, like friends. As we all know, women are generally more sociable and person-oriented than men. We tend to enjoy family relationships more, our friendships are more self-disclosing and confiding, and when we lose friends through moving away, death, or other separations, we tend to replace them more often than men do. Kathleen McCormick, who completed a dissertation with me on "best friends" versus "just friends," found that some of her older men respondents could not give her the address of their designated best friend because, they said, they did not know where he was now. None of the older women had lost touch with her best friend. Many men, in this and other research on friendship, list their wives as their best friend; no woman lists her husband. Essentially, there are many trade-offs in sex differences in later life. For example, women live longer than men, but men have more money. Women are healthier, but men can remarry. Women have friends to keep them from being lonely, but men can remarry.

The Future of Old Age

Has there been any change between 1970, when I first came up with the epithet "poor, dumb, and ugly" and now, fifteen years later? Not an awful lot. A significant proportion of people below the poverty line are still women over sixty-five. Younger generations still have more schooling than their mothers and grandmothers, even though women of all ages went back to school and took jobs during the flood period of the late 1960s and the 1970s. And, in spite of Blackglama mink ads, old women labeled attractive still have to look youthful.

Is this something to do with what Vern Bengtson and Joseph Kuypers termed the "generational stake"? In their review of data on actual versus perceived generational differences in attitudes and values (the "generation gap"), they found that younger generations have a need to exaggerate the *differences* between themselves and their parents and grandparents in order to stress their uniqueness and separateness from previous generations. This seems to be particularly true in the years of entry into adulthood, in the process of identity formation. At the same time, older generations seem to need to exaggerate the *similarities* between themselves and their children and grandchildren, perhaps to assert their wish that others will carry on their values. Having dedicated years of their lives to affirming and support- ing their values and beliefs, they do not wish these efforts to have been in vain.

Do young women, in this respect, want to see their mothers and grand- mothers as poor, dumb, and ugly so that they can see themselves as rich, smart, and beautiful? Do I, as an old woman, exaggerate my own wealth, intelligence, and attractiveness so that I can see the same qualities in my daughters and granddaughter? While I might like to pursue this fancy, I remind myself that few old women really believe they are rich, smart, and beautiful. In fact, it is reasonable to presume that if I do exaggerate my own positive attributes I want to maintain an equality with my daughters and granddaughters rather than try for superiority.

Jeanne Brooks-Gunn, a Princeton psychologist, and Barbara Kirsch use the term "plot line" to describe how people evaluate and predict their lives. One problem old women face today is that their plot lines end at middle age and that their life plots are completely predicated upon marriage and parenting. Today's cohort of old women, whose parenting ended before mid- life and whose marriages sometimes did, too, are thus likely to be left stranded for the future. We need models of old women who show us how to be old. In the last few years, as more and more women have lived longer,

such models have become available; but because these models themselves
have been pioneers in longevity, their experiences and feelings may show us
more what we don't want to do than what we want to do.

One model of the old woman, a consequence of the stereotype, is polite
blankness, a masked personality. Another is the opposite, which I think of
as the antistereotype. The flamboyant women on that "other" bus in Banff
are examples of this, as is the cult heroine in the movie *Harold and Maude*.
Maybe there is another way, one of creative achievement that continues
from earlier life even though it goes through transformations to suit altered
conditions of vitality, opportunity, and interest. I have suggested here that I,
at least, am turned off by polite blankness. I hope I don't go in for it too
often, even though I have found myself also acting that way often enough.
But I am not altogether charmed by flamboyant old ladies either. I give
them credit for their obvious élan and sometimes even manage to adopt that
mode myself. There are times when I get together with old friends and we
go off in gales of giggles as we at least metaphorically strut across our stage.
Last year I bought a trendy jumpsuit and feel as jaunty as the next woman
when I wear it with dangling earrings.

But why do we have to be either of these extremes? Why can't we let
ourselves be diverse? Why can't we find a way that allows us to flourish in
our own individuality without being either masked or flamboyant? Then we
would really be free of stereotyping. Until then, old women must be pioneers. And all pioneers face special dilemmas along their uncharted course,
including those pioneers on the frontier of age.

LILLIAN E. TROLL, professor of psychology at Rutgers-The State University, is an authority in the field of life span development, particularly in the area of family life, on which she has written and lectured extensively. She is a Fellow of the Gerontological Society of America, in which she has held several offices, and a Fellow of the Adult Development and Aging Division and of the Psychology of Women Division of the American Psychological Association. She is also the director of the Undergraduate Gerontology Certificate Program at Rutgers.

Before coming to Rutgers in 1975, she was an associate professor in the Psychology Department of Wayne State University and a senior research assistant at the Merrill-Palmer Institute. She received her B.S. (1937), M.A. (1966), and Ph.D. (1967) degrees in psychology and human development from the University of Chicago. Before beginning her academic career, she worked in personnel psychology, school psychology, and child psychology. She has been a visiting professor at the University of Michigan, the University of Southern California, and the University of British Columbia. Dr. Troll's books include *Looking Ahead: A Woman's Guide to the Problems and Joys of Growing Older* (with Joan Israel and Kenneth Israel) (Prentice-Hall, 1977); *Families in Later Life* (with Sheila Miller and Robert Atchley) (Wadsworth Publishing Co., 1979); *Continuations: Development After Twenty* (Brooks/Cole, 1982); and *Early and Middle Adulthood* (Brooks/Cole, 1985).

Further Reading

Baruch, Grace, and Brooks-Gunn, Jeanne. *Women in Midlife.* New York: Plenum, 1984.

de Beauvoir, Simone. *The Prime of Life.* Cleveland: World Publishing Co., 1962.

Fisher, M.F.K. *Sister Age.* New York: Knopf, 1983; in paperback, Vintage, 1984.

Olson, Tillie. *Mother to Daughter; Daughter to Mother.* Old Westbury, N.Y.: Feminist Press, 1984.

CONFLICTS AND CRISES:
Coping with Stress

14

Humor

CAROLE WADE

A smile is a curve that sets everything straight.
                              —Phyllis Diller

Experience is not what happens to you; it is what you do
with what happens to you.

                              —Aldous Huxley

Consider the following irritations of everyday life, and some hypothetical
responses:

- You are trying to tell your "significant other" something important, but
  the TV has him in a semihypnotic trance and he's ignoring you. To get
  his attention, should you (a) shout your message in his ear; (b) cry and
  storm out of the room; (c) walk purposefully over to the television set
  and turn it off; or (d) concoct an outrageous story about the lusty time
  you had that afternoon with your secret lover, piling on one salacious
  detail after another until your TV addict looks up from the tube?
- Your teenager has decorated her room with a year's supply of class
  notes, four rotting apple cores, an old cup of coffee with green stuff
  growing in it, and the entire contents of her closet. To communicate
  your disapproval, should you (a) launch into your 576th tirade on her
  slovenliness; (b) deliver a reasoned lecture on the relationship of cleanli-
  ness to godliness; (c) resentfully clean the room yourself; or (d) pile
  everything into the middle of the floor, stick an American flag on top,
  and hang a sign on the mound that reads Monument to the Battle of the
  Bilge?
- Your boss, who makes Genghis Khan look like Alan Alda, has sum-
  moned you to his office for an impromptu evaluation. To prepare your-

self for the ordeal, should you (a) work up a righteous sense of indignation over what a tyrant he is; (b) rehearse your resignation from the firm; (c) sneak out to the bar across the street for a quick infusion of liquid courage; or (d) imagine how the ogre looks when he's in the john?

• At a party you're giving, a guest accidentally drops a good crystal goblet on the floor, smashing it to pieces. Should you (a) moan and groan until the klutz offers to replace the goblet; (b) cast a reproachful look, but say nothing as you clean up the mess; (c) carry on for ten minutes about how it's perfectly all right, *really;* (d) throw up your hands and proclaim, "There goes another one of my best jelly jars!"

If you answered "d" to the above questions, you may be one of those lucky people who have learned to grin under stress, the better to bear it. A sense of humor is not merely the ability to come up with a quick quip; it is a playful frame of mind that permits you to see the ironic side of serious situations and to assert your control over them. Once thought too frivolous a topic for serious psychological study, humor is finally gaining recognition as a healthy way to cope with tension, depression, and pain, and as a fundamental component of emotional well-being.

How Humor Helps

The idea that humor is healthy is not new. Hippocrates, the ancient Greek credited with being the father of medicine, advised that a "physician should have a certain ready wit, as dourness is repulsive both to well and ill." The Bible, too, tells us that "a merry heart doeth good like a medicine, but a broken spirit drieth the bones" (Proverbs 17:22). Historically, a few sourpusses have looked on humor with suspicion or disdain: "He who laughs," harrumphed the German poet and dramatist Bertolt Brecht, "has not heard the terrible news." But in general, poets, philosophers, and pundits have praised the wisdom of the wisecrack.

One of the first psychologists to analyze *how* levity raises the spirits was Sigmund Freud. In an early monograph Freud argued that jokes are a way of expressing sexual and hostile tendencies that are usually repressed or driven from consciousness. By disguising such tendencies in a joke, we make them acceptable to ourselves and others, and thus derive pleasure from them. Freud called aggressive humor "wit" and distinguished it from "humor," which he considered a healthy way of dealing with painful situations, but he focused mainly on the former. Years later, though, he devoted an essay to humor, this time noting that humor clearly has something "fine and elevating" in it. When a person has a humorous attitude, wrote Freud, the ego—the part of the personality that adjusts instinctual and social demands to reality—asserts its invulnerability: "It refuses to be hurt by the arrows of reality or to be compelled to suffer. It insists that it is impervious to wounds dealt by the outside world, in fact, that these are merely occasions for affording it pleasure." It may be no coincidence that at the time Freud wrote those words, he had only recently embarked on what was to be a long and painful struggle with cancer.

Freud's early emphasis on humor as a safety valve for the darker drives attracted more attention than his later focus on the triumphant nature of humor, but both themes were taken up by writer Arthur Koestler. Humor, Koestler claimed, always contains at least a faint hint of aggression or apprehension: "It is the aggressive element, the detached malice of the parodist, which turns pathos into bathos, tragedy into comedy." But like any act of creativity, Koestler wrote, humor also shakes us out of automatic ways of thinking and behaving, making us truly alive.

Gorillas and chimpanzees produce something like a laugh when they are tickled, but our species seems to be the only one that laughs in amusement. Humor may have developed as a uniquely human activity to handle the stresses of civilized life. Back in the days when *Homo sapiens* had to contend with woolly mammoths, dramatic physical responses to stress were appropriate, but as we moved from caves to huts, these responses tended to lose their value. In modern life, where the typical stressor is a mammoth traffic jam, not a mammoth mammal, they are definitely overreactions. When you face your tyrannical boss, you don't really need to sweat to dispose of the excessive body heat that might develop in battle. When your daughter uses her room as a trash receptacle, you don't really need to breathe hard to get oxygen to your muscles. Laughter (and weeping too) developed, said Koestler, as a "luxury reflex" to dispose of surplus emotion.

Other theories of humor emphasize its mental or cognitive elements. When you laugh at a difficult situation, what you are really doing is putting it in perspective by seeing it—and perhaps yourself—from the outside. In *Man's Search for Himself*, psychologist Rollo May noted that spontaneous humor (in contrast to forced gags performed solely for effect) are a way of preserving the sense of self: "It is an expression of our uniquely human capacity to experience ourselves as subjects who are not swallowed up in the objective situation." It also makes a statement, to yourself and others, about the true importance of the situation.

One of my aunts is an expert at using humor in this way. A few days before she was to undergo a modified radical mastectomy on her left breast, I saw her at a relative's wedding and marveled at her calm. Though hardly happy about the impending operation, she seemed to be enjoying the celebration. "Listen," she said with a twinkle in her eye, "I told your uncle not to complain; he's had forty good years on that side."

Rod Martin, a Canadian psychologist who has studied the value of humor as a stress buffer, believes that we can best understand the healthy effects of humor if we take both the physical and cognitive aspects of emotional tension into account. When you feel tense, it's because you have evaluated a situation as stressful and because your body has responded with certain subjectively unpleasant changes. Martin suggests that humor mounts a two-pronged attack. First it helps you reappraise the situation and the degree of control you have over it. Then it activates certain beneficial physical responses, possibly stimulating the immune system or starting the flow of endorphins, brain chemicals that act as the body's natural painkillers. Interest in the physiology of humor is growing; studies by several researchers, most notably Dr. William F. Fry, Jr., of Stanford, show that vigorous laughter gives internal organs a brief workout, releases muscle tension, pumps air through the lungs, and improves blood flow.

Joel Goodman, who holds a doctorate in education and heads the Humor Project at the Sagamore Institute in Saratoga Springs, New York, likens the use of humor under pressure to aikido, the Japanese martial art that teaches you to turn aside an adversary by "going with the flow" of the attack. Like aikido, humor provides a way of avoiding passive submission on the one hand and a futile battle with reality on the other. For example, one man I know dealt with his grief over a friend's terminal illness by bounding out of bed in the middle of the night and concocting the "Henny Youngman Post-surgical Inventory," a wonderfully clever takeoff on psychological tests. At the time this man thought his "inventory" was solely for his sick friend's amusement, but later he realized that the act of writing it had also helped dissipate his own depression.

Humor-as-aikido not only defuses stressful situations, but can be used to disarm human adversaries, which is why minorities and oppressed groups who cannot fight back directly have often forged humor into a verbal weapon. A Jewish joke tells of a Jew who accidentally bumped into a Nazi in Hitler's Germany. "Swine!" bellowed the Nazi. "Cohen," the Jew replied. "Pleased to meet you."

Most of us think of the perfect zinger when it's too late ("If only I'd said . . ."). Occasionally, though, inspiration strikes. A friend—I'll call her Rita

Green—told me that as a graduate student in geography she was required to take a field course from Dr. M., who was known for such endearing qualities as racism, sexism, and all-around meanness. (This was in the days before students lodged formal complaints about such things.) "His style," Rita recalls, "was to run his course like boot camp, barking out questions no one was supposed to answer because they were just a way to keep people in their place. Most of us were older than thirty—many were veterans or reentering women—yet we were forced to submit meekly to ten 8-hour field trips given by this intimidating bastard." One day the class was touring a Southern California lemon and orange plantation, and paused next to some migrant housing shacks:

Dr. M.: Yes siree, this land had lotsa different folks working it—wops, Okies, beaners, neegrows . . .

(Class reacts with surreptitious snickering, eyes cast down at shoes. One student, an Italian man, giggles nervously.)

Dr. M.: What's so funny, Petrini?

Petrini: Er, ah, er, I think those terms are only used in the pejorative sense these days.

Dr. M. *(in a rage):* You son of a bitch, how many missions did the Jesuits build in California? What's the chemical composition of granite? *(He continues with several other who-gives-a-damn-type questions.)*

(Long silence.)

Dr. M.: You guys think you're so goddamn funny. I'll show you; this day's gonna be rough. Green, who produces the best citrus in the world?

Rita *(in a little voice):* I guess I don't know, Dr. M.

Dr. M.: Israel, Green. And do you know what makes that citrus the best in the world?

Rita: It's the chosen fruit.

I'm pleased to report that my friend's gambit worked. Everyone burst out laughing, and she quickly followed up with, "I've copyrighted that one, Dr. M., so you can't use it." What was Dr. M. to do? Defanged by her humor, he behaved in a relatively civilized fashion for the rest of the afternoon.

In addition to coming to our rescue in particular circumstances, humor also has the broader function of releasing us from social restraints. In *Laughter and Liberation,* psychologist Harvey Mindess persuasively argues that jokes are a way of irreverently thumbing our noses at all the rules and regulations, written or unwritten, that keep us stuck in the status quo. Word play defies linguistic convention; ribald jokes mock moral inhibitions; nonsense jokes rescue us from reason; playful humor dissolves the deadly seriousness of adult responsibilities. And by ridiculing those we consider oppressors, we assert our own dignity and overcome, at least momentarily, our feelings of inferiority and subordination.

But the ultimate value of humor, in Mindess's view, is that it enables us to laugh at our own flaws and foibles with good-humored self-acceptance. (Bitter self-mockery is a different story.) A patient of Mindess's once concluded her tale of woe by saying, "My problem's simple. I'm a total mess." Somehow, in context, it seemed funny, and both patient and therapist broke up laughing. By exaggerating her plight, the woman had paradoxically managed to reduce its significance; as Mindess noted, compared to a *total* mess, a partial mess did not seem so bad.

Laughter in the Laboratory

Mindess and a handful of other psychotherapists use humor deliberately with patients in psychotherapy to help them overcome anger, grief, and depression. But until recently, there was little hard scientific evidence that humor does people any good. There were some hints, though. In *Adaptation to Life* (1977) psychiatrist George Vaillant reported on a four-decades long study of male college graduates. He found that the best-adjusted of these men dealt with anxiety and depression by using five "mature" defense mechanisms, or adaptive styles, and one of them was humor. (The others were anticipation of future needs, altruism or service to others, suppression or postponement of actions that might be inappropriate, and sublimation or channeling of energy into productive activities.) The healthiest use of humor, Vaillant wrote, was ironic rather than clownish or masochistic. One man, when asked what he would most like his children to have that he didn't, replied, "Someone to look after their children." And when asked to describe the chief hobbies he had developed, he responded, "I have developed considerably less spare time."

You might suppose that those men who had a robust sense of humor were blessed with easy lives. Perhaps their humor was a response to, rather than a cause of, happiness. But that was not the case. Men who used humor as a coping strategy had as much to cope with as anyone else, if not more. For example, four men who had been editors of the college humor magazine had, during childhood, all lost a parent through death. What distinguished these men was the ability to transform their own suffering into wit. Thus, one of the former humor editors, after spending a summer with his alcoholic mother, commented, "My mother got on after a fashion—after an old-fashioned." Studies of professional comics also find that humor frequently develops during childhood as a way of making peace with what might otherwise drive one to despair. Mark Twain said it best: "The secret source of humor . . . is not joy but sorrow."

In a similar study, writer and researcher Gail Sheehy examined the coping strategies of male and female "pathfinders"—people who risk change or deal with it creatively when it is foisted upon them. Why, she asked, do some people get through life's struggles and disappointments with confidence and courage, and with their *joie de vivre* intact, while others go to pieces or turn into emotional zombies? To find the answer, Sheehy put together a Life History Questionnaire that was ultimately completed by sixty thousand people. She also conducted hundreds of telephone interviews and several face-to-face ones. In her 1981 book *Pathfinders,* she reported that emotionally hardy persons of both sexes turn most often to four coping devices: They work more; they seek out friends; they pray; and they look for humor in their situations. People who are not hardy indulge in food, drink, and drugs; pretend their problems don't exist; develop physical symptoms; and escape into fantasy.

Humor, though, does not imply putting on a "happy face." Women, in particular, often think they have to smile, smile, smile, no matter what the situation, in order to put others at ease. But in Sheehy's sample, women who wore a smiling mask felt trapped and unhappy. Female pathfinders, in contrast, were gutsy types who established, often with great effort, their own identities and resisted the impulse always to please others.

Vaillant's and Sheehy's observations on humor were relatively informal. The first strong statistical evidence for humor's healing power appeared only recently. Rod Martin, the Canadian researcher I mentioned earlier, had noticed that when very old people are interviewed in newspapers about their longevity, they often make remarks such as "I owe my long life to a sense of humor and a good supply of Scotch." To pin down the emotional advantages of humor, Martin and psychologist Herbert M. Lefcourt constructed a special test to tap the tendency to use humor as a coping strategy in everyday situations. They gave college students this test, along with two others. Then they had college students take the test; complete a questionnaire on current levels of tension, anxiety, depression, anger, fatigue, and confusion; and report on events that had had a negative impact on their lives during the previous year. (To find out your own "humor quotient," see page 299.)

Other researchers had already established that when people experience a series of unpleasant or stressful events, they tend to suffer subsequent mood disturbances. This association between stress and mood turned up in Martin and Lefcourt's study, too. But—and this is the important point—the association was significantly *weaker* for people with high sense of humor scores than for those with low ones. In other words, a sense of humor seemed to provide a protective umbrella against the emotional fallout of stress.

Later, Martin and Lefcourt designed a clever experimental study to confirm these initial results. Students had to watch a film called *Subincision,* which showed young male aborigines having the undersides of their penises split as part of an initiation rite. Some students were told to make up a running narrative for this anxiety-producing film. Others were instructed to concoct a funny commentary. Those students who tried to be amusing reported less stress after watching the film, and also grimaced, squirmed, and fidgeted less during it.

Since psychological stress is associated with physical illness, the stress-buffering qualities of humor probably help protect physical as well as emotional health. So far, the evidence for this is mainly anecdotal, but some of the anecdotes give one pause. For example, in *Anatomy of an Illness as Perceived by the Patient,* Norman Cousins told how he used laughter to fight ankylosing spondylitis, a disease of the connective tissue that binds the body's cells together. The medical prognosis was bleak; according to one specialist, chances of full recovery were only one in five hundred. But Cousins refused to give up hope. From his own reading on stress and illness, he concluded that his fate depended on the ability of his hormone system, and especially the adrenal glands, to function properly. He knew that negative emotions could cause adrenal exhaustion and an out-of-kilter body chemistry. Perhaps, he reasoned, positive emotions would produce healthy adrenals and positive chemical changes.

There is not much funny about lying on your back in constant pain in a hospital. So to rev up his positive emotions, Cousins moved out of the hospital (with his doctor's support) and began to watch old "Candid Camera" programs and Marx Brothers films. He also had a nurse read to him from E. B. and Katharine White's *Subtreasury of American Humor* and Max Eastman's *The Enjoyment of Laughter.* To Cousin's delight, a mere ten minutes of genuine belly laughter had an analgesic effect and allowed him to get at least two hours of pain-free sleep. What's more, after each laughter session there was a small but cumulative drop in his sedimentation rate—the speed with which red blood cells settle in a test tube. (In general, the lower the sedimentation rate, the less severe an inflammation or infection.)

Cousins combined periodic injections of mirth with massive doses of ascorbic acid, administered intravenously. Within a few months he was able to return to work, and eventually he achieved a nearly complete recovery.

Can Women Be Funny?

A healthy sense of humor, then, makes good sense, both emotionally and physically. But this book is addressed to women, and it behooves us to ask ourselves whether women encounter any special obstacles on the way to the guffaw.

Historically, female humorists have been rare. When I leafed through Elaine Partnow's *Quotable Woman,* I found only nineteen comedians or humorists among the 1,334 women quoted—about as many humorists, it seemed, as hymnists. Of course, Partnow's selections were based on her personal tastes and interests, and she was not looking specifically for funny women. More important, the absence of famous women humorists proves little about the average woman's sense of humor: Women haven't produced a lot of famous chefs either, but that doesn't mean they can't cook. In both fields social barriers to achievement can explain why women haven't entered the top ranks.

Recent psychological findings are more enlightening. The clearest one is that men are far more likely than women to tell jokes in mixed-sex social situations. This sex difference in the initiation of humor appears to have roots in early childhood. Paul McGhee, associate professor of human development at Texas Tech University, has found that among three-to-five-year-olds, boys initiate more "behavioral" humor—clowning around, acting silly, making faces, and so forth. And by age six, boys also make more attempts at joking, silly rhyming, and other forms of verbal humor than girls do, either because boys increase their output with age, or because girls decrease theirs.

It's not that little girls don't *appreciate* humor. In most studies their ratings of jokes and cartoons are similar to boys', and they usually laugh and smile as much as boys do in response to humor. But one study found that after age six, boys laughed more during free play. Further, the responses of girls and women seem to be associated more closely with a desire to be socially correct than those of boys and men. In a number of studies, females' humor ratings and reactions to something funny were more strongly influenced than males' by whether *other* people were smiling or laughing.

There are many ways to explain such findings. For example, boys may become more practiced at producing humor because humor tends to be a social behavior, and little boys play in larger groups than girls. Girls often stick to what psychologists Eleanor Maccoby and Carol Nagy Jacklin call "chumships." Or girls may produce less humor than boys because there are few funny females to serve as models. But certain features of the female role also work against the public display of humor. For example:

• *Sexual reticence.* If you are trying to preserve an image of sexual chastity and naïveté, you are cut off from one of the favorite topics of American humor—sex. Or, as the immortal Mae West once said, "It's hard to be funny when you have to be clean." (Fortunately, Mae never let sexual reticence dampen *her* wit. Remember one of her most memorable lines: "Is that a gun in your pocket, or are you just glad to see me?")

• *The need to be nice.* Author Rebecca West once wrote, "All the world over, the most good-natured find enjoyment in those who miss trains or sit down on frozen pavements." Not to mention those who slip on banana peels or get stranded on flagpoles. In McGhee's studies, children with the heartiest sense of humor have been those with a prior history of being verbally and physically aggressive with their peers. These children may have learned to use humor as a socially acceptable outlet for aggression. But hostility, like sex, is not ladylike. By the time they are in elementary school, children know this; boys are significantly more likely than girls to initiate hostile humor—for example, in name calling or defiance of adults.

• *Intellectual modesty.* Elephant jokes don't require any special intelligence, but wit does. Traditionally, though, women have been expected to appear mentally inferior. Whether on a date or as the hostess of a dinner party, the traditional woman's function is to make her male partner look smart, not to shine herself.

• *Social decorum.* English poet and literary critic Alice Meynell (1847–1922) once daintily observed that "the sense of humor has other things to do than to make itself conspicuous in the act of laughter." Indeed, there is something unladylike about outright mirth. (Remember all those film images of ladies giggling discreetly behind their fans?) In elementary school, girls who do have a strong sense of humor tend to be those who are out on the field playing ball or climbing on the jungle gym—and making themselves conspicuous—rather than those who are quietly working on puzzles or arts and crafts.

• *Taboos against self-assertion.* When Paul McGhee polled college students, those who perceived themselves as funny also saw themselves as dominating and socially assertive. The connection makes sense: When you tell a joke or make a witticism, you put yourself into the limelight and implicitly ask for approval and admiration; laughter is the humorist's applause. Telling a joke can also be a way of controlling a social situation or establishing power. But the traditional female role bars social dominance and self-display; men may not approve. I have been struck by how many of my women friends and acquaintances are clever and entertaining when they are with other women, but restrained and subdued whenever a boyfriend or husband is present.

Is There a "Women's Humor"?

In spite of sex-role restrictions, there have always been great women comedians (Mae West, Fanny Brice, Gertrude Berg, Beatrice Lillie, Gracie Allen, Lucille Ball, Totie Fields, Phyllis Diller, Joan Rivers) and humorists (Dorothy Parker, Peg Bracken, Jean Kerr). Though few black women have gained national fame as humorists (Whoopi Goldberg is a recent exception), many black writers and entertainers have commented on racial oppression with a wry, incisive wit: women such as Lena Horne, Nell Carter, and Alice Walker. And in the past few decades the number of women who make their living in whole or in part through humor seems to have grown: Elaine May, Lily Tomlin, Carol Burnett, Goldie Hawn, Gilda Radner, Louise Lasser, Valerie Harper, Bette Midler, Judith Martin (Miss Manners), Nora Ephron, Judith Viorst, Fran Lebowitz, Ellen Goodman. . . .

A head count of professional comics and humorists doesn't tell the whole story about women's humor, though. Humor that heals must spin gold from the apparent dross of ordinary experience. Jewish humor and black humor are famous for this. Is there also a "women's humor" that draws on the unique experiences of women as they grow up, struggle with relationships, look for jobs, rear children?

An experience about a decade ago made me think not. I was teaching in a community college, and the wife of one of my students invited me to an all-female comedy show put on by the Ladies' Auxiliary of a national fraternal organization. "Aha!" I thought. "A chance to see grass-roots female humor at its source!" The fact that the review was called "Hag's Night" should have warned me, but off I went with notepad and tape recorder in hand.

When I arrived at the huge hall used for the occasion, I found hundreds of women milling about in excited anticipation. I learned that the annual show ran for five nights, that it was always sold out, that the performers prepared for months, and that no men were allowed (though a few always stuffed their shirts with Kleenex, smeared on some makeup, and tried to sneak in). There was a conspiratorial atmosphere among the women in the room; this was *their* night, when they could pull out all the stops and be as daring as they pleased. The lights dimmed, the curtains parted, and I prepared to learn what female humor was like.

I never found out. Most of the jokes and skits were borrowed from Las Vegas shows and the kinds of humor books meant to be kept by the toilet. I was struck by the fact that many of them were clearly from the male viewpoint; for example, they expressed complaints about women—the "Take my wife . . . please" type of joke. There were no "Take my husband" jokes. Some routines had to be performed in men's clothing to make any sense. Few if any lines were delivered about kids, women's lovers, husbands, jobs, childbirth, birth control, divorce, or any of the other realities that matter to women. To my dismay, there was a smattering of rape jokes, and more than a smattering of jokes disparaging women's sexuality and intelligence.

After the show several women who had noticed me taking notes came up to ask if I planned to write an article on their production. They were friendly, open, generous women, and obviously proud of their effort. I didn't have the heart to repay their hospitality with a consciousness-raising session.

Of course, the women who put on the "Hag's Night" were not professional comics. They did not attempt to produce much original humor, and so they were limited to the jokes, gags, and skits then available in the mass media. Since that time some profound changes have occurred in attitudes toward women's roles. Women have thronged to the workplace. They are making steady progress in fields once the sole province of men, such as law, medicine, and business. As I write, a woman is running for Vice President and, incidentally, showing that she is an expert at using humor as aikido. Perhaps, then, the self-disparagement I heard ten years ago is a thing of the past?

Alas, not quite. The evidence comes from humor research on responses to jokes about aggressors and victims. In general, people find such jokes funnier when the aggressor comes from their own group and the victim comes from another than if the roles are reversed. For example, a Republican is likely to prefer a joke that puts down Democrats to one that puts down Republicans. Men consistently follow this pattern: They prefer jokes in which women are the butt to those in which men are. Some women also prefer to see the opposite sex put down. But studies find that many women, and in particular traditional women, show more appreciation for jokes in which men put down women than for jokes in which the reverse is true. In fact, such women seem to find more humor in female victimization, whatever the sex of the aggressor, than men do.

Again, these sex differences start early—by about kindergarten. Paul McGhee and Nelda Duffey asked young children to choose the funnier cartoon in pairs of cartoons that differed only in the sex of the victim. For example, the children had to choose between a cartoon picturing a boy on a ladder accidentally spilling paint on a girl as she held the ladder for him and a cartoon showing a girl spilling the paint on a boy. In another pair either a boy or a girl fell while skateboarding and got an ice cream cone in his or her hair. Boys who had a preference usually thought these mishaps were funnier when the girl was the one who (literally) got dumped on. As a group, middle-class girls had a slight preference for cartoons in which boys were victimized, but lower-income girls, who presumably would be more likely to learn the traditional sex role, agreed with the boys that female victims were funnier.

On the other hand, outside the laboratory there are signs that women are developing a new, self-affirming brand of humor. Growing numbers of talented and funny women are braving the loneliness of the road and the lingering prejudices of some club owners and audiences to break into professional comedy. And these up-and-coming female comics will have little to do with the self-disparaging brand of humor associated with Joan Rivers and many of the older comedians. Gone, too, are the portrayals of childlike scatterbrains once common in television shows such as "I Love Lucy." Instead, young female comics draw their material from politics, male-female relationships, the Pill, modern courtship rituals, periods, and the trials of aging.

Two very different female humorists illustrate the change. Cathy Guisewite, who draws the syndicated cartoon strip "Cathy," harvests hilarity from the daily trials and tribulations of the single career woman. Whether she's coping with her boss, struggling with a diet, worrying about her "biological clock," or trying to decide what to do about Irving, her maddeningly noncommittal boyfriend, Guisewite's Cathy makes us laugh at the truth and at ourselves. But we laugh with Cathy, never at her. Cathy may have her weaknesses, especially when she's around the refrigerator or a dress shop, but we know she's a survivor who can take care of herself—no matter *what* her mother thinks!

The other quintessential woman humorist is that sage philosopher of marriage and motherhood, Erma Bombeck. She jokes about age (she says she's "somewhere between estrogen and death"); the loneliness of housewifery ("The kids come in, look you in the eye, and ask you if anybody's home"); babies (they get so wet "their diapers give off rainbows"); pregnancy (a pregnant woman is "like a kangaroo wearing Earth Shoes"); and husbands ("Transporting children is my husband's 26th favorite thing; it comes somewhere between eating lunch in a tearoom and dropping a bowling ball on his foot"). Bombeck pokes fun at herself, too; when asked in supermarket parking lots whether she is Erma Bombeck, she has been known to blush and retort, "No, I'm Ann-Margret, but thank you anyway."

At first glance, Bombeck may seem to be merely a chronicler of the traditional female role, but in fact she is its supreme satirist, proving, as *Time* magazine observed in a cover story on her, that laughter is the best revenge. By lampooning waxy yellow buildup, children who flunk lunch, and washing machines that eat one sock in every pair, Bombeck is saying that the joys of housework and momhood are not all they're cracked up to be. But they have their treasured rewards, too, and anyway, what's the use of wallowing in self-pity? Laughter is a subtle way of lobbying for change without going bonkers in the reality of the present. It's completely in character that this spokeswoman for the suburban set spent two years at the end of the seventies stumping around the country for the Equal Rights Amendment.

Learning to Laugh

Women, then, can and do come to terms with the frustrations and disappointments of life by using humor. Most of us, though, do not have the comic vision of a Cathy Guisewite or an Erma Bombeck; we have to learn to resist the force of gravity by deliberately cultivating levity. Unfortunately, it is not always easy to look at life through Groucho Marx glasses. Recently, I found myself late for an appointment and stuck in a traffic jam. "You've been up to your laugh lines in humor," I told myself. "It's time to practice what you preach." But my sense of humor let me down when I needed it, and I arrived at my destination hot and hassled. Clearly, recognizing the need for humor in one's life is not enough; enlarging a funny bone, like building up triceps, takes time and effort.

There are no scientific studies that reveal the best way to improve your laugh life, but I have collected some suggestions from people who do research on humor or who use it in psychotherapy, and have added a few techniques that I have personally found effective.

First, some general tips for appreciating humor or using the humor of others as a stress buffer:

- Don't wait until the sky is covered over with clouds of gloom to look for the sunny side. Humor is most effective when used as preventive medicine. Once the darker emotions take over, they are hard to turn off. Joel Goodman suggests thinking of potentially upsetting situations and preparing humorous responses to them in advance.

- One person's yuck is another's yawn, so learn what kinds of humor appeals most to you—whether risqué, philosophical, political, or silly.

- Write up a list of favorite books, television programs, and people that you can seek out when you begin to feel crushed by the weight of your worries. You might even keep a scrapbook or file of humorous pick-me-ups. I have a file of "Cathy" cartoons snipped from the morning paper, and they never fail to pull a chuckle out of me. I've also found some gems in, of all places, "Dear Abby." For example, a woman wrote to Abby to express her anger at strangers who made "funny" comments about her son's parentage because his hair was a different color than either hers or her husband's. Another woman then wrote to say that she was in the same situation, but she thought it was a riot. It seems that the man who drove the local bakery delivery truck was a handsome fellow with flaming red hair. When the woman's daughter was born, the baby had a full head of red hair. The expressions on the neighbors' faces struck the woman as hilarious and so did their comments ("Boy, when you get *bread,* you really get *bred!*"). "People aren't trying to be mean," the writer wisely commented. "The world is full of comedians!"

- Don't try to laugh all your troubles away. Humor should not be used to trivialize serious problems or put a lid on justified outrage. As Harvey Mindess notes, the goal of using humor is not to avoid all tears, but to learn to laugh through them. And some situations are never funny—the death of someone you hold dear, sexual exploitation, physical and psychological abusiveness.

- Recall events in your life that seemed serious at the time but that you now appreciate as funny. Nearly everyone I've asked can remember at least one such episode, and most recall several. These memories provide personalized lessons in how to find the silver lining of laughter. You might even ask yourself during an infuriating episode, "Will this make a funny story later?" Or draw up a list of petty annoyances that could be viewed as amusing, if not funny: for example, milk cartons that won't open cleanly, plastic wrap that sticks only to your fingers, phone callers who have a sixth sense about when you're sitting down to dinner, mothers who can't enter your house without grabbing a broom.

• Ask others what makes them laugh. All too often, people who get together for social chitchat wind up exchanging complaints about their problems. By swapping jokes and humorous experiences instead, you'll get some additions for your collection and also have a great time.

To develop your own ability to produce humor:

• Allow your comic side free rein, without censoring yourself. You don't have to compete with the professionals; even groaners are effective stress reducers. Remember, the goal is to improve your own frame of mind, not to entertain or please others.

• Look for incongruities and ironies. Humor usually depends on a juxtaposition of ideas that are not ordinarily associated. Allen Klein, who runs humor workshops in Northern California, suggests the following exercise: Make a list of unrelated nouns, including some that strike you as funny, and divide the list into two groups. Choose a word from the first group as the subject of a joke, and use one from the second group in the punch line. For example, suppose you have these groups:

fruitcake	goat
garbage truck	peanut butter
death	floor wax
odor eaters	Jockey shorts
water buffalo	vacation

Your joke might be: "When you die it's like taking an extended vacation, except that you don't have to worry about what luggage to take or what to pack. You are in your luggage and you are what you pack." I doubt that this exercise will produce anything that Woody Allen could use, but it may encourage the habit of creatively combining different ideas.

• Play with words. Paul McGhee observes that producing humor is "like running your thoughts through a double-meaning filter." Children first learn this skill when they develop the "riddle disease" in about the first grade. Kids also practice their verbal humor skills with puns and word play. For example, once when my ten-year-old son and I stopped at a "Don't Walk" sign, he suggested that we *run* across the street instead. The incongruities of most adult humor are much more sophisticated, of course, but they are also harder to think of. Besides, plenty of amusing lines can be constructed from simple puns—like W. C. Fields' routine, "Do you believe in clubs for children?" "Yes, but only when kindness fails." Novice humor makers, then, might take a lesson from first-graders and look for double meanings in words.

• Rehearse favorite stories or funny lines that you've heard or read. No genetic defect keeps people from remembering jokes; the ability is acquired. Start with simple one-liners that you find particularly appealing. (I always thought I couldn't remember or tell jokes, but I find that Mae West's little gems are always at the top of my cognitive deck.)

• Spend a rainy afternoon with a friend constructing some homemade humor. One idea: Write your own captions for one-frame cartoons. Or make up a funny job description for the work you do. In one of Joel Goodman's workshops, a group of teachers came up with this: "A teacher is someone who can drink three cups of coffee before eight o'clock and hold them until three."

• Beware of humor that is overly hostile. As we've seen, hostile humor sometimes has its place, but most people do not appreciate having a Don Rickles type in their life. All too often, "But I was only kidding" is merely a lame excuse for a vindictive verbal jab. And really mean-spirited "humor" is not likely to do the perpetrator any good either; studies of emotion show that when people are physiologically aroused, hostile humor tends to increase anger, not reduce it.

Finally, don't take *any* of this advice too seriously. The healing power of humor resides in your attitude, not in your comic cleverness. And conversely, without this attitude, all the one-liners in the world won't help— witness the sad cases of Freddie Prinze and John Belushi. In the end, it's not exercises or laugh lessons that cure our sobersidedness, but the wisdom to appreciate our own foibles and limitations and to find amusement in them. This truth is beautifully captured in an old Jewish story:

An aged rabbi was lying on his deathbed, surrounded by his admiring students. The students had arranged themselves in the order of their accomplishments, with the most brilliant at the rabbi's shoulder and the densest at the end of the line. "Tell us, Rabbi," said the brilliant student, "what are your final words to us?"

"My final words," whispered the old man, "are . . . that life is a river."

"The rabbi says that life is a river," said the brilliant student to his neighbor, and the message quickly passed down the line: "The rabbi says that life is a river." "The rabbi says that life is a river."

Finally, the rabbi's words reached the simpleton at the end of the line, who scratched his head in puzzlement when he heard them. "What does the rabbi mean, that 'life is a river'?" he asked the student next to him. His question passed back up the line: "What does the rabbi mean, that 'life is a river'?" "What does the rabbi mean, that 'life is a river'?"

When the question reached the most brilliant student, he bent over the rabbi and said, "Rabbi, what do you mean, 'life is a river'?" Anxiously, he put his ear next to the old man's mouth, for the wise one was drawing his last breaths.

And the wise man shrugged and croaked, "So it's not a river!"

A Test of Humor Under Pressure

This test contains selected items from a longer test, The Situational Humor Response Questionnaire, used by psychologists Rod A. Martin and Herbert M. Lefcourt in their research on humor and stress.

Directions for Part I: We all have our own ideas about what situations are funny and when humor is appropriate. The following items describe hypothetical situations from everyday life. For each item, try to recall a time when you were in the situation. If you cannot remember an actual experience, try to *imagine* yourself in such a situation. Then circle the appropriate letter to indicate how you responded or would have responded. Do not spend too much time on any one item. There are no right or wrong answers.

1. If you were awakened from a deep sleep in the middle of the night by the ringing of the telephone, and it was an old friend who was just passing through town and had decided to call and say hello—
   a. I wouldn't have been particularly amused.
   b. I would have felt somewhat amused but would not have laughed.
   c. I would have been able to laugh at something funny my friend said.
   d. I would have been able to laugh and say something funny to my friend.
   e. I would have laughed heartily with my friend.

2. You had accidentally hurt yourself and had to spend a few days in bed. During that time in bed, how would you have responded?
   a. I would not have found anything particularly amusing.
   b. I would have smiled occasionally.
   c. I would have smiled a lot and laughed from time to time.
   d. I would have found quite a lot to laugh about.
   e. I would have laughed heartily much of the time.

3. When you have been engaged in some lengthy physical activity (e.g., swimming, hiking, skiing), and you and your friends found yourselves to be completely exhausted . . .
   a. I wouldn't have found it particularly amusing.
   b. I would have been amused, but wouldn't have shown it outwardly.
   c. I would have smiled.
   d. I would have laughed.
   e. I would have laughed heartily.

4. You were travelling in a car in the winter and suddenly the car spun around on an ice patch and came to rest facing the wrong way on the opposite side of the highway. You were relieved to find that no one was hurt and no damage had been done to the car . . .
   a. I wouldn't have found it particularly amusing.
   b. I would have been amused, but wouldn't have shown it outwardly.
   c. I would have smiled.
   d. I would have laughed.
   e. I would have laughed heartily.

5. *If you were watching a movie or TV program with some friends and you found one scene particularly funny, but no one else appeared to find it humorous, how would you have reacted most commonly?*

    a. I would have concluded that I must have misunderstood something or that it wasn't really funny.

    b. I would have "smiled to myself," but wouldn't have shown my amusement outwardly.

    c. I would have smiled visibly.

    d. I would have laughed aloud.

    e. I would have laughed heartily.

6. *You thought you recognized a friend in a crowded room. You attracted the person's attention and hurried over to him/her, but when you got there you discovered you had made a mistake and the person was a total stranger . . .*

    a. I would not have been particularly amused.

    b. I would have been amused, but wouldn't have shown it outwardly.

    c. I would have smiled.

    d. I would have laughed.

    e. I would have laughed heartily.

7. *If you were eating in a restaurant with some friends and the waiter accidentally spilled a drink on you . . .*

    a. I would not have been particularly amused.

    b. I would have been amused, but wouldn't have shown it outwardly.

    c. I would have smiled.

    d. I would have laughed.

    e. I would have laughed heartily.

8. *If you were crossing a street at a crosswalk and an impatient car driver, who had to stop for you, honked the horn . . .*

    a. I would not have been amused.

    b. I would have been amused, but wouldn't have shown it outwardly.

    c. I would have smiled.

    d. I would have laughed.

    e. I would have laughed heartily.

9. *If there had been a computer error and you had spent all morning standing in line-ups at various offices trying to get the problem sorted out . . .*

    a. I wouldn't have found it particularly amusing.

    b. I would have been able to experience some amusement, but wouldn't have shown it.

    c. I would have smiled a lot.

    d. I would have laughed a lot.

    e. I would have laughed heartily.

10. *In the past, if your girlfriend/boyfriend decided to break up with you because she/he had found someone else, and a few days later you were telling a good friend about it . . .*

    a. I wouldn't have found any humor in the situation.

    b. I would have been able to experience some amusement, but wouldn't have shown it.

    c. I would have been able to smile.

d. I would have been able to laugh.

e. I would have laughed quite a lot.

Directions for Part II: The remaining items consist of personal descriptions. For each item, circle the number that reflects your agreement or disagreement with the statement as it applies to you.

	Strongly Agree	Mildly Agree	Mildly Disagree	Strongly Disagree
11. I often lose my sense of humor when I'm having problems.	1	2	3	4
12. I rarely look for something comical to say when I am in tense situations.	1	2	3	4
13. I must admit that my life would probably be easier if I had more of a sense of humor.	1	2	3	4
14. People who are always out to be funny are really irresponsible and are not to be relied on.	1	2	3	4
15. Even though they may look different, humorous and depressed people really have many common traits.	1	2	3	4
16. In my experience humor is rarely a very effective way of coping with problems.	1	2	3	4
17. When I engage in discussions where one person pokes fun at other people's arguments, I get the impression that he is trying to cover up his own ignorance.	1	2	3	4
18. It is my impression that those who try to be funny really do it to hide their lack of self-confidence.	1	2	3	4

Total Points: _____

To score yourself: In Part I, for each item, an *a* answer earns 1 point, *b* earns 2, *c* earns 3, *d* earns 4, and *e* earns 5. In Part II, the number circled indicates the points earned for each item. Add up all your points to get your total. The lowest possible score is 18, the highest 82. A score of 47 is about average, and about two-thirds of all people score between 40 and 54. If your total is over 54, you probably put an exceptionally high value on humor and use it in a variety of stressful situations. But a score lower than 40 may mean that you are taking life's little annoyances too seriously. If so, you may want to ponder the traditional Jewish advice for coping with problems: "Your health comes first; you can hang yourself later."

CAROLE WADE is a psychologist and social science writer with a special interest in sex roles and human sexuality. After taking her Ph.D. at Stanford University in 1973, she taught for a year at the University of New Mexico, then spent two years as an editor at *Psychology Today,* where she broadened her purview of psychology and became addicted to science writing. A confirmed West Coast person, she returned to teaching when the magazine moved east, and spent the next eight years at San Diego Mesa College. During this period the challenge of teaching several thousand undergraduates, continuing her writing, and rearing two wonderfully spirited children forced her to develop a previously dormant sense of humor. Dr. Wade now lives in the San Francisco Bay Area, where she continues to teach part-time at the College of Marin but spends the bulk of her time writing. She is the author of *Human Sexuality* (Harcourt Brace Jovanovich, 1982) and is coauthor (with Carol Tavris) of *The Longest War: Sex Differences in Perspective,* (Harcourt Brace Jovanovich, 1984) as well as a forthcoming psychology textbook. When she is not at her word processor, she enjoys hiking, cooking, and laughing at her own jokes.

Further Reading

Cousins, Norman. *Anatomy of an Illness as Perceived by the Patient.* New York: Norton, 1979. Cousins describes how he used humor and vitamin C to fight a debilitating disease, and speculates on the role of humor in mental and physical health.

Laughing Matters magazine, available from The Humor Project, 179 Spring Street, Dept. A, Saratoga Springs, NY 12866. A quarterly publication that is full of jokes, stories, and practical tips on finding humor in ordinary situations. The Humor Project also sells books of and about humor, and runs humor workshops and courses for educators, helping professionals, businesspeople, and other groups.

McGhee, Paul E. "The Role of Laughter and Humor in Growing Up Female." In *Becoming Female,* edited by Claire Kopp. New York: Plenum, 1979. A scholarly review of research on sex differences in humor and how they develop.

Mindess, Harvey. *Laughter and Liberation.* Los Angeles: Nash Publishing Corp., 1971. Although marred by the inclusion of a few sexist jokes and cartoons and an unsatisfactory chapter on humor and women's liberation, this book is nonetheless an eloquent, enlightening, and entertaining treatise on the role humor can play in our lives.

Rosten, Leo. *Leo Rosten's Giant Book of Laughter*. New York: Crown, 1985. Any book of humor that suits your own comic tastes.

15

Coping with Stress:
Problems in Perspective

PHILLIP SHAVER AND
CARY O'CONNOR

Women Under Stress

• When her husband was killed six months ago in an accident at his workplace, Melinda A. lost not only her partner and closest confidant, but also any chance of keeping the family's income above the poverty line. She received some compensation from her husband's death benefits, but the amount wasn't even equal to what they had paid in rent on their three-bedroom house, and Melinda was forced to move to a much cheaper two-bedroom apartment. In the new neighborhood her boys, seven and five, were having trouble adjusting to the change in schools and playmates, and were often irritable and unhappy. Melinda was beginning to feel overwhelmed, hopeless, and exhausted.

• Cheryl B. thought when she accepted her current job as an administrative assistant for a medium-sized computer company that she was beginning a satisfying long-term career, one with great potential for advancement. After two years, however, she had recently been overlooked for the third time when a higher position in the company became available, a job for which she felt well qualified. Each time upper management had brought in a bright but inexperienced young man from outside the company and spent much time and money training him in work that Cheryl was already familiar with. She felt it was unfair and possibly discriminatory, and she was spending more and more time sitting at her desk too upset to concentrate, sometimes even crying in the bathroom. She felt resentful, suffered from insomnia and headaches, and when she did sleep, dreamt of sabotaging the company.

• Joan C. expected to be able to leave her infant daughter with her widowed mother every weekday while she returned to her job as an artist in a rapidly growing advertising firm. The company was glad to have Joan back after her short maternity leave, and she had been excited about both her new child and her continuing career. After her first month back and without any warning signs, Joan's mother became seriously ill and not only was unable to care for the baby, but required a great deal of care herself. Her mother moved into their guest room, and while Joan's husband went to a demanding job that required him to spend most of his time away from home, Joan felt it necessary to quit her job to stay home with mother and daughter. She felt terrible about missing a key phase in the growth of the company and worried that she would lose seniority and be left behind as time went on.

Stress, Illness, and Well-Being

Death of a spouse, problems of single parenthood, sex discrimination in the workplace, the burdens of caring single-handedly for children and needy relatives—these are some of the problems that weigh heavily on American women in the 1980s. They are some of the major causes of women's *stress.*

What is stress exactly? Although the term has quickly come to occupy a central place in the national vocabulary, few people realize how difficult it is to define.

The term was first made popular by medical physiologist Hans Selye in a 1956 book, *The Stress of Life.* Selye noticed that many different kinds of events—extreme heat, cold, noise, food deprivation, painful injury, and exposure to illness-causing toxins, viruses, and bacteria—have similar effects on the body. At first, he said, the body shows an "alarm reaction," involving increased activity of the heart, arteries, and adrenal glands; a shrinking of the lymph nodes; and interference with digestion. These are signs of the body's efforts to meet an intense and demanding challenge to its equilibrium; they are part of the fight-or-flight response that must have frequently saved our ancestors from sudden death and disaster. If the stressor persists, however, and is not powerful enough to severely damage or kill the person, a "stage of resistance" sets in, during which many of the adverse symptoms of stress disappear or are actually reversed. This is a sign that the body has, for a while at least, successfully met the challenge. Unfortunately, if the stressor persists, the body eventually enters a "stage of exhaustion," indicating that the costs of resistance and adaptation were simply too great. As stress researcher Robert Sapolsky explains:

> The stress response is magnificently designed to get the body through an acute crisis—providing quick energy, shutting down inessentials, buffering pain, sharpening the mind—but it is a poor way to deal with chronic stress. . . . Chronic stress depletes the body of stored energy, causing muscle wastage and fatigue. The short-term adaptiveness of increased blood pressure becomes, during chronic stress, the maladaptiveness of hypertension. The short-term need for supression of digestion, reproduction, and disease surveillance leads, after prolonged periods, to stress-induced stomach ulcers, impotency and amenorrhea, and increased risk of illness.

In Selye's words, "Just as any inanimate machine gradually wears out, so does the human machine sooner or later become the victim of constant wear and tear." The goal of stress-management efforts, then, is to postpone the inevitable breakdown until "later"—preferably well into old age.

Since 1956 the emphasis in stress research has become increasingly psychological. Although Selye mentioned that psychological stressors—virtually anything that causes strong and prolonged *emotional* reactions—are at least as important as physical stressors (heat, cold, noise), his research did not explore the psychological aspects of stress in any detail.

His general idea, that stress is part of the person's *attempt to adapt to important environmental changes,* suggested to social scientists that they identify and measure the major events that call for human adaptation. Table 1 lists some of these events, taken from two of the most popular measures of the "life events" that require significant personal adjustment, change, or adaptation. Researchers constructed the lists partly by noticing that certain events seemed frequently to precede the onset of physical illness (suggesting that the stress of dealing with these events *caused* the illness) and partly by asking large numbers of people to name stressful events or events that require significant personal changes or adjustments. The list in Table 1, like all such lists, includes universal events of human significance (for example, marriages, births, illnesses, injuries, deaths, and changes in occupation or wealth), plus several stressors common in advanced industrialized societies (legal battles, problems in the corporate workplace, mortgage foreclosures).

Notice that the list, while largely negative in tone, contains some events that are usually considered positive: getting married, birth of a child, being released from jail, etc. These are included because researchers believed originally that *any* event requiring personal adaptation or adjustment could cause stress; and marriage, childbirth, and release from jail certainly cause changes that call for adaptive responses. Nevertheless, several recent studies have shown that negative events predict subsequent illness much better than positive events do, suggesting that prolonged negative emotions (such as anxiety, fear, anger, resentment, and depression) are the problem, not challenges and readjustments per se.

While the original interest of those who study stress and its relation to illness was the effect of major life events, recent work indicates that stress is also caused by everyday disappointments, conflicts, frustrations, and threats. Researchers call these "daily hassles." (Table 2 lists some of them.) Everyday hassles actually predict the onset of stress-related illnesses *better* than major life events do, and major life events are often stressful just to the extent that they cause an increase in hassles. Perhaps "daily hassles" predict illnesses better than life events because hassles are closely related to a woman's *negative feelings* about what is happening in her life. An event such as discovering that your lover has been unfaithful would almost always be interpreted as negative or "bad," but *how* bad it is, how many and what types of negative emotions it generates, and whether there are any possible benefits to be found in the situation are all variable and depend on the person and the situation. On the other hand, by labeling the planning of meals a *hassle,* the respondent reveals her negative feelings about it. Clearly, it represents a negative or stressful experience for her, otherwise she would view it simply as a nondisturbing, neutral part of her day.

Notice that stress, or negative emotion, usually results from *interpretations* of events, not directly from events themselves. This is why researchers have a hard time saying in general whether becoming pregnant, getting married, changing jobs, and so on, will be stressful or not; it all depends on whether the person in question views these events as threatening, worrisome, or undesirable.

Although we often think of emotions as irrational and uncontrollable—as powerful forces that hit us from "outside"—actually they are caused largely by our own interpretations of events. While many of the events do hit us from outside, our interpretations of them are "internal" and not nearly as

TABLE 1.

Kinds of Events Included in Popular Life-Events Stress Scales

Death of a child or spouse; death of a close relative or friend

Serious physical illness or injury; being raped or assaulted; inability to get adequate treatment for a serious illness or injury

Being arrested; being on trial; being convicted of a crime; going to jail

Marital separation or divorce; breakup of a love relationship; deterioration in the quality of a marriage or love affair

Pregnancy; birth of a child; onset of menopause; discovery that one cannot have children; miscarriage or stillbirth; adoption of a child

Losing a home through fire, flood, or other disaster

Discovering that one's spouse or love partner is unfaithful

Getting married; being reunited with a separated spouse or lover; a major improvement in the quality of a marriage or love affair

Being acquitted of a crime or released from jail

Building or remodelling a home; moving from one residence to another

Suffering a major business loss or failure; getting fired; going on welfare; losing a substantial sum of money; getting robbed

Enjoying a major business success; getting promoted; going off welfare; winning or inheriting a substantial sum of money

Retiring

Starting a new job, business, or profession; graduating from an educational program

Obtaining a large mortgage or loan; having a mortgage or loan foreclosed

Someone moving into or out of the household; someone not moving out after being expected to

Major conflicts with family members, coworkers, in-laws, neighbors

TABLE 2.
Examples of Stress-Producing Daily Hassles

Social obligations, unexpected company, nonfamily members living in your house, financial responsibility for others not living with you

Inconsiderate smokers; troublesome neighbors

Your children quarreling; their noise, complaints, and messes

Troubling thoughts about failure; concerns about meeting high standards or getting ahead; regrets over past decisions

Thoughts about death, concern about the meaning of life; conflicts over what to do about your future; inner conflicts, having trouble making decisions

Concerns about owing or being owed money, about taxes, about getting credit, about money for clothing, food, health care, housing, basic emergencies, etc.

Too many responsibilities; too much to do; too many meetings; too many interruptions

Unchallenging work; dissatisfaction with boss or job; problems with coworkers, clients, or employees; problems on job due to being a woman

Not enough time for family, for entertainment and relaxation, for doing things you need to do

Being lonely; too much time on hands; friends or relatives too far away; not seeing enough people

Physical illness or decline; concerns about own health or health of a family member; side effects of medication; problems about sex, weight, appearance, energy level; difficulty seeing or hearing

Planning or preparing meals; shopping; caring for pets; yardwork; home maintenance

Wasting time; having to wait; transportation problems; filling out forms

Misplacing or losing things; silly practical mistakes; difficulty with arithmetic, reading, writing, or spelling skills

Noise; crime; traffic; pollution; the weather; television; news events; rising prices; neighborhood deterioration inexplicable or uncontrollable as we think. For example, suppose the company you work for is unexpectedly going bankrupt, and you are about to lose your job. Needless to say, that is a potentially stressful event, one about which you are likely to have many negative feelings. In fact, you (like Melinda A. in our first example) may feel overwhelmed by these feelings, as if they were an outside force inundating you. If you pause to notice the interpretations that cause these emotions, however, you will discover something like this: "Oh, my God! If the company goes bankrupt, I am out of a job. Without a job, I can't pay my rent. If I have to move, my children will have to change schools. They won't like that, and my life with them will be miserable. I will be helpless and hopeless. What am I going to do?"

This chain of thoughts is (a) not irrational in itself, but actually quite logical; (b) not imposed from the outside, but constructed by you; and (c) not immutable or necessarily overwhelming. In principle, since you are generating the chain of thoughts that is triggering the flood of negative emotions (shock, dread, fear, anxiety, helplessness, loss, etc.), you can alter its course to a considerable extent. You are not a passive victim unless you allow yourself to be. In this sense emotions are no more unreasonable than the thoughts that cause them. If the thoughts are inappropriate or exaggerated, then the resulting emotion will be, too.

One of the common triggers of negative emotions is a *violation of expectations.* You thought your job would continue for years and you built your image of yourself and your future on that assumption; now suddenly the assumption proves incorrect and your vision of the future is shattered. If this unpleasant surprise seems *unfair* to you, your main emotional reaction will be anger. If what bothers you more is the nature and degree of *pain and discomfort* you will suffer in the future, your main emotion will be anxiety. If the whole affair makes you feel *helpless, hopeless, and lost,* like just giving up and lying down to die, then your main emotion is sadness or depression. If your interpretation vacillates among these three (injustice, uncertainty, and helplessness), your feelings will include a parade or mixture of anger, apprehension, and depression. Far from being inexplicable or imposed on you from outside, all of these feelings are natural consequences of your own thoughts.

Anger, including all of its physiological and behavioral components, is a sensible response to injury, especially if it motivates you to correct an *alterable* source of injustice. Fear or anxiety is a sensible response if it causes you to prepare efficiently for an uncertain future; it tells you that you may need help or protection and should motivate you to find it. Sadness is a natural consequence of failure, defeat, or loss. If you really are defeated, it may be wise to give up a hopeless plan, rest and reconsider, and then adopt a more productive course. Which of these responses makes the most sense depends entirely on an accurate appraisal of the situation. Thus, the supposed unreasonableness or irrationality of emotion only holds when emotions are caused by unreasonable interpretations or appraisals of events. An important part of coping with stress is learning to make accurate, constructive appraisals.

Coping with Stress

By now it should be clear that stress is usually caused by something more complicated than life-altering events or even daily pressures and hassles. It comes largely from interpretations of and reactions to events and hassles. But even considering that events in the environment are filtered through your appraisals, there is another important factor that mediates the effects of stress on well-being—your *coping resources.*

According to Richard Lazarus, a distinguished psychologist who studies stress and coping, the term "coping" refers broadly to *efforts to manage* environmental and internal demands and conflicts among demands. There are different types of coping, some more successful in a particular situation than others. Some methods attack the problem directly; some work on the appraisal process; and some, such as relaxation or exercise, intervene between the negative event or situation as the person interprets it and the effects it could have on health—exhaustion or ulcers, for instance. The role of coping in the overall stress process is shown in the accompanying diagram.

As an example, think of Cheryl, whose frustration at being overlooked for promotion has led to an inability to concentrate, sleep comfortably, or even get much pleasure out of life. She undoubtedly has a large number of options for coping with her situation, and some are sure to be more useful than others. She could attempt to solve the problem directly by confronting those in charge, suggesting that she should be seriously considered for the next vacancy, and waiting to see what happens. She could decide that she was lucky to learn how this organization works before she spent too much time there, then use her acquired skills as a basis for landing a new job. Or she could stay where she is, not say anything and still hope for the best, meanwhile enjoying her friends, exercising vigorously to release tension and di-

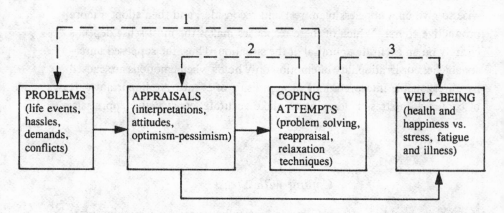

How Stress Works: This diagram summarizes links between all of the factors discussed in this chapter. "Problems" (including life events and hassles) lead to "Appraisals" or interpretations that can *directly* affect "Well-Being" or can affect "Coping Attempts," which (by solving problems, reappraising, or inducing relaxation) *indirectly* affect "Well-Being." The dotted coping arrow labeled "1" represents problem solving, the one labeled "2" represents reappraisals, and "3" represents relaxation techniques.

vert her energies, and adding to her self-esteem in the areas of friendship and athletics.

These are examples of the three major kinds of coping: (1) problem solving; (2) rethinking, reappraising, or reevaluating the situation; and (3) reducing or avoiding the physical effects of stress.

PROBLEM SOLVING: ALTERING OR ELIMINATING THE STRESSOR

The first kind of coping, if successful, makes any further coping unnecessary. The best solution, if it is feasible, is to deal directly with the stressor and seek to alter or eliminate its problematic aspects.

To return to the earlier example of losing your job, instead of becoming overwhelmed by negative emotions and fantasies of disaster, you could begin immediately to *analyze the problem thoroughly, generate potential solutions,* and *choose the best available alternative.* The first phase of problem solving, analyzing the problem, is likely to be the most difficult if you are overwhelmed with negative images and feelings. This is why a *combination* of problem-focused and emotion-focused coping strategies (that is, expressing your feelings, interpreting the event in the most favorable possible light, and relaxing and keeping yourself fit while also trying to solve the problem) is almost always desirable. And indeed, recent research shows that people generally do cope in all three ways simultaneously. Most of us have learned to try to keep problems in perspective while seeking actively to solve them.

Begin by figuring out exactly what the problem is. Be aware that there is a difference between sorting out a problem and being obsessed by it. Your employer is going bankrupt—when? How long do you have, realistically, to seek alternative employment? Are you entitled to termination benefits? Do you have savings or investments to tide you over while looking for a new job? Can you sell your house and move into a cheaper apartment or condominium?

Are there hidden advantages to the problematic situation? Maybe this job has been less than satisfactory for years, but you were too entrenched to consider alternatives. Maybe your house has become a burden, requiring more and more attention and time-consuming repairs. Maybe moving would be a relief.

Is there anyone who can help analyze the problem? Many times when trouble strikes, people are reluctant to share their problems with friends, family members, or professionals. Yet research shows that social supports, including both practical help (for example, financial assistance or professional advice) and psychological support, are among the most effective reducers of stress. Attempting to explain the problem to someone else, especially while expressing or examining your feelings, is a good way to get it clearer in your own mind. Are you entitled to consultation with a personnel manager? Does your insurance cover visits to a therapist or counselor? You have probably already paid for some forms of help in one way or another: through deductions from your paycheck, visible or invisible, or by doing favors for your friends and relatives. Don't feel bad about collecting when you need to.

Once your alternatives become clear, start exploring the best ones in detail. When you are pretty sure you know which is best, take action. Conflict is costly and delay can be disastrous. If the problem is medical, seek the best advice available (from whatever source you trust) and then follow it. If the problem is social—for example, you are dissatisfied with your marriage to an alcoholic or are chronically lonely—take action. Join your spouse in a couples' treatment program, if you still love him, or seek competent individual counseling to talk about separating from him if you feel that love is no longer possible. Join social groups if you are lonely; no one ever met a favorite friend or a Prince Charming while sitting home alone watching TV.

The immediate goal is to solve the problem at hand, to eliminate or alter the stressor. But there are also some long-term costs and gains at stake: your self-esteem, your sense of control and effectiveness, and your feeling that life is rewarding and meaningful. Wallowing in self-pity, unnecessarily delaying action, vacillating indefinitely, falling into perpetual helplessness—these are the terrible costs of failing to attack the problem boldly. In the long run, they are likely to be more deadly than the problem immediately at hand.

In some cases, sad to say, there simply is no solution to the problem, at least as initially conceptualized. A woman's lover has found someone new and is definitely going to leave; a woman's mortgage is being foreclosed, and neither she nor her family and friends have the money to prevent it. A woman may learn she is terminally ill and be forced to confront death. In such cases there are only two workable "solutions": Admit that you are stymied and go ahead and cry (preferably on the shoulder of someone who really cares about you), and then pick yourself up and decide what to do next. Recast the problem from "How can I beat this rap?" to "What of value can I do now that I've lost that one?" There are alternatives available (alternative psychological stances, at least) even in the worst situations.

REASSESSING THE STRESSFUL SITUATION

As we have said, all negative feelings, except physical pain (and sometimes even that), are reactions to interpretations or appraisals of events, not to the events themselves. Therefore, one of the most effective ways to cope with stress, short of eliminating the stressor by direct problem solving, is to choose one's appraisals wisely. The following list of psychological coping mechanisms, which could be expanded almost indefinitely, illustrates the range of strategies available.

Problem or Challenge? Loss or Learning Experience? According to Lazarus and other stress researchers, the appraisal process contains two parts: primary and secondary appraisal. Primary appraisal is an immediate, global judgment concerning whether the event in question is good or bad for you. Secondary appraisals are more detailed evaluations of the good or bad implications of an event, including judgments concerning your capacity to respond effectively. Primary appraisal might include the global sense that your employer's bankruptcy is bad for you; secondary appraisal might include the realization that the problem isn't really so severe, since your savings are adequate to cover a prolonged job search.

To the extent that your primary and secondary appraisals can take account of the potentially positive side of events in question, your emotional reactions will be less uniformly negative and hence less stressful. One way to do this is to be always on the lookout for what is challenging, interesting, or humorous about life's unexpected twists and turns. Challenge, interest, and humor are varieties of happiness; they stimulate coping energy, increase the likelihood that other people will enjoy helping, and increase the probability of a happy conclusion.

We know from extensive research with both animals and humans that an anxious sense of helplessness leads frequently to depression. Curiosity, challenge, interest, optimism, and humor are powerful enemies of helplessness and defeat.

Psychologically Containing the Problem. Researchers who study people's reactions to success and failure, as well as those who study the determinants of depression, have discovered three particular kinds of thinking that determine emotional reactions. The first is whether you believe that the cause of a problem lies *in* you, in other people or the environment. For example, when you fail at some task you have set for yourself or when life just doesn't seem to be going well for you, you can attribute the problem primarily to yourself or to events outside yourself. Say you are having difficulty completing tasks at work. Is this your fault or is it the fault of coworkers who fail to satisfactorily manage their end of assignments? If you judge the problem to be your fault, your risk of depression is increased.

Second, do you see the problem as temporary or long-lasting? If temporary, the costs of coping and the risks of depression are low; if permanent ("Things are lousy and will never get better"), the risk of depression is much higher. Such pessimism is rarely justified, and its consequences can be deadly.

Third, do you see the problem as specific to the work realm or is it just one of many signs that you are hopelessly inept *in general?* (In the researchers' lingo, is the problem specific or global?) If the problem is specific, you can take comfort from all of the other areas of life in which you are doing well. "All right," you say, "maybe I'm not much good as a report editor but I'm an excellent artist, decorator, and amateur tennis player; I'm a good friend and an accomplished lover." Probably all you need is a weekend or several-evening course in editing; no call for depression here. If you tend to generalize from one failure or shortcoming to your entire life, you are a candidate for depression.

In his helpful book *Feeling Good: The New Mood Therapy,* psychiatrist David Burns calls the tendency to overgeneralize failures "catastrophizing." We exaggerate our own ordinary mistakes into enormous personal failings, and minimize our personal strengths by seeing them as trivial. Every error becomes a catastrophe, and the way we feel about ourselves becomes dangerously distorted simply because we view our "performances" in life too negatively.

The worst reaction is the one involving, all at once, internality, stability, and globality: "I am a klutz, it's my fault; I've always been a hopeless klutz and probably always will be; and I'm a klutz from arithmetic to zoology, there's almost nothing I do well." The corresponding analysis of one's social life is just as self-defeating: "I'm an unlovable, hateful person; I'll always be unlovable; almost everything about me is inadequate and unlovable." This kind of thinking can push its victim into a well of depression from which escape seems impossible.

It pays, then, to be very careful about the explanations you accept for negative events in your life. Whenever possible, notice the external factors that contribute to your trouble; rarely is it all your fault. Not every failed conversation occurs because you were awkward or uninteresting—it's just as likely to be the other person's shortcomings, or simply a mismatch of interests and personalities. Second, even when you *are* at fault, don't succumb to the depressing thought that your fate is unchangeable. Figure out what you can do to correct the error next time. And don't make the mistake of allowing this specific error to mask, in your own mind or in your dealings with others, your many good qualities, which have nothing to do with this single mistake.

Putting the Stressor in Perspective. A related coping strategy involves stepping back from your current problem and viewing it in relation to your most important priorities. This is difficult to do, because one feature of negative emotions is that they naturally and forcefully pull your attention toward the problem that, through your interpretation of it, caused the negative reaction in the first place. The human nervous system is built so that the perception "angry bear in the campsite" interrupts your concentration on cooking dinner, playing backgammon, or dancing around the campfire. Unfortunately, the same mechanism can crowd out items of logically higher priority.

How many headaches are caused each day by people's urgent frustrations with traffic jams, slow bank clerks, and broken vending machines? Very rarely do the lost fifteen minutes, or fifty cents, matter when viewed in perspective. The narrow view causes fears about new gray hairs and wrinkles to crowd out the many chances for positive life changes still before us. Each of us probably spends more hours worrying about minor signs of aging than contemplating the more important but less concrete ways to make the coming years more meaningful, happier, and healthier.

One way people can counteract the narrowing of attention that negative emotion produces is to purposefully pull back from the annoyance or disturbance and psychologically "distance" themselves from it. With a little effort and practice, anyone can learn to do this. Try interrupting your train of thought when it begins to pull you into a dark tunnel of upsetting ideas. Remember that they are *your* thoughts and you can change them. Then try to put the problem in perspective; think about it in relation to the rest of your life, including your eventual death. Think of other possible outcomes besides the one you are afraid of or angry about, and consider what you can do to make the positive ones materialize.

Positive Comparisons. Psychologist Shelley Taylor and her colleagues have studied women's methods of coping with breast cancer, concluding that one of the most common and effective methods is to notice how well one is doing in comparison with real or imagined other people. This is a well-known strategy, unfortunately made unpalatable by parents telling their children, "Eat! The children in [whichever country seems most destitute at the time] are starving." You are supposed to feel lucky by comparison even if you can't stand lima beans. As irrelevant as this argument seems to children, it is a venerable coping strategy for adults.

The women in Taylor's studies coped successfully by continually noticing how well they were doing compared with others who suffered from cancer. Married women who had lost a breast, for example, said they felt better off than single women because they didn't have to worry about telling future boyfriends of their loss. Women who had had lumpectomies (removal of the lump only) felt fortunate that they hadn't had mastectomies. Mastectomy patients thought themselves well off compared to women with cancer throughout their bodies. These positive comparisons not only made the women feel better, but also enhanced their self-esteem and sense of control over events.

Distraction and Denial. For a long while denial had a bad name. Psychologists viewed it as a primitive defense mechanism whose consequences included being out of touch with reality. But in cases where reality serves up a problem for which there is no solution, or at least no immediate solution, what's so bad about losing touch with it? In recent years, as psychologists have moved from the concept of "defense" to the more constructive concept of "coping," they have looked more sympathetically on people's attempts to ignore problems they cannot solve. This strategy frees their energies for other, more rewarding activities.

Recently, we witnessed an auto accident near our office building. Three cars collided at a busy intersection and all were badly damaged, although fortunately no one was injured. The group in one car got out, surveyed the damage, called the police from a phone booth, and, hearing that the police wouldn't arrive for fifteen minutes, shrugged their shoulders, smiled, and went into a nearby café for Italian ice cream. The other two drivers, one of whom was primarily at fault, scowled, whined, and bitterly accused each other of despicable driving habits. Who do you think inched closer toward stomach ulceration—the resigned and distracted ice-cream eaters or the problem-preoccupied grumblers? Maybe the former were temporarily distracting themselves and denying the damage that had been done to their car, the damper that had been placed on their immediate plans, and so forth. But they saved themselves a mountain of stress in a situation where worrying and complaining wouldn't have helped.

Several years ago, when Daniel Patrick Moynihan (now a senator) was a social policy adviser to President Nixon, he received a lot of flak for writing a memo in which he suggested "benign neglect" as a temporary strategy for dealing with racial issues. The flak was justified because, in that case, solutions or at least partial solutions *were* available. But the phrase "benign neglect" was a good one. Many parents give themselves stomach pains and headaches as well as insomnia worrying, say, about how to control the lives of their teenage children. Part of the difficulty is the parents' inability to accept the fact that their children are growing up. The best strategy in many cases is benign neglect, because there simply is no more effective alternative, no solution that would benefit either the teenagers or the parents. Benign neglect can be well exercised while the parents play golf, go to the movies, or do anything else of value that gets them out of their children's hair. Distraction? Yes. Denial? Maybe. But sometimes a very healthy strategy.

People differ in the degree to which they generally seek information about threats to their well-being. Some, for example, want to know before an operation as much as possible about the nature of their malady, the surgical procedures to be employed, the dangers inherent in the procedure, and what they can expect in the way of sensations and regimens once the operation is over. Others would just as soon get on with the operation; the less said or thought about it, the better. Psychologists call the former "sensitizers" and the latter "repressors" or "deniers."

If being sensitive to and mulling over a problem contributes to its solution, then sensitizing is beneficial and denial is dangerous. For example, denying that a lump in your breast might be malignant can contribute to a very dangerous delay in diagnosis. But when nothing constructive can be done about a problem, distraction and denial often prove beneficial. Research shows that before most operations, when nothing can be done but wait, "sensitizers" waste time and energy worrying, while "deniers" relax—

a difference in attitude that contributes measurably to the more rapid recovery of the deniers.

Forgiving and Forgetting. One of the most stressful clusters of negative emotions is unresolved resentment, hostility, humiliation, and hatred based on an event that happened long ago. For her book *Pathfinders*, writer Gail Sheehy set out to discover how people who negotiate life's major transitions successfully differ from those who don't. One of the things she learned is that "pathfinders" let go of old negative feelings. They don't hold grudges, don't invest their energies in settling old scores, don't dwell on past failures, and don't feel that the world owes them.

This reminds us of a Tibetan Buddhist attitude called *maitri,* "unconditional friendliness toward oneself," along with the corresponding attitude of openness and trust toward others and toward nature. When someone you love and respect blunders, your attitude is likely to be one of supportive sympathy and forgiveness. After all, this is a genuinely good person who didn't mean to harm anyone. The same attitude should hold for oneself and for life in general. After all, you are a good person; you are genuinely trying, sometimes under extremely difficult circumstances, to do what you believe is right. If occasionally you make a mistake, as everyone does, have sympathy for yourself and offer yourself supportive forgiveness. You will then find it easier to do the same for others, and ultimately for humanity in general. Wise people realize, and feel in their hearts, that humanity, though clearly imperfect, is genuinely good, creative, funny, and worthy of love. When foibles and failings prevail temporarily, be quick to forgive—preferably because you are truly generous and loving, but if for no better reason because you don't need the headaches, ulcers, and feelings of bitterness that holding onto resentment will bring you. Let them go, pass them by.

Maintaining a Sense of Humor. Considered separately, the different coping strategies seem quite distinct: getting distance from the problem, distracting oneself, reconceptualizing the problem, attempting to increase positive feelings (through positive comparisons, for example, or by maintaining hope and optimism). Remarkably, nature has provided human beings with a health-enhancing blend of all four—*humor.* Joking and laughing about a frustrating or frightening situation breaks its hold on our thoughts and feelings and allows us to ignore the seriousness of the problem for a moment while we gain a new, more relaxed perspective on it. (See Chap. 14.)

If you doubt that relief from stress is a major purpose of humor, take a few minutes to scan the titles in the humor section of your local bookstore. Erma Bombeck, the well-known newspaper columnist, has collected her warm and funny observations in several volumes: *At Wit's End; If Life Is a*

Bowl of Cherries, What Am I Doing in the Pits?; and *The Grass Is Always Greener over the Septic Tank.* The first two reveal immediately that the source of Bombeck's humor is in the stresses and hassles she has suffered; the third reminds us that from deep and rotten troubles, beautiful results sometimes spring.

Think about the pains and strains hidden behind some of these other titles: *Life Is What Happens When You're Making Other Plans* (Teresa Bloomingdale), *Small-Busted Women Have Big Hearts* (Herbert I. Kavet), *How to Jump-Start Your Husband* (Langdon Hill), *Eat Your Way to a Better Relationship* (Cathy Guisewite), *One Hundred One Reasons Not to Have Sex Tonight* (I. M. Potent, M.D.), *How to Get a Teenager to Run Away from Home* (Martin A. Ragaway), *Marriage Is an Invasion of Privacy & Other Dangerous Views* (Jules Feiffer), *How to Raise Your IQ by Eating Gifted Children* (Lewis Burke Frumkes), *Moisturizer Is My Religion* (Victoria Black), and *Who Needs Midlife at Your Age? New Evidence of Life After Thirty!* (Jack Roberts, Dick Gunther, and Stan Gortikov). These titles immediately offer readers a lighter, healthier perspective on problems created by our culture's fanatic concern with bust size, wrinkles, IQ, and extra pounds, and on the unavoidable stresses and strains of sex, marriage, and family life.

Since humor has its roots in suffering, individuals and groups who have suffered a great deal are frequently drawn to humor. Jews are a good example. Although persecuted for centuries and therefore deeply familiar with pain and suffering, they have also created a rich legacy of humor. (Sholem Aleichem's Tevye says to his maker: "God, I know we are the chosen people, but couldn't you choose somebody else for a change?") Within our own time and society, we have had the pleasure of sharing laughs with Groucho Marx, Jack Benny, Milton Berle, Lenny Bruce, Jerry Lewis, Henny Youngman, Mel Brooks, Joan Rivers, Mike Nichols, Bette Midler, Dr. Seuss, Woody Allen, Art Buchwald, Rodney Dangerfield, Goldie Hawn, and Gilda Radner, to name a few. Woody Allen—who makes fun of his own guilt and neuroticism, his crazy Jewish family background and ethnically determined doubts and obsessions, his troubled sex life and endless psychoanalysis— illustrates the transformation of personal and ethnic suffering into humor. From another American minority group, blacks, we have been blessed with, among others, Bill Cosby, Flip Wilson, Richard Pryor, and Eddie Murphy.

While most of us are not as talented as these comedians and humorists, we have the potential to see the funny side of our own problems. It's a potential worth exploring, developing, and expressing. To a large extent, the appreciation and creation of humor can be deliberately and lovingly cultivated. As with other coping strategies, the choice is always ours: cherries or pits, grass or septic tank.

Reducing the Physical Effects of Stress

One woman we know, despite spending more than fifty hours a week at a demanding and stressful job, always finds time for relaxing, distracting, and pleasurable activities. She claims these are absolutely necessary to counteract the pressure of her work. She keeps a journal in which she writes about her daily dealings with people and the feelings these evoke. She reads novels and listens to music in the evenings, and on weekends tries to get out of the city at least one day to the beach or mountains. Her activities are effective because they take her mind and body away from the stressful situation and allow her to relax—they undo stress-related damage before it progresses too far.

In the chart on page 312, which summarizes the stress process, you will see that we have talked about two of the three coping arrows, the one dealing directly with the stressor or problem (problem solving) and the one dealing with appraisal (rethinking the problem). The third has to do with reducing the negative effects of stress on the body.

The physical components of negative emotions include increased or irregular heart rate, elevated blood pressure, tension headaches, backaches, insomnia, inability to concentrate, fatigue, increased stomach acidity, intestinal cramps, over- or undereating, and diarrhea. Less visible but just as important, if negative feelings persist, are decreased resistance to illnesses and lowered ability to fight malignant cells in the body. Often these undesirable reactions are exaggerated or aggravated by increased consumption of stimulants such as nicotine and caffeine, and sometimes by reckless, inattentive driving, arguments with relatives and coworkers, or other activities that push the stress spiral upward. Regardless of the specific stressors and appraisals that give rise to these symptoms, it is often desirable to cope directly with the symptoms themselves—in a word, to *relax*. Table 3 lists some of the many enjoyable ways to do it.

Relaxation methods fall into four basic categories. Some attack the stress responses directly by countering them with what medical researcher Herbert Benson calls the "relaxation response." Resting, napping, and sleeping are the obvious ways to do this, but stress often rules out this simple solu-

TABLE 3.
Some Useful Relaxation Methods

Resting; napping; sleeping

Walking; hiking; contemplating nature; contemplating serene works of art or architecture

Listening to relaxing music; listening to the ocean; listening to high-quality recordings of natural sounds such as surf washing over the beach or rain falling in a forest

Engaging in vigorous exercise (jogging, swimming, martial arts, aerobic dance) and then resting

Hypnosis; verbally induced deep muscle relaxation

Vivid visualization of relaxing scenes

Meditation; elicitation of the "relaxation response"

Biofeedback

Massage; stretching exercises; using a vibrator (or vibrating chair or bed) to relax tense muscles

Hot tubs, Jacuzzis, warm baths, saunas

Sexual activity

Writing in a journal or diary; writing to a close friend

Working on a relaxing (nonfrustrating) hobby; reading a pleasant and interesting but nonarousing, nonaggravating book, poem, or article

Viewing, listening to, or reading something humorous

Talking with a sympathetic, calming person about your concerns

Praying; reading religious or inspirational literature

Occasional, sparing use of relaxing or pain-reducing drugs

tion by creating insomnia. That's where hot tubs, massages, biofeedback, hypnosis, and meditation (when used for relaxation) come in: They encourage the relaxation response (deep breathing, lowered heart rate and blood pressure, deep muscle relaxation) and encourage sound sleep.

The second category of relaxation techniques allows the stress response to be expressed and released physically. Recall that stress is related to the negative emotions anger and fear, and to the bodily reactions that were originally designed to aid fighting or fleeing from predators, enemies, and natural disasters. In modern living situations, the causes of anger and fear cannot be eliminated by fighting or fleeing, and we are left with pent-up energy, tense muscles, and racing thoughts with nowhere to go. Nonaggressive physical exercise—for example, brisk walking, jogging, weight lifting, aerobic dancing, biking, and swimming—allow the energy and tension to be released in ways similar to fighting or fleeing. They leave a person feeling naturally released, cleansed, and better able to rest (see Chap. 16).

A third category of relaxation techniques—including the contemplation and enjoyment of nature, music, and the visual arts, along with mentally visualizing relaxing scenes—work in ways similar to rethinking a problem and viewing it as having positive as well as negative features. The natural response to beauty, grandeur of nature, and humor is positive emotion. Positive emotion is expressed in expansive, open, and free movements (think of what it's like to laugh, sing, and dance with pleasure)—just the reverse of the tension, constriction, and rigidity of anxiety and anger. So contemplation of positive images, whether real or imagined, replaces stress with relaxation.

Finally, the fourth group of relaxation techniques—writing in a journal; corresponding with or talking to a friend, relative, or counselor; praying (talking with God)—can be relaxing because they are the psychological counterparts of physical exercise; they too release pent-up feelings, reduce conflicts by getting them out in the open, and provide perspectives on problems, which usually don't seem so bad when viewed from a calm vantage point.

These methods of coping with stress, when not used excessively, are highly recommended, but it is important to realize that they deal only with the tail end of the stress process. You may play tennis after work, have a glass or two of wine with dinner, and talk with your partner by the fireside or down at the beach, maybe even make love with great satisfaction; but if you view your job as inundating you with pressing, important, unsolvable problems the next morning, your body will react again with stress symptoms. Ultimately, there is no substitute for solving the problem.

The ideal approach to handling stress is to use all three methods in combination. Relaxation and exercise are good for you, mentally and physically, even if all your problems are solvable and you see life through the rosiest glasses. When you *are* under stress, relaxation methods can help you get through the worst of it with less physical damage. And being relaxed probably helps with the other two kinds of coping (problem solving and reinterpreting the problem), by giving you the time and psychological distance necessary to reflect on your problems more realistically and with less anxiety.

Stress-Resisting Attitudes and Personal Styles

Up to this point we have been describing many specific coping strategies that can be used by anyone. You may correctly suspect, however, that these strategies are not independent; they are likely to be organized in some way within the personality, equipping some *kinds* of people much better than others with the resources necessary to avoid or combat stress. Most people probably have a favorite personal anecdote about someone they know or have heard about who made a "miraculous" recovery from a serious, life-threatening illness. One of us knows someone who has had lung cancer disappear between diagnosis and scheduled surgery—not once, but twice!

Psychologists Suzanne Kobasa and Salvatore Maddi were curious about the fact that not all people who undergo stressful life events develop illness symptoms as a result. In studies involving mainly business executives and attorneys, they compared two groups of people subjected to about equal numbers of stressful life events: those who developed disease symptoms and those who did not. Members of the latter group turned out to have what the researchers call "hardy" or stress-resistant personalities.

Hardiness has three psychological components: *commitment,* the feeling that life, one's work, and close relationships are interesting and worthwhile; *control,* the belief that one is not helpless, that events can usually be influenced in one's favor; and *challenge,* the willingness to accept, indeed savor, novelty and change.

Hardy people feel engaged and energized by the challenges they face; they tackle them with a sense of confidence that the results will be acceptable, if not downright exciting. They react to potential stressors with predominantly *positive* emotions and with generally constructive problem-oriented behaviors. Nonhardy people, in contrast (those who score low on measures of commitment, control, and challenge), typically feel alienated, directionless, relatively powerless, and afraid of change. They are bundles of negative emotions, and prime candidates for stress, strain, and physical illness.

You are probably at least somewhat familiar with the highly publicized distinction between Type A and Type B personalities. The former are hard-driving, competitive, irritable and hostile, deadline-conscious, and prone to heart disease; the latter are more balanced, levelheaded, relaxed, and healthier. Hardy personalities and Type A personalities are both energetic and ambitious. Research reveals, however, that the two categories are *independent;* a person can be a hardy or a nonhardy Type A or Type B. Some Type A's are intrinsically committed to their work, and they are the healthy ones; others are desperately driven by fear of failure. Some Type A traits (high standards, the urge to be productive) are acceptable from the perspective of well-being, then, as long as they are shaped by hardiness.

Eastern Wisdom

In nearly all of the recent research and writing on stress and coping, one notices the clear stamps of Western civilization. First, many stressors arise primarily because our culture emphasizes speed, competition among individuals and human groups, and the subjugation and control of nature. Second, our culture views stress "management" as a matter of dominating the environment and of controlling or managing oneself, as if one's own feelings were unruly parts of nature that required taming. Third, a common goal, according to Western psychology, is enhancement of one's feelings of *control* and *self-esteem* (often interpreted as self-glorification). The not so hidden goal of all this control, "management," and ego enhancement is clear: victory over death, aging, and change—in other words, blissful immortality. Consider as evidence the Western image of heaven, where "worthy" individuals are believed to contemplate a "perfect" world in which nothing at all happens or changes, for all eternity!

It is impossible not to notice how different all of this is from Eastern philosophy and psychology. The difference might be just a curiosity if the combined findings of Western research did not point to the essential correctness of the Eastern views. For example, some forms of Buddhism begin with the assumption that death and change ("impermanence") are inevitable, and that no one who fails to recognize this can possibly be balanced, healthy, or at peace. Much of the stress experienced by Americans is due, the Buddhists say, to attempts to enhance the "illusion" of self and deny death. Fear often stems from a threat to this illusory, puffed-up self and from hints of the inevitability of death. Anger and resentment are reactions to real or imagined slights to the self; and sadness is a reaction to the reluctant realization that youth is fleeting, like life itself.

If we really accepted the fact that life is finite and brief, would we want to spend it arguing with loved ones over relatively small matters and stewing over slights and quarrels long past? If we accepted aging as a natural, unavoidable process, would we spend a sum total of months at the makeup table trying to hide wrinkles rather than devoting those months to meaningful enjoyment? Before *choosing* a full-blown stress reaction to a minor slight, frustration, or disappointment (and, as we have argued, choosing it is what we actually do), wouldn't it be better to view these hassles within the grand scheme of things? This simple, subtle maneuver would knock the props out from under the tension-headache business.

Tibetan Buddhists have a word, *ziji*, which is their version of "self-confidence." It is often translated as "confidence-trust" and refers to a combined attitude of openness, fearlessness, and mental clarity that contains no elements of arrogance, selfishness, or hidden insecurity. The woman with *ziji* moves into life's situations with the quiet assurance that things will generally go well—and with this attitude they usually do! Her stance includes trust in other people and in the world's general goodness, which often brings out the best in her companions. She feels generally loving and sympathetic toward people, and is quick to see the potential for humor in every situation. She has a kind of sparkling dignity; and in fact, the word *ziji* literally means "shining or glittering" *(zi)* "splendor or dignity" *(ji)*. When things go well, the person with *ziji* acknowledges this quietly, thinking not "How wonderful and clever I am," but "Once again, life is kind." When things go badly, she tries clearheadedly to identify the unintended mistakes or accidents that caused the problem, not berating herself or anyone else.

The concepts of *ziji* (confidence-trust) and *maitri* (unconditional self-acceptance) seem closer to the heart of stress avoidance and stress resistance than our Western concepts of self-esteem, control, stress management, and hardiness. "Management" is a business term and "hardiness" (like Sheehy's term "pathfinders") seems more suited to Daniel Boone or the Lone Ranger than to a person living in a twentieth-century city. We can be pretty sure that Western stress-management schemes haven't quite hit the center of the target, because (as a teacher at a Buddhist institute pointed out to us) employees of stress-management firms, who sell everything from records and tapes to vibrators and biofeedback machines, look just as stressed as stockbrokers and insurance sales people.

The stress-resistant person, in the Eastern conception, is one who loves and appreciates life and other people, acknowledges impermanence, aging, and eventual death, seeks a sense of internal balance and peace, desires self-knowledge, and realizes that the total control of nature and emotion is devastating to life and ultimately impossible. Nature is the source and sustainer of life, and human feelings are one of its brightest creations.

Because we live in a Western society and are psychological creations of it, there is probably no way to shun it completely in favor of another culture's traditions. Most of us would not want to do that even if it were possible. Still, the conclusions of future stress research will be based, we suspect, as much on concepts such as wisdom, love, clear vision, and confidence-trust as on management, control, and subjugation. Every woman who is seeking balance, peace, and personal growth has to grope her way toward them, taking advantage of the best hints that both East *and* West have to offer.

PHILLIP SHAVER, Ph.D., a social psychologist, has taught at Columbia University and New York University and is currently professor of psychology at the University of Denver. He is coauthor (with Carin Rubenstein) of *In Search of Intimacy* (Delacorte Press, 1982), a book about loneliness and how to cope with it, and editor of a special issue of the *Review of Personality and Social Psychology* entitled "Emotions, Relationships, and Health." To reduce stress, Dr. Shaver imagines and writes about peaceful mental states.

CARY O'CONNOR, M.A., is a doctoral student in social psychology at the University of Denver and is taking courses on Tibetan Buddhist psychology at the Naropa Institute in Boulder, Colorado. Her recent research concerns the nature and structure of human emotions and the development of a Buddhist approach to stress.

Further Reading

Antonovsky, Aaron. *Health, Stress, and Coping.* San Francisco: Jossey-Bass, 1979.

Benson, Herbert. *The Relaxation Response.* New York: Morrow, 1975.

Burns, David D. *Feeling Good: The New Mood Therapy.* New York: Morrow, 1980.

Cousins, Norman. *Anatomy of an Illness as Perceived by the Patient.* New York: Norton, 1979.

———. *The Healing Heart.* New York: Norton, 1983.

Goldberger, Leo and Breznitz, Shlomo, eds. *Handbook of Stress: Theoretical and Clinical Aspects.* New York: Free Press, 1982.

Kobasa, Suzanne, and Maddi, Salvatore. *The Hardy Executive.* Homewood, Ill.: Dow Jones-Irwin, 1984.

Lazarus, Richard. *Psychological Stress and the Coping Process.* New York: McGraw-Hill, 1966.

———, and Folkman, Susan. *Stress, Appraisal, and Coping.* New York: Springer Publishing Co., 1984.

Novak, William, and Waldoks, Moshe, eds. *The Big Book of Jewish Humor.* New York: Harper & Row, 1981.

Seligman, Martin E. P. *Helplessness: On Depression, Development, and Death.* San Francisco: W. H. Freeman, 1975.

Selye, Hans. *Stress Without Distress.* Philadelphia: Lippincott, 1974.

———. *The Stress of Life.* 2nd ed. New York: McGraw-Hill, 1976.

Sheehy, Gail. *Pathfinders.* New York: Morrow, 1981.

Tavris, Carol. *Anger: The Misunderstood Emotion.* New York: Touchstone Books, 1984.

Taylor, Shelley E. "Adjustment to Threatening Events: A Theory of Cognitive Adaptation." *American Psychologist* 38(1983):1161–73.

Thoits, Peggy. "Coping, Social Support, and Psychological Outcomes: The Central Role of Emotion." In *Review of Personality and Social Psychology,* edited by Phillip Shaver. Beverly Hills, Calif.: Sage Publications, 1984.

Trungpa, Chögyam. *Cutting Through Spiritual Materialism.* Berkeley, Calif.: Shambhala Publications, 1973.

Weisz, John R.; Rothbaum, Frank M.; and Blackburn, Thomas C. "Standing Out and Standing In: The Psychology of Control in America and Japan." *American Psychologist* 39(1984):955–69.

Welwood, John, ed. *Awakening the Heart: East-West Approaches to Psychotherapy and the Healing Relationship.* Boulder, Colo.: Shambhala Publications, 1983.

16

Body Fact, Body Fiction:
Exercise, Diets, and Well-Being

JOEL GURIN

Maybe you'd like smaller hips. Or a larger bust. You probably, almost certainly, would like to lose weight. (Maybe just five or ten pounds, but they are pounds that never seem to drop.) Maybe you'd like more muscles, or maybe you're embarrassed by your already muscular thighs. But whether your self-image is closest to Lily Tomlin, Dolly Parton, Jane Fonda, or somebody else, you probably aren't overjoyed with your body.

Most American women aren't. A recent *Glamour* magazine poll, for example, got some thirty-three thousand responses to the question "How do you feel about your body?" and related queries. Only 6 percent of the women were "very happy" with their bodies; 41 percent were "moderately unhappy" or "very unhappy." And while 71 percent felt their breasts were fine, only 39 percent were satisfied with their hips, 36 percent with their stomachs, and 28 percent with their thighs.

This problem hits women young. Psychiatrists Daniel Offer and Melvin Sabshin, who have studied adolescents extensively, find that boys have a much more positive body image than girls do. While most girls are proud of their bodies, a significant number—43 percent—often feel "ugly," "unattractive," and "ashamed" of their bodies.

But the most universal dissatisfactions, and desires, have to do with weight. That was "the most striking finding of the survey," according to the *Glamour* pollsters. "Married or single, employed or not, at all ages, education and income levels, a steady 73 to 77 percent of the respondents feel they are too fat, although according to even conservative height and weight tables, only one-quarter are actually overweight."

Academic research backs this up. Yale psychologist Judith Rodin and her colleagues tested male and female undergraduates, selected at random, and found that "weight and body shape comprised the *central* determinants of a woman's perception of her physical attractiveness." Weight was also important to men, but much less so. No wonder that a Nielsen survey found 56 percent of women between twenty-four and fifty-four were on a diet *at the time they were asked.*

It's not surprising. In every way, American culture tells women that they should be thin. Fashions are designed, as Bloomingdale's advertised a few years ago, for women who are "bean lean, slender as the night, narrow as an arrow, pencil thin, get the point?" Executive women in the pages of business magazines are almost uniformly slender. And the health clubs they go to promote a new kind of lean, well-muscled look. Thinness hasn't just become a way of attracting men; it has become an area where women compete among themselves.

The thin body may be valued for a simple, perverse reason: It is difficult to attain. In poorer countries, where food is scarce, fatness can be a sign of status. But in America it's easy to be fat; it's harder to be thin. Thinness is seen as a sign that a woman can take the time to exercise, or can spare the psychic energy needed to stay on a diet. In short, it's seen as an achievement.

The problem, though, is that it's not an achievement everyone can aspire to. There really do seem to be biological differences that keep some people fat even if they watch what they eat, while others can have dessert with every dinner and never gain a pound. The worst irony is that women in general, who are under the most pressure to be thin, are built to be fatter than men. Evolution has programmed women with fat reserves that are useful for pregnancy and breast-feeding, but inconvenient when you're trying to fit into a nonmaternal society. The female sex hormones start to build up fat reserves during adolescence, precisely the time that young women start to become most concerned about their appearance.

As a result, dieting is epidemic among teenage girls—perhaps dangerously so. Adolescent dieting has probably caused a drop in nutritional status and normal fat reserves, thereby delaying the average age of menarche (onset of menstruation), according to research psychologist Anke Ehrhardt. Eating disorders are on the rise, particularly the binge-and-purge cycle of bulimia. A recent survey of young women in high school showed that 21 percent were binging at least once a week, and 7 percent controlled their weight with purging—by vomiting or by abusing laxatives. Estimates of binge eating among college women range even higher, from 35 percent to 60 percent. Eating disorders and dieting are linked; out-of-control eating patterns often start with a stringent diet.

But science now suggests another reason that women (and men, too) should give up the diet habit. In spite of their popularity, diets—even "sensible" diets—just don't work. By the most popular estimate, about 95 percent of dieters regain their lost weight within a few years.

Though most dieters don't like to admit it, dieting usually starts a vicious cycle. You lose, gain the weight back, and blame yourself for being a weak-willed glutton. Worse than that, the latest evidence shows that the "yo-yo" cycle of losing and regaining can actually make you fatter, and lead to medical problems as well. You diet because you want to be thin, happy, and healthy, and you end up irritable, less healthy, and plumper than before.

The only way out of this mess is to understand why diets don't work and how the body really controls its weight. Dieting *seems* sensible; if you give your body fewer calories, it should oblige you by becoming thinner. The problem is that the body has a mind of its own. While you may think of fat as the filling for unwanted saddlebags, your body sees fat tissue as an important organ, necessary for energy reserves, temperature control, even manufacturing hormones. When you starve yourself by going on a diet, your body fights back in a number of ways designed to keep the fat on.

Once you understand the ins and outs of this balancing act, it becomes clear that exercise is a much better way of controlling weight. Exercise is a way of working *with* the body, not against it. Rather than a form of starvation, it is a way of helping the body reach a new, thinner balance point. More important, it has a number of health benefits that outweigh (so to speak) having a slimmer figure.

This is crucial to keep in mind. Because if your only goal is thinness, then exercise can become as grim and unrewarding as the grapefruit diet. The latest celebrity exercise books—which suggest you can look like your favorite TV star with just ten minutes of exercise a day—are as unrealistic as old-fashioned diet books. Exercising too hard, like dieting too hard, can become a drag, or injure the body.

Whether you are contemplating a diet, starting an exercise program, or just worrying about your weight, the first step is to think hard about what is right for you. You may naturally gravitate to a weight that's somewhat higher than that of the models in *Vogue*. But that weight may be perfectly comfortable, and attractive, for you.

What's more, it may be a weight that is perfectly healthy. Though height-weight tables have dictated "ideal" weights for years, they were based on cultural prejudices as much as science. The latest research shows that being plump may not only be more comfortable for many women—it may also be healthier than most people think.

Why Fat Isn't Always Fatal

It has been hard to untangle the health effects of fatness, dieting, and exercise, because most people (doctors included) come to the subject with a lot of biases. We have been so conditioned to think of fat as a Bad Thing that we think any way of taking it off should be worthwhile. In fact, the risks of dieting have been understated, and the risks of fatness have been overstated.

Early in 1985, a panel of experts convened by the National Institutes of Health (NIH) announced that any degree of "overweight" is a disease. The chairman declared that "obesity is a killer" and warned against weighing even five or ten pounds above the standard height-weight tables. But the evidence behind this proclamation was shaky, and those standard weight tables are even shakier.

The committee stated, for example, that overweight increases the risk of heart disease. But the best evidence for the connection comes from studies of young white males. For women, the evidence is less clear. As the NIH panel admitted, different studies have produced "widely divergent results."

Is obesity linked to cancer? Many doctors think so. And extremely fat people do have a higher than average risk of certain types of cancer. But on the whole, moderately fat people have a relatively low cancer risk, while very thin people may have a higher risk.

In general, very fat people have a shorter life expectancy than average-weight individuals; the insurance companies have known that for years. But their statistics also show that very *thin* people don't live as long as those in the middle ranges. Though this could be partly because smokers tend to be thinner, there is evidence that thinness by itself is not a very good sign.

Some surveys even suggest that you will live longer if you are a little plumper than average.

So the healthiest goal is not to be as thin as possible, but to be somewhere in the great middle ranges. And when it comes to a healthy weight, the safe "middle range" is probably broader than you thought.

Those familiar insurance company tables divide the world into small, medium, and large frames, and give an acceptable range of only ten to fifteen pounds for each height and frame size. But the frame divisions originally were added to make the charts more acceptable to the public; they have no scientific basis. The statistics today show that at any weight within a range of about *thirty or forty pounds*—roughly from the bottom of "small frame" to the top of "large frame"—your life expectancy should be average, or better.

The insurance tables also assume that you should weigh the same throughout life—an assumption that goes against the common experience that people get fatter as they get older. Dr. Reubin Andres, clinical director of the Gerontology Research Center at the National Institute on Aging, believes the healthiest weight may rise with age. He reanalyzed the data collected by insurance companies, and in 1984 he published the accompanying table. While it is a little stricter than the standard tables for people in their twenties, it is much more lenient for older folks, and implies that we shouldn't all start dieting frantically when we begin to see some middle-aged spread.

Because the insurance statistics measure the life expectancy of healthy people, they don't apply to people who have a weight-related disease, such as diabetes. But even in that case, obsessively watching the scale isn't the healthiest way to manage weight. The shape your pounds take may be more important than their number.

Potbellies increase the risk of diabetes in women (and heart disease in men), while broad bottoms are not implicated, according to Dr. Ahmed Kissebah and his colleagues at the Medical College of Wisconsin. They do not know whether abdominal fat actually damages the body, or whether it is a sign of something else that is harmful, such as a slight imbalance in sex hormone levels. But either way, the diabetes connection with abdominal fat stands.

To find your own risk, measure your waist and hips with a tape measure, and divide waist size by hip size. The average ratio for women is about .7. Women whose ratio is above .85 have a threefold higher risk of diabetes, and might consider having a glucose tolerance test. The good news is that the fat around the middle is much easier to lose than that on the bottom and hips.

The Right Weight for Your Age

Height	Metropolitan 1983		Age-Specific Weight Range for men and women				
ft. and in.	Weights (25-59 years) Men	Women	20-29 yrs.	30-39 yrs.	40-49 yrs.	50-59 yrs.	60-69 yrs.
4'10"		100-131	84-111	92-119	99-127	107-135	115-142
4'11"		101-134	87-115	95-123	103-131	111-139	119-147
5'0"		103-137	90-119	98-127	106-135	114-143	123-152
5'1"	123-145	105-140	93-123	101-131	110-140	118-148	127-157
5'2"	125-148	108-144	96-127	105-136	113-144	122-153	131-163
5'3"	127-151	111-148	99-131	108-140	117-149	126-158	135-168
5'4"	129-155	114-152	102-135	112-145	121-154	130-163	140-173
5'5"	131-159	117-156	106-140	115-149	125-159	134-168	144-179
5'6"	133-163	120-160	109-144	119-154	129-164	138-174	148-184
5'7"	135-167	123-164	112-148	122-159	133-169	143-179	153-190
5'8"	137-171	126-167	116-153	126-163	137-174	147-184	158-196
5'9"	139-175	129-170	119-157	130-168	141-179	151-190	162-201
5'10"	141-179	132-173	122-162	134-173	145-184	156-195	167-207
5'11"	144-183	135-176	126-167	137-178	149-190	160-201	172-213
6'0"	147-187		129-171	141-183	153-195	165-207	177-219
6'1"	150-192		133-176	145-188	157-200	169-213	182-225
6'2"	153-197		137-181	149-194	162-206	174-219	187-232
6'3"	157-202		141-186	153-199	166-212	179-225	192-238
6'4"			144-191	157-205	171-218	184-231	197-244

Note: All figures given are for height without shoes and weight without clothes.

This table, devised by Dr. Reubin Andres, gives the range of weights associated with the greatest longevity at each age. It is based on Andres's reanalysis of data collected by the Metroplitan Life Insurance Company. For comparison, Andres has also listed the weights suggested by Metropolitan Life's own tables, which ignore the age factor.

The actual Metropolitan Life tables give different ranges of weight for each frame size. Here, in the columns marked "Metropolitan 1983," Andres has merged the figures for different frame sizes, and listed the full range from the bottom of "small frame" to the top of "large frame." The Metropolitan tables also give different weights for men and women; Andres's analysis suggests that is unnecessary.

(For men, by the way, the average waist-hip ratio is about .9 to .95; potbellied men much above this range have a higher risk of heart disease and stroke.)

Though the picture is still confusing, the evidence shows that there is no magic number on the scale that guarantees health and long life. A better goal is to try to find a weight that is comfortable for you. This may sound unscientific, but it is not as mysterious as it seems. When you diet *below* your naturally comfortable weight, you feel it, in your hunger, your energy level, and even in your mood. In a very real sense, dieting too long can make people a little crazy.

How Diets Affect the Mind

Listen to what people say: "I stay overweight because, deep down, I'm afraid of being too attractive." "I eat when I'm lonely, nervous, or depressed." "When things go well, I celebrate with a hot fudge sundae." "My mother always pushed food on me; it was her only way of showing love." "My mother was cold and ungiving; she never fed me enough."

All the explanations sound sensible enough—until you realize that they are mutually contradictory. Indeed, mountains of psychological research fail to support the notion of a neurotic basis for overweight. New research on the psychology of weight loss has turned the conventional wisdom upside down. Emotional problems are more likely to be a consequence of dieting than a cause of overeating.

Even most truly obese people are mentally healthy, considering the fact that they live in a world that hates fat and values the thin. Surveys over several decades have shown that the obese are generally no more neurotic or sexually repressed than thin people. And some studies have found that fat people are somewhat *less* anxious and depressed than thin ones.

At the same time, dieting puts such a strain on the system that it can lead to "neurotic" problems. Three decades ago Dr. Albert Stunkard, a pioneering obesity researcher, described the "dieting depression" that afflicted many of his patients when they tried to lose weight. At the time, Stunkard thought these emotional problems arose from unresolved conflicts, which bubbled up when people could no longer use food as a defense.

But since that time many obesity experts (including Stunkard) have come to believe that the psychological problems of dieting may have a physical cause. Researchers at Rockefeller University have shown that obese men who reduce become anxious, depressed, and obsessed by food fantasies— even *after* they have stabilized at a lower weight. In other words, it's not just the experience of losing weight that is troublesome, but the stress of staying at a weight below what is comfortable.

The same symptoms showed up in a major study conducted during World

War II to determine the effects of semistarvation. The volunteers, who were conscientious objectors, were normal young men. Yet they, too, became depressed, irritable, constantly hungry, and obsessed by food when they were put on a severely restricted diet for several months.

Dieting can do more than make you unhappy; it also makes you eat in strange ways. When you go on a diet, you are trying to eat by some rigid set of rules: cutting carbohydrates, eating a protein powder, sticking to fifteen hundred calories a day, or whatever. That automatically means that you are not eating when your *body* tells you to: when you are hungry. In fact, if you diet for long enough, you will probably find that you become hungry all the time.

What happens then? You could manage to live your life in a state of chronic deprivation, never breaking your resolve. But it is more likely that you will start eating—and sometimes overeating—in ways that don't match your body's needs. You may eat, for example, only when the clock says it's dinnertime. Or you may finish everything on your plate, whether you want it or not. Or go on a little binge whenever a food is especially tasty.

For many years psychologists thought that only overweight people ate in these ways. The "externality" hypothesis said that people became fat because they ate according to "external" cues—the amount of food on the plate, the time of day—rather than the "internal" cues of their own bodies. Many behavior modification techniques were designed to help people lose weight by teaching them to deal with external cues differently, by putting food on smaller plates, for instance, or chewing more slowly.

The problem with the theory, though, is that both fat and thin people often eat when they're not really hungry. Chronic *dieters* of any weight— not necessarily overweight people—are the ones who eat by external cues. And behavior modification, which has proved less successful than originally hoped, was based on a theory that has become obsolete.

The new theory, though, explains why dieting disrupts both your eating habits and your psyche. Two psychologists at the University of Toronto, Peter Herman and Janet Polivy, have studied what they call "restrained eaters"—chronic dieters. They have found that restrained eaters may actually be setting themselves up for eating binges.

Restrained eaters are constantly using their willpower to eat less than they would like. But if anything breaks their resolve, the accumulated hunger can make them binge. A few cocktails, for example, can set up an eating bout. And when restrained eaters break their diets—with a piece of cake, perhaps, or an ice-cream sundae—they may decide "What the hell" and overeat for the rest of the day.

Most Americans are restrained eaters to some extent. But Herman and Polivy have developed a self-test, given below, to tell how much you're restraining yourself. In general, women who score at least 16 points out of a possible 35, and men who score at least 12, are restrained eaters.

Are You a Restrained Eater?

1. How often are you dieting?
(0) Never (1) Rarely (2) Sometimes
(3) Often (4) Always

2. What is the maximum amount of weight (in pounds) that you have ever lost within one month? (0) 0–4 (1) 5–9 (2) 10–14 (3) 15–19 (4) 20+

3. What is your maximum weight gain within a week? (0) 0–1 (1) 1.1–2 (2) 2.1–3 (3) 3.1–5 (4) 5.1+

4. In a typical week, how much does your weight fluctuate? (0) 0–1 (1) 1.1–2 (2) 2.1–3 (3) 3.1–5 (4) 5.1+

5. Would a weight fluctuation of five pounds affect the way you live your life? (0) Not at all (1) Slightly (2) Moderately (3) Very Much

6. Do you eat sensibly in front of others and splurge alone? (0) Never (1) Rarely (2) Often (3) Always

7. Do you give too much time and thought to food? (0) Never (1) Rarely (2) Often (3) Always

8. Do you have feelings of guilt after overeating? (0) Never (1) Rarely (2) Often (3) Always

9. How conscious are you of what you are eating? (0) Not at all (1) Slightly (2) Moderately (3) Extremely

10. How many pounds over your desired weight were you at your maximum weight? (0) 0–1 (1) 1–5 (2) 6–10 (3) 11–20 (4) 21+

Binging isn't the only risk of chronic dieting. Restrained eaters, according to Herman and Polivy, put so much effort into the quest for thinness that they are "chronically in a state of stress/arousal . . . There may well be cause for concern about the implications of this semichronic stress for their behavioral, emotional, and even medical well-being." One experiment, for example, showed that restrained eaters have elevated levels of free fatty acids, an indication of body stress.

Why Diets Don't Work

The strongest argument against dieting, though, is not just that it is stressful and unpleasant. The best reason not to diet is simple: Diets don't work. Experience and statistics show that the vast majority of people who lose weight on a diet will gain it back almost as quickly.

Though most dieters know the odds, they may think that everyone *else* fails just because they lack willpower. If I try hard enough, the reasoning goes, I can get thin and stay thin.

But a new theory of weight control, which seems to fit the evidence better than any other, explains why willpower isn't enough. According to this theory, everyone's body has a "setpoint," a set level of fatness that is biologically natural for the individual. People really were meant to come in different sizes: petite, large, and all gradations in between. The setpoint works like a thermostat to keep the body at the weight range it was "set" to be. This is why it is as hard for skinny people to gain weight as it is for large people to lose it. The theory says that anatomy is destiny, but only up to a point. You can change your setpoint, and your shape, to a certain extent. But only exercise will do the job. Self-starvation won't.

When you lose a significant amount of fat on a diet, your body rebels and tries to bring you back to your natural, "set" level. Under the control of your brain, mainly an area called the hypothalamus, your feelings of hunger increase—feelings that largely account for the psychological problems of dieting. At the same time, your metabolic rate, your body's baseline rate of burning calories, slows down.

The problem becomes even worse with yo-yo dieting: the up-and-down cycle of gaining, losing, and gaining again that many dieters go through. With each cycle the metabolic slowdown becomes more severe and the body takes longer to return to normal. Moreover, losing a lot of weight—perhaps 20 percent of what you started with—can kick off a metabolic "overcompensation" that makes you regain more weight than you lost. And while you lose muscle weight on a diet, the weight you regain is more likely to be fat.

There is also some evidence that yo-yo dieting can be bad for the heart. At Northwestern University, Paul Ernsberger put rats on a version of the yo-yo scheme: getting them thin by underfeeding them, refeeding them, and going through the cycle several times. What he found was frightening: Their blood pressure went up significantly by the third cycle of weight regain. Ernsberger thinks that overweight people may be prone to hypertension because they are likely to have gone on and off many diets, not because weight itself necessarily raises blood pressure.

Frustrated by their bodies' rebellion, many dieters have looked for a magic pill to make dieting easier and more effective. What they are looking for, in essence, is a pill to lower the setpoint—something to change the body metabolically so that it feels natural and comfortable to be thin. And in fact, some of the drugs that have been used in weight loss, such as amphetamine and related chemicals, do seem to work on the nervous system in a way that lowers the setpoint.

There are two obvious, major problems. First, the pills work only as long as you take them. Once you stop, your weight bounces back up to where it was, probably faster than if you had lost the weight through dieting alone. And second, these pills aren't safe to take for a long period of time. Even over-the-counter diet pills, which contain an amphetaminelike drug called phenylpropanolamine, can be dangerous. This compound can cause everything from anxiety and dizziness to high blood pressure and heart problems.

Another deadly drug also lowers the setpoint: nicotine. People often gain some weight when they stop smoking, and the usual interpretation is that they're eating more to meet their oral needs. But, in fact, surveys have shown that many smokers gain when they quit even if they *don't* eat more. Apparently, nicotine keeps a smoker at a lower setpoint by speeding up the metabolic rate. Quit smoking, and the comfortable weight rises somewhat as metabolism slows down. Thus, many women today smoke as a means of "weight control." And their rates of lung cancer, ulcers, and other serious diseases are reaching a deadly equality with men's: a big price for a few pounds.

People who want to become thinner need a safe, effective way to help their bodies balance out at a lower level of fatness. Dieting won't do it. Drugs won't do it. The only approach that works is exercise. Do the right kind of workout for long enough, and the body will naturally readjust to be leaner.

Exercise has other benefits that go far beyond thinness. While many people start exercising to lose weight, they stick with it because they feel better or because they are convinced that they are actually healthier. Exercise is a way to use the body enjoyably, not a grim exercise in self-deprivation. While dieting can send you into a neurotic tailspin, exercise can help your mental health—whether you are skinny, plump, zaftig, or average. In fact, regular exercise is probably the closest thing to a cure-all that modern science has to offer.

Why Fitness Will Stay in Style

Though it is tempting to see fitness as a fad, it is probably more correct to see it as a remedy, a reaction to a lifestyle that had become abnormally sedentary. By about ten years ago, on-the-job automation, television, and the automobile had conspired to make us a nation of sitters. According to government statistics, Americans ate, on average, about 10 percent *less* in 1977 than they did in 1965—but weighed a few pounds more in the early seventies than they had in the early sixties. The only possible explanation is that we had become much less active.

The fitness movement, which took off in the late seventies, may have reversed the trend to inactivity. Most of us no longer *have* to get exercise by walking to work, doing heavy manual labor, or chopping wood for the fireplace. So now we choose our own ways of sweating and, in the process, bring our bodies back to the activity level they were meant for.

The most important kind of exercise, from the viewpoint of weight control as well as health, is aerobic, or "oxygen-using," exercise—the kind you do continuously, without stopping to catch your breath. You have to do aerobic exercise to burn fat effectively, build up your cardiovascular system, or get other health benefits. Jogging, swimming, cycling, cross-country skiing, fast racket sports, aerobic dancing, even *brisk* walking all qualify. Weight training doesn't; though it builds muscle, it is generally not aerobic.

There is now a lot of evidence that exercise lowers the risk of heart disease in several ways. It increases the heart's capacity for work; improves the cholesterol balance in the blood; and it lowers blood pressure, both by helping people lose weight, and probably also through hormonal effects (though these are not quite understood).

While women rarely get heart attacks, they are prone to osteoporosis, the progressive thinning of the bones that comes with age and calcium loss. Here, too, even light exercise, a few times a week, seems to help younger women strengthen their bones. Calisthenics, jogging, or a workout with light weights are all useful; a possible exception is swimming, which may not stress the bones enough to prevent bone loss.

Aerobic exercise can also help prevent or treat diabetes; not the "juvenile" diabetes that strikes children, but the kind that starts in adulthood and is linked with overweight. The adult form of diabetes isn't due to a lack of insulin, but to a loss of cellular sensitivity: The body's cells become less responsive to the insulin that is already there. Aerobic exercise, combined with a diet rich in complex carbohydrates, can improve the body's insulin response and help correct the blood sugar problem that endangers diabetics.

How Much Exercise Is Enough?

400 Calories Per Week	800 Calories Per Week	1,200 Calories Per Week	1,600 Calories Per Week	2,000 Calories Per Week
Heart Long-term risk of a first heart attack is 10% lower at the 400-calorie burn level than in sedentary men, according to a Harvard study.	**Weight** Body weight drops without changes in diet, but the loss is only around two ounces per week. 800 calories equals two or three weekly workouts.	**Heart** Long-term risk of a first heart attack is 20% to 25% less than for sedentary men.	**Weight** Exercise four to five times per week drops weight about one-half pound per week without dieting. Since you add muscle as you shed fat, actual fat loss may be greater. Weight loss is faster for those who start out fatter.	**Heart** For men, the Harvard study shows the risk of first heart attack continues to fall with increasing exercise. At 2,000 calories, heart risk drops 35% below that for sedentary people. At 5,000 calories, risk drops to 50% less.
Aerobic Fitness How much oxygen the body can burn in a given time period is a measure of overall fitness. With one or two exercise sessions per week (about 300 to 600 calories burned), aerobic capacity rises 8% above sedentary levels.	**Aerobic Fitness** Overall fitness rises 15% above sedentary levels, the minimum recommended by the American College of Sports Medicine.	**Bone Loss** Preliminary data from the University of Wisconsin suggest postmenopausal women build additional bone at this exercise level—without estrogen or calcium supplements.	**Aerobic Fitness** Rising ability to use oxygen begins to level off at about 25% above sedentary levels. Further increase comes hard and slow.	**Injuries** Overuse injuries like shin splints become a problem, especially in runners. Exercising more than five times per week triples the injury rate. Increasing exercise sessions from 30 to 45 minutes doubles the risk.
Bone Strength For the young to middle-aged, light exercise can maintain bone strength. Work the whole body; for example, alternate jogging with lifting light weights. (Swimming may not stress bones enough to prevent bone loss.)	**Blood Pressure** For obese people, especially diabetics, exercise reduces blood pressure and may decrease the need for antihypertensive drugs.	**Metabolic Changes: Cholesterol** Relative levels of high-density lipoprotein (HDL) cholesterol—a form that seems to protect against heart disease—go up at the 1,200-calorie burn level, according to work at Stanford and Baylor. (Other studies say you need 2,000 calories a week or more.) This shift takes weeks or months to occur and fades within weeks if you quit exercising.		**Metabolic Changes: Amenorrhea** Menstrual irregularities become more common in women who run off much more than 2,000 calories a week. Lower estrogen levels in these women may contribute to loss of calcium from the bones.
Psychology: Sex Interest Increased physical activity brings greater interest in sex, according to studies at Ohio University and the University of California (and lots of anecdotal evidence). Interest, however, doesn't guarantee opportunity.	**Metabolic Changes: Fatty Acids and Insulin** Blood fatty acids (triglycerides)—a risk factor in heart disease—drop within days of beginning rigorous exercise. The body's cells gradually become more sensitive to insulin, so diabetics may need less of it. **Psychology: Type A** Gradual shift from Type-A personality, with a high risk of heart disease, to easygoing Type-B personality.	**Psychology: Depression and Anxiety** Within a few weeks or months, depression and anxiety ease. Improvement can be as great as with drug treatment or psychotherapy.		**Psychology: Compulsive Runners** Some athletic overachievers, long distance runners in training, show signs of compulsive self-denial similar to anorexia nervosa.

This chart shows the benefits, and possible drawbacks, of different levels of exercise. Many benefits, such as protection against heart disease, increase with more activity. But drawbacks of exercise, such as injuries and amenorrhea (cessation of menstruation), also increase at high levels of activity (more than 2000 calories a week).

To help you estimate the number of calories you burn in exercise, here's the number used up by some common sports and activities. These estimates are for a 150-pound person; the less you weigh, the less calories you burn per hour.

Walking (4.5 mph): 400 cal./hour
Tennis (moderate): 430 cal./hour
Swimming (45 yards/min.): 530 cal./hour
Handball, squash: 590 cal./hour
Jogging (5.5 mph): 630 cal./hour
Bicycling (12 mph): 800 cal./hour
Cross-country skiing: 900 cal./hour

Chart reprinted from *American Health* magazine, July/August 1983. Copyright © *American Health*. 1983.

Finally, aerobic exercise, and only aerobic exercise, can help control weight. When you exercise regularly (and aerobically), your body rebalances appetite, metabolism, and activity and becomes leaner. Your appetite and metabolism change as your activity level does. Unless you understand this, exercise looks like a pretty dumb way to try to lose weight. If you just count the calories you burn *while* you're running around a track, swimming, or whatever, it's not very much. Jogging half a mile to a mile only burns off the calories in a single apple. So why not just skip the apple, stay home, and watch TV?

The reason is that regular exercise changes the body's rate of burning calories *between* workout sessions. Because of the increase in muscle tissue, or perhaps because of a hormonal change that is yet to be discovered, a fit body burns more calories than a fat one, even while it is eating, sleeping, or just hanging around.

It is hard to measure the metabolic rate—the rate of burning calories just to keep the body going—so no one is sure just how much metabolism is boosted by exercise. But there is general agreement that activity stokes the metabolic fires in various ways, in sharp contrast to dieting, which generally *lowers* the metabolic rate by about 20 percent. That is one reason dieters hit a plateau; they reach a point where their bodies are burning calories too slowly for them to keep losing weight.

You can see the metabolic boost, for example, after you eat a meal. When you have dinner, your metabolic rate goes up for a few hours as your body works to burn off some of the calories. People who have been through aerobic fitness training have a higher postmeal metabolic rate than those who are less fit.

To take another example, the heat you feel after vigorous exercise may help you burn calories off. Strenuous running—say, four miles in thirty minutes or less—can shoot your temperature to 102 degrees. Apparently, exercise boosts the body's level of a substance called endogenous pyrogen (EP), which raises body temperature. Curiously enough, this is the same protein that triggers fever, which is really the body's defensive way to kill bacteria when you are sick.

To be the perfect weight-control remedy, exercise shouldn't just boost your metabolic rate; it should decrease your appetite. But this part of the picture is less clear. For about three decades doctors and athletes have argued about whether exercise makes you more hungry, less hungry, or neither. The answer now seems to be: It depends.

It is always hard to tell how much people are really exercising and eating; we'd all like to think we exercise more than we really do, and eat less. But at

St. Luke's Hospital in New York, a major center for obesity research, two groups of women volunteered to be scrupulously, indisputably honest. One group of obese women, and later a group of lean women, each lived in the hospital for several weeks while they were put on a carefully monitored exercise program and every bite of their meals was counted.

They proved that how you eat when you exercise depends largely on how fit you are to begin with. The obese women ate about the same amounts even when they began daily treadmill workouts. But the lean women, in contrast, reacted to exercise like finely tuned machines. The more they worked out, the more they ate, adding fuel for their new level of activity. This fits with other studies that have shown that runners eat to match their activity level (marathoners are notorious chowhounds).

What does this mean? First, it proves that you don't have to diet to be thin. Runners, like the lean women in the St. Luke's lab, eat plenty, but their exercise level—and the accompanying metabolic changes—burn off those calories. And second, the research helps show why fatter people lose weight faster on an exercise program than thin people do. Somehow, their bodies seem to know they have more to lose, and they refrain from eating more even when they are burning more calories.

What to Expect from Exercise

Whether you are fat or thin, you can't expect to see a fast change on the bathroom scale. Though exercise will take weight off without dieting, it does it slowly. Exercise is more helpful than it looks, however, because the bathroom scale doesn't tell the whole story. When you exercise, you build muscle while you burn up fat. In contrast, roughly a third of the weight you lose on a diet, and two thirds of the weight you lose on a total fast, is a loss of muscle. Some recent research shows that even moderate dieting—say, 1,800 calories a day—can wither your muscle tissue.

It is not only healthier to lose fat and build muscle, it makes you leaner, since a pound of muscle is smaller than a pound of fat. That is why you can go down a clothing size or two when you exercise without losing a single pound. You just replace fat with muscle.

If you want to plan an exercise program to give the greatest possible fat loss, the first thing is to make it aerobic: continuous, deep-breathing exercise. A start-and-stop, huff-and-puff workout with weights won't affect fat (though it may build muscle). You can also forget about "spot-reducing" exercises, the ones that promise to take fat off your stomach, thighs, or wherever in just ten minutes a day. True, these exercises can improve the muscle tone in different parts of your body. But you could do a hundred sit-ups a day and develop stomach muscles like a rock, and still have three inches of flab on top of them. The only way to lose fat is through aerobic exercise, which takes the fat off your whole body at once. You will probably lose the most fat, though, from the places where you have the most to lose.

Exercising frequently is also important, perhaps because it keeps your metabolic rate high from day to day. The standard recommendation is to exercise at least twenty minutes at a time, burning at least 300 calories a session, and to do it at least three times a week. Each session your pulse should get up to 70 to 85 percent of its maximum rate (the maximum is 225 minus your age). But one summary of the available exercise studies showed that people who exercised four or five times a week lost weight three times faster than those who exercised three times a week. Exercising just once or twice a week was ineffective.

It may be tempting to try to speed things along by going on a strict diet when you start to work out. Don't do it. The typical low-carbohydrate, quick-weight-loss plan simply won't give you what you need to support a vigorous exercise program. Your body needs carbohydrates as well as fat to be active, and you need to supply them.

You may find, however, that your tastes change as you work out. You may crave *more* complex carbohydrates, such as fruits, vegetables, and pasta, and find you can get by with less meat than before. That's fine, because a diet high in complex carbohydrates is best for both activity and health.

The most important thing in approaching an exercise program, perhaps, is your frame of mind. You have to take the long view and look forward to the long-term benefits. A recent Stanford study, for example, found that runners were still losing fat two years after they started to exercise, even though they were no longer increasing their activity levels. When you become active, you program your body to become leaner, but it takes a while for it to fully reach that new point.

Exercise, in short, should be a lifetime commitment. But unlike dieting, it *can* be something you stick with for life. Dieting can bring short-term euphoria, as the numbers on the scale drop day by day. But very quickly, any diet gets to be a drag. Exercise, in contrast, is hard to start—and hard to stop. Once you get past the first few weeks of pushing your body, you may find that exercise feels more like fun than like a chore. Though people usually start exercising for their physical health, it's the effect on mental health that keeps most of them on the track.

Sweating Away the Blues

Over the past few years psychologists have found that exercise can be good therapy, not only for people who are clinically depressed or anxious, but also for people who have the normal blues, blahs, decisions, and stresses of everyday life.

In a recent study at the University of Kansas, for example, forty-three depressed undergraduate women were divided into three groups at random: a group who got aerobic training, one that practiced relaxation training, and a group that got no treatment at all. After ten weeks the women who went to aerobics classes and started doing other exercise showed significantly more improvement than the other two groups.

Other studies have been designed to find the amount and type of exercise that give the most psychological benefits. In general, the standard minimum —twenty-minute workouts three times a week—seems to hold here, whether the problem is depression or anxiety. A shorter, twelve-minute workout can relieve muscle tension, but not psychic tension, which shows that exercise does more for your mind than loosening your muscles. More frequent or prolonged exercise may give you more benefit, up to a point. But exercising *too* intensely, to a point of exhaustion, may actually *increase* your anxiety, at least during and just after the workout.

The psychological benefits apparently aren't tied to just one specific exercise. Swimming seems to be fine for anxiety and depression. And according to a University of Rochester study, even nonaerobic exercise, such as weight training, can help lift the blues.

If you would like to improve your mood, a few other exercise guidelines can help. It may help to exercise at the time of day you're most anxious (midafternoon or later for most people). Try to set specific goals for yourself —a distance to run, or amount of weight to press—in addition to the more amorphous goal of feeling better. If you run, try to run with someone of about the same ability, not a faster friend who will be bad for your self-esteem. And consider listening to your favorite music; it really can help take some of the stress out of exercise, according to recent research.

Hard-driving Type A personalities may find that exercise helps their hearts in two ways: through the physical effect on the circulatory system, and through a calming effect on the mind. At Stanford, a group of middle-aged faculty members were interviewed before and after a year-long exercise training program. Men who were Type A to begin with, and who started jogging at least eight to ten miles a week, showed a significant shift in the Type B direction.

If you are Type A, though, it is important not to be too driven while you are out on the track. Racing against the clock, or becoming too competitive and upset when you're losing, may put a real strain on your heart. One psychologist has shown that athletes who think competitive thoughts produce more of the stress hormone norepinephrine, which damages the cardiovascular system.

What if you just want to feel sharper, brighter, more alert? Again, there is evidence that exercise can help. A Purdue researcher put twenty ordinary people on a six-month exercise program, and found that they not only became fitter, they also became much better in a test of complex decision making. At California State University in Long Beach, psychologist Robert Thayer found that a ten-minute treadmill walk made people more energetic for half an hour afterward. In contrast, eating a candy bar boosted their energy only briefly, and the sugar made them more tense after thirty minutes.

If you can force yourself to work out in the morning (though many people can't) then you may get a special bonus. The aerobic dawn patrol has hit on something valuable. Regular early morning workouts may actually reset your biological rhythms in beneficial ways. They boost your body temperature earlier, and keep it high for longer, than your normal body rhythms would. And since a rise in body temperature makes you more alert, that means that you actually have a more productive day.

Exercise may not do all these things for you, or even most of them. But if you can get yourself onto a regular routine, you should find that it becomes a positive experience, positive enough to get you hooked. Dieting is a way of *fighting* the body, and thus it becomes much more difficult after the initial pleasure of losing a few pounds. But exercise is a way of *using* the body, and gives greater rewards over time. For well-being, mental and physical, the choice should be obvious.

JOEL GURIN is editor of *American Health* magazine, a general-interest magazine about health and everything that affects it. *American Health,* which has been published since March 1982, focuses largely on exercise and nutrition, the subjects of this chapter. Mr. Gurin's interest in these areas—and his iconoclastic approach to them—predate his involvement with the magazine. He is coauthor, with William Bennett, of *The Dieter's Dilemma* (Basic Books, 1982; paperback edition 1984). Billed as "the scientific case against dieting as a means of weight control," the book presents the "setpoint" theory, and received wide publicity.

Mr. Gurin has now been covering science and medicine as a journalist for more than ten years, since he graduated from Harvard with a degree in biochemistry in 1975. He has written for *The Atlantic, Smithsonian, The Nation,* and the New York *Times,* as well as various science and fitness magazines. He is also coeditor of *The Horizons of Health* (Harvard University Press, 1977), an overview of medical research.

Further Reading

Bennett, William, and Gurin, Joel. *The Dieter's Dilemma.* New York: Basic Books, 1982; in paperback, 1984.

Cooper, Kenneth, and Cooper, Mildred. *Aerobics for Women.* New York: Bantam Books, 1973.

Katch, Frank, and McArdle, William. *Nutrition, Weight Control, and Exercise.* Philadelphia: Lea & Febiger, 1983.

Polivy, Janet, and Herman, C. Peter. *Breaking the Diet Habit.* New York: Basic Books, 1983.

17

When Disaster Strikes

IRENE HANSON FRIEZE AND
MAUREEN C. McHUGH

The beatings started two weeks after we were married. . . . Sometimes he kept me up all night. He would stand me up against the wall for hours and wouldn't let me smoke, get a drink of water, or go to the bathroom. He would keep asking me the same question, such as "You deliberately left the cap off the soda bottle, didn't you?" When I would say no, he would hit me and say I was lying. If I said yes, he would really hurt me. He never broke any bones, but I almost always had bruises all over my face and body, split lips, patches of hair torn out, and black eyes.

The lights were out in the elevator and there was someone on it that I didn't know about. He tried to assault me sexually, but the elevator stopped and he ran away. It was totally dark and I couldn't see him at all. [I felt] disgusted, violated, and dirty. . . . I'm totally alert now and extremely cautious.

When we [the victim and her sister] were preschoolers, my grandfather would sit in a dark room in his rocking chair and call us over. He would finger our vaginas. I told our father, and wondered why he didn't say anything. Then he started the same kind of thing in a few years.

Violent Crimes and Natural Misfortunes

Every day in our society, people are victimized by violence, crime, serious accidents or disease, and natural and technological disasters. Although few if any of us expect to be victims, many of us, and our family members and friends, will be victimized at least once, if not many times, in our lives.

Rape. According to the 1981 FBI *Uniform Crime Report,* a forcible rape occurs every six minutes in this country. When this estimate is corrected for underreporting, it is believed that a rape occurs every two minutes. Recent community surveys suggest that a woman living in an American city has a one-in-four chance of being raped in her lifetime, and almost a one-in-two chance of being the victim of an attempted rape.

Wife abuse. A recent national survey suggests that 1.8 million wives are beaten by their husbands in any one year, and that at least 25 percent of American families have at least minimal levels of husband-wife violence.

Incest and the sexual abuse of children. Social worker Florence Rush called these the "best kept secret." Kinsey found that 24 percent of his female respondents had been approached sexually by an adult male prior to their adolescence; a recent survey of college undergraduates, done by sociologist David Finkelhor, revealed that one in five females and one in eleven males were sexually victimized as children. Seventy-five percent of the experiences reported by respondents were with older persons known to the child. Females were especially likely to have been victimized by a member of their family.

Personal property victimization is also a common experience for Americans, affecting one out of every twelve females, and one out of every ten males. Nearly 25 million American households, 30 percent of the nation's total, were somehow touched by a crime of violence or theft during 1981. This would translate into about 41 million individual victimizations.

Sexual harassment. Although some people think that "nice women aren't harassed by men," case studies show that sexual harassment cuts across socioeconomic lines, age, race, marital status, physical appearance, and educational levels. Recent surveys suggest that this harassment is not uncommon. One woman told psychologist Pearl Dykstra her experience:

> That's why I left my last job . . . I couldn't get moved up unless
> I did favors for him. I didn't want to move up in any company
> that way . . . he touched, he made comments . . . if you met
> him there [on a back staircase], you'd be going down the stairs,
> he'd be going up, he'd grab you . . . it was horrible.

Exhibitionists, voyeurs, obscene telephone callers, and harassers on the street. Statistics on the frequency of such events are not regularly collected nor are many of these events reported. A study of female undergraduates indicated that 61 percent had received obscene phone calls, 44 percent had been sexually molested, 27 percent had been a victim of exhibitionism, and 24 percent reported being followed. Often victims treat such experiences lightly or even in a humorous way. However, some writers contend that such events contribute to female fears of victimization and humiliation. One of our interviewees said:

> I was seated in a chair out in the hall and there was no one else around because classes were in session. A man walked around the corner, shabbily dressed and carrying no books. He paced nervously back and forth near me, and I tried to ignore him. All of a sudden I realized he was standing still, and I looked up to see him standing, masturbating about a foot in front of me.

The sense of vulnerability to crime is particularly acute among women of all ages, blacks, Hispanics, the elderly, and the poor. While the fears of blacks and the poor have a strong basis in reality (i.e., they do, in fact, have higher rates of victimization than other segments of the population), men are actually nearly twice as likely as women to be victims of robbery, assault, and other violence. But women are frequently victimized by physical and sexual violence and by nonviolent sexual intimidation or harassment; social scientists such as sociologist C. J. Sheffield fear that our society is becoming one of sexual terrorism for women.

How Society Views the Victim

These statistics offer a discouraging picture. Most of us feel uncomfortable about victims, and we defend against serious consideration of the possibility of victimization for ourselves or those we know in several ways. We may *deny* the evidence, *trivialize* the experiences of victims, or *blame the victim.*

DENIAL

Most people underestimate the frequency with which females in our society are victimized. Partly, this is because female victimization is often hidden "behind closed doors"; many crimes of sexual violence are not reported to the police. Underreporting is common to all crimes against females and has been linked to both female passivity and the negative reactions that women have received when they *do* report such events.

But people also deny the facts about victimization because the truth is too hard to bear—it means, for instance, that something is deeply wrong with our society. Even victims themselves may deny the importance or implications of their own experiences to avoid feelings of anger or fear that might otherwise occur. As one of our young female students said: "I was harassed by someone who called me on the telephone. . . . At first, I was a little scared and angry, but then I forgot about it. . . . [Any advice?] No, just don't let things get to you so much."

Denial of the nature and extent of female victimization inhibits our ability to develop strategies to eliminate sexual violence. It also results in the female victim feeling isolated and *personally* responsible, despite the commonness of her experience.

TRIVIALIZING THE PROBLEM

In addition to denying the high level of victimization of females, we also deny the gravity of such events, whether the victim is female or male. As a twenty-year-old male told us: "Somebody threw a brick through the windshield of my car . . . I was very upset. . . . Some [other people] thought it was pretty funny."

Trivialization or laughter is an especially common response to reports of exhibitionism, obscene telephone calls, and street harassment. Females learn to respond to such events as if they didn't matter, or as if they were funny. Jokes about sexual harassment, rape, wife abuse, and the sexual assault of children are also common. The chase around the boss's desk, Chester the Molester, and the physical violence of Andy Capp toward his wife all belittle the seriousness and destructiveness of this violence. Trivialization can also occur with other forms of victimization. An eighteen-year-old male student described almost dying from a virus. He said the reactions of other people were that "it was not considered anything major because I am still alive."

BLAMING THE VICTIM

Our society does not take a positive view of any type of victim; most people tend to blame the victim for his or her misfortunes. Perhaps the victim did something to deserve her plight? One of the first questions people ask when they learn of someone being raped, beaten, robbed, harassed, or murdered is "Why did this happen?" Comments such as "She asked for it," "Why was she there in the first place?" or "She must have done something to lead him on" are all examples of the types of things people say that lead them to search for something the victim did to deserve his or her fate. This pervasive belief that victims deserve what happens to them affects the victims in two important ways. Before the victimizing experience, most victims once *shared* this belief that the victim is to blame. The victim herself may seek to determine what she did wrong. Second, the biased attitudes of others will be communicated to the victim, making it harder for her to recover.

Why do people denigrate the unfortunate sufferers of crime, acts of nature, disease, or other traumatic events? First, people want the world to run so that good things happen to good people and bad things happen to bad people. Psychologist Melvin Lerner calls this the "just world hypothesis." If a good person is victimized, this seems unfair, but as long as the victim is somehow to blame, we can continue to believe in a "just" world. As one of our students described it:

> I was taught to believe that one, if proper, did not even discuss sex, let alone incest. I was given to believe that things such as rape or incest only happened to the bad girl. If you are a bad girl, who the hell is going to believe you, and if you are a good girl, it wouldn't have happened in the first place.

People also want to protect themselves against the belief that they might be future victims of some catastrophe. Very few people believe they are potential victims of any misfortune; on the contrary, they generally feel that they are *less* likely than most people to be victims. Psychologist Linda Perloff has labeled this perception as a belief in one's "unique invulnerability." Perceiving others as victims is threatening, particularly if the others are hit by a random blast of fate: "If it could happen to anyone, it could also happen to me." People feel especially fearful and vulnerable if the victim is like them—in age, race, education, or other factors.

Thus, knowing someone who is a victim arouses one's sense of injustice and creates fears for one's own safety. By finding specific things the victim did and by then avoiding doing these things ourselves, we can once again feel secure.

The Victim Herself: Emotional and Behavioral Reactions

Studies of crimes, accidents, environmental disasters, and harassment have all found common reactions. The most common, and debilitating, is intense feelings of helplessness. For individuals who think of themselves as "in control," being a victim violates their basic sense of autonomy. Reacting with anger or retaliation may reflect some victims' attempts to regain control; individuals who already perceive themselves as powerless and passive may be traumatized by their feelings of even greater helplessness.

After a few hours or days, these reactions change. Typical now are mood swings, from sadness to elation, or from guilt and self-pity to a desire for retaliation. Rape victims sometimes shift from feeling confident about their abilities to cope to feeling unable to deal with their lives, from fears about the past rape to fears of future attacks. Many victims also suffer continuing symptoms such as severe depression, decreased interest in social and sexual relations, recurrent nightmares, and drug abuse. For example, several months after the eruption of Mount St. Helens, local residents showed increases in illness, alcohol abuse, family stress, violence, and aggression.

How should people respond to upsetting and tragic events? In our society there are no clear standards. Although we expect victims to feel distress, there are no guidelines as to how intense the victim's reactions "should" be, or how long they "should" last. This ambiguity makes it difficult for victims to assess the "normalcy" of their own reactions. Feelings that one's reaction is more extreme than typical or is deviant further increase distress.

Many people are surprised to learn about the long-term persistence of symptoms related to victimization. Rape and incest victims, in particular, may have emotional problems that linger for years. In one study victims of a flood were still experiencing a variety of symptoms up to two years later, and so were victims of a nuclear power plant accident.

The debilitating physical or material consequences of a victimizing event are bad enough; the emotional and psychological consequences may be far more serious. The victim's worldview changes: Rather than assuming that the world is safe and just, the victim now faces an uncertain and threatening world. She wonders, "Why me?" In order for her to once again feel secure, she must "mentally restructure" the experience.

FEELINGS OF INEQUITY

Most people believe that we should be fair in our dealings with others, and that others should be fair with us. When someone violates this principle, we feel angry and upset and seek to punish the offender.

Equity theory, a formal model of our need for balance and justice, suggests that the inequity arising from the experience of being victimized can be reduced *cognitively* by reevaluating the event. Victims might feel better after deciding that their injuries were really minor, that the property stolen was of only minimal value, or that they contributed to their own misfortune and therefore deserved their fate. Inequity can also be reduced *behaviorally*: by improving one's own situation, or by doing something to harm the offender, or by having that person punished by the law. Retrieving one's stolen property or obtaining compensation from an insurance company for an "act of God" likewise restore equity. In some form, the scales of justice must be rebalanced after the blow that left them lopsided. As a twenty-two-year-old male described it: "My car was stolen in Oakland. I felt cheated, pissed off, revengeful. . . . [Afterward] Dog eat dog. . . . They steal off me—I'll steal off them."

REDEFINITION OF THE EVENT

Whether or not the individual perceives herself as a victim depends, in part, on her appraisal of what happened. She may decide that the event was not so bad. As a nineteen-year-old female student described it: "Someone robbed our house and made off with $5000 of video equipment which was all insured anyway. . . . [Do you feel you were a victim?] No, it was just material items stolen that can always be replaced."

Psychologist Shelley Taylor and her colleagues have identified some of the processes by which female cancer patients have redefined their illness; for example, they compare their own situation to that of others who are less fortunate (see Chap. 15). Rape victims also make downward comparisons. By comparing herself with another woman who suffered even more than she did, the rape victim is able to build her own self-esteem. One long-suffering abused wife told us: "I took the beatings for two and a half years. Now that's really too much, but what about the women that stayed with their husbands for much longer than that?"

Sociologists Pauline Bart and Kim Scheppele provide an example of these processes in their study of rape victims. Although all these women were victims of acts legally classified as rape, those who had been forced to perform sexual acts other than those involving the penis defined themselves as "escaping" rape. Conversely, most of those who were penetrated vaginally, orally, or anally did define the crime as rape; they also had the most negative reactions to the crime and were the most likely to report it to the police.

Another way of redefining the event is to look at the experience as having a greater meaning—a test of strength and character perhaps. "When I look back on this and other things that happened," a student who had been sexually abused as a child told us, "I realize that they made me strong and independent as a person."

We read about one woman who had been severely beaten, shot in the head, and left to die. She survived, and described in a newspaper interview how the assault had led to a "joyful reconciliation with her mother." Other victims report that they gained a sense of "mystical consciousness."

SELF-BLAME

As we have seen, others are likely to blame the victim as a way of assuring themselves that they are safe from being victimized themselves. But what happens if they become victims? They ask: "Why me?" "What could I have done differently?" "What can I do about this now?" The answers to such questions will vary—and will affect emotional reactions. A woman may blame herself ("I shouldn't have gone out with him") or her abuser ("How dare he!"). She can see herself or others as responsible.

As we reviewed the research dealing with the reactions of *all* types of victims, we found a general tendency for victims to blame themselves. It is not uncommon, for example, for victims of unprovoked sexual assaults or of battering to take personal responsibility for the crime. Thus, a battered woman may say to herself, "If only I had gotten dinner ready on time." A rape victim may focus on the clothing she was wearing or on not being vigilant enough in observing others around her. Even victims of natural disasters tend to blame themselves by saying such things as "We should have moved sooner." Our informants said:

My boyfriend beat me up and broke my nose during an argument. [I felt] very hurt, felt guilty as though it were my own fault, like I provoked it.

I just had my purse stolen. It could happen to anyone, and besides, in a way it was my fault for being so careless.

The need to be protected [from the sexual advances of the choir director] without causing a scandal drove me to confide in my friend, the deacon. My trustworthy, adult, loving friend told me I was at fault—I appeared suggestive. . . . I began to feel that the image I projected was suggestive.

I'm ashamed of the fact I was victimized. When and if I told one of my girlfriends, I did so in a hushed whisper and swore them to secrecy . . . I still even now think I should justify my reputation and morals to you . . . As irrational as it seems, I still felt somehow I deserved it and search my mind for what thing I had done to make me guilty of this.

It might seem that holding oneself responsible for one's victimization would be self-defeating and maladaptive. However, such self-blame can be quite functional, especially if it focuses on behavior ("I was careless") rather than character ("I am always too attractive to men"). Characterological self-blame attributes one's victimization to aspects of one's personality, a relatively permanent matter; so these attributions give a woman little confidence that she can avoid future victimization, and can produce feelings of depression and helplessness. Psychologist Ronnie Janoff-Bulman found that rape victims who made characterological attributions also tended to feel they *deserved* the rapes. Not only did these women see themselves as the types of women who get raped, but also, sadly, as the types of people who should be raped.

But rape victims who attributed their rapes to behavioral reasons were more confident about avoiding future attacks. By seeing particular actions or behaviors they had done as responsible (such as saying they should have been more careful about going out alone at night or dating someone they did not know well), they were able to psychologically take control over the event: To avoid future victimization it is necessary for them only to act in a different way. Similarly, crime victims who blame themselves for not preventing the crime report fewer psychological problems both two weeks and four months after the crime than those who did not blame themselves.

It is important for a victim to distinguish between *responsibility for the problem,* which connotates blame, and *responsibility for the solution,* which connotes control. This can be seen in the case of a young female student involved in an auto accident:

> We were hit by a drunk who fell asleep at the wheel. We were victims of a careless human being. . . . I have become more cautious as a driver.

In another case involving a female college freshman, she told us:

> I was at a party and a guy kept giving me more drinks. . . . Then he said he would walk me home. . . . He attacked me, but I got away before he did anything too severe. . . . I feel I should not be so naïve when it comes to trusting people, although I do not think it was my fault.

Battered women often blame themselves for their husbands' violence, but this does not mean they feel that they alone have caused the violence. Rather than asking the "Why me?" question posed by other victims, they may instead ask, "What did I do tonight that set him off?" Once they answer this question, battered women then try very hard not to initiate the violence again. Unfortunately, these efforts are rarely successful in stopping the battering. Many battered women continue to be hopeful that the violence will stop, even though it is more common for the violence to become more severe and frequent over time.

Once a pattern of violence is established in the marriage, the battered woman then begins to ask herself another attributional question: "Why do I stay in this relationship?" With repeated unsuccessful attempts to control the battering, some battered women give up and sink into lethargy and helplessness. As this occurs, they become less and less able to change their situations for the better. The battered wife may fear that her husband will retaliate against her, their children, or her family if she tries to leave. Such fears are often justified, because many women who have left abusive husbands have been followed by them and harassed or even killed. The severely battered woman may finally leave her husband, often only because she is desperate and fears for her life or that of her children if she stays. Women who are battered *and* raped by their husbands suffer some of the strongest reactions and are most likely to leave. Some women feel so trapped in a violent marriage that they may resort to killing or attempting to kill their battering husbands.

LOSS OF A SENSE OF SAFETY OR OF INVULNERABILITY

Most people assume that disasters will not happen to them or to those close to them; they feel invulnerable. But many women feel especially vulnerable to crime and harassment; they feel weak and helpless and unable to defend themselves physically. One way women respond to these fears is to develop protective strategies or rules designed to reestablish their sense of invulnerability. "I won't wear jewelry on the street to tempt muggers." "I won't wear short skirts in Central Park." "I'll put new bars on the windows." All of this may backfire, though, if these rules do not protect them.

Many women, for instance, have rules they follow in their daily lives to avoid being raped. These rules make them feel safe as long as they follow them. If a woman is raped in spite of following her personal safety rules, the emotional consequences can be devastating; now she has no basis for feeling safe in the future. Rape victims who are able instead attribute the rape to their having broken those safety rules ("I took the short cut through the alley") have fewer long-term aftereffects. For them it is still possible to feel invulnerable to future rapes. But women who are raped at home, in spite of locks and other precautions, have a more difficult recovery.

Feelings of safety or invulnerability are also affected by one's own experiences with victimization. Once one does become a victim, it is easy to imagine oneself in the victim role again. "I was scared to death of everything," said a twenty-year-old woman who had been assaulted, "and jumped if anyone came up behind me unexpectedly."

Research on other crimes finds the same processes at work. People who have been robbed are more likely to report being afraid of crime than their neighbors; interviews with victims of crime in New York City revealed that 48 percent were fearful of future victimization. Burglary victims have a particularly strong fear, feeling that the one place where they felt safe—their homes—is no longer secure.

The sense of vulnerability also matters because it affects crime-prevention efforts. People who feel that they can take steps to avoid victimization are most likely to use door locks and other crime-preventative measures such as participation in neighborhood watch programs.

REACTIONS DURING AND AFTER THE EVENT

If you are about to be mugged, raped, beaten, or harassed, what are you likely to do? Do you take protective or defensive action? In one national crime survey, women were about as likely as men to take self-protective measures during the commission of a crime against them. Men were more likely to use physical force to protect themselves, whereas women were more likely to try to get help or frighten off the offender. Although women often use less violent techniques of resistance than men do, they typically do something.

Women sometimes report having been taught or encouraged to respond to victimization passively, especially with regard to minor offenses such as street harassment and exhibitionism. Two young college women told us:

> I was taught that women are supposed to be passive and compla-
> cent. I was also taught not to be forceful or use self-defense at all.
> Now I realize that women don't fight back because their socializa-
> tion causes them to be afraid of being hurt by force and also causes
> them to be afraid of hurting others, even those who are assaulting
> them.

> I can see where my reluctance to respond comes from fears that
> have been ingrained in me that if I do respond, the male will
> physically put me in my place.

Some researchers, such as psychologist Louise Kidder, have suggested that such training or advice makes it difficult for women to respond actively to rape and other abuses. Several recent studies have indicated that even low levels of resistance, such as running or screaming, may distinguish women who were assaulted, but escaped rape, from rape victims.

> I think the thing that kept me from getting raped was the fact that
> I was very alert. I didn't ignore the sounds I was hearing [of
> someone following her].

In a similar vein a young female victim of an attempted mugging told us: "I screamed loudly and took a karate stance and the mugger ran off."

What can a woman do after being victimized? As a response to their fear or shock, some women retreat into their homes, not going out, not seeing others. Others move to a new residence or change their telephone numbers. Two young female college students described this to us:

> A kid used to call me up on the telephone and use extreme profan-
> ity. It was someone I knew, apparently, because he knew my
> name. It bothered me because I didn't think anyone I knew would
> do anything like that. I also began to withdraw from quite a few of
> my male friends and other males that I knew.

Two friends and I were in Port Authority [Bus Terminal] catching a bus and two black girls stole our wallets . . . [I] haven't gone back to the Port Authority building since. I used to go there all the time.

Other victims take self-defensive measures to reduce their sense of vulnerability. Some robbery victims get weapons; rape victims become more cautious or enroll in self-defense courses. Programs to prevent rape have been developed to train women in self-defense, in how to walk on the street and be aware of their surroundings. These programs are often effective in making the participants more self-confident. Some actions may reduce her feelings of inequity. Reporting crimes to the police, applying for compensation, or filing an insurance claim also help the victim cope.

Getting Help, Getting Justice

Many victims turn to others for help—for medical assistance, emotional support, information, or assistance with physical tasks resulting from the victimization. Other people can help the victim to assess the situation clearly and to determine if victimization has occurred. Others also give advice to the victim.

Not all victims seek help, and those who do may not receive the assistance they want. Sadly, friends and acquaintances as well as bystanders may ignore victims, whom they see as "losers" or because they fear guilt (or victimization) by association. People with whom the victim comes in contact often blame her or have other negative reactions discussed earlier. Others avoid victims because victims, naturally, are so often depressed, and most people prefer not being around unhappy people. People want to help the victim, but at the same time feel uncomfortable because of her sadness, complaints, and anxiety. When they attempt to reduce their friend's distress, they often communicate to the victim that she is more upset than she "should" be, and is not recovering properly. When a woman does turn to others for help, and the others refuse or respond with distancing or dislike, the woman may find their reactions even more distressing than the original victimizing event.

FAMILIES, FRIENDS, AND NEIGHBORS

The first place many women go for help is to their families and friends. In a study of abused wives, two thirds relied on family or friends for emotional help or shelter; 43 percent of the abuse victims in a Milwaukee study done by sociologist Lee Bowker received help from family members and 52 percent from friends.

Positive social support helps a victim cope, recover, and restore her self-esteem. Family members and friends give this help in several ways. By simply being available to talk with the victim about the event, friends allow the victim to express depression, sadness, and other emotions; the need for such emotional expression may continue for months or even years. Friends and family also assist the victim in solving problems: referring her to agencies, showing her how to behave, getting proper help, figuring out what to do next. This kind of social support is related to the likelihood that victims of wife abuse will obtain a divorce or fight back.

In addition, family, friends, and neighbors can help victims reduce their feelings of injustice by helping her identify, locate, and prosecute the offender. As one young woman described it to us:

> Six months ago someone stole my purse . . . [Other people who learned of it] were angry for me. They were outraged to think that someone would do that to me. . . . Some told me to go out and get revenge. Go back and do the same thing to them.

Victims may also rely on others to help reduce their fears of being victimized again. One popular form of increasing feelings of safety is the "neighborhood watch" program, in which neighbors join together to keep an eye out for suspicious events.

Support is a particular issue for rape victims because of the common negative reactions of their husbands or lovers. Rape victims typically react to the crime with fear, guilt, or anger and hostility toward men; their male partners are more likely to feel anger or rage toward the rapist. Many male partners have recurrent fantasies of killing or maiming the rapist. The woman's feelings of shame, guilt, and fear of negative consequences are further reinforced by objectively unpleasant reactions she may further endure—a sizable number of disrupted relationships or divorces are initiated by husbands who were unable "to adjust." Even in couples who stay together, sexual relations are often disrupted for months or even years.

THE CRIMINAL JUSTICE SYSTEM

Overall, about one third of all crimes are reported to the police. What do those who call the police expect to gain? Notifying the police reduces the victim's stress in several ways. Her sense of injustice, outrage, or offense can be reduced if she actually reports, and her sense of control is restored if the police catch the offender, recover the stolen property, or find the mugger, or if the offender is convicted, punished, or forced to make restitution. Prosecuting the criminal helps the victim realize that she has a legitimate grievance and can, therefore, help her feel less guilty and apathetic—and less vulnerable to future attacks.

Despite these benefits, the fact that only a third of all crime victims call the police suggests that many victims see little likelihood of being helped by the police or that they do not wish to incur additional costs and stress. Indeed, two of the most frequently cited reasons that victims give for not calling the police are that "nothing can be done" and that "the police would not want to be bothered." Other victims try to downplay the seriousness of the crimes against them. In a recent study of rape victims, it was found that the women who failed to report a rape were those who denied or rationalized their experience, or who attempted to find an explanation for the event in their own behavior.

Crimes of sexual violence are the least likely to be reported to the police; victims doubt that they will be believed or that the offender will be punished. To some extent such fears are realistic. Rape has the lowest conviction rate of all violent crimes: On a national average, one rapist in twenty is arrested, one in thirty is prosecuted, and one in sixty is convicted. Court appearances are stressful, too, because testifying forces the victim to relive the experience, and it may also evoke fears of retaliation from the criminal.

To make matters worse, some rape victims feel frustrated, embarrassed, guilty, and angry in their encounters with the police and courts. They often feel violated a second time—that they are the ones on trial, not the rapists. A college student recalled her experience with the police after a sexual assault:

> When the police arrived to file a report, I was dressed in jeans and a T-shirt. The one officer asked me if I had been wearing this at the time of the attack. . . . I told him I really didn't think it mattered if I was naked, nobody had the right to lay their hands on me. . . . He then said I must have been wearing something revealing to be so defensive. . . . The other officer then asked me

if I had been touched in any way. When I told him yes, he asked me if I had enjoyed it. . . . The officers of the law were just as verbally abusive [as the attacker], if not more so.

Similarly, wife-abuse victims often have difficulties with the police. In two studies abused wives rated the police as the *least* helpful of available sources of help. Police officers often do not define battered women as the victims of violent crime, and they often refuse to arrest the abusive husband even when the wife requests them to do so. Two battered women told sociologist Lee Bowker that:

When I did go to the police, they did nothing.

The police stood on my front lawn and allowed us to be beaten with a lead pipe knowing we were all in there helpless.

When the police are responsive to the victim's needs, she will often feel comforted and reassured. The good news is that the majority of rape victims have positive experiences with the police, who, they report, are helpful and make them feel better. Moreover, one step that is effective in preventing violent husbands from beating their wives is arresting them. When the police do agree to intervene, they can be very effective.

The decision to report must be left up to the victim. She is best able to evaluate her need for prosecution, her ability to cope with the procedures involved, and the other resources on which she can rely. Her decision to report may prevent other victimizations and will improve the accuracy of our estimates of these crimes.

HELP FROM MENTAL HEALTH PRACTITIONERS

Although their work is designed to help people, very often nurses, doctors, therapists, and other mental health professionals share the common social beliefs about victims; they may blame her, want to avoid her, and even feel contempt toward her:

During all this time I was still going to group therapy meetings. I kept telling them what was happening and they kept saying I must be doing something to cause these beatings to happen. I told them I tried everything. . . . The group couldn't figure out why these things weren't working.

For a while I went to some psychiatrists who just sit there and listen and never say a word.

Victims may, in turn, internalize this contempt in the form of self-loathing. This is a particularly complex situation, because the types of victims who are most likely to seek therapy are often the ones who demonstrate the most self-blame. An abused woman in our class told us:

Once when we had another fight and I was pretty badly beaten, I called my husband's psychiatrist and told him I was leaving my husband. He said, "Why are you leaving him? He hasn't beat you up in a month."

The mental health industry has, for the most part, not involved itself in the planning and implementation of services for victims; it has tended to ignore victims' issues; it has thus continued to be ill-equipped to handle the special treatment needs of victims. County mental health services, for example, have not been victim-oriented, with the exception of concern for problems of rape victims. Some have extended their services to drug users, runaway youths, and potential suicides, but they have lagged noticeably in extending services to victims of crime or sexual harassment. Many victims continue to feel invisible and frustrated at the relative unavailability of skilled professionals to handle their special problems.

SELF-HELP GROUPS

Many women turn to self-help groups, an intermediate step between professional services and friends. Self-help groups have a formal structure and serve specific types of victims. Operating on the assumption that people who have endured some victimization are the best experts on how to cope with it, these groups offer women the opportunity to meet and talk with others who have been through the same thing. Peer support groups help the victim to feel less deviant, to find meaning in the horrible experience, and to reach better long-term adjustment; but, studies find, groups may not help her overcome depression.

One example of a successful self-help group is a woman's shelter, typically staffed by women, many of whom have been abused themselves. Such shelters are not available everywhere, and many women are unaware of their services. A study of wife-abuse victims in southwestern Wisconsin found that only 10 percent of the women went to a shelter after the first incidence of abuse but, with repeated abuse, 29 percent sought help there. A woman student who had witnessed her mother's abuse and later had been abused herself said:

> Things are better now, though. At least some women have some shelters to go to and be safe. My mother and I never had a place to seek shelter and counseling. . . . Someday I hope to be involved in some form of wife-abuse shelter so I can try to help other women get out of this painful trap, especially women with no education or who have kids and don't think they can make it alone.

Another abused woman who did go to a shelter reported:

> I will always be grateful to that group, for I am sure I would be dead now if it wasn't for them. Although I still had problems, they taught me to deal with my feelings, and that I was not to blame.

Many people think that it is important for victims to keep their stress within tolerable limits, to maintain a positive self-concept, to ventilate their emotions, and to develop a realistic (non-self-blaming) view of their experience. But research does not always support this reasoning. Each of these conclusions has been challenged by research on the long-term adjustment of victims. For example, in general, it is more effective for the victim to *regulate* her emotions than simply to *ventilate* them endlessly. Emotional discharge (i.e., "letting out your feelings"), a popular coping strategy among women, tends to produce continued upset. However, at least in the short-term reaction stage, intense distress and anger can be major motivations in getting women to react constructively.

Based on research with all types of victims, we offer the following suggestions for the victims. However, remember that different coping strategies work for different individuals in different situations. If one strategy fails, try another. *Victims who can define their situation as a challenge rather than a loss or a threat cope most effectively.*

Advice for Victims and Care Givers

- Realize that victimization of females is not uncommon, and is not funny.

- Understand why people blame victims. This can help you deal with the negative or blaming reactions you may receive from others.
- Know about the common reactions and experiences of other victims; realize that your reactions are not bizarre or unusual, and are not indications of poor coping.
- It may be helpful for you to view your experience as "not so bad," or to focus on any positive aspects of the event. It is probably *not* helpful for friends or relatives to make such observations.
- Consider whether your behavior may have contributed to your victimization. Are there any ways you can protect yourself better in the future? But don't think that you are the type of person who is victimized or that you in some way deserved to be victimized.
- You may feel less vulnerable if you design a new set of rules or strategies to prevent future victimizations.
- You need to reestablish your sense of justice in the world. You might join an organization that is helping other victims, or that is fighting the causes of what victimized you.
- When possible, *resist* victimization. Yell, scream, kick, shout "Fire!" (that brings people). *Listen* for men possibly following you. Once victimized, take note of what you did to resist, or why it was impossible for you to behave otherwise.
- Taking appropriate retaliation or self-defensive action is an important aspect of coping.
- Seeking help from others is healthy, not a sign of weakness.
- Victims rarely benefit from the "Cheer up" messages given by others; do not use such messages as an indication of the appropriateness or inappropriateness of your reactions.
- Understanding some of the reasons that others fail to provide support may help you deal with your friends' reactions.
- The police may be able to assist you in many ways, but it may be prudent for you to anticipate negative attitudes.
- Look for self-help groups that deal with the problem you have. If you can't find one, start one!
- To decide whether to report your victimization to authorities, weigh the potential gains for yourself and others (future victims) against the stresses involved and the limits of your resources.
- You can restore your sense of control by rejecting social programs that are inadequate to your needs; realizing when your friends and family can help, and when they cannot; recognizing the need for collective action when you can't do everything on your own.

Sources of Help

Professional Sources of Help
Family Services
Children's Services
Human Services
Salvation Army
Private Mental Health Referrals
Welfare
Hospitals

Self-Help Groups
Women's Centers
Rape Centers
Alcoholics Anonymous
Community Hot Lines

Specific Referrals
Sexual Harassment Center
  for Women in Government
1400 Washington Avenue
Draper Hall
Albany, NY 12222
(518) 442-3900

Domestic Violence
National Coalition Against
  Domestic Violence
1500 Massachusetts Avenue, NW
No. 35
Washington, DC 20005

Criminal Justice System Sources
  of Help
Police
District Attorney
Legal Aid
Private Attorneys
Victim Compensation Board

General Referrals
National Organization for Victim
  Assistance
717 D Street, NW
Washington, DC 20004
(202) 393-6682

National Victims Resource
  Center
Office of Justice Programs
Suite 1352
633 Indiana Avenue, NW
Washington, DC 20531
(202) 724-6134

Response to the Victimization of
  Women and Children
A publication of:
  Center for Women Policy
    Studies
  2000 P Street, NW
  Suite 508
  Washington, DC 20036

IRENE HANSON FRIEZE, Ph.D., is professor of psychology, business, and women's studies at the University of Pittsburgh, where she is also Chair of the Social Psychology Program and director of the Women's Studies Program. Dr. Frieze's research has included studies of women who are victims of batterings and marital rape. She has also done research on beliefs about the causes of success and failure, applying her findings to understanding the reactions of victims. She is a past president of the Division of the Psychology of Women of the American Psychological Association and was a member of the American Psychological Association Task Force on Victims of Crime and Violence. Dr. Frieze is the author of numerous publications and articles on victimization and domestic violence, and in 1983 was a coeditor of a *Journal of Social Issues* volume on reactions to victimization.

MAUREEN C. McHUGH is an assistant professor of psychology at Duquesne University. Gender roles are her primary teaching and research interest. She has taught courses in the psychology of women and in human sexuality at several colleges and universities. She became particularly interested in the victimization of women from reading and listening to her students' experiences (in their journals and in class discussions). Dr. McHugh has received numerous awards for her research and teaching and has published many papers on women's issues.

Further Reading

Bard, Morton, and Sangrey, Dawn. *The Crime Victim's Book*. New York: Basic Books, 1979.

Barkas, J. *Victims*. New York: Scribner, 1978.

Bowker, Lee. "Coping with Wife Abuse: Personal and Social Networks." In *Battered Women and Their Families,* edited by Albert R. Roberts. New York: Springer Publishing Co., 1984.

Chappell, Duncan; Geis, Robley; and Geis, Gilbert. Forcible Rape: *The Crime, the Victim, and the Offender*. New York: Columbia University Press, 1977.

Farley, Lin. *Sexual Shakedown: The Sexual Harassment of Women on the Job*. New York: McGraw-Hill, 1978.

Finkelhor, David. *Sexually Victimized Children*. New York: Free Press, 1979.

Frieze, Irene. "Investigating the Causes and Consequences of Marital Rape." *Signs* 8 (1983):532–53.

———. "Perceptions of Battered Wives." *New Approaches to Social Prob-*

lems: Applications of Attribution Theory, edited by I. Frieze, D. Bar-Tal, and John Carroll. San Francisco: Jossey-Bass, 1979.

Jones, Ann. *Women Who Kill*. New York: Fawcett, 1980.

Lerner, Melvin. *The Belief in a Just World*. New York: Plenum, 1980.

MacKennon, Catherine A. *Sexual Harassment of Working Women: A Case of Sex Discrimination*. New Haven: Yale University Press, 1979.

McCahill, Thomas W.; Meyer, Linda C.; and Fischman, Arthur M. *The Aftermath of Rape*. Lexington, Mass.: Heath, 1979.

Pagelow, Mildred. *Women-Battering: Victims and Their Experiences*. Beverly Hills, Calif.: Sage Publications, 1981.

Rush, Florence. *The Best Kept Secret*. Englewood Cliffs, N.J.: Prentice-Hall, 1980.

Russell, Diana. *The Politics of Rape: The Victim's Perspective*. New York: Stein & Day, 1974.

Sheffield, Carole. "Sexual Terrorism." In *Women: A Feminist Perspective*, edited by Jay Freeman. Palo Alto, Calif.: Mayfield, 1984.

Silver, Roxanne; Boon, Cheryl; and Stones, Mary. "Searching for Meaning in Misfortune: Making Sense of Incest." *Journal of Social Issues* 3, no. 2 (1983):81–102.

Skogan, Wesley, and Maxfield, Michael. *Coping with Crime: Individual and Neighborhood Reactions*. Beverly Hills, Calif.: Sage Publications, 1981.

Straus, Murray; Gelles, Richard; and Steinmetz, Suzanne. *Behind Closed Doors: Violence in the American Family*. Garden City, N.Y.: Doubleday, 1980.

Walker, Lenore. *The Battered Woman*. New York: Harper & Row, 1979.

WHEN PROBLEMS PERSIST:
Change and Therapy

18

The Challenge of Change

HARRIET GOLDHOR LERNER

Dianna began psychotherapy on her thirtieth birthday. "It occurred to me," Dianna explained during our first appointment, "that the *next* ten years could be just like the *last* ten years. The thought filled me with dread, and so I decided to get help." I learned that Dianna had been feeling stuck for a long time, and the more she tried to change things, the more things stayed the same.

Dianna's presenting complaint was "depression"—a woman's problem of epidemic proportion. "I feel like my life is going nowhere," reported Dianna, with an obvious effort to hold back tears. Dianna explained that she was bored and exhausted by her substitute-teaching job and that she entertained frequent thoughts about going back to graduate school to increase both her paycheck and her career options. Her husband, Jonathan, however, vetoed the idea. In Dianna's words, "Jonathan just won't hear of it until our daughter Cara is in kindergarten. No matter how much I fight with him, his final word is always 'No.'"

Dianna's depression was only part of the picture. She was also feeling bitter and resentful. In fact, Dianna viewed both her mother and husband as the sources of her unhappiness. According to Dianna's description, her widowed mother was a controlling, demanding, and critical woman who was impossible to get along with. Dianna portrayed her husband in similarly unflattering terms: Jonathan was an emotionally distant workaholic who ignored his family and then moved in with an iron hand. "When he does lower himself to get involved in family affairs," explained Dianna with undisguised sarcasm, "he makes decisions as if he rules the roost."

Over the years, Dianna had engaged in numerous unsuccessful attempts to shape up her husband and change her mother. The outcome was that nothing changed at all.

Dianna's specific complaints may or may not ring a bell, but she touches on some universal themes in women's lives:

• She is depressed.
• Her self-esteem is suffering.
• She feels blocked from moving ahead at work.
• She blames her mother and her husband.
• She engages in nonproductive fighting that goes nowhere.
• She feels dominated and controlled by others.
• She is unaware of her contribution to her own dilemma.
• She feels helpless and powerless to change the status quo.

All of the above are common "women's problems"—but why? What blocks us from moving ahead with our own growth? Why do we have difficulty identifying and assertively claiming our own needs and wants? Why would so many of us participate in relationships at the expense of our own self? And can we have *both* an intimate relationship and a self? These are questions that women struggle with daily, whether we are aware of it or not. By taking a closer look at Dianna's story, we can learn more about our own selves.

When "We" Means Loss of "I"

Dianna was eager to return to graduate school, but her husband wouldn't hear of it. I learned that their conflict about graduate school was only one example of a long-standing marital pattern in which Dianna fought with Jonathan but nonetheless adapted to his wants rather than standing firmly and assertively behind her own.

Dianna had not always been a fighter. Early in their relationship her philosophy was "peace at any price." "Looking back," said Dianna, "it was as if we shared a common brain and bloodline. We operated as if there were only one way to see the world, and that was Jonathan's way." Not only did Dianna avoid conflict at all cost—she also avoided making clear statements about her own thoughts and feelings when she feared that such clarity would expose differences between herself and Jonathan and disrupt the harmonious "oneness" of their relationship. "I suppose I had the urge to merge," said Dianna. "When we were first together, I would not even have told *myself* that I wanted to go back to school if I sensed that Jonathan would be threatened or disapproving."

Dianna was describing the process of *de-selfing* that occurs frequently in marriage. "De-selfing," a term from Bowen Family Systems Theory, means that too much of the self (the "I") is sacrificed in the service of a relationship (the "we"). Obviously, all close relationships require compromise, negotiation, and give-and-take. We cannot always get our way or do what we want to do. The problem arises when one partner—frequently the woman—does more than her share of giving in and going along. When too much of the self—one's thoughts, feelings, wants, and ambitions—becomes negotiable under relationship pressures, the de-selfed partner may develop symptoms. In Dianna's case her symptoms included depression, fatigue, apathy, and a growing sense of bitterness, helplessness, and low self-esteem.

At the time Dianna began psychotherapy with me, the honeymoon was over and her behavior with Jonathan had shifted dramatically. In Dianna's words, "I've gone from being a good girl to a flaming bitch." Dianna was now better able to define who she was, apart from what her husband wanted and expected her to be, and she was no longer afraid to identify differences and face conflict in her marriage. Despite all appearances, however, not that much had changed in her marriage, because Dianna was engaging in repetitive cycles of ineffective fighting and blaming that still served to keep her stuck in a dependent and de-selfed position. To make matters worse, Dianna was beginning to fit the stereotype of a nagging, bitchy wife, which increased her feelings of depression and low self-esteem.

Venting anger is not much different from staying silent if our expressions of anger serve to block change rather than facilitate it. Like many women, Dianna was fighting in a manner that actually protected her husband and the status quo of their relationship. In a nutshell, Dianna was putting her emotional energy into trying to change a husband who did not want to change. In trying to do the impossible, she relinquished the power that she did have—the power to change her own self and to take a new and different action on her own behalf.

Let's take a closer look at the domestic battle scene. As Dianna described it, a typical fight would unfold as follows: Dianna would voice her frustration with her substitute teaching job and would express her wish to enroll in a master's program at a local university. Jonathan would then argue that

Dianna should put her plans on the back burner until their daughter entered kindergarten—"for Cara's sake." Dianna would then quote her feminist friends and bring forth evidence from child development experts in an attempt to argue her case. The more Dianna tried to prove her point, the more tenaciously Jonathan clung to his original opinion. When things became sufficiently intense, Dianna and Jonathan would angrily withdraw from each other. Eventually, they would cool off and later the sequence would begin again.

What was the problem here? First of all, Dianna's "urge to merge" was still in operation. She was behaving as if there were only one correct way to view a situation, and she was trying to convince Jonathan to see things her way. Perhaps it is difficult for all of us to maintain enough "separateness" in our close relationships, to recognize that people think, feel, and react differently. Too often, we equate closeness with sameness—an equation which is a hallmark of fused relationships, where the individual "I's" get blurred within the "we." Dianna was failing to recognize that *both* she and Jonathan had a right to their perspectives on the graduate school issue. We all have a right to everything we think and feel.

Dianna and Jonathan were also fighting about a pseudo-issue, as couples frequently do. The real issue was not how Cara would be affected by having a mother in graduate school. Jonathan's focus on Cara reflected his difficulty expressing his own fears directly. "Cara needs you at home," he would say. "I support your going back to school, but I do not like to see the baby and the household neglected." It took a long while for Jonathan to address the real issue, "I am scared and worried about your making this change," even to himself. To state his fears directly would have made him feel weak, dependent, and emotional, and these were "feminine" qualities that he did not wish to acknowledge within himself. Tangible things, like the household or small children who have a right to need people, were far more acceptable concerns. Dianna, too, kept the spotlight off her own anxieties about returning to graduate school by arguing with her husband about Cara.

Finally, Dianna's attempts to change Jonathan only protected him from change. Dianna fought with her husband, but she continued to actively maintain her dependent and de-selfed position. She did not challenge the basic rule in the relationship, which was that Jonathan made the rules. Why would Dianna participate in nonproductive fights that only served to hold the clock still? Why would any of us choose to stay stuck in a dependent, de-selfed position in a relationship?

The Fear of Change

If Dianna chose to operate from a position of power and strength, she could refuse to participate in the old fights entirely and instead stand firmly behind her own position. After all, it is Dianna's job to clarify her own thoughts and feelings, and to behave in a manner that is congruent with her convictions and beliefs. It is *not* her job to change Jonathan or make him see things her way. The more she tries, the more she will insure that nothing will change.

Let us suppose that Dianna were to approach Jonathan when things were relatively calm between them, and tell him the following, without apology or blame: "Jonathan, I know you don't approve of my going back to graduate school at this time and I understand that you are concerned that Cara will suffer. Nonetheless, I've decided that I need to do this for myself and I plan to go ahead." Should Jonathan invite her to reinstate the old fights about their daughter's well-being, Dianna could refuse to take the bait. For example, she might say: "Perhaps you're right about Cara or perhaps you're wrong. I can't know for sure. What I do know is that I want to go to graduate school at this time, and if I put it off, I will end up feeling bitter and resentful. I am hoping for your support, but I certainly understand that you may see things differently." Let us suppose that Dianna could stand behind her position with firmness and dignity, and without trying to change her husband's feelings or convince him to see things her way.

If Dianna could calmly maintain this new stance, without getting buffeted about by Jonathan's reactions to her change, she might find herself confronting some anxiety-arousing issues in her marriage: "How is power and decision making shared in this relationship?" "Who is in charge of making decisions about my own life?" "How will it affect my marriage if I become a stronger, more assertive person?" "What are my own fears about taking more responsibility for my choices?" "If my choice is to save my marriage or save myself, which do I choose?" These are difficult questions that Dianna herself preferred to avoid by participating in the old familiar fights.

How might Jonathan react to his wife's new behavior, and what would his next move be? Would he become withdrawn, depressed, or sullen? Would he drink or have an affair? Might he say, "If you go back to graduate school, I will leave you"? One thing is for sure. Jonathan will make some attempt to reinstate the familiar, reassuring fights, and to test out whether his wife would then return to the old pattern. There are few things more anxiety-arousing in a relationship than when a dependent spouse stops the old pattern of silent submission, or ineffective fighting and blaming, and begins to move to a higher level of independence and self-definition. It is simply inherent in the nature of human systems that change of this sort is a scary business and will be resisted from both inside and out.

For many months in psychotherapy Dianna remained stuck in a narrow space in which she could not move. If she continued in the old marital pattern, she was betraying and sacrificing her own self, which impaired her self-esteem and left her feeling bitter and depressed. If, however, she shifted to a position of greater self-assertion and independence, she feared threatening, if not losing, her marriage. Caught between a rock and a hard place, Dianna got trapped in repetitive cycles of fighting and blaming, fights that served both to protest and protect the status quo.

Why do many women spin their wheels in unhappy relationships? The answer is not because our masochistic souls secretly like it that way, but because we may be too anxious and guilty to take even a small step toward greater separateness and independence. We may unconsciously view our own change and growth as a hurtful and destructive act that will diminish others and shatter the predictable security of our relationships. This was true in Dianna's case. Underlying her complaints that Jonathan was a domineering husband who "ruled the roost," she experienced him as a fragile individual who might not easily tolerate her moves toward greater separateness and autonomy. This belief lurks in the unconscious of countless women —the belief that our self-assertion, clarity, autonomy, competence, and growth will weaken, rather than strengthen, our most important relationships, especially with men.

Where does such a belief come from? In many instances this fear of change reflects the rules of the systems in which we operate. Our very definitions of "femininity" teach us to inhibit any strengths or abilities that might be threatening to men and to cultivate instead those very qualities (e.g., dependency, passivity, and vulnerability) that men fear in themselves. In countless ways women are encouraged to assume a dependent and de-selfed position in order to bolster and protect men, just as men learn to derive their sense of masculinity and self-esteem from their partner's one-down position.

The unspoken psychological contract in Dianna and Jonathan's marriage was a common one, prescribed and reinforced by culture: Dianna protected Jonathan by assuming the role of the dependent, de-selfed child, thus allowing Jonathan to deny and disown these qualities within himself. Jonathan, in turn, assumed a dominating and controlling position in the relationship which protected Dianna from facing the challenges of greater autonomy and achievement, which she feared. Dianna held the clock still with Jonathan not only because she harbored the secret conviction that her marriage had little flexibility to tolerate her growth. She also wanted to protect both her husband and herself from the feelings of anxiety, guilt, and loss that inevitably accompany the process of change. This marital arrangement lowered anxiety in the short run, but Dianna's chronic depression and mounting resentment spoke to the long-term cost.

Looking Deeper

We bring to a marriage—or to any intimate relationship—the same level of independence, autonomy, and selfhood that we have achieved in our family of origin. Dianna's stuck position in her marriage reflected the fact that she had never really left home, and her behavior with Jonathan mirrored her interactions with her mother, Lillie. Here, too, Dianna would argue and blame on the one hand, or distance herself and withdraw on the other, rather than calmly and clearly define her own position on important issues. Both blaming and emotional distancing prevented Dianna from making a real declaration of independence from her mother—who also experienced Dianna's change and growth as a potential threat and loss.

A typical interaction between mother and daughter might go as follows: Lillie had strong reactions to Dianna's lack of interest in religion and she would lecture Dianna about her failure to attend church, elaborating at length on the adverse effects this would eventually have on Cara. Dianna, in response, would become extremely tense. She would then criticize her mother and the church, or refuse to discuss the subject entirely.

How might Dianna move differently if she were ready to shift to a higher level of independence and bring the separateness between herself and her mother into bolder relief? In a voice that conveyed neither intensity nor blame, she might say, "Mother, I know that it upsets you that I do not go to church. If I were in your shoes, I might feel the same way. I know how important religion is to you and how helpful it has been in your life. But I'm me, and I need to make my own decisions for myself and my family. At this point Jonathan and I have both decided not to attend church."

Dianna could also do her best to stay inside her own skin and resist getting sucked back into the old pattern of distancing or arguing when her mother reacted strongly to her declaration of separateness and independence. For example, if Lillie's anxiety led her to intensify her lectures and criticism (which is the predictable response), Dianna could listen respectfully and then say: "I understand how you feel, Mother, and I appreciate your involvement with the church. But I need to sort out my own perspective on religion. I know that it's not the same choice that you would make, but I guess that you and I have different views on this subject."

If Dianna were feeling courageous, she could ask her mother questions to further open up this important emotional issue in the family by putting her mother's strong reactions into an historical perspective. Dianna, for example, might inquire about the following: "How religious was your mother, compared to you?" "Did Grandma ever disapprove of your attitudes toward religion and how you taught religion to your own kids?" "How did Grandma react when Uncle Bob (Lillie's younger brother) stopped going to church?" "Did you ever go through a struggle in your own life about the church or question some if its views?"

What we are talking about here is something different from, and greater than, "assertiveness" in the popular sense of the word. *This is what achieving separateness and independence is all about.* It is about maintaining emotional contact around "hot issues" in the family, without cutting off or distancing. It is about defining a clear "I" ("This is what I think"; "This is what I feel"; "This is what I will and will not do") without trying to change, control, or take responsibility for the thoughts, feelings, and reactions of others. It is about learning the *facts* about our parents' history rather than just reacting emotionally to family members. And, finally, it is about changing our *own* part in the old patterns that keep us stuck, rather than blaming and diagnosing others. When Dianna began to move in this direction with her first family, she began to proceed more calmly and clearly with her second, which was, after all, her most important goal.

Maintaining this higher level of separateness and self-definition with her mother was anything but easy. Dianna unconsciously appreciated that her mother would be threatened by her changed position—at least in the short run. Dianna, too, feared that she would lose her mother if she persisted in behaving in a more separate and self-directed manner. Indeed, both mother and daughter were uncertain about what kind of closeness would replace the old hostile-dependent pattern which, although painful, kept them bound tightly together with invisible threads. Here again, Dianna's de-selfed position with her mother reflected her very best attempts to maintain closeness and security in this important relationship, and to protect her family, as well as herself, from the anxieties of change. Of course the subject of religion was not the only "hot issue" in the family. Let's look further.

Graduate School Revisited

In helping Dianna become untangled from the graduate school knot ("Jonathan won't let me . . ."), I began to inquire how her parents reacted to her achievements and accomplishments. In response to my inquiry Dianna focused almost exclusively on her mother, and recited an old folk poem:

> "Mother, may I go out to swim?
> Yes, my darling daughter.
> Hang your clothes on a hickory limb
> And don't go near the water."

For Dianna this poem captured the mixed messages that Lillie communicated, perhaps without conscious awareness or intent. "Be independent!" her mother's words would say—but then "Be like me!" or even "Be for me!" was the contradictory message. "Be successful!" was one communication, but then Lillie would subtly ignore or undermine her daughter's successes. As Dianna explained, "When I graduated from college with honors, my mother got a migraine headache and missed the ceremony. When I told her that I was thinking about getting my master's degree, she told me about her friend's daughter who just got into medical school. Now I tell her nothing. She really doesn't want to hear it."

Surely the theme is a familiar one. A mother who has been blocked from her own self-development and growth may ignore or devalue her daughter's competence, or she may encourage her daughter to be a "special" or "gifted" child whose successes mother will vicariously enjoy. Lillie was doing a bit of both, without awareness that her mixed messages to her daughter had something to do with the fact that her own talents were going down the drain. Nor was Dianna aware that she (Dianna) was restricting her own professional growth, in part, to protect her mother from envious and competitive feelings. It was not only Jonathan whom Dianna secretly feared would be hurt and threatened by her successes. For several generations the women in Dianna's family had worked hard and made large sacrifices for their children, asking little for themselves in return. What did it mean for Dianna to break from this family tradition and begin to put her energy into her own personal goals? A part of Dianna said "Go!" and another part said "No!" Just as fighting with her husband about graduate school helped Dianna to avoid examining her own anxiety and guilt about success, blaming her mother did the same.

Dianna began to work constructively on her problem when she stopped criticizing her mother and sought instead to understand her mother's reactions and place them in some perspective. Why were Dianna's intellect, ambition, and achievements a source of anxiety and discomfort for Lillie? Without gathering some family history, Dianna would remain in the dark.

When Dianna mobilized the courage to really *talk* with her mother, rather than just *react* to her, she learned the following. Lillie was the first girl and the second child of five siblings. As the oldest female child, her considerable competence and sense of responsibility were channeled into caring for her brothers and sisters. Lillie did an enormous amount of "mothering" while she was growing up, and by her own report, she did so willingly and without protest. Although she graduated second in her high school class, only her older and younger brothers were able to go to college.

As Dianna began to learn about her mother, she took the important step of sharing her dilemma about graduate school, inviting Lillie to share her own experience and wisdom. "You know, Mother," Dianna said one day over tea, "I've been fighting with Jonathan about the graduate school business, but I'm beginning to recognize that I have mixed feelings about it myself. I want to go ahead and have the best career possible, but I think I'm also scared to death. I'm not asking you for answers or advice, because I have to make my own decision in the end. But it would be very helpful to me to hear more about your perspective and experience." For the first time in her adult life, Dianna asked questions that validated her mother as a person who could help her by sharing more about herself: "Have you ever struggled with anything like this yourself? If so, how did you try to deal with it?" "Do you think other women in our family have struggled with a fear of success?"

Dianna also asked many questions about her mother's family in order to learn more about how this important family theme was played out a generation back.

> "How did your mother and father react to your talents and achievements?"
>
> "Were you seen as smart in your family?"
>
> "Which of your brothers and sisters were viewed as smart or not smart?"
>
> "Did you ever think about going to college? What was your parents' attitude about that?"
>
> "If you had started a career early in life, what would have been your first choice?"
>
> "Do you think you would have been successful at it? What might have stood in your way?"

"How was it decided that your brothers were able to go to college and you weren't? What are your feelings about that?"

"What was it like for you to have so much responsibility in your family as you were growing up?"

Dianna was surprised by her mother's growing eagerness to talk about her past. Family members usually *do* want to share their experience if we first share something we are currently struggling with and express a sincere wish to learn more about how other members of our family have managed similar problems. Lillie revealed to Dianna that she once had her heart set on being an English teacher, but this goal was eclipsed by her responsibility for others in her first family, and later in her second. Lillie's self-disclosures shed more light on her distant, ambivalent attitude toward Dianna's accomplishments. No wonder her mother had a difficult time praising her, when Dianna's achievements and opportunities were reminders of what Lillie herself could not have!

As Dianna learned more about her extended family, she discovered that she was the only woman on her mother's side of the family (cousins included) who had even considered going for a graduate degree. This fact in itself helped Dianna to better appreciate her own anxiety and guilt about success. It is not easy to be a pioneer and to allow ourselves to have, without apology, what the women who came before us could not.

Perhaps Dianna's most courageous moment came when she could openly share some of her insights about her graduate school dilemma as it related to her relationship with her mother. She was able to detoxify the issue of mother-daughter competition by getting it out on the table in a direct, yet nonblaming fashion: "You know, Mother, this may sound kind of crazy, but as I learn more about myself in therapy, I realize that I'm a little scared and guilty about being successful. There is a part of me that feels guilty or worried about having opportunities that bright and competent women like you and your own mother were not able to have. You've said that you are satisfied with your choices and that you like your life as it is. But I still feel a little funny about allowing myself to have what my own mother and grandmother could not have. And you're so bright and competent that sometimes I can't help but think what a fantastic teacher *you* would have been, if you had gone in that direction."

In response to Dianna's self-disclosure, Lillie looked puzzled. She shook her head and said, "Well, that doesn't make much sense to me." Then she changed the subject. A week later Dianna received a phone call from her mother. "You know," said Lillie, "all week I found myself thinking about women who went back to school after their kids were born. I can't decide whether I just didn't have the courage to put myself to the test or maybe I was just born a generation too early. By the way, I just signed up for this course on Shakespeare and I'm wondering if you think I should audit it or take it for credit. Goodness knows why I'm doing something like this at my age!" When Dianna got off the phone, she felt an unexpected surge of love for her mother. Then she burst into tears without even knowing why.

These changes that Dianna made with Lillie freed her to pursue her own goals without having to either fail or succeed *for her mother's sake*. More important, this work was part and parcel of the lifelong developmental task of achieving greater separateness and autonomy from her family. We cannot truly separate from family members until we are able to share our own selves and learn about others, without trying to change others or tell them how they should think, feel, or behave. For Dianna angry reactions toward her mother were eventually replaced by more empathic and thoughtful ones, as she began to see her mother's behavior in the broader context of her mother's own family.

Where Have All the Fathers Gone?

Dianna's father, Frank, died of lung cancer one year after her marriage to Jonathan. In psychotherapy Dianna talked about her dad only when questioned, and then with disconcerting blandness: "I just didn't miss him when he died because he was never really available when he was alive." According to Dianna, her father had always been withdrawn from the family, but he became increasingly distant and uninvolved in her life from her eleventh birthday onward. "We didn't fight," Dianna explained, "we just hardly talked at all."

When Dianna first started therapy, her blaming stance toward her father blocked her from appreciating the ways in which *all* family members had participated in maintaining her father's role as the emotionally distant parent. In particular, it was difficult for Dianna to begin to identify her own part in maintaining the very distance she complained of and to examine her anxiety and guilt about navigating an emotionally close bond with her father.

What had blocked Dianna from negotiating a closer relationship with both Lillie and Frank? Daughters have a radarlike sensitivity to the wants and needs of their parents and to the complex, unspoken rules that govern a family system. In Dianna's family the pattern over several generations had been that of intense mother-daughter relationships with fathers occupying a distant, outside position in the family. This multigenerational legacy affected Dianna deeply. Even as a young child she had sensed that her father would feel anxious and at a loss if she moved toward him, just as her mother might feel threatened and betrayed by such a move.

It was only after Dianna achieved greater separateness from her mother that she was able to reexamine her relationship with her father as well. His death deprived her of the opportunity to relate to him differently and to directly address important emotional issues in their relationship. Nonetheless, there was much work to do. Over time, Dianna began to contact relatives on her father's side of the family whom she had not seen since his funeral. By talking separately to his older brother and younger sister, she began to gather some history and to learn each of their unique perspectives on her father's life. Her father began to emerge as a real person to Dianna as she learned more about him. Reconnecting with her dad's family predictably stirred intense feelings in Dianna, which she occasionally handled by distancing. In the long run, however, it was Dianna's courage and perseverence in staying in emotional contact with her father's family that allowed her to mourn his loss successfully.

Becoming a family historian also gave Dianna a richer context in which to understand her father's retreat from parenting. She learned that her father lost his own dad, Frank Sr., in a farming accident two weeks after his eleventh birthday. This fact helped Dianna to understand why her father had withdrawn from her when she herself reached the highly charged age of eleven. Dianna also learned that her grandfather had lost *his* father (Dianna's paternal great-grandfather) at the age of eight. For at least two generations sons did not have fathers. Dianna's blaming position toward Frank softened considerably as she began to understand her father's distance from her as an expression of anxiety, and not lack of love. In addition, Dianna came to appreciate how she herself had kept her distance from her father in order to protect her mother and preserve the close (although conflictual) bond between them.

What does Dianna's relationship with her deceased father have to do with the problems that brought Dianna into psychotherapy to begin with? A great deal. How we navigate our current intimate relationships depends on the degree to which we have successfully navigated our separateness and independence from *both* parents. A relationship with a parent that has been characterized by emotional distance and superficiality is actually no different from an intense, fused relationship. Distance and fusion are simply flip sides of the same coin. A true declaration of separateness and independence can only occur in the context of emotional connectedness and a rootedness in the facts of our own family history.

As a result of the work that Dianna did with her first family, she began to move with greater clarity and calm in her marriage. Energy that had previously gone into blaming her husband or trying to change him now went into making thought-through decisions about her own life. When Dianna became certain that it was in her best interest to return to graduate school, Jonathan did indeed become threatened and upset, and a new level of marital conflict emerged. Jonathan first tried to draw Dianna back into the old fights; when that didn't work, he became withdrawn and depressed. As we have seen, it is predictable—or rather, inevitable—that a move forward by a de-selfed individual will be met by a "Change back!" reaction from a partner. Jonathan's anger, as well as his depression, was his way of testing out whether his wife was serious about real change.

At first, Dianna took responsibility for her husband's withdrawn, sullen behavior and she unconsciously attempted to "rescue" him through her self-sacrificing moves. Rather than allowing herself to enjoy graduate school, she found it an overwhelming drain, and during the evening she would complain to Jonathan that it hardly seemed worth it. Jonathan felt less threatened and more useful to his wife who was expressing a need for his help and making it clear that she was not having a very good time. As Dianna explored this dynamic in psychotherapy, she became a bit braver and began to show more enthusiasm about her studies. She also learned to allow Jonathan the space to handle his reactions to the changes she was making, which were his problem to deal with and not hers. She stopped trying to rescue him or fix him, but she did not fight or emotionally withdraw from him. Predictably, Jonathan began to manage his own envy, anxiety, and depression, and he calmed down. Rather than continuing to focus on what his wife was doing wrong, he began to put more of his emotional energy into examining some problems in his own job.

Nothing came quickly or easily. When Dianna asserted her position about attending graduate school, she began to gain clarity about the fact that she bore the ultimate responsibility to make other important decisions about what she would and would not do. Thus, the balance of power and decision making began to shift in all spheres of the marriage. This meant a high level of anxiety for Dianna and Jonathan in the short run. In the long run, it meant a more mature, gratifying, and calmer relationship for them both. Most important of all, Dianna had consolidated a clearer and stronger "I" to bring to her marriage—and to every other close relationship she would enter.

The Family Systems Approach

My work with Dianna reflects my training in psychoanalytic theory and Bowen Family Systems Theory. Bowen Family Systems Theory holds that in order to change a stuck pattern in a current relationship, we may first need to work directly on the task of clarifying a self and renegotiating relationships with persons on our own family tree. As we have seen, this does not mean diagnosing, blaming, or withdrawing from family members. Nor does it mean trying to change others. Rather, work with our family of origin involves the following: gathering facts about the extended family over several generations, reconnecting with family members, defining a clear position on important emotional issues, and learning to observe and change our own part in the old relationship patterns that keep us stuck. Because of the complexity and rigidity of family patterns, and the high level of anxiety that is evoked when one family member changes, it can be especially helpful to work with a therapist or trained "coach."

A family systems perspective has nothing to do with whether a therapist works with an individual client or sees ten family members together in one room. What defines a systems perspective is not a head count, but rather a way of *thinking* about people in context. A family systems therapist is much like an anthropologist who approaches each client as an emissary from a complex culture, which over many generations has developed a set of values, beliefs, and rules that govern its members' behavior and prescribe a particular tolerance for change as well as requirements for sameness and stability. From a systems perspective no one person is ever viewed as "causing" another person's difficulties or as being "the problem" in a family. Rather, a family systems therapist helps the client to observe the complex circular patterns in which *all* family members participate. Within this broader perspective an individual can begin to evaluate both the positive and negative implications of changing her own part in the entrenched family patterns that keep her stuck.

In regard to the human condition, psychotherapists can count on only two things that will never change—the will to change and the fear of change. It is the will to change that motivates us to seek help, and it is the fear of change that motivates us to resist the very help we seek. From a systems perspective our resistance to change has positive, adaptive aspects that cannot be understood in isolation from the most crucial of all human contexts, the family. Nor can the family be understood in isolation from the roles and rules of the society in which it is embedded. As Dianna's case illustrates, behavior that appears to be dysfunctional and even "masochistic" may reflect an attempt to "play by the rules," to protect and bolster others and preserve important emotional ties. Certainly, the very structure of both family and culture predispose women to thwart our own growth and "hold the clock still" in the service of preserving harmony in relationships. And our old behavior patterns are at least familiar—change is an anxiety-arousing business for us all. It is scary not only for the person changing, but also for those closest to her, who themselves will no longer be able to continue in the old ways.

Separateness and Togetherness

The unifying, if not universal, thread in Dianna's story is the struggle to define a clear, whole, and separate "I" within close relationships. Obviously, we all need *both* the "I" and the "we," which ideally nourish and give meaning to each other. As we have seen, however, women frequently sacrifice the "I" for the "we" and betray the self in order to protect the other and preserve the bond. Men, on the other hand, learn to sacrifice the "we" for the "I." Many men build a shaky sense of pseudoindependence based on emotional withdrawal, lack of intimacy, and their female partner's de-selfed or subordinate position. For both sexes, and especially for women, the task of negotiating separateness and togetherness is a difficult business.

Before the current wave of feminism women were discouraged from even thinking about the "I." Selflessness (meaning "without a self") and self-sacrifice (meaning "the sacrifice of the self") were feminine virtues of the first order. Our job was to steady rocked boats, to please and protect others at all cost, and to hold relationships in place as if our lives depended on it. And often, women's lives *did* depend on it, and still do. Without financial independence and marketable skills, the dissolution of a marriage may mean not only the loss of identity, esteem, and social status, but the possibility of a lifetime of poverty as well. Many women today continue in de-selfed and dependent positions because of the unarticulated fear that the high cost of change may be greater than the pain of continued sameness. Nor does it help matters that women who *do* challenge the status quo are often accused of diminishing and castrating men, hurting children, and threatening the very fabric of family life. Communications of this sort reflect the high level of anxiety that is stirred when a subordinate individual or group moves to a higher level of autonomy, self-definition, and growth. Even intellectually liberated women may harbor the deep-seated belief that strengthening the self will be hurtful to others at worst and "selfish" at best.

The ultimate power for change lies within the self. Only *I* can define what I think, feel, and want, and what I will and will not do. No one else can do this for me, although others may certainly try. Yet personal change, like political change, must occur in a context of connectedness, rather than isolation. The feminist movement taught us the crucial importance of sharing our stories and experiences with other women in order to get clearer about the self. The same is true within our own family of origin. The process of revealing ourselves and learning about the experience of our parents, siblings, and relatives is a crucial part of the lifelong developmental task of defining a clear, whole, and separate self.

A clear and separate "I" goes hand in hand with the capacity to form a more gratifying and intimate "we." Our separateness need not mean isolation and loneliness. Togetherness need not mean fusion and sameness. Our responsibility to our own selves need not be at the expense of our loving regard for others. Traditionally, women have been taught that having a relationship is more important than having a self. The challenge for all of us is to have both.

HARRIET GOLDHOR LERNER is a senior staff psychologist at the Menninger Foundation. Her work on the psychology of women has earned her a national reputation in this field, and she was named Outstanding Woman of the Year in Topeka, Kansas. Her professional training is in psychoanalytic and family systems theory, and her writing, teaching, and clinical work reflect her integration of the two approaches. Dr. Lerner has published widely in professional journals and popular magazines such as *Cosmopolitan, Nation's Business, Ms.,* and *Working Mother.* Dr. Lerner encourages women interested in the subject of anger and change to read her recent book, *The Dance of Anger: A Woman's Guide to Changing the Patterns of Intimate Relationships* (Harper & Row, 1985). Having studied and trained in New York City and San Francisco, Dr. Lerner now enjoys the simple life in the Midwest flatlands where she lives with her husband, Steve, and their two sons, Matt and Ben.

Further Reading

Carter, Elizabeth et al. "Mothers and Daughters." *Monograph Series I.* Washington, D.C.: Women's Project in Family Therapy, 1981. Order from: The Women's Project, 2153 New Port Place, NW, Washington, DC 20037

Kerr, Michael. "Family Systems Theory and Therapy." In *Handbook of Family Therapy,* edited by A. Gurman and D. Kniskern. New York: Brunner/Mazel, 1981.

Lerner, Harriet Goldhor. *The Dance of Anger: A Woman's Guide to Changing the Patterns of Intimate Relationships.* New York: Harper & Row, 1985.

Miller, Jean Baker. *Toward a New Psychology of Women.* Boston: Beacon Press, 1976.

19

Depression:
Theories and Therapies

JUDY IWENS EIDELSON

Depression is full of paradoxes. It can be very simple, yet very complex. At times it is a state of mind that everyone understands, and at times it is a mysterious syndrome that defies explanation. We can all understand the feelings of sadness and the wish to retreat from the world that we experience when we lose someone we love or when we fail at something important to us. But why do some people feel depressed when "nothing terrible" has happened? And why do others function quite well even after tragedy?

Some of this confusion is caused by the fact that the term "depression" is used to refer to many different emotional states. Some of these are mood changes that occur from day to day in response to events in our lives and fluctuations in physical well-being. You might hear a tragic story on the news and feel sad for a while afterward. Or you might have a bad cold and feel unhappy about your discomfort. Sometimes internal events and external events interact. Many women become more susceptible to the "blues" when they are premenstrual. They describe themselves as feeling very vulnerable and can cry "at the drop of a hat" if something is said that might otherwise be shrugged off.

Yet we also use the term "depression" to talk about people who lose all interest in the world around them—even their families—people who retreat and give up on life, sometimes to the point of wanting to die. These depressed persons usually are overwhelmed by feelings of worthlessness and guilt. They see the future as hopeless and feel utterly helpless about overcoming their problems. Severely depressed individuals may notice that even the most basic functions of life have become disrupted. They may lose their appetites or find themselves binging in search of pleasure. Some depressed persons sleep almost continuously (without feeling rested) and some can hardly sleep at all. Many depressed people lose interest in sex and most have very little energy to engage in productive, pleasurable activities.

How are the so-called "normal" blues related to the deep incapacitating depressions I just described? Some mental health professionals believe that these are two ends of the same continuum. They see severe depression as an exaggerated form of the "garden variety" depression that we're all familiar with. Other experts in this field believe that severe depressions are *qualitatively,* not just *quantitatively,* different from mild states of sadness. How can you differentiate normal sadness from severe depression? What can you do to help yourself learn from your depressions? I'll try to help you answer these questions and then discuss the most promising forms of treatment for depression.

What Is Depression?

Although depression is typically considered a *mood* disorder, it actually involves our *thoughts, behavior,* and *physical well-being* as well as our emotions. The degree to which each of these components is present in each person's depression may vary, but in severe depressions all four symptom areas are usually involved.

EMOTIONAL COMPONENTS

The changes in feelings that occur in depression include sadness, guilt, remorse, disappointment, defeat, hopelessness, and helplessness. Anger and anxiety often go along with depression, but, as we will see, they are not necessarily part of the depression itself.

BEHAVIORAL COMPONENTS

Depression has an inhibiting effect on behavior. When people become depressed, they tend to be passive and nonproductive. One of my patients, Anne, described it in this way: "I used to be a really active person—always on the go—so people really noticed it when I started doing less and less. At first, I thought I was sick with a virus or something. You know how it is, I just felt run-down all the time. I didn't feel like doing things. Just getting up and getting dressed took a tremendous effort." Psychiatrist Aaron T. Beck and others have referred to the inertia that Anne and other depressed people feel as "paralysis of the will." This behavioral inhibition is a crucial part of depression because it perpetuates the problem. As Anne became less and less active, she became more critical of herself, she lost touch with friends who might otherwise have been supportive, and she robbed herself of the physical benefits of activity.

PHYSICAL COMPONENTS

Often physical feelings of well-being are affected during a depression. Disturbances in sleep, eating, and sexual functioning are commonly reported. Some people also experience fatigue, constipation, headaches or other chronic pain. Since any of these symptoms may be caused by an illness, people who suffer these problems should have a thorough physical examination before concluding that depression is their cause. Conversely, people who have continuing, inexplicable physical symptoms and loss of energy in the absence of any diagnosed medical condition should investigate a diagnosis of depression.

COGNITIVE (THINKING) COMPONENTS

When people are depressed, they tend to see things in a very negative light. Aaron Beck, the originator of the cognitive approach to depression, refers to the three main themes in depressive thinking as the "cognitive triad"—a negative view of the self, the world, and the future. For example, when my client Sarah was depressed, she would tell herself: "I'm a complete failure. I'm worthless, I deserve to be punished." Her thoughts about other people included "No one really cares about me, they're just out for themselves. People always let me down." Sarah's thoughts about the future were: "The future looks black to me . . . just more of the same . . . I'll never feel happy again." Cognitive therapists believe that the negative thoughts that people have while depressed are actually distorted perceptions of reality, which affect the way people feel and act. These clinicians believe that there is no limit to irrational beliefs that people might have, but that there are systematic "errors in thinking" that produce them. In his book *Feeling*

Good, psychiatrist David Burns describes these cognitive distortions as forms of "twisted thinking." Three of the most common distortions are catastrophizing (making disasters out of small problems), mind reading (imagining arbitrarily that someone dislikes you), and "all-or-nothing" thinking (you are either perfect or a total failure).

Depression, therefore, can be thought of as a cluster of symptoms. No one of the symptoms *must* be present for depression to be present, and virtually any of these symptoms *can* be present on its own without a depression being diagnosed. Severe depression, called "clinical depression," is diagnosed according to the number, severity, and duration of the symptoms.

Although a reliable diagnosis of clinical depression can only be made by a qualified professional, the questionnaire on pages 413–14 may give you a general idea of which symptoms you are experiencing and how severe your problem is.

Causes of Depression

There is a tremendous amount of disagreement currently in psychiatry and psychology about the "real cause" of depression. Like the blind men who tried to describe an elephant, experts see different parts of the animal. Theories of depression variously emphasize biological causes, psychological issues, the social status of women, and sex role learning.

Although we know very little about what causes depression, the forms of treatment that practitioners offer have typically been determined by what each clinician believes is the cause of the problem. Our main source of information about the causes of depression has been the relative effectiveness of the treatments used to help depressed patients. Using a medical analogy, we might conclude that a feverish patient who recovers after taking antibiotics was suffering from a bacterial infection. By the same reasoning, a depression that subsides after exploration of unconscious conflicts might be thought to be *caused* by unconscious forces. A patient who feels better after taking drugs that alter the levels of certain chemicals in the brain might be thought to be suffering from a chemical or hormonal depression. A therapist who sees patients recover after behavior therapy might conclude that depression is caused by insufficient rewards in life. A cognitive therapist who observes patients recovering from depressions after modifying irrational beliefs might conclude that these distorted thoughts *caused* the depression.

All of these conclusions would be suspect. Clinicians who observe their own patients are not always truly objective about their patients' improvement. Most therapists believe in what they do and are highly motivated to see improvement in their patients and to attribute this improvement to their own efforts or theories. However, even the most effective treatment need not be directly related to the cause of the problem. Aspirin is effective in lowering a fever but this is not because the patient suffers from an aspirin deficiency!

Furthermore, there is new evidence that all of these systems may interact. Thus, a patient who learns to think and behave in a more positive manner may be changing his or her body chemistry. At the same time, recent studies have shown that antidepressant drugs—which presumably change brain chemistry—also help to reverse negative thinking patterns. These studies suggest that we need to become more aware of the interaction between mind and body, rather than looking for a single cause of depression. With this caveat in mind, let's consider the most prevalent theories of depression.

ANGER TURNED INWARD

The traditional approach to depression has been psychoanalytic, which is based on the concept of "anger turned inward." Sigmund Freud and his followers, including Karl Abraham and Melanie Klein, believed that people who are highly dependent on others are most likely to become depressed. When such dependent people (especially women) feel angry toward a loved one who is lost—either in reality or symbolically—they find it unacceptable to express the anger toward the person who is lost (and who they feel *abandoned* them). So instead, they identify with the loved one and direct their anger inward, against themselves.

Studies of the psychological research on anger, however, find very little empirical evidence in support of this theory. Instead of *replacing* outward hostility, depression often exists along with anger. Depressed people are more than capable of being angry or resentful toward others, as well as self-hating. There are different causes of anger and different causes of depression; neither necessarily "causes" the other. Anger and depression may be learned responses to adverse circumstances. My friend Toni, for example, gets angry whenever something goes wrong, but she rarely gets depressed. Others, like my friend Pam, feel angry first but later depressed. When Pam found that her son was being beaten up by other children in his class, she first was furious at the teacher for not protecting her child. After complaining to the teacher and the principal, Pam's anger died down, but she felt drained and defeated. As she put it later, "I just get tired of fighting. I start to feel worn out and then I just feel depressed." (I will discuss the relationship between anger and depression further below.)

LOSS OF SELF-ESTEEM

The common themes running through most theories of depression, including the psychoanalytic theory, are the themes of loss and of low self-esteem. We all understand the pain associated with the loss of a loved one. Yet the mourning process is time-limited and has a predictable cause. When a loved one is lost through death or separation, the pain that follows the loss is a necessary part of mourning, a pain that helps us to recognize the meaning of the lost relationship. But this natural grief does not involve prolonged loss of self-esteem. An emotionally healthy grieving woman may remove herself from the normal flow of life for a period of time, but she will not see herself as worthless and unlovable. She will recognize that she has the ability to develop and maintain relationships in the future, though she may not feel ready to do so currently. A clinically depressed grieving woman, in contrast, may blame herself for the loss, decide she is a terrible, unlovable person, and sink into a prolonged despair.

Why do some people experience depression in response to a loss? And why does depression affect women from two to six times more frequently than men? Perhaps there is a connection between these two questions.

Most theories of depression stress the important but elusive concept of self-esteem—the way we see ourselves, how much we like ourselves, and what we think we are capable of (see Chap. 2). Self-esteem or self-concept is not always related to reality. Maria, an anorexic model, told me she had to diet because she was fat. Sarah, a depressed college professor who had won several coveted awards for her research, worried that some day soon a bright student would review her work and uncover her "stupidity."

We do not know at this point what causes depression, but it seems that a shaky self-concept makes people more vulnerable to it.

WOMEN'S ROLES AND STATUS

Some feminist writers, such as Phyllis Chesler, believe that the lower status given to women in the workplace and at home directly robs them of self-esteem. Sociologists and psychologists have conducted some studies that support the idea that the higher rate of depression among women is related to the societal roles that women are in. Sociologist Jessie Bernard has found that marriage is "healthier" for men than it is for women: While married men are both physically and psychologically better off than single men, the reverse is true for women. In order to control for the possibility that healthier men are more likely to get married in the first place, Bernard compared widowers to married men. She found that widowers are miserable. They have higher death rates and levels of psychological distress. Even married clergy are better off than priests.

Married women have more mental and physical problems than single women, and the situation is even worse for women who do not work outside the home. Depression is most prevalent among housewives who have small children, but paid employment has a beneficial effect on mental health. One reason is that income-producing jobs provide more validation of a woman's competence than, sadly, housework and child care do; another is that when women earn money they raise their status and power in their marriages and are treated with more respect (see Chap. 11). In a very compelling study of the factors that contribute to the different rates of depression in men and women, Susan Gore and Thomas Mangione found that these differences could be accounted for by the combined presence of marriage and a full-time occupation—and more men than women had both.

LEARNED HELPLESSNESS AND LOSS OF EFFICACY

According to psychologist Martin Seligman's learned helplessness theory of depression, when we find that nothing that we do makes a difference, we not only give up trying to have impact on the environment; we feel helpless and stop caring about the goal we were pursuing. Even worse, we have great difficulty learning to try again, even when things have changed and our efforts *would* be fruitful.

The work of social psychologist Albert Bandura suggests that depression may be a failure of self-efficacy. Bandura's research shows that people are motivated not just by how responsive they see the environment as being (as in the learned helplessness theory), but also how confident they are that they *have what it takes* to do the things that make a difference. Bandura's work suggests that our level of functioning is determined by what we believe we are capable of. Second, we form opinions about ourselves by using the same kinds of information we use to decide how capable *other* people are. We learn the most about what we can do in the future by observing what we have done in the past or what we are doing currently. We also get information about what we can do by observing others with whom we identify. The third source of information about our abilities is what others tell us about ourselves, and the fourth is our own physiological state. If we feel tired or anxious, for example, we are less likely to feel "up to" the demands of the job we are considering.

The four sources of information about competence are fairly reliable for most people most of the time. However, they are highly *inaccurate* during a depression. As I noted earlier, depression is characterized by selective focusing on negative perceptions. As a result, depressed people do not observe their own behavior objectively. Instead, they focus on the mistakes that they made. Similarly, they compare themselves negatively with others. They do not derive self-confidence from watching others, because they are busy putting themselves down. When others try to be encouraging, depressed people discount their efforts, grumbling, "They're only saying these things to be nice."

SEX DIFFERENCES

One important explanation for the sex differences in depression rates begins in childhood, when boys are taught to be good at *things,* while girls are taught to be *good!* Boys get relatively clear, external feedback about how successful they are (in sports, school performance) and eventually they are encouraged to set their own standards and evaluate their own performances. Girls are taught to be "nice"—likable and attractive. These qualities, which are vague and difficult to internalize, are tied to approval from others. Women tend to value themselves in the context of their interpersonal relationships—especially for their success in their roles as mothers and homemakers. This arrangement is problematic for several reasons: First, the continuing reliance on being appreciated by others becomes the primary road to self-esteem; second, the role of mother fades with time, just as physical attractiveness does; and third, if relationships are of primary importance in our lives, then the loss of these relationships can be expected to affect us very deeply. In her book *Unfinished Business* Maggie Scarf argued that depression in women is related to difficulty in resolving the relationship conflicts that are posed by different stages of life. She concluded that the underlying themes in depression "had to do with the loss or letting go of crucial emotional relationships and with the letting go of the idea of oneself as the person in and defined by those relationships."

BIOLOGICAL FACTORS

The case for a biochemical basis for depression and other emotional problems is stated with great force in Paul Wender and Donald Klein's book *Mind, Mood, and Medicine.* Support for the notion that depression is caused by some sort of organic dysfunction comes from two main sources. First, the presence of physical symptoms in many depressions suggests a biologically based illness. More convincing evidence comes from a variety of studies that demonstrate that depression and its close relative, manic-depressive illness, tend to run in families. This finding alone could be explained by the common environmental factors that family members are exposed to, rather than by a genetic link, but preliminary studies of twins and children who were adopted at birth suggest that our genetic endowment does play a role in predisposing some people to depression.

A hormonal basis to depression is suggested by the fact that depression in women is commonly associated with states that alter endocrine functioning. Menstruation, use of oral contraceptives, the postpartum state, and menopause all have been associated with increased depression. Despite the strong clinical support for the effect of these hormonal shifts on mood, researchers have not yet been able to identify the exact mechanisms that are involved. In their review of research in this area, Myrna Weissman and Gerald Klerman concluded, "The pattern of the relationship of endocrine to clinical states is inconsistent. . . . There is little evidence to relate these mood changes and clinical states to altered endocrine balance or specific hormones." Nevertheless, most of the studies on depression and the endocrine system are now outdated because of very recent advances in research methods in the field of endocrinology. Perhaps future research will tell us just how and why hormonal changes affect our moods.

The most popular biological model of depression is the biogenic amine deficiency theory. Biogenic amines, or neurotransmitters, are the substances that are involved in the communication of nerve cell impulses from one cell to another. The theory that depression is caused by a shortage of these transmitters in certain parts of the brain originated with the finding that certain drugs that increased the amounts of the biogenic amines available in the limbic region of the brain seemed to alleviate depression.

Effective Treatments

The more we learn about depression, the more we see that there is not one single cause. Further, identifying the causes of the problem does not guarantee change. Think of the human being as a system with interrelated parts: When we change one part (chemistry, thoughts, behavior, or feelings) the other parts eventually change as well. When I decide how to treat a depressed person, I look for an effective point to intervene, because I know that any change in the system will bring about other changes. Many women believe that in order to solve their problems they must discover the unconscious reason for their suffering. They see all attempts at self-help as useless because they are "superficial." They believe their "symptoms" will disappear as soon as the *true* roots of the problem are uncovered. These beliefs are simply unfounded. Regardless of the reasons that women do get depressed, their recovery from both mild and more severe depressions is greatly influenced by how they deal with their thoughts and feelings. Even if a woman's depression is not *caused* by accepting the passive, compliant role traditionally allotted to women, acceptance of this role will certainly interfere with her ability to resolve her depression on her own or to find the professional help and social support that she may need from others.

At the same time, research has shown that cognitive and behavioral strategies are highly effective in the treatment of depression. Many of these techniques can also be used by *mildly* depressed individuals on their own to help them cope with problems. Antidepressant medications have also been shown to be effective in the treatment of certain kinds of depression.

COGNITIVE-BEHAVIORAL APPROACHES

Cognitive-behavioral therapists do not recommend that all pain be eradicated. Emotional pain, just like physical pain, can serve as a signal that something in our lives is out of kilter. We stress the importance of goal-directed introspection to determine whether the pain originates in actual or imagined circumstances.

The first step is defining the problem. How have your thoughts and behavior changed since you started feeling down? Was there an event that triggered your negative thoughts and feelings? Is there something you can do about the situation that is upsetting you? Often the circumstances that upset us are partly external and partly internal. There may be concrete actions that would make you feel better, but you may not allow yourself the chance to change the situation. Linda, a twenty-eight-year-old nurse, was unhappy with her job; her supervisor was extremely demanding and non-supportive of her staff. Yet Linda would not allow herself to look for another position because of her belief that she *should* be able to resolve the conflicts, and if she couldn't it was *her* fault. By writing her thoughts down on paper and reading them as if they belonged to someone else, she was able to see the errors in her thinking:

Negative Thoughts	Rational Responses
If I leave this job, I'm a quitter.	What's so bad about quitting? I've given this job more than enough time and effort. Why not find something more satisfying?
If I tried hard enough, I could work things out.	It takes two to tango! You can only be responsible for your own actions, not everyone else's.

While Linda began to focus on her problems at work, she also started to make some changes in her daily life. Like many depressed people, she had stopped doing things she used to enjoy because she "didn't feel like doing them." She had the belief that there is no point in going out with friends or by yourself when you're down. She didn't want to be seen "that way" and thought she'd be a phony "just going through the motions." In fact, being active can improve your mood. *Becoming inactive and withdrawing from others will make things worse.* Depression can be a downward spiral: The worse you feel, the less you do; the less you do, the more negative your thoughts are about yourself; the more negative your thoughts are, the worse you feel, and so on.

In contrast, your efforts to help yourself will spiral upward. As you function, self-efficacy returns; you will respect yourself more and your mood will improve. Remember that feelings can be deceptive. You can feel very uncomfortable about going to a party but still go to it. If your motivation to do things is biased by your misperceptions of your competence, an important part of helping yourself consists of *identifying* and *challenging* your negative automatic thoughts that prevent you from *feeling* more competent and therefore *being* more competent.

THE PERFECTIONIST PARADOX

Perfectionism—the tendency to set high, unrealistic goals for oneself—represents the opposite of the attitude of self-acceptance. Perfectionists are vulnerable to depression because the unreasonable demands they make of themselves give them ample opportunity to fail and disappoint themselves. They often feel overwhelmed from trying to do too much too well.

What can you do to cope with these feelings in a more effective way? Start by making a list of the problems that are overwhelming you. Now translate each problem into a *realistic* long-term goal. Next, break each *long-term goal* down into smaller *short-term goals.* The more concrete and specific these goals are, the better. Assign priorities to your short-term goals and estimate the amount of time required to complete each of the subgoals. Finally, make a schedule for the coming week beginning with the goals to which you have given the highest priority. If you cannot find enough room in your schedule for all of the tasks that you have given priority to, your goals are, by definition, *unrealistic.* Reevaluate your priorities and choose something to put off for the time being. Until you have a realistic plan, you will continue to feel overwhelmed, and, as a result, you will get very little accomplished. The paradox here is that the more you can accept your limitations, the more you can do.

Lisa, a twenty-four-year-old student, sought therapy because of her increasingly severe problems functioning at school. Lisa was bright and cared greatly about her performance, but she had more and more trouble completing her assignments and handing them in because of her perfectionistic standards. Lisa found herself afraid to put words on paper because she was plagued by doubts about the quality of her work. As she began to write, she imagined her professor reading her paper and ridiculing her work. She tried to anticipate all possible criticisms, thinking that turning in an inferior paper would be worse than not turning anything in at all. As the deadline for Lisa's papers passed, her standards became even higher. Now she told herself, "Since the paper is late, it has to be even better to make up for its lateness."

Lisa came to me for cognitive-behavioral therapy when the dean of students at her university told her she was on the verge of flunking out because her "incompletes" were turning into F's. During her therapy Lisa learned to adjust her expectations and to focus on the process of working more than on the outcome. She also learned to give herself credit for her accomplishments along a continuum, where success is relative rather than all-or-nothing.

Even though Lisa understood the principles I described to her quite readily, she was not able to put them into action until we identified and challenged her underlying assumption about perfectionism: "I must be perfect in order to be loved." By carefully examining this belief Lisa was able to question it and test the possibility that it was not true. Gradually, she collected evidence that she could be lovable in spite of her flaws and sometimes even because of them.

Learning self-acceptance was an important step for Lisa in changing her behavior. In order to make these changes she also found it helpful to respond to her negative thoughts since they came to her so automatically. Here are some examples of Lisa's automatic thoughts and her responses to them.

Automatic Responses	*Rational Responses*
That sentence isn't good enough. I better rewrite it.	Good enough for what? True, it won't get the Pulitzer Prize for literature, but it's just fine for an English 300 essay that's only 5 percent of your grade.
It's terrible not to do my best. I'm wasting my potential.	It's terrible to waste your life rewriting English 300 essays. Do your best at accepting your imperfections and living your life fully, not perfectly.

David Burns has identified the concept of "emotional perfectionism," a lack of tolerance for negative emotions such as normal anger, sadness, and worry. This form of perfectionism is one of the biggest obstacles women face in dealing with stress and depression. By criticizing yourself for feeling upset, you further erode your self-esteem and undermine your ability to solve the problems that are troubling you.

Cognitive therapists view anger just as they would see other negative emotions—as the result of our perceptions. Anger—like any other emotion —can be constructive or destructive, useful or excessive. Anger is usually related to one of two perceptions: First, we become angry when we believe that we have been hurt or offended by someone; second, we become angry at people (including ourselves) when we believe that they have violated a *rule* or expectation for how people *should* act. Both of these angry reactions are common among depressed people; because depressed people selectively focus on negative events, they usually have a lot to be angry about. Depression and anger also go together because of the depressed person's tendency to dwell on the past. This exaggerated focusing on the past frequently contributes to hostile brooding or rumination about past hurts or injustices.

Distorted Thinking About Depression

Since depression is characterized by distorted thinking, it is not surprising that depressed people often have distorted beliefs about depression! Unfortunately, these beliefs often interfere with a depressed person's ability to cope with problems and get help from others. The most common distorted beliefs people have about depression fall into the categories of "all-or-nothing" thinking and "blame versus responsibility," and the overlap of these two distortions.

1. *Depression is all-or-nothing.* Many people fail to understand that the symptoms of depression exist on a continuum from very mild to very severe. They think they either are depressed or they are not. Therefore, people who have had a severe depression tend to overreact when they realize that they are reexperiencing some of their old symptoms.

Jean, a twenty-nine-year-old nurse, experienced a serious depression after the death of her mother. One of her symptoms was insomnia. Two years later, when Jean began having difficulty sleeping again, she became extremely upset because she was convinced that her depression had reoccurred.

When I questioned Jean carefully, it became clear that the only thing she was depressed about was the possibility of being depressed again. Her insomnia seemed to be due to the fact that she had been put on a different shift and was drinking a lot of coffee to stay alert at work. Although Jean was simply misinterpreting her symptoms, she and others with a history of depression have to be aware that life is full of ups and downs. There are many things to feel sad about, but this normal sadness need not be seen as a relapse into deep depression.

2. *Blame versus Responsibility.* Too often we confuse blame with responsibility. Is it your own fault if you get depressed? If it's not your fault, does that mean there is nothing you can do about your depression? No! The belief

that people become depressed or stay depressed because they are lazy or because they want attention (they *"enjoy* being depressed") is common among friends and relatives of depressed people. These people might start off being supportive, but eventually they get fed up and start blaming the depressed woman for being the way she is. Because self-blame is so much a part of depression, the patient is likely to believe this as well. In reality, no one enjoys depression. For some people feelings of hopelessness and fear of the unknown may keep them from trying to do things that might be therapeutic. In this case it is the hopelessness and fear that must be attacked, not the person herself.

Another distorted belief about depression is "If I didn't make this happen, I can't do anything to make it go away." This belief is particularly common among women who have become depressed suddenly, or in response to gradual or sudden hormonal changes. Giving up all responsibility for your recovery is as unrealistic as blaming yourself for being depressed. Many people find that once they are depressed what they do about it determines the severity and the duration of the episode.

For example, Suzanne, a thirty-eight-year-old homemaker, suffered from periodic depressions since the birth of the first of her three children. Since these depressions seemed to come "out of the blue," she felt completely helpless to do anything about them. Instead, she would stay in bed as much as possible and withdraw from her friends and family, telling herself that "I can't stand being around people when I'm feeling this way. I can't let them see me this way." On two occasions Suzanne was "forced" to function in spite of her depression: once when her ten-year-old son, Tim, was injured in a skiing accident, and again two years later when her husband, Larry, was laid off from his job. During both of these crises Suzanne found herself rising to the occasion in spite of being depressed. She arranged medical care for Tim and cared for him at home when he was released from the hospital.

What Suzanne came to understand in her therapy as she reviewed these periods of her life was that during these crises her concern for her family overrode her poor self-image. Once she became more active, she was able to see *evidence* that she was a capable and compassionate human being. This observation made her more motivated to continue participating in her family and social life. She learned that it was the way she thought about herself that kept her depressed. This was not "her fault" in the sense that she did this *intentionally.* Her thinking style was ingrained in her by her upbringing and reinforced by her perception of herself as lazy and worthless when she was depressed. Even though this thinking pattern was automatic by the time she reached adulthood, she was able to gain control of it by identifying her self-defeating thoughts and the basic assumptions that set them off—for instance, that her only role in life was to take care of her family, that she must always put others first, and that she was "doing her job" when they were happy, healthy, and had all their needs met.

Suzanne may have a biochemical predisposition to depression. Yet she can minimize her depression in the future by learning skills and doing work that allow her to experience pleasure and mastery directly, not just through her family. Being active and seeing evidence of our competence is important to everyone, especially when we are feeling low.

SOMATIC TREATMENTS

Somatic treatments for depression include electric shock treatments and antidepressant medication. Shock treatments (sometimes called electroconvulsive therapy, or ECT) have had a terrible reputation in the past; the image most people have of ECT is that of torture—a helpless patient being held down on a table, screaming while being electrocuted. Years ago this picture might not have been too far off. I knew a man who was crippled for the rest of his life because he received shock treatments in the 1950s. His convulsions were so violent that he was thrown off the table; he broke both legs so badly that he never walked again without two canes.

But shock treatments have changed since the fifties. The amount of electricity that is used is much less than it once was, and it is administered in a safer, more controlled, and presumably painless manner. Advocates of ECT point out that it is a very fast-acting treatment and may have saved the lives of many suicidal patients who could not wait to be helped by slower-acting therapies or drugs. Critics of this method argue that we still don't really understand how it works, that it often causes temporary confusion and memory loss, and most important, that the beneficial effects seem to wear off in three to six months. Occasionally, when I recommend hospitalization to severely depressed patients, they initially refuse it because they are afraid that they will be forced to receive shock treatments. I explain to these people and their families that ECT cannot be administered without informed consent. If a physician recommends shock treatments, he or she must discuss this option with the patient, arriving at a decision based on the realistic advantages and disadvantages of this form of treatment.

THE QUESTION OF DRUGS

The most commonly prescribed medications for depression are the tricyclic antidepressants (such as Tofranil, Elavil, and Sinequan), which act on the neurotransmitters norepinephrine, serotonin, and dopamine by blocking their reabsorption by the cells that have released them. Other commonly used antidepressants include the monoamine oxidase (MAO) inhibitors (such as Parnate, Nardil, and Marplan) and lithium carbonate. MAO inhibitors directly elevate the level of biogenic amines in the brain. They can be extremely useful in the treatment of atypical depressions, including depressions that are associated with very severe fears or panic attacks (see Chap. 20). Since certain strict food restrictions must be observed while taking the MAO inhibitors, tricyclics are usually tried first.

Lithium carbonate is considered to be the treatment of choice for manic-depressive (bipolar) illness. Lithium is a form of salt that was accidently found to have a calming effect on animals and was then used with manic patients. Since it has a narrow therapeutic range—too little is useless, too much can be toxic—people who take it must have blood tests on a regular basis to make sure they are at a therapeutic dosage level. Although lithium tends to be more useful in controlling manic episodes than in treating depressions, it has also been used effectively with some unipolar depressives, particularly those with family histories of manic-depressive illness.

Treatment outcome studies indicate that antidepressant medication is effective in treating from 60 to 65 percent of individuals suffering from clinical depression. Many physicians believe that medication is the obvious first choice in treating depression because it is relatively effective, inexpensive, and easy to administer. For these reasons many internists and general practitioners as well as psychiatrists readily prescribe antidepressants. Yet many people, laymen and professionals, are wary about the use of medications to treat depression. Some are concerned about side effects. For most people these are relatively minor, such as dry mouth and constipation, but for a small number of people they can be more serious, such as cardiac irregularities. Minor side effects (or people's awareness of them) seem to fade after three to four weeks. Others question the wisdom of using a drug when no one really knows how it works.

Ellen, a thirty-six-year-old patient of mine, described her fears about medication clearly. I had encouraged her to consult with a specialist in psychopharmacology because my initial evaluation revealed that she was deeply depressed, having trouble concentrating well enough to engage in psychotherapy, and that she had a strong family history of depression. The following is an excerpt of our discussion of this issue.

ELLEN: I just couldn't do that [take drugs].

J.E.: Why is that?

ELLEN: Because even if I felt better, it just wouldn't be *me*. It would be the drug I was taking. I would feel like a phony. I'd rather go on feeling lousy than have false pleasure. Besides, I'd probably get addicted to the drugs and have to take more and more of them just to feel okay.

After discussing this issue in therapy for some time, Ellen was able to consider the possibility that she could be just as much herself—maybe even more—without her depression as she was with it. I explained to her that the antidepressant medications that are commonly used are not addictive. In fact, many people are able to use them for several months and then stop, without relapsing into depression. Ellen eventually tried medication and found that it helped her to mobilize herself to use the therapeutic techniques she was learning. Being an independent, "I'd rather do it myself" person, Ellen was anxious to get off the medication as quickly as possible and found she was able to do this by working actively on changing her self-defeating behavior patterns and style of thinking.

Ellen is one of a large number of people who are able to benefit from a combination of cognitive-behavioral therapy and antidepressant medication. For them, both types of treatment are important. The medication seemed to improve Ellen's sleep, appetite, and energy level, but initially she regarded these changes as evidence that she was a "defective" person, who would always have to be on drugs "just to do what any normal person can do on her own." Ellen discounted the steps she had taken to help herself, attributing all of her improvement to the medication. By using cognitive therapy techniques, Ellen was able to challenge these beliefs. Her therapy included behavioral and cognitive experiments in which she included more pleasurable activities in her weekly schedule; when she had self-critical thoughts, she would generate at least one alternative thought for each guilt-inducing one. Here is an example from Ellen's list:

Automatic Thoughts (Self-criticism)	*Rational Responses* (Self-acceptance)
Taking drugs shows how weak I am. I can't do anything on my own.	Actually, it took a lot of courage for me to ask for help. I do many things on my own, but there's no need to do everything on my own. I

avoid relying on others because that has hurt me in the past, but as an adult with pretty good judgment I can choose to ask for help when it makes sense to do so. If it doesn't work out, I can always change my mind.

Getting Help

If you have been moderately or severely depressed for several weeks without relief, you should know that many effective forms of treatment are available to you. No guaranteed method of therapy works for everyone, and what works for someone else might not work for you. Start by asking people you know for names of therapists who have helped them. Call several therapists on the phone and ask them some basic questions. What is their therapeutic orientation? Will they consider drug therapy? Many clients find it helpful to arrange a consultation (this may take from one to three or four visits). In addition to giving the therapist information about yourself, save some time to ask him or her for recommendations. How does she see your problems? What type of treatment would he recommend? How long does treatment last, on the average? If you do not feel some rapport with your therapist after a few sessions, think about leaving and consulting someone else. If your therapist doesn't seem to understand what you're talking about or is reluctant to answer your questions, don't assume it's your fault. Just because your cousin Mary believes she owes Dr. Smith her life because of how helpful he was to *her,* this doesn't mean that Dr. Smith will be able to communicate the time of day in a way that makes sense to *you.*

What if it doesn't work? Depressed people, especially women, are good at blaming themselves for anything that goes wrong. They doubt their own judgment and have trouble questioning their therapists. It is difficult to set a standard for "how long it should take" to start feeling better. A general rule would be to say that if you see no improvement after four to six weeks regardless of the form of treatment, start asking questions. Sometimes the therapeutic relationship is very comfortable and the patient doesn't want to alienate her therapist by questioning the usefulness of the therapy. Remember that a competent and ethical therapist will be happy to discuss your progress with you, and he or she will be open to the idea of arranging for a consultation with an experienced clinician or physician in order to revitalize your therapy or recommend alternative forms of treatment.

Cultural, political, physiological, and psychological forces all play a role in the development of depression. There are many different forms of depression, ranging from normal sadness to severe incapacitation. Much of the confusion about depression occurs because the cluster of symptoms that make up the syndrome of depression can all occur for other reasons. A mild but continuing case of the blues may be a sign that something is amiss in your life. Leslie Farber, a psychiatrist and writer, wrote that depression is always about something that has gone wrong in one's life. He argued that we have come to see depression as being the problem rather than a woman's *response* to problems, which may be marital, job-related, or financial.

By yourself, careful introspection may help you to identify what is really troubling you, and many cognitive-behavioral techniques are available for use on your own or with the assistance of a psychotherapist. But depression that is *pervasive,* and produces many symptoms that interfere with your ability to function, requires professional help. *Severe* depression that prevents a woman from coping with her problems is not a healthy response; in circumstances where women are abused emotionally, physically, or socially, depression serves only to *keep them where they are.* It is an involuntary form of giving up.

As the pressures of everyday life increase, so does the number of women who experience depression. Although our knowledge of the causes of depression and our ability to predict which treatments will be most helpful to each patient are sadly limited, a variety of treatment options are available and successful. All of us can protect ourselves from depression to some extent by examining the ways in which we maintain our self-esteem—and by striving towards self-acceptance rather than relying on the approval of others.

BECK DEPRESSION INVENTORY

On this questionnaire are groups of statements. Please read each group of statements carefully. Then pick out the one statement in each group which best describes the way you have been feeling the PAST WEEK, INCLUDING TODAY! Circle the number beside the statement you picked. If several statements in the group seem to apply equally well, circle each one. **Be sure to read all the statements in each group before making your choice.**

1 0 I do not feel sad.
   1 I feel sad.
   2 I am sad all the time and I can't snap out of it.
   3 I am so sad or unhappy that I can't stand it.

2 0 I am not particularly discouraged about the future.
   1 I feel discouraged about the future.
   2 I feel I have nothing to look forward to.
   3 I feel that the future is hopeless and that things cannot improve.

3 0 I do not feel like a failure.
   1 I feel I have failed more than the average person.
   2 As I look back on my life, all I can see is a lot of failures.
   3 I feel I am a complete failure as a person.

4 0 I get as much satisfaction out of things as I used to.
   1 I don't enjoy things the way I used to.
   2 I don't get real satisfaction out of anything anymore.
   3 I am dissatisfied or bored with everything.

5 0 I don't feel particularly guilty.
   1 I feel guilty a good part of the time.
   2 I feel quite guilty most of the time.
   3 I feel guilty all of the time.

6 0 I don't feel I am being punished.
   1 I feel I may be punished.
   2 I expect to be punished.
   3 I feel I am being punished.

7 0 I don't feel disappointed in myself.
   1 I am disappointed in myself.
   2 I am disgusted with myself.
   3 I hate myself.

8 0 I don't feel I am any worse than anybody else.
   1 I am critical of myself for my weaknesses or mistakes.
   2 I blame myself all the time for my faults.
   3 I blame myself for everything bad that happens.

9 0 I don't have any thoughts of killing myself.
   1 I have thoughts of killing myself, but I would not carry them out.
   2 I would like to kill myself.
   3 I would kill myself if I had the chance.

10 0 I don't cry any more than usual.
   1 I cry more now than I used to.
   2 I cry all the time now.
   3 I used to be able to cry, but now I can't cry even though I want to.

11 0 I am no more irritated now than I ever am.
    1 I get annoyed or irritated more easily than I used to.
    2 I feel irritated all the time now.
    3 I don't get irritated at all by the things that used to irritate me.

12 0 I have not lost interest in other people.
    1 I am less interested in other people than I used to be.
    2 I have lost most of my interest in other people.
    3 I have lost all my interest in other people.

13 0 I make decisions about as well as I ever could.
    1 I put off making decisions more than I used to.
    2 I have greater difficulty in making decisions than before.
    3 I can't make decisions at all anymore.

14 0 I don't feel I look any worse than I used to.
    1 I am worried that I am looking old or unattractive.
    2 I feel that there are permanent changes in my appearance that make me look unattractive.
    3 I believe that I look ugly.

15 0 I can work about as well as before.
    1 It takes an extra effort to get started at doing something.
    2 I have to push myself very hard to do anything.
    3 I can't do any work at all.

16 0 I can sleep as well as usual.
    1 I don't sleep as well as I used to.
    2 I wake up 1–2 hours earlier than usual and find it hard to get back to sleep.
    3 I wake up several hours earlier than I used to and cannot get back to sleep.

17 0 I don't get more tired than usual.
    1 I get tired more easily than I used to.
    2 I get tired from doing almost anything.
    3 I am too tired to do anything.

18 0 My appetite is no worse than usual.
    1 My appetite is not as good as it used to be.
    2 My appetite is much worse now.
    3 I have no appetite at all anymore.

19 0 I haven't lost much weight, if any, lately.
    1 I have lost more than 5 pounds.   I am purposely trying to lose weight
    2 I have lost more than 10 pounds.   by eating less. Yes _____ No _____
    3 I have lost more than 15 pounds.

20 0 I am no more worried about my health than usual.
    1 I am worried about physical problems such as aches and pains; or upset stomach; or constipation.
    2 I am very worried about physical problems and it's hard to think of much else.
    3 I am so worried about my physical problems that I cannot think about anything else.

21 0 I have not noticed any recent change in my interest in sex.
    1 I am less interested in sex than I used to be.
    2 I am much less interested in sex now.
    3 I have lost interest in sex completely.

Beck uses these guidelines in interpreting total scores on the Beck Depression Inventory: 0–9 Normal range; 10–15 Mild Depression; 16–19 Mild to Moderate Depression; 20–29 Moderate to Severe Depression; 30–63 Severe Depression.

JUDY IWENS EIDELSON received her B.A. degree with honors from
Princeton University and her Ph.D. in clinical psychology from Duke University. She received postgraduate training in cognitive therapy at the University of Pennsylvania. Dr. Eidelson has conducted research on the effect
of self-image on productivity and family relations. Since 1984 she has been a
clinical supervisor in the departments of psychology and psychiatry at the
University of Pennsylvania. From 1984 to 1986 she was the clinical director
of the Institute for Cognitive and Behavioral Therapies at the Presbyterian-
University of Pennsylvania Medical Center. Dr. Eidelson maintains a private practice in Philadelphia, where she lives with her husband and son.

Further Reading

Beck, Aaron T. *Depression: Clinical, Experimental, and Theoretical Aspects.*
New York: Harper & Row, 1967. Republished as *Depression: Causes
and Treatment.* Philadelphia: University of Pennsylvania Press, 1972.

Burns, David D. *Feeling Good: The New Mood Therapy.* New York: Morrow, 1980; in paperback, New American Library, 1980.

Emery, Gary. *A New Beginning: How You Can Change Your Life Through
Cognitive Therapy.* New York: Simon & Schuster, 1981.

———. *Own Your Own Life: How the Cognitive Therapy Can Make You Feel
Wonderful.* New York: New American Library, 1982.

Klerman, Gerald L., et al. *Interpersonal Psychotherapy of Depression.* New
York: Basic Books, 1984.

Scarf, Maggie. *Unfinished Business.* Garden City, N.Y.: Doubleday, 1980; in
paperback, Ballantine Books, 1981.

Tavris, Carol. *Anger: The Misunderstood Emotion.* New York: Touchstone
Books, 1984.

20

Fears and Anxiety

DIANNE L. CHAMBLESS

Everyone has fears and anxiety. Why in a woman's health book do we have a whole chapter on the subject? Phobias and anxieties, overall, have been found to be more common in women than in men, although this is not true for every type of fear. A recent study of nine thousand Americans revealed that phobias are the most common mental health problem among women. In this chapter I will focus on those fears that are particularly prevalent in women, consider some of the reasons why women are more likely than men to be anxious, and review some of the treatments for these problems.

Keep in mind, however, that psychological difficulties always lie on a continuum from normal to pathological. The common notion that there are two separate categories of "healthy people" and "emotionally disturbed people" is a misconception. Hence, we may all recognize something of ourselves in the descriptions that follow. A woman should consider herself as having a problem worthy of treatment or other action only if a fear or anxiety is severe enough to make her lead her life in ways she is unhappy about, to cause her to lose abilities that she has had before or to fail to grow in optimal ways.

There is another misconception we need to dispense with: that anyone who has a psychological problem such as a phobia is crazy, mentally ill, or emotionally disturbed. Fears and anxiety problems are very common and can (and often do) exist in people who are generally psychologically healthy. This particularly frightening misconception only serves to dissuade people from recognizing their problems and from taking steps to change them. Thus, when someone says to you, "You must be crazy to be afraid of _____ [substitute your favorite fear here]," that person is in effect saying, "Your fear is different from my fear, and I don't understand yours."

Agoraphobia

Agoraphobia is the most disabling of the phobias, accounting for 50 to 80 percent of the phobias for which people seek therapy. Disregard the dictionary definition of fear of open spaces. The Greek *agora* was not only an open space, but also the social, political, business, and spiritual center of town. A person in the *agora,* therefore, is in a public place and is away from home. It is characteristic of agoraphobics to fear such situations, while only a minority of them literally fear open spaces. Agoraphobics have a great many fears, including fears of public transportation, driving (especially on expressways), tunnels, bridges, eating in restaurants, attending church or entertainment events, or being alone. There are many situations that agoraphobics fear, but not all agoraphobics fear all of them.

All these fears may seem bewildering, but they are actually quite orderly: The agoraphobic fears being away from her safe place (usually home) or her safe person (usually a parent or spouse) and fears being in any place where she feels confined, whether physically or by social convention, from leaving quickly should she become anxious. For example, going to a dinner party is anxiety-provoking because she can't run out after the soup course if she begins to feel uncomfortable. An elevator may be frightening because the agoraphobic imagines it may stick between floors, and then how will she get out if she gets panicky? Driving away from home on an expressway is hard because she can't turn around immediately and head for home if anxiety should strike; she must wait for the next exit, search for the entrance ramp going back, and so forth.

By now you have noticed that I keep saying the agoraphobic wants to be able to leave situations where she might become anxious. Why should she fear becoming anxious? Agoraphobia begins with a series of anxiety or panic attacks that seem to come for no reason. Upon closer examination the attacks are found to arise during a period of general emotional or physical stress, but because the woman sees no immediate trigger for the attack, she feels all the more frightened. Unable to see the anxiety attack as a symptom of stress, the agoraphobic-to-be usually interprets the feelings as a sign that she is going crazy or is seriously ill, and perhaps will die. Thus, an event which is thoroughly unpleasant, but not life-threatening, is interpreted as catastrophic.

Shaken in confidence, the agoraphobic begins to retreat from the world, seeking to maintain contact with reassuring places or persons in case she should experience another attack. The more she retreats, the more she finds she cannot do the things that were once commonplace because of the great anxiety she feels when even anticipating doing them. If, as many agoraphobics do, she loses social contacts, quits her job or is fired because of absences, stops volunteer activities, becomes unable to participate fully in her children's lives or to shop for herself and her family, she may begin to see herself as a seriously disturbed and worthless person. This only adds to her fear that she will become insane and increases her dread of another panic attack. For this reason we think of agoraphobia as more of a fear of fear itself than as primarily a fear of places.

After a time anything that sets off feelings that are like those associated with panic becomes intolerable and is avoided. Women may stop sticking up for their rights because the rush of adrenaline that comes during an argument feels too much like anxiety; even pleasant excitement, which involves some of the same feelings of emotional arousal, may come to be frightening. Because agoraphobia is a fear of fear, it tends to spread rapidly. The agoraphobic is really afraid of her own reactions, and because these reactions could occur anywhere, no place may feel completely safe. In the worst cases, agoraphobics are not only housebound, but also may not be able to tolerate being alone even in their own homes. One woman I saw had to accompany her husband outside when he carried the garbage out, or else she would have a panic attack.

The great majority of people with agoraphobia are considerably comforted by the presence of a trusted companion. For some of them, almost anyone, even a pet, can serve that role. For others it must be a particularly safe person, typically a family member, who knows about the agoraphobia. Some can go anywhere and do anything if accompanied by a safe person. Most, however, find that their safety zones (the area around the home in which the agoraphobic can function with tolerable levels of anxiety) are notably increased by the presence of the companion, but that there are still definite limitations on their activities. The agoraphobic may become very concerned about losing her trusted person, fearing what would happen to her if that person would become ill or die. Moreover, she becomes reluctant to confront the other with anger or demands because she is dependent on the companion's goodwill to meet her basic needs. Thus, unspoken resentments may build, poisoning the relationship, and the agoraphobic feels powerless not only in the face of her fear, but also in her intimate relationships.

Are all agoraphobics housebound? Absolutely not. There is a wide range of disability involved. One woman who consulted me recently worked at a high-level position, rode buses comfortably, and shopped easily, but she had difficulty driving in congested areas and on expressways, being alone more than thirty minutes away from home, and going through tunnels and over bridges. She had also begun to avoid high places because the dizziness that most of us experience when looking down from a high place had come to remind her of the dizziness she felt in a panic attack. Because she was not housebound and could go into stores, she had never thought that treatment for agoraphobia might help her. All the articles she had read focused on the suburban housewife who couldn't go to the shopping mall. In fact, I find that the often-depicted "housebound housewife" accounts for the minority of agoraphobics and is a holdover from the days when women weren't so involved in the work force. Like this woman, many agoraphobics may be able to hide their problems and function well in many spheres. Most agoraphobics have a safety zone in which they can operate fairly comfortably. The size of that safety zone may vary from the confines of one's own house to a geographic area as large as a hundred square miles. The employed agoraphobic may have a second safety zone around the workplace. Some people, therefore, can carry on for years and only seek treatment when a move or a promotion forces them to begin to travel, or when the frustration of not being able to see friends and family members in other cities grows too great.

There is yet another group of agoraphobics, sometimes called "white knucklers." To the external world, these people seem perfectly normal, for they force themselves to keep going and doing. Inside, however, they are afraid and torture themselves with terrifying ideas of the possibility of humiliating loss of control should they lose the grip on their anxiety. The continued stress takes its toll on their emotional life, but they continue to hold a job and do what they must do. Men seem somewhat more likely to operate this way. Unfortunately, the white knuckler may use alcohol, tranquilizers, or other drugs to contend with the anxiety, and substance-abuse problems may result.

ASSOCIATED PSYCHOLOGICAL PROBLEMS

Because agoraphobics begin to experience problems with their relationships and feel a general demoralization as the phobia progresses and endures, it is not surprising that most of them are also mildly to moderately depressed. For a time, this was confusing to mental health professionals, who thought that agoraphobia might be a special case of depression. Occasionally, agoraphobics are still told this. People who are severely depressed do sometimes become phobic for the duration of the depression and lose the phobias when the depression lifts. In the great majority of cases, however, agoraphobia is the primary problem, and the depression improves when the agoraphobia is successfully treated. Severe depression does at times interfere with treatment in that it is hard for someone in such a state to have the necessary energy and persistence to improve. Consequently, it is particularly important for the depressed agoraphobic to see a competent professional who can treat all the problems involved.

On the whole, agoraphobics are not only nervous when they are in their phobic situations, they are anxious most of the time. Feeling inadequate and anticipating humiliation from a panic attack, they are anxious in social situations and very fearful of the criticism of others. Usually, the agoraphobic becomes frightened about her health, not only fearing catastrophe during a panic attack, but also being shaken by minor illnesses because she is so hyperalert to any unusual sensations in her body. She may spend a great deal of money and time seeking reassurance from physicians about her health or hoping to find a physical cause for her anxiety symptoms. Her family physician may tell her it's "nerves" or may refer her for extensive workups to a neurologist or other specialist. Paradoxically, she may also become afraid to take medications she might need when physically ill, fearing that a strange substance in her body will make her lose control. Later in the process of agoraphobia many agoraphobics become afraid of going to physicians and dentists, feeling trapped in the waiting and examining rooms as well as by various procedures such as having a cavity filled. The thought of being in a hospital or receiving anesthesia is terrifying. Consequently, these people may fail to get important medical care.

This chronic anxiety, from so many sources, takes its toll on the agoraphobic's ability to enjoy life and often results in her losing interest in sex, as many anxious and depressed people do, thus further straining intimate relationships. As part of her anxiety, the agoraphobic may become excessively worried about her children and their safety, communicating an attitude that the world is an unsafe place. Some children can shrug this off, but others are affected and become anxious themselves.

Family relationships are further impaired by the agoraphobic's difficulty in fulfilling her share of the necessary load. She may be unable to drive the children to their endless round of activities, to participate in family outings, to go on vacations, to visit family members, to attend school meetings, and to go to social functions with her spouse. Loss of her income puts a strain on the family finances, and the standard of living may have to be lowered.

Since agoraphobics usually try to hide their problem from relatives, friends, and sometimes even their spouses, misunderstandings often result, with significant others feeling rejected or confused. Typically, the agoraphobic is concerned that others will think her crazy, and withdraws or comes up with excuses that become untenable over the years. She deeply regrets the resulting social isolation and lists it as the most distressing consequence of her phobias; but she doesn't risk the rejection she fears will come if she is honest. In truth, there are people who will not understand and who will retreat from the agoraphobic. Many will not understand but will still care and remain close. However, most agoraphobics I have seen find that when they eventually share their problems with those close to them, they are met with acceptance and relief. A typical response from relative or friend is, "I'm so glad you told me. I knew something was wrong, and I didn't know how to talk to you about it." People are often eager to read articles or books the agoraphobic might provide to help them better understand the problem.

The decision to announce to the world that one is agoraphobic is, after all, a personal thing; but I encourage my clients to realize that if a person is judgmental or rejecting, that is a reflection on that person's insensitivity or own fearfulness, not on the agoraphobic. Moreover, one doesn't benefit from trying to be close to people who lack compassion and understanding.

Agoraphobics usually try to hide their fears from their children, or if the fears are apparent, they do not explain what they are experiencing. They say that they are afraid that the children might catch agoraphobia somehow if they were told. Most often the children know something is wrong and are more frightened by what they imagine or don't understand than they would be by the truth. Most agoraphobics in treatment eventually tell their children and are relieved when they do. Being able to admit to a fear that one is trying to overcome is a much more positive model for children than treating a problem as a shameful secret; consequently, it is especially unfortunate that so many agoraphobics are secretive with their children.

Single agoraphobics have their own particular problems. They generally find dating excruciating, as they have to contend with feared events such as

movies, concerts, going to restaurants and crowded bars, and driving or
being driven who knows where. Moreover, they must do these things with
an unfamiliar person, from whom they are trying to conceal the phobias.
Faced with these obstacles, the single agoraphobic may stay in a highly
unsatisfactory relationship with someone who knows about and tolerates
her phobias rather than risk rejection with a new person. If she is unable to
work, she may have to seek disability status or public assistance or move in
with relatives, who vary in the degree to which they are able to be emotionally or financially supportive. Needless to say, this is extremely demoralizing. The adolescent agoraphobic may not be able to leave home to go to
college or join the work force. Depending on the age of onset, the young
agoraphobic may not finish junior or senior high school. It is particularly
hard for the agoraphobic who has never experienced normal adult life to
conceive of being part of the world, of ever functioning like other people.

PHYSICAL PROBLEMS ASSOCIATED WITH AGORAPHOBIA

From time to time, articles appear in the popular press, or papers are
presented in professional forums, asserting that the physical cause for agoraphobia has been found. Agoraphobics tend to seize upon this news, hoping
that they have a problem that, being physical in nature, will be more acceptable to their family and friends. After a time, the evidence mounts that this
is not so, but often this does not filter down to the public, and much confusion results. Unfortunately, there are no answers to agoraphobia that are so
simple, and it pays to be skeptical upon hearing that such a solution has
been found. Physical problems and agoraphobia can be interrelated in several ways:

- Physical problems can be part of the stress that leads to agoraphobia.
  For example, onset during the postpartum period is not unusual. Obviously, most women who give birth do not become agoraphobic, and we
  cannot say that pregnancy and childbirth cause agoraphobia. We can
  say, however, that pregnancy and childbirth bring about a great deal of
  stress, both physical and psychological, even in cases where the child is
  eagerly wanted.
- The anxiety associated with being agoraphobic can, in some people,
  increase the severity of physical problems such as high blood pressure.
- The stress that leads to agoraphobia can, at the same time, or at an
  earlier time, produce physical problems such as (according to one
  study) hyper- or hypothyroidism.

It is important for people with agoraphobia to take good care of themselves physically and psychologically, but it is unusual for a physical cause to be found and for treatment of that physical cause to cure the problem. For example, hypoglycemia (low blood sugar) is rarely a primary cause of agoraphobia. Nevertheless, there are complex interactions between blood sugar levels and stress, and shaky feelings associated with low blood sugar may lead to panic attacks in agoraphobics or make existing anxiety worse. Similarly, caffeine causes feelings of agitation that, for someone afraid of fear, can increase the tendency to panic. For these reasons I always try to get my clients to eat a healthier diet and to limit caffeine intake. Feeling better reduces the overall anxiety level, making one less likely to panic and making change with treatment easier.

Mitral valve prolapse (MVP) is a generally benign abnormality in one of the valves of the heart; that is, it is not likely to cause a heart attack. At one time, it seemed that people with panic attacks were much more likely to have MVP than the average person, and it was thought that MVP might be a cause of panic attacks. The more recent and more carefully conducted medical research has led to different findings: Agoraphobics are no more likely to have MVP than anyone else, and MVP does not play a major role in panic anyway. Mitral valve prolapse is very common among the population at large, and most people who have it never even know that they do, for it causes no symptoms other than reducing exercise tolerance somewhat. However, people who have panic attacks and constantly fear they are dying are exquisitely sensitive to any unusual sensations in their bodies. Consequently, there may be subtle sensations associated with MVP that most people ignore, but that people with panic disorders find frightening. Perhaps what is most important to know is that people with and without MVP seem to respond equally well to treatment.

WHO BECOMES AGORAPHOBIC?

Whether we count agoraphobics who seek treatment or those studied in community surveys, we consistently find that the great majority are female (about 80 percent). Typically, agoraphobia begins in young adult life (eighteen to thirty-five), but it may begin as early as twelve years of age. According to the most recent figures, about 4 percent of women in the United States are currently agoraphobic. Poorly educated women and nonwhite women may be twice as vulnerable to agoraphobia. Both of these factors are associated with being economically disadvantaged and having fewer re-

sources, in terms of knowledge and finances, for handling the stressors associated with the onset of agoraphobia. Thus, the common image of the agoraphobic as a pampered, middle-class housewife with nothing to do but dwell
on herself and let her imagination run wild is a myth. Like other psychological problems, agoraphobia is worse for the disadvantaged.

Agoraphobics are likely to have come from families where parents are
alcoholic and/or severely depressed and where other family members also
have many anxiety problems, including agoraphobia. Further, a significant
number of an agoraphobic's children (particularly the daughters) will have
panic attacks and develop agoraphobia themselves. These findings, as well
as those from studies of twins, suggest that the tendency to have panic
attacks runs in families. Some researchers conclude that agoraphobia is an
inherited disease, which must be medically treated; I disagree with them. I
think that the best way to conceptualize this problem is to realize that all of
our bodies respond to chronic stress with some symptoms. For some of us
that symptom is headaches, for others ulcers, and so on. It is quite likely
that the particular vulnerable point we have in the body is inherited; how we
cope with stress is learned.

For example, under prolonged stress some people will respond with a
panic attack, which, as we have seen, often leads to agoraphobia. The famil-
ial depression and alcoholism statistics reinforce what we hear from agoraphobic clients: that their upbringing was lacking in a stable, supportive, and
safe environment in which to grow to a confident adulthood. So the panic
attack reinforces their feelings of insecurity and fear. But a person who
knows what a panic attack is and who has learned to feel competent in the
world is a person much better equipped to cope without becoming phobic.

Are agoraphobics lifelong weaklings and cowards? Not at all. We do see
some clients who have been extremely overprotected and simply never
learned to cope independently. More often the women we see were the
strong ones in their families, who ignored their own feelings and handled the
family problems. They pay a price later for learning to set aside their own
needs, particularly if they enter intimate relationships that are not emotionally supportive. They then lack the reserves on which to draw if stresses
mount, and the collapse may come in the form of panic attacks. Moreover,
as adults they may be unable to recognize important needs and feelings and
consequently may not readily apprehend the conflicts that lead them to be
so stressed. A typical one for agoraphobic women is unhappiness with their
relationships with a spouse, lover, or parent. This is hardly unique to agoraphobia; women place a great deal of importance on relationships and are
distressed when they are unsatisfactory. What does seem to be different for

the woman who becomes agoraphobic is that she has panic attacks when under prolonged strain, and that she is so prone to ignore her feelings that she attributes the panic to some unknown disease rather than to her own unhappiness.

TREATMENT

After one or more panic attacks, the agoraphobic usually goes to see her family physician. Depending on the doctor's awareness of agoraphobia and panic, she will usually get a checkup, reassurance that her problem is not physical, and the diagnosis that her problem is due to anxiety. Very frequently, she will get a prescription for a tranquilizer such as Valium. If she continues to complain of her symptoms, she may be referred for extensive physical workups to all kinds of specialists. When these produce no evidence of physical abnormalities (or when the treatment done for any physical problems found leads to no change in the agoraphobia), the physician may suggest that she see a psychotherapist.

Until the 1970s, agoraphobics were treated with standard (usually Freudian) psychotherapy. That is, they went to see a psychologist, psychiatrist, or psychiatric social worker from one to five times a week and talked about their problems, their childhood, and so forth, while the therapist tried to help them understand the source of their problems. The assumption was that with insight the phobias would improve. Although many agoraphobics learned a great deal about themselves that was useful, on the whole this approach did little for the phobias. With no success in therapy despite considerable expense and effort, the agoraphobic usually becomes discouraged and feels that she is hopeless. In fact, what she needs is specialized treatment.

More and more therapists are learning to recognize agoraphobia and to refer the problem to a phobia specialist; unfortunately, most practitioners still use the ineffective method of "talk therapy." This is why successful treatment is most often obtained when the agoraphobic herself becomes an educated consumer and locates the right person to see. Two approaches have been found to be helpful in the treatment of agoraphobia: behavior therapy and drug therapy.

Behavior Therapy. Until the 1970s behavior therapists, although successful in treating other phobias, usually did little better than traditional therapists when working with agoraphobics. An effective treatment for other "simple" phobias (such as fear of dogs), called systematic desensitization, did not work for agoraphobia, perhaps because it did not address the fear of fear adequately. (I will describe this treatment in the section on other phobias.) In choosing a behavior therapist, therefore, it is important to find one who has kept up with the times rather than someone who still tries to use this old technique.

What has proved very effective is a treatment developed in the last decade called *exposure therapy*. In exposure treatment, the therapist takes the agoraphobic person into the actual situations she fears, helps her to cope with her anxiety, and to remain in the situation until her anxiety declines. In this way she learns that the panic will not harm her if she doesn't run from it. The treatment is conducted in a step-by-step, orderly fashion, beginning with easier things and working one's way up to harder tasks. With repetition, the anxiety fades, the therapist gradually withdraws, and the client is able to master these situations on her own. Exposure is combined with education about agoraphobia and the nature of panic, to lessen the agoraphobic's fear that she is going to die or become insane. The majority of those treated with exposure improve markedly in their ability to get about, become less depressed, and less likely to have panic attacks.

Training in breath control is also very important, because many symptoms result from chronic hyperventilation as well as from the acute attacks of hyperventilation during a panicky moment. Slow, diaphragmatic breathing greatly reduces anxiety in phobic situations, but most agoraphobics are unaware that they are breathing improperly, even when asked about hyperventilation. The therapist can coach the agoraphobic to breathe properly during exposure sessions and, in order to change the overall hyperventilation pattern, to use correct breathing as the new, normal way of breathing at all times.

Exposure treatment is time-consuming: An ideal length for a session is usually ninety minutes or so. If your therapist uses the standard fifty-minute psychotherapy hour, it becomes hard for him or her to provide effective treatment. For this reason, and because in some locales there are not enough trained behavior therapists to meet the demand, alternatives to individual therapy have been developed.

First, treatment may be provided in a group situation. This approach is equally as effective as individual therapy and has the added benefit of reassuring the agoraphobic person that others, who are definitely sane people, share her problem. This reduces her fear of insanity as well as her sense of isolation. It is important, however, in joining a group to make certain that there are enough therapists to allow for individual attention in the group. Unless the group members are extremely similar in the situations they need to work on (for example, everyone has trouble with public transportation and shopping malls), there should be one therapist for approximately every three clients.

A second alternative is for the therapist to teach the client to carry out her own treatment. The therapist meets with her weekly, giving assignments to complete during the week and training her in coping techniques. The actual exposure is done by the client on her own, perhaps with the help of a friend or relative. This approach produces good results for about one third of agoraphobic clients, as opposed to the two-thirds improvement rate for those actually accompanied on exposure sessions by the therapist. This is not, however, an effective method for severe cases such as the housebound agoraphobic. Similar problems are likely for those who work on their problems alone with books, manuals, and tape-recorded treatment programs. Nevertheless, this may be the only treatment available in some communities.

Third, some clinics employ paraprofessionals to conduct the exposure treatment. These are people who are not professional psychotherapists but who are trained to do the exposure work with phobics and who commonly work under the supervision of a professional. Often the paraprofessional is a former phobic. It is not difficult to learn to conduct exposure treatment, and paraprofessionals are generally quite effective. Problems do arise when they are not adequately supervised, because agoraphobics have so many significant problems beyond the situations they fear and avoid. Some caution should be used, therefore, in working with the paraprofessional who has set up an independent practice unless the agoraphobic person also seeks consultation from a professional therapist.

Drug Therapy. As behavior therapists were developing effective treatments, medical researchers were advancing in finding drugs that are helpful in the treatment of agoraphobia. Tranquilizers had proved to be of little help and sometimes led to addiction. The so-called major tranquilizers (antipsychotic drugs that have powerful sedating effects), such as Thorazine, made agoraphobics worse. Consequently, it was a major breakthrough when a tricyclic antidepressant (Tofranil) seemed to reduce panic attacks and make it easier for therapists to persuade agoraphobics to go out again. Similar beneficial effects were found for a drug in another antidepressant family called the monoamine oxidase (MAO) inhibitors (Nardil). Because these drugs are called antidepressants, agoraphobics are often confused when their use is recommended, feeling that they suffer from anxiety much more than depression. As yet it is not known why these drugs help agoraphobics, but in general it is important to realize that most drugs have a range of effects: The drugs may well help depression in one way and anxiety through some different action. These drugs were a considerable improvement over tranquilizers because they were not only more effective but were also not drugs that people would abuse and become physically dependent upon.

A new arrival on the drug market, Xanax, is a close cousin of the tranquilizer Valium. Although there is limited evidence on its effectiveness as this chapter is written, it is being touted as the new miracle drug for the control of panic. Its similarity to Valium suggests that there will ultimately be problems of abuse with this drug, and that Xanax will lose its effectiveness over time, requiring higher and higher doses to fend off anxiety. Indeed, I am already seeing these problems in those who apply to my clinic for treatment, in addition to extreme difficulty withdrawing from the drug. For this reason, my psychiatric consultant sticks with the antidepressant drugs, even though their side effects are more troublesome. Until we know much more about the long-range effects of Xanax, prudence is the best policy.

Studies show that the antidepressants, *combined* with the sort of systematic instructions from a therapist to carry out an exposure program and monitoring that I have previously described, constitute an effective treatment for agoraphobia. For the agoraphobic person who is not able to obtain exposure treatment *with* a therapist, this is an important treatment alternative. Unfortunately, there have been many biased claims in the popular press of late to the effect that agoraphobics *must* take drugs if they are to improve, because otherwise they will not be able to control the panic. One journalist went so far as to liken agoraphobia to diabetes and the drugs to insulin, implying the agoraphobic has a disease which will last and require medication for the remainder of her life. Not true.

As I noted, behavioral treatment without drugs reduces panic attacks, avoidance habits, and depression. Indeed, the majority of clients in my treatment program report that they are having no more panic attacks within six months of beginning treatment. The most carefully conducted research indicates that medication adds little to the effects of an exposure program carried out with a therapist, although it does help when the client is merely given instructions to go out on her own. Medication is an alternative, not a requirement.

In considering the medication alternative, women need to think about several issues. First, uncomfortable side effects such as dry mouth or dietary restrictions are annoying to some users. Second, 80 percent of agoraphobics are women of childbearing age. None of these drugs are recommended for the pregnant or nursing woman, and pregnancies are often not planned. Third, relapse rates have been quite high with the drugs, probably because the agoraphobic has learned no other method of coping with her anxiety and attributes any changes she has made to the medication. The current thinking is to reduce the relapse rate by extending the length of time that one takes the medication to a year or even much longer. To our knowledge the antidepressants are safe drugs for prolonged use; however, researchers have ultimately been unhappily surprised in the case of other drugs. For this reason some caution may be called for before advocating that millions of American women take these drugs on a regular basis. On the other hand, agoraphobia can be such a crippling problem that if drugs are the only available treatment, their use may be invaluable.

A woman who wants to investigate drug treatment should see a psychiatrist or other physician who has expertise in using antidepressant medication for panic attacks. Most American physicians are unfamiliar with the use of Nardil, and those used to prescribing the tricyclics (such as Tofranil) for depression may use the wrong approach with agoraphobics. In treating depression one typically starts out with a fairly large dose (50 to 75 mg) and doubles or triples that dose within a week. Agoraphobics, however, are so sensitive to and frightened by the side effects of the medication that they generally need to start out with 10 to 25 mg daily, building up over three to four weeks to their effective dose level. Moreover, 20 percent of agoraphobics respond best to *low* dosages of the medication, much less than the level that would be effective for depression, and in all cases of agoraphobia too much of the drug makes the condition worse. Thus, the prescribing physician must help the agoraphobic look carefully for what is called the "therapeutic window," the amount of drug that is enough but not too much. For these reasons many agoraphobics have had bad experiences with tricyclics in the past and think they cannot benefit from them, when with better handling of the drug, perhaps the results would have been different. In the absence of other options, the agoraphobic may decide to work with her family physician on finding an effective range of the drug for her condition.

Simple Phobias

Most children have specific fears—of the dark, of separation from their parents, of animals. Most of these fears disappear in the normal process of maturation. By early adolescence, both boys and girls report fewer fears, but fears drop more rapidly for boys than for girls. In adulthood, fears of particular situations or objects such as thunderstorms or animals that are so severe as to require treatment, are rather unusual. Of those who do need such treatment, the majority are women.

How do we understand this discrepancy? Our society seems to be much more tolerant of fears in girls and women. As a result, girls are probably less likely to push themselves to overcome a lingering fear, whereas boys will do so to avoid humiliation by their peers. In laboratory experiments men and women who are equally fearful of an animal such as a snake have been given the opportunity to approach the animal as closely as they can tolerate. Consistently, men force themselves nearer to the animal. The nature of this fear is such that if a person stops avoiding the animal he or she fears, the anxiety decreases and the phobia is ultimately erased. The female sex role, therefore, in allowing women to avoid what they fear, encourages them to remain fearful.

Although usually not as crippling as agoraphobia, specific phobias, such as fears of animals, may be highly distressing. The phobic person may have frequent nightmares concerning this animal and may restrict her recreational activities to avoid contact. Anyone living in the suburbs or a small town who is afraid of dogs or cats may have many humiliating experiences when visiting neighbors or when simply going out of doors. Those afraid of storms may hesitate to leave home in summertime and listen incessantly to weather reports, terrified there will be a storm that day.

Treatment for Fear

Considerable research has shown that a person who has a specific phobia is no more or less psychologically healthy than the average person. For this reason it is completely inappropriate for such people to be in talk therapies to overcome their problem, nor does anyone advocate the use of medication for these fears. Fortunately, over the past thirty years behavior therapy has proved to be very successful in treating these problems.

The first treatment devised was called systematic desensitization. The phobic person is taught to relax deeply and then begin to progress mentally through a hierarchy of her phobic situations. The situations are arranged from the easiest to the hardest, and she is taught to imagine them clearly as they are described by her therapist, one at a time. Remaining relaxed, she imagines each situation until she can visualize it calmly, and then progresses to a slightly more difficult image. As she realizes that she can cope adequately with the phobic situation, she is more likely to accept her therapist's assignments to carry out in reality the things she has imagined doing successfully.

Systematic desensitization is effective, but it is time-consuming. Moreover, some people have difficulty learning to relax; others find it hard to experience fear when imagining their phobic situation rather than actually being in it. For this reason, exposure therapy is often used when possible with simple phobics as well as agoraphobics. Changes may be very rapid using this approach. With treatment not only are waking life changes apparent, but the nightmares disappear as well.

Generalized Anxiety

Anxiety is not far behind the common cold in sending people to their general practitioners. Not all of those who have anxiety problems develop phobias. About 8 percent of all women have severe, chronic, but nonphobic, anxiety problems within a given year, about twice the rate of that seen for men. That is, they don't fear a specific situation; rather they are almost constantly tense. Less severe anxiety problems are commonplace, being reported by 30 to 40 percent of those surveyed in the United States. Anxiety is not only psychologically uncomfortable, it also is accompanied by many unpleasant physical sensations such as headaches, rapid heartbeat, and problems falling asleep. Not surprisingly, women are the major consumers of tranquilizers in the United States.

Does all this mean that women are more mentally unstable than men, as Freud suggested? Not at all. Rather, men and women seem to express their psychological distress in different ways: Women get anxious, depressed, and phobic, while men have problems with alcohol, drug abuse, and criminal behavior. Overall, the rate of psychological problems is equivalent for the sexes, but, perhaps due to the influence of societal forces, the form of the problem varies in predictable ways according to one's sex.

At present, less is known about how and why people develop anxiety problems because anxiety has been studied less than the phobias. Anxiety seems particularly likely to arise when a person has to assume some new responsibility: caring for a new child, a promotion to a more demanding job, or changing roles in life (for example, returning to the work force after a break to raise children). It is more common in those with lower socioeconomic status and seems to become more likely with advancing age. Like agoraphobics, people who develop severe anxiety problems often report having had uncaring or overprotective parents and that their anxiety became a significant problem after some sort of loss or after moving to a new location. Again, the insecure upbringing seems to be implicated. Finally, people who become severely anxious, like those with other emotional problems, are less likely to have solid, supportive relationships to sustain them through bad times.

People who suffer from anxiety have a heightened perception of danger in the world. They are remarkably likely to see the worst in any given situation, worrying for days before an event of all the possible things that could go wrong. In this way they feed their anxiety, keeping it at a high pitch when, realistically, the situation is much less threatening than they perceive it to be.

Although some women with anxiety problems may be alarmists, many of their worries are realistic. Women are more and more likely to hold full-time jobs while also keeping a home and raising a family, thus having a seventy-hour work week and virtually no time to relax from the strains of the week. In the workplace women face demoralizing and frightening sexual harassment and economic discrimination. Women who are single parents face an even higher level of stress, coping with diminished financial resources and children who may have developed behavioral problems during the divorce. Women and their children make up the bulk of those living below the poverty line.

Physical safety is also a concern for the anxious woman. In perhaps one family in fifteen, women are being physically abused by their husbands or boyfriends. Such women are of course chronically anxious, fearing for their lives and the safety of their children. Even once they escape from the violent situation, women who have been battered require months before their anxiety levels approach normal. Severe anxiety reactions are also typical of women who have been sexually assaulted (as about 10 percent of women living in cities will be). While the worst of the anxiety and depression following assault tends to be over in six to eight months, fears of being alone on the streets, of men or of strangers, indeed of any situation reminiscent of the assault, persist for years (see Chap. 17).

Treatment for Anxiety

I have already noted that women are the major consumers of tranquilizers; this is hardly surprising in light of their greater anxiety and lower tendency to use alcohol and street drugs. Millions of American women receive prescriptions for these drugs—such as Valium, Tranxene, Ativan, Xanax, and Librium—when they complain to their physicians about trouble sleeping, feeling anxious, or the physical complaints associated with anxiety. Unfortunately, the effectiveness of these drugs, when taken on a regular basis, may only last a few weeks, or at most a few months. In addition, the drugs may have side effects such as drowsiness and subtle disruption of cognitive functions and speech. Taking a pill may be easy, but it is not a good long-term solution to chronic anxiety.

Effective therapies *are* being developed, although these received less attention than therapies for phobias until recently. Obviously, an important step is for the woman to resolve the particular stresses in her life that are fueling her anxiety. She may have to learn new skills, such as how to be assertive with an unreasonable employer. She may need to learn general problem-solving skills to generate solutions to future or current distressing problems, such as how to get herself prepared to leave an abusive spouse (see Chap. 15).

A woman who is anxious to an exaggerated degree given the reality of the situation may benefit from a cognitive-behavioral treatment variously called anxiety management training, stress management training, or stress inoculation training. These procedures have been found to be helpful to those with generalized anxiety, including rape victims. There are several components to this treatment. First, women are educated about anxiety, its symptoms, and its effects. This is particularly important for those bewildered by physical complaints they have been told result from "nerves" or for victims of violence who don't know the course of their stress response.

Second, the clients learn how to relax both mind and body, generally through progressive relaxation training. During this training clients learn to tense and relax the various muscle groups of the body, until, with practice, they can relax by giving themselves the instruction to do so. In some clinics biofeedback is used in this training. There is no evidence that the use of biofeedback equipment is necessary to learn the relaxation response, but in some cases it may be helpful. Once a woman can relax while reclining, she learns to do so sitting up, standing, and eventually while carrying out her daily routine. When she has reached this point, she is ready to use the relaxation response to cope in stressful situations of any kind. She learns to use anxiety as a prompt to begin relaxing her body rather than starting a vicious cycle of tension.

But what of her head? Her body may be relaxed; however, if she continues to "catastrophize," or mentally rehearse frightening scenarios and anxious thoughts, she will remain anxious. The third component of the program is training in controlling these anxious thoughts and images. This is easier to do when the relaxation training has made the anxiety less severe. The client learns to identify thinking patterns that lead to more anxiety and to stop them early on—to nip them in the bud before they become full-blown anxieties. She is trained to spot irrational worrying about all the dreadful things that might happen and to counter these negative thoughts with a more rational and positive approach. Applying the relaxation and new thinking patterns whenever the anxiety occurs, rather than just during the treatment sessions, is crucial to the success of this treatment.

Many relaxation programs are available on tape for the public. These may be helpful, but it is important to recognize that if the tapes are not beneficial, this does not mean that similar procedures with a trained professional would not work. While these treatments can be clearly specified, they are not always so easy to apply on one's own. There is evidence, however, that someone who has received anxiety management training is able to apply it in situations other than those her therapist has helped her with. This makes it a particularly valuable procedure.

Getting Help

To learn more about these problems one can seek treatment from a professional therapist who specializes in anxiety disorders. There are now many clinics specializing in phobias, some of which also have treatment for nonphobic anxiety problems. Information about the nearest treatment center can be obtained by sending a self-addressed, stamped (for 2 oz.) envelope to The Agoraphobia and Anxiety Program, Temple University Medical School, 110 Bala Avenue, Bala-Cynwyd, PA 19004. Some of these centers, such as the one at Temple, have special intensive treatment programs that are particularly useful for people from out of town.

Second, look into local self-help efforts. In some communities phobics have banded together to form self-help groups. Such groups may be very supportive, but it is essential to determine that the members of a group are actively working to change rather than simply to complain about their problems. Otherwise, the group may become a negative rather than a positive force. It is generally desirable that the group have some professional consultation. The Phobia Society of America publishes a newsletter for its professional and lay members and holds an annual conference where one may get up-to-date information about phobias and their treatment. Information is available by writing to the society at 5820 Hubbard Drive, Rockville, MD 20852.

Finally, keep in mind that no one need suffer from fear and anxiety in private torment. These problems are part of life, they are all too common, and they can be conquered.

DIANNE CHAMBLESS is the director of the Agoraphobia and Anxiety Program of the Department of Psychology at American University and a clinical psychologist in private practice in Washington, D.C. Dr. Chambless received her master's degree in 1972 and her doctoral degree in 1979 from Temple University. In 1976 she was a cofounder of the Agoraphobia Program of Temple University Medical School, one of the first facilities providing specialized treatment for phobias. She continues to be affiliated with that program as director of research.

Dr. Chambless is author of some twenty professional papers on agoraphobia and other anxiety disorders and editor of the volume *Agoraphobia: Multiple Perspectives on Theory and Treatment.* In 1979 she was awarded the Presidential Research Award of the Association for Advancement of Behavior Therapy for her work on agoraphobia. A cofounder in 1972 of the Feminist Therapy Collective of Philadelphia, she has long been involved in the treatment of women's emotional problems and has published research on depression among women and on female sexual dysfunction.

Further Reading

Agras, Stewart. *Panic: Facing Fears, Phobias, and Anxiety.* New York: W. H. Freeman, 1985.

Goldstein, Alan, and Steinbeck, Barry. *Overcoming Agoraphobia.* New York: Viking, 1986.

Marks, Isaac. *Living with Fear: Understanding and Coping with Anxiety.* New York: McGraw-Hill, 1978.

Weekes, Claire. *Hope and Help for Your Nerves.* New York: Bantam Books, 1979.

————. *Peace from Nervous Suffering.* New York: Bantam Books, 1979.

Zane, Manuel D., and Milt, Harry. *Your Phobias: Understanding Your Fears with Contextual Therapy.* Washington, D.C.: American Psychiatric Press, 1984.

21

A Consumer's Guide to Psychotherapy

CARIN RUBENSTEIN

In the mid-1800s, the time of settling the Kansas frontier, husbands were often far away for long periods of time. In *Pioneer Women*, author Joanna Stratton describes women's lives during that time:

> Such long absences were wearing for the waiting mother. Burdened with both the maintenance and the protection of the family homestead, she could rely on no one but herself. In these lonely circumstances, she fought the wilderness with her own imagination, skill, common sense and determination. . . . [Her] loneliness, usually borne with dignity and silence, could at times express itself in unexpected ways. Mary Furguson Darrah recalled a time when "Mr. Hilton, a pioneer, told his wife that he was going to Little River for wood. She asked to go with him. . . . She hadn't seen a tree for two years, and when they arrived at Little River she put her arms around a tree and hugged it until she was hysterical."

The women who pioneered the West more than a century ago battled against wolves, weather, Indians, solitude, dangerous childbirth, floods, and famine without the comfort and support of a local psychotherapist. For them the need to survive superseded the need to relieve anxiety, loneliness, depression, and unhappiness. Indeed, they were probably too preoccupied to worry about such emotions.

The practice of looking inward and analyzing one's feelings, thoughts, and fears is relatively new. If our foremothers had a personal problem, they would have kept it to themselves or perhaps asked a clergyman for spiritual support. Occasionally, they may have expressed their distress by hysterical tree hugging or frantic Bible reading. But they would most probably have been horrified at the idea of hiring a stranger to listen to their problems.

Sigmund Freud changed all this with his invention of the "talking cure." Around the turn of the century he began to treat hysteria patients—a majority of whom were women—by having them talk about their childhood, their dreams, their fantasies. With the use of what he called "psychoanalysis," Freud believed that he could reach the unconscious emotional and sexual underpinnings of his patients' physical symptoms and psychological woes. His view of the dynamics of personality was one of the major intellectual revolutions of the twentieth century. Yet most Americans now take the idea of psychotherapy for granted, as if it has always been the best way to solve personal distress.

Modern psychotherapy has gone through many metamorphoses since Freud's era and has evolved into a major force in the American medical establishment. Even more important, therapy has become a business; a woman who seeks help for a psychological problem is a consumer of a product called psychotherapy. And she should choose her therapist with at least as much care as she would choose a ripe melon. After all, she will spend a considerable amount of money on the therapist, whom she will see more often than she sees any physician, dentist, or hairdresser.

Like other professionals who have services to sell, therapists must market their particular brand of therapy, since they need a steady supply of new clients to stay in business. Because the number of psychotherapists is growing every year, therapists need you more than you need them. Thus, don't think of the therapist as someone who is doing you a favor by taking you in. The situation is quite the contrary. For this reason, you have a greater ability to be selective in your choice of a therapist than do therapists in their choice of patients. Also, remember that the label of "therapist" or "psychologist" or "psychiatrist" is no guarantee that a practitioner is competent. It should be your job as a consumer to select the most suitable therapist for your problem—a choice based on much more than just professional titles or credentials.

This chapter will offer the reader guidance and insight on psychotherapy, enabling her to become an informed consumer. At times, the view of therapy taken here may seem harsh or overly critical, but that is only because questions about its efficacy have never been answered completely. Still, therapy has a great deal to offer people, depending on their particular needs and goals. It is *your* task to decide what it is you want from therapy and which kind of therapy will be most likely to help you.

Who Goes to Therapy and Why They Go

The recent "psychologization" of America has made psychology and the emphasis on introspection a primary basis for people's evaluations of themselves and others. Many Americans have begun to think psychologically and to judge people on their inner qualities, such as honesty, trustworthiness, and warmth, rather than on external traits such as profession or what kind of car they own. Over the past generation or so, according to a study conducted by the Institute for Social Research (ISR) at the University of Michigan (hereafter, "the Michigan study"), more and more Americans have also become able to admit to having psychological problems. In addition, they have grown more willing to seek professional help to solve those problems. In 1957 about 14 percent of a random sample of Americans said they had seen a professional about a mental health problem; by 1976, 26 percent said that they had done so.

In a 1984 study by the National Institute of Mental Health (NIMH), researchers interviewed nearly ten thousand adults in three cities and found that about one in five suffered from at least one mental problem. These problems were, in order of prevalence, anxiety disorders (such as phobias, panic attacks, obsession-compulsion), alcohol or drug abuse, depression, and schizophrenia. Among those people diagnosed as having a mental disorder, between one quarter and one third (depending on the city in which they lived) had sought professional help for the problem.

Although the use of professionals to treat psychological problems is growing, women are more likely than men to seek out and use such help. The Michigan researchers suggest that women may suffer more from social and emotional distress and so actually *need* such help more than men do. It is also possible that women are more likely than men to think of their problems in psychological terms. A woman having trouble at work, for example, may feel that her problem lies in low self-esteem; a man with similar woes might be more likely to attribute them to an incompetent boss. The recent NIMH study also found that twice as many women seek help for mental problems as men. Yet they found that men were equally troubled: The women were most likely to suffer from phobias (an unreasonable fear of anything from snakes and spiders to elevators and heights) and depression; the men were more troubled by alcohol or drug abuse and antisocial behavior.

In addition to women, there are several types of Americans who are most likely to seek psychological help, according to the Michigan research. Those who are under fifty years old, those who live in urban or suburban regions, those who live or grew up on the West Coast, Jews, church attenders, and those whose parents were divorced or who are themselves divorced are most open to accepting professional help for psychological problems. The actual visit to a therapist, however, requires that a person have a psychological orientation and perceive that help is available. It is also important that her social group (friends, colleagues, relatives) view therapy as acceptable and beneficial.

The two most common reasons that people give for seeking help are for marital troubles and for personal problems in adjusting to daily life. In some circles such concrete reasons are not necessary, since everyone has "a shrink." In these groups, having a therapist has become a kind of status symbol. (The success of Judith Rossner's novel *August* was due in part to the chord struck in the hearts of all patients who must be parted from their therapists during that popular vacation month.)

Who Needs Psychotherapy?

According to psychologist Bernie Zilbergeld, author of *The Shrinking of America*, psychotherapy is "any systematic course of action under expert guidance designed to alter a person's thoughts, feelings, attitudes, behavior and relationships, without drugs or surgery."

Quite simply, psychotherapy should make people feel better about themselves and should also promote change—in behavior, attitudes, or feelings. Most experts agree that its primary purpose is *not* to "cure" psychological disorders, probably because in many cases people's emotional problems cannot be completely and permanently cured. The hidden benefit of therapy, writes Zilbergeld, is that it offers people meaning, control, and hope. "All change processes provide ways of viewing and understanding the world and one's place in it . . . a framework for viewing all the important aspects of life—mental processes, emotions, relationships, work, love, and so on. . . .

Meaning itself brings a measure of control." The sense of hope comes from the feeling that the problem can be resolved, which (many people believe) will ultimately lead to living happily ever after.

People enter psychotherapy for everything from adjusting to divorce to losing weight to conquering a fear of flying to gaining a deeper understanding of themselves and their problems. Almost all of these people have one thing in common—they think psychologically, defining their problems both internally and interpersonally. Our culture has become so psychologically tuned in partly because of the preponderance and influence of psychologists. Indeed, psychotherapy may be the only form of treatment, says eminent psychologist Jerome Frank, that creates the illness it treats. "By calling attention to symptoms they might otherwise ignore and by labeling those symptoms as signs of neurosis," says Frank (in *Persuasion and Healing),* "mental health education can create unwarranted anxieties, leading those to seek psychotherapy who do not need it. The demand for psychotherapy keeps pace with the supply, and at times one has the uneasy feeling that the supply may be creating the demand."

Author Zilbergeld also warns that therapists keep themselves in demand by making definitive problems out of simple difficulties and spreading the alarm—unhappiness at forty-five becomes a mid-life crisis, postdivorce disturbance becomes divorce trauma, unhappiness at work becomes burnout. Then, although psychologists deem it acceptable to have such problems, they make it seem as if people cannot resolve their problems by themselves. After all, an expert's help is always preferable. Finally, says Zilbergeld, psychotherapists offer salvation in terms of simple prescriptions for happiness, high self-esteem, and lifelong success. They make it seem almost criminal *not* to seek help. Many of the problems you think you have, in short, could have been created by the very experts from whom you are seeking help. If you are alert to this possibility and knowledgeable about exactly what it is you hope to get from therapy, you will be less likely to be disappointed in it.

Before deciding on psychotherapy, it is essential to rule out physiological illness as the cause of psychological symptoms. A reputable therapist will make certain that a patient's problems are not due to an undiagnosed physical ailment. A variety of diseases (such as endocrine abnormalities, liver trouble, and multiple sclerosis) and drugs (such as LSD, cocaine, and some hypertension medication) can trigger all sorts of psychological problems that disappear completely when the illness is cured or the drug treatment stopped. For example, depression (if it occurs for the first time after the age of fifty-five) is the only early symptom of pancreatic cancer, appearing six months before the correct diagnosis. Reserpine, a drug used to treat hypertension, often causes severe depression; beta-blockers (used for hypertension, angina, migraine headache) often result in lethargy, sluggishness, and a general low feeling. Other commonly used drugs (such as steroids and Tagamet for ulcers) can actually cause psychotic episodes, including hallucinations and intense agitation.

Even Sigmund Freud made the mistake of treating the symptoms of a physical illness as if they were the result of deep psychological problems. For one of his most well-known illustrations of the sexual origins of hysteria, Freud used the case of Dora, an eighteen-year-old girl who came to him with convulsions, attacks of loss of consciousness, delirious states, and a tendency to drag one leg. As described in *The Freudian Fallacy,* by medical historian E. M. Thornton, Freud discovered that a close friend of Dora's father had tried to seduce her. Not only that, but her father himself was probably having an affair with this man's wife. After many analytic sessions with Dora—analyzing her dreams in great detail, as well as probing into her proclivity to masturbate—Freud deduced that Dora's hysteria was probably related to her secret desire to have sex with her father. Her physical symptoms, however, indicated that she probably had epilepsy. In another case, Freud treated a fourteen-year-old girl for hysteria when she came to him with chronic stomach pains. Two months after he finished treating her, believing that her hysteria had improved a great deal, she died of stomach cancer.

With these caveats in mind, there are several standard psychological problems that can signal a need for professional help. First, and perhaps most common, is chronic depression. Depression is characterized by serious disturbances in eating and sleeping habits: loss of weight without really trying and insomnia or waking early without being able to fall back to sleep, feeling lowest early in the morning with slight improvement as the day goes on. Other physical symptoms include deep fatigue and a loss of interest in sex. Psychological signs of depression can be intense feelings of helplessness, despair, and emptiness that last for at least a month or more. Thoughts of death and suicide are also common among the chronically depressed. These feelings may recur throughout adulthood or may have been triggered by a specific event, such as the loss of a spouse through death or divorce, but will not have dissipated even after a reasonable amount of time (see Chap. 19).

Other common signals that psychotherapy might be needed (according to health writer Jane Brody in *The New York Times Guide to Personal Health*) include the following:

• Feelings of hopelessness and demoralization or overwhelming boredom;

a sense of the meaninglessness of one's existence along with recurring thoughts of suicide; uncontrollable mood shifts.

- Being afraid that people are out to get you; feeling that events seem unreal or that you don't feel like yourself; serious inability to get along with other people.
- Compulsive, self-destructive behavior such as drinking, overeating or undereating, gambling, or using drugs; compulsive rituals such as hand washing; phobias, including the fear of heights, elevators, or going outside the house.
- Sexual problems, such as impotence, premature ejaculation, or inability to reach orgasm.
- Constant insomnia or nightmares.
- In children, chronic disruption at home and school; senseless destruction of objects or flagrant criminal acts; inability to get along with others; continuing physical complaints for which no medical cause can be found.

If you find that minor problems become major emotional upsets, that small pleasures are no longer satisfying, that you have constant feelings of anxiety, that you are persistently afraid of other people or situations, that you are suspicious of others, or that you have strong feelings of inadequacy and self-doubt, any one of these symptoms is a potential reason for seeking a psychotherapist. Next, the type of problem you have should determine which kind of therapist you choose (see "Types of Psychotherapy").

Seeking a therapist for a friend or relative is more difficult than doing so for yourself. First, that person must agree that she has a problem that needs to be treated. If a client lacks the motivation or desire to change, therapy will probably be ineffective. Second, it is best for the person who needs a therapist to make her own selection. No matter how close you are, you can't tell which therapist will be most compatible with someone else. The best you can do for someone you think has a serious problem is to convince her that it is serious and that she should do something about it.

Is Change Possible?

Even with years of therapy, can an insecure, anxious man ever become an outgoing life of the party? Will an aggressive, cold woman be able to transform herself into a warm earth mother? More and more of the latest research shows that such metamorphoses are unlikely, if not impossible. Most experts now believe that adult personality is remarkably stable, especially when it comes to key traits like extroversion, neuroticism, sociability, excitability, and anxiety. If a man is slightly neurotic, introverted, shy and not easily excited at twenty-one, he will probably be much the same, at least psychologically, at eighty-one. (For a discussion of these issues, see Jerome Kagan's *The Nature of the Child* and Orville Brim and Jerome Kagan [eds.], *Constancy and Change in Human Development.)*

Yet popular beliefs don't seem to agree with the research. In our culture we like to assume that people can do anything if they try hard enough. *If he really wanted,* so we like to believe, that twenty-one-year-old could become a different and better person. Bernie Zilbergeld points to three such assumptions of malleability of which Americans seem particularly fond. First, they believe that people *should* change, that they become better through self-improvement. It is always possible, goes this tenet, to be happier, less anxious, a more well-adjusted person. Second, we feel that there are few limits to personal change—no matter what is wrong, you can fix it. "If we can defy gravity, ignore the seasons, conquer great distances, and do all the other things which we have done, it is easy to assume that we need not accept anything as given," writes Zilbergeld, "not our frustration, our lack of ability or success, our pain, our unhappiness, or anything else." Finally, says Zilbergeld, we believe that these personal transformations are relatively easy —just get some therapy and you get better, like taking penicillin for an infection.

But change is not all that simple or easy. If it were, no one would be in analysis for ten or twenty years (as many are) and no one would need to see more than one therapist (as many do) and no one would need to be treated for more than a few sessions (as most are). The truth of the matter, which makes many advocates of therapy very uneasy, is that human beings are not easily malleable, like clay. One of the most unpleasant truths is that physiology and heredity provide strict limits: A man who is five feet four inches tall will never be a professional basketball player; a woman who has a tin ear will never be an opera singer. Likewise, some psychological qualities, such as shyness, sociability, and extroversion, are probably influenced by heredity. (For a comprehensive discussion of this issue, see *Temperament* by Arnold Buss and Robert Plomin.) Disorders such as schizophrenia, depression, and alcoholism may also have a genetic component. Someone born with an inherited predisposition to these diseases may be more vulnerable to them during stressful times in life than would someone without such a genetic proclivity.

A woman who wants to change in some way must devote considerable time and energy to the process. Some people, says Zilbergeld, just don't invest enough of themselves in the effort. Major change also requires learning new ways to think, feel, and behave that many people are either incapable or unwilling to be taught. As a result, they often don't comply with the requests or demands of the therapist—somewhat akin to not taking medication prescribed by a physician. Finally, people need social support for making major changes. A woman who is ridiculed by her family for being in therapy and mocked if she makes a statement that "doesn't sound like you," will probably have a great deal of difficulty making a significant personal change.

There are, it seems, serious limitations to how much people can change. Moreover, perhaps not everyone or everything *should* be changed. Suffering, anxiety, and unhappiness are parts of human life that will never go away, even through the alleged magic of psychotherapy. The key is to learn to accept events over which you have no control and to live with your own limitations. "Acceptance of ourselves as we are, and this would include acceptance of our desire to be different than we are," writes Zilbergeld, "would mean less disappointment and less self-hatred for not being all the things we believe we should be."

How Effective Is Psychotherapy?

Even when some changes are possible, how effective is therapy in producing them? Can it really change behavior, attitudes, and feelings? The honest answer to these questions is that no one really knows, but therapy probably cannot do as much as many people think it can. The effectiveness of therapy depends on what people expect from it; complete personal transformation is less easily achieved than the simple relief that comes from being able to discuss one's problems and fears with a sympathetic listener.

Until very recently there was almost no research on how and if therapy worked. The only evidence that it did work came from case reports written by the therapists who had treated the patient in question. No wonder, then, that most of these patients seemed to improve dramatically. One reason that few systematic studies had been done was that they posed seemingly insurmountable problems. First, it is very difficult to know if someone "gets better" in therapy. How should improvement be defined and measured?

Who is to judge it, the therapist or the patient? How long after the therapy is completed should success be determined—right away, six weeks later, one year or five years later? Second, it is usually very difficult to get patients to say anything negative about their therapy sessions, to say nothing of getting therapists to admit to having failed in treating a patient. Patients tend to assume that improvement is their responsibility, and not the therapist's. In addition, after having spent so much time and money on something, they are reluctant to admit that their effort was wasted. Finally, a reliable study requires that control groups be used to compare to those actually in therapy. Many researchers were reluctant to deny therapy to a group of people who wanted it, simply for the sake of doing a study. (The alternative, now used quite often, is to offer therapy to those in the control group after the study has been completed.)

Pressure from the federal government and insurance companies—who were paying for a growing proportion of psychotherapy treatment—finally forced experts to begin research on the efficacy of therapy. One of the first such studies was done in 1952 by psychologist Hans Eysenck. He found that about two thirds of patients in therapy improved—nearly the same as the number who improved in untreated control groups! It is not surprising that Eysenck's study caused a great deal of controversy; it also prompted a number of other scientists to begin to study the efficacy of therapy.

Almost all recent studies of therapy, using a variety of criteria for success, show that about 60 to 80 percent of clients derive some benefit from it. Recently, the American Psychiatric Association published a report called *Psychotherapy Research* that discussed the findings of the best studies on the effectiveness of psychotherapy. Most of these studies concluded, unlike Eysenck, that those in treatment do better than those in control groups. Among participants in the 1976 Michigan study who had used professional help for a personal problem, 56 percent said it had either "helped a lot" or "helped." Another 19 percent said it had helped, with qualifications; 16 percent said that therapy did not help. The ones who felt therapy had not been useful were most likely to have sought help for marital problems. Those who said therapy had been helpful gave different reasons for why they thought that had been the case. Some four in ten said the talking and advice had been useful; two in ten said that something had been cured or that their troublesome relationship had changed; another two in ten said that the therapy had simply been comforting and gave them the ability to endure their problems. Other studies also show that many therapy clients do not seem to require that anything concrete actually change in order for them to believe that their therapy has been successful. Some clients feel good just to be able to talk about themselves for a while and to achieve greater personal understanding, even if they can't do anything about it. The talking and awareness give them a sense of control, of being able to cope with their problems.

Several hundred studies on the effectiveness of therapy have been conducted over the past few decades; most of their findings are relatively consistent. Here is a summary of the conclusions of those studies.

- *No one brand of therapy seems to produce better results than another.* Studies comparing individual and group therapy, for example, show no significant differences between results for each. Neither do comparisons between client-centered therapy and psychoanalysis or between behavior therapy and verbal therapy. (Each type of therapy will be discussed later on.) The only exception to this rule, which most of the studies seem to find, is that behavior therapy is clearly most effective in treating phobias, sexual problems, some compulsions, addictions, and some anxiety states. This method is not as helpful if the client is interested in self-exploration or a search for meaning.

- *Psychotherapy is most effective for treating less serious, less persistent psychological problems.* These include simple fears, anxieties, and phobias, a temporary blow to self-esteem (usually the result of a situational crisis such as a divorce or loss of a job), some marital and family problems, and lack of assertiveness.

- *The length of treatment seems to have little influence on how effective it is.* Studies comparing time-limited therapy (usually fewer than twenty sessions) and unlimited therapy show no significant differences. Many people believe that the longer someone is in therapy the better off she will be. There is no evidence that this is true, with the possible exception of the benefit of the therapist who will need to find fewer patients to keep busy.

- *The effects of therapy seem to be neither permanent nor long-lasting.* Relapse rates in sex therapy, for example, range in several studies from 7 percent up to 54 percent (for a discussion of sex therapy, see Chap. 3). In an examination of behavior therapy, about one third of the clients lost gains they had made in a very short time. In treating addictions to alcohol or food, some studies show that 90 percent of those who seek therapy for such problems return to their former habits after the therapy has concluded. Relapse rates tend to be much lower among those who take it upon themselves to break out of their own addictions.

- *Professional psychotherapists may be no more effective in helping clients than lay people.* In a study conducted at Vanderbilt University by Hans

Strupp and his colleagues, psychologists and nonprofessionals (who had less than one hundred hours of training) each treated a group of patients. Patients in both groups judged the therapists as equally empathic and warm. Both groups improved equally. In another study untrained college student interviewers were rated just as warm, genuine, and empathic as experienced counselors. In fact, the clients felt more accepted by, and less anxious with, the nonprofessionals. In a review of forty-two studies comparing professionals and paraprofessionals, only one showed that the professionals were more effective; the paraprofessionals came out best in twelve of the studies, and the two groups were equal in all the others. Therapists do not have a monopoly on caring and empathy; in fact, they do what priests, ministers, and rabbis have been doing for hundreds of years. They listen. They offer advice. They are sympathetic.

• *For the treatment of prolonged, clinical depression, drug treatment alone reduces symptoms while traditional psychotherapy alone does not.* The best results are obtained when drugs and therapy are used in combination. However, this depends on the type and seriousness of the depression. (For a more complete discussion of cognitive-behavioral and drug treatments for depression, see Chap. 19.)

Studies of the efficacy of psychotherapy conclude that in some cases therapy can actually be harmful. In a review of 101 studies of therapy outcome, Julian Meltzoff and Melvin Kornreich found that about sixteen of the studies found some negative results. In studies of marital and family therapy, for example, 5 to 10 percent of the relationships *worsened* as a result of therapy. In a study of encounter groups, one in five of the clients felt that they were worse off than before as a result of being in the group. One group of researchers asked seventy therapists about the negative effects of therapy they had seen in their own practices. Most agreed that bad things do happen: The clients' symptoms worsen or new ones develop; clients become overly dependent on therapy; clients develop negative attitudes to themselves or become disillusioned. The therapists believe that this occurs if the therapist is cold, hostile, seductive, or pessimistic, or if the patients are not motivated. Finally, they admitted that sometimes therapists make mistakes in doing therapy, with disastrous results for clients. One man, for example, took Valium to control his anxiety on the advice of a therapist he had been seeing for years. After a time the client realized that he had become addicted to the drug and weaned himself of the need for it. When he went to his therapist to announce that he no longer needed the man's services, the therapist contradicted him, saying, "Now you need me to cure your addiction to Valium."

Many of the studies on the effectiveness of therapy find that a majority of patients have been in more than one type of therapy. Many of these people say that they were satisfied with their previous therapy but that they just wanted to try something new. An overdependence on therapy is another of its negative effects, which can lead to anxiety, guilt, and unhappiness. Zilbergeld believes that the message of therapy is that "there is something wrong with the way you are and you ought to do something about it." The implication is, of course, that you are not okay and that whatever is wrong with you is your fault. This fear can turn some people into "therapy junkies" (see "Knowing When to Stop").

Alternatives to Psychotherapy

On balance, it appears that psychotherapy may or may not do what you hope it will. If the time and expense of therapy seem cumbersome, or if you believe that your community and social group attach a stigma to those who seek professional psychological help, there may be alternatives to make you feel better and to help you solve problems.

In some cases a change of circumstance can be just as effective as therapy, possibly more so. Leaving a violent husband, quitting a job, joining a club or adult-school class, or putting a child into a different school can work wonders for spouse abuse, trouble at work, a need for friendship, or school difficulties. These solutions, while sometimes difficult to initiate, solve the problem by going directly to its source. Indeed, many people go into therapy to acquire the assertiveness or self-esteem necessary to take these practical steps.

Support and caring might also be available, without cost, from friends and relatives. In fact, according to the nationwide Michigan study, more people rely on friends and family to help them get through personal crises than on professional help. (Forty-five percent use informal resources; 39 percent use both; 13 percent use neither; 3 percent use only professional help.) Men are less likely than women to have a network of friends they can rely on for help; younger people have more resources to count on than older people. Other studies show that while men tend to rely most heavily on their wives for support and comfort, wives usually have other sources of help, such as close friends and relatives.

The people interviewed in the Michigan study said that aside from psychologists and psychiatrists, they rely on clergymen, doctors, marriage counselors, and lawyers for help in dealing with marital and child-related problems, work or school problems, personal adjustment issues, and psychological reactions to new or troubling situations. In addition, a large number of people believe that they can manage their own problems and cannot imagine ever needing to seek out a professional for help.

If much of the value of psychotherapy is that one has hired a professional listener, the alternatives involve finding someone whom you can recruit to listen to your problems for free. This kind of informal counseling goes on all the time, with everyone from bartenders and hairdressers to friends and brothers and sisters. Many problems can be worked out either by talking to a friend, spouse, or relative, or by joining a problem-specific self-help group (such as Alcoholics Anonymous, Parents Without Partners, or Weight Watchers). (If your unpaid listener is yourself, you might try writing in a diary or talking it out into a tape recorder.) If these methods fail or if your problems require medication, then you might seek professional help. In any event, writes Zilbergeld, "since there is undoubtedly a relationship between one's faith in the treatment and the results obtained, those who believe strongly in professionals will probably get more from them than from others."

Finally, if money is your only deterrent in seeking professional help, there are several sources of very inexpensive (or even free) help. Most neighborhood clinics, such as crisis centers and hot lines, can offer free or very low-priced treatment. Likewise, professional training centers and universities with graduate programs in psychology have clinics that they use for training students. For a low fee you can receive psychotherapy from a student-in-training, who will be supervised by a more experienced teacher. And remember, research indicates that such relatively inexperienced therapists are no worse—and may actually be better—than professionals with many years of training.

Types of Psychotherapists

Unlike many other professions, people who are trained to do psychotherapy come from a variety of very different backgrounds. Almost anyone can call him- or herself a "therapist"—from health food advocates to Indian gurus. But special licensing and credentials are necessary for a therapist to be called a psychiatrist or psychologist.

Psychiatrists, who have M.D. degrees, have spent four years in medical school, one year in internship, and three years as hospital residents in psychiatry. Their license to practice medicine is also their license to practice therapy. You can check a psychiatrist's license and certification by contacting the American Board of Psychiatry and Neurology (One American Plaza, Evanston, Illinois 60201). Psychiatrists are the *only* therapists who can legally prescribe drugs. They are also most well qualified to administer or recommend laboratory tests to diagnose organic problems. Almost all insurance policies that cover treatment for mental health problems will pay, at least in part, for the services of a psychiatrist.

Some psychiatrists practice various behavioral and cognitive types of psychotherapy. Others, called *psychoanalysts,* have received further training in psychoanalytic techniques based primarily on the theories of Freud and his followers. Psychoanalysts are not always psychiatrists, however. Anyone accepted into a psychoanalytic training institute can become a psychoanalyst.

Psychologists have spent four or five years earning a doctorate (Ph.D.) in psychology and a year in a supervised training program. They have also passed a state certification examination that gives them a license to practice and the legal right to call themselves a "psychologist." Each state sets different criteria for passing the licensing test, which usually consists of a multiple choice section and an essay or oral part. In New York State, for example, the qualifying mark is determined so that between 20 and 25 percent of the Ph.D. psychologists who take it will fail. To find out if a psychologist is licensed, contact the American Board of Professional Psychology (2025 I St. N.W., Washington, D.C. 20006). The therapy that psychologists provide is usually acceptable for reimbursement by most medical insurance policies. Psychologists' fees are generally lower than those of psychiatrists.

Social workers have usually received a master's degree (M.S.W.) or a doctorate in social work. They, too, receive certification as psychiatric social workers and their services may or may not be covered by insurance policies. To check their accreditation, contact the Academy of Certified Social Workers at the National Association of Social Workers (7981 Eastern Ave., Silver Springs, Md. 20910).

Other therapists with master's-level degrees include psychiatric nurses and pastoral counselors. Neither are formally accredited and both are usually associated with hospitals, clinics, community mental health centers, and local churches or synagogues. Although relatively inexpensive, their services are usually not covered by medical insurance.

While a fancy degree and state certification are respectable credentials, they by no means guarantee that one therapist is better or more competent than another. To choose the right therapist, you must use your common sense and your consumer instincts to decide who will best treat your problem in a way that makes you feel most comfortable.

Choosing a Psychotherapist

Keep in mind that you are a consumer shopping for a widely available service offered by a variety of vendors. Also, remember that the type of problem you have should determine, at least in part, the kind of therapist you choose, based on the type of therapy practiced.

The personal qualities to seek in a psychotherapist are similar to those you look for in choosing a close friend. Both should provide support, understanding, and warmth. A Harvard psychiatrist recently asked twenty-three therapists what *they* looked for when selecting a therapist. (The therapists had been treated by an average of four therapists.) According to therapists themselves, the most important quality is a therapist's reputation for competence. (This information is not usually available to most consumers.) These therapists also stressed the importance of a therapist's personal qualities, particularly warmth, liking, caring, and supportiveness. They also said that they wanted someone who approved of, appreciated, and respected them, characteristics of a close friend or even a good parent. They were especially harsh on therapists who seemed distant, cold, or ungiving. Personal qualities and idiosyncrasies can be reflected, so these fellow therapists believed, in the way a therapist dresses and decorates his or her office. They refused to use a therapist whose manner of dress or office decor was not to their taste.

A good therapist is not necessarily easy to find. Ask people who are satisfied with their therapist for referrals; other recommendations might come from family doctors, clergymen, local university or hospital mental health departments or clinics, and local hot lines. Some radio psychologists are good sources of information about where to get local help for all kinds of specific problems. (But beware of those who only recommend themselves.) A local telephone book will list the number of the Mental Health Association of your county, which will have information about nearby therapists.

Always shop for a therapist; don't just get one name and then assume that he or she will be right for you. Once you have the names of several therapists, shop first by telephone. Tell the therapist what you need therapy for and what you hope to accomplish in the process. Ask the therapist if he or she has worked with similar problems and what kinds of clients he or she works best with. Although it is difficult to judge a person over the telephone, you should be able to listen to the therapist's voice and tell if you like it. Perhaps more important, find out the therapist's location and hours (especially if you prefer evening or weekend sessions), and if the treatment will be covered by your insurance policy. Once you weed out therapists (by telephone) according to convenience, you can begin more personal distinctions. Be wary of a therapist who will not give you any information over the telephone but who insists that you pay for a visit.

After you have narrowed your list down to two or three names, take the time to visit each therapist in person. This will help you judge the therapist's personal style, warmth, and general compatibility. Such consultations may cost as much as a regular visit, but are worth the time and money. Try to see all the names on your list before you make your decision. You should ask about the kind of therapy the therapist practices and make an informed decision on whether it is appropriate for your problem. (See "Types of Psychotherapy.") You should also ask about any relevant beliefs the therapist has—concerning marriage, sex, or drinking, for example, if those are your problem. Someone who believes that marriage is an outmoded institution, for example, might not be the marriage counselor you want if you are trying to save your marriage.

One of the most important questions to ask a potential therapist is about the fee and the policy toward missed or canceled appointments. (Some will require that these also be paid for.) Paying for therapy is unlike buying a dress or visiting a dentist, in that almost all therapists use a sliding scale to determine how much a client should pay. Indeed, some therapists feel somewhat ambivalent about taking money for a service that may have no concrete or immediate results. Fees can range from ten dollars to several hundred dollars an hour, and it is important to begin therapy at an appropriate price. Since therapists receive virtually no training in how much to charge for therapy, as the consumer you can take the upper hand in the negotiations for what your hourly fee will be. Most therapists are especially sympathetic toward, and therefore willing to take lower fees from, struggling students, newly divorced women and their children, and anyone with a particularly unusual problem. Some therapists will waive the part of the fee that is not covered by insurance (usually at least 50 percent is not covered), so that, in essence, the patient pays nothing. While many therapists consider this dishonest and unethical, it has become standard in some parts of the country. (No one seems to know if it is actually illegal.) Before choosing a therapist, make sure that your medical insurance policy covers the type of therapist you are interested in; some policies will pay only for treatment by a psychiatrist or psychologist. Also check on whether there is a maximum payment per year or a maximum number of visits per year covered.

Sigmund Freud himself was the first to emphasize the importance of the therapist's fee in the healing process. He believed that the patient should pay a lot, as a strong source of motivation and conviction in the treatment's technique. He even suggested that the fee should hurt a bit, providing what his followers have called "optimal frustration." *Nevertheless, there is no proof that the amount of the payment affects the success of the therapy.* In a study of the records of 432 patients receiving psychotherapy at a community mental health center, the amount the patient paid had no relation to how well the patient did later on. In another study 52 patients either paid twenty dollars for counseling or got it for free. The two groups did not differ in how satisfied they were with the counseling, how much they had learned, or whether they wanted to continue.

Never trust a therapist who suggests that a sexual relationship with him (or her) will help your problem. The practice is not only unethical, it may also be illegal. Therapists can be ejected from their professional associations and lose their license to practice if they are found to be having sex with a patient. A good general rule: A therapist should never do anything to you or make you do anything that makes you highly uncomfortable or that you don't like. An extreme case, for example, is the therapist who treats rape victims by strapping a dildo onto himself and reenacting their attacks. This is supposed to help them relive the experience and allow them to fight back.

You should also be extremely wary of any therapist who asks to borrow money from you. Several years ago a California therapist was taken to court by several clients who had never been repaid the several hundred thousand dollars he owed them. Therapists are professionals whose services you hire. They should treat you with as much respect and propriety as you treat them.

Knowing When to Stop

Only you can really know when enough is enough. Breaking with a therapist can be a painful, traumatic experience, somewhat like leaving home for the first time. But doing it at the appropriate time is also a sign that the therapy has been at least somewhat successful. (Overdependence on the therapist is one clue that it has failed.) If you have only just begun therapy, but feel that you are making no progress, you might consider changing therapists or at least telling the one you have how you feel.

Some people see an unending stream of therapists, becoming "therapy junkies." This describes you if (1) during the past several years you have been in at least two or three different types of therapy, all of which made you feel good only while they lasted; (2) therapy seems to dominate your life to the point where everything else seems less important; (3) your need to be cared about and comforted is unavailable anywhere else. Perhaps you don't necessarily want to change; you want company. Zilbergeld quotes one woman who had been a member of several group therapies: "I guess I was looking for a surrogate family without any of the hassles of a real family. In the groups I was free to do pretty much what I wanted. I could speak up or not, get involved with other people's problems or not, hang out with other members after the meetings or not. I kept my freedom but always had a feeling of belonging to and being cared for by the group I was in." There is nothing wrong with this attitude, provided that you don't completely substitute a surrogate family for the real thing. After all, will the members of your group help or comfort you in the outside world?

Therapy is also, writes Zilbergeld, "one of the few places where it is perfectly acceptable to think only about yourself." This can, however, go too far, as in the case of a man who was going to his therapist four times a week and began to feel irritated when his wife or children wanted attention. He confessed that he felt they were getting in the way of his therapy!

Not only an antidote for loneliness and a central motivation for life, therapy can also become an addictive form of entertainment. Group therapy provides live, weekly soap operas about real life. As one group therapy addict told Zilbergeld, "It was the most exciting show I've seen in a long time. Here are all these people talking about their problems, hangups and weaknesses. . . . It was a voyeur's delight."

Types of Psychotherapy

There are at least 250 different kinds of therapy available for the treatment of psychological problems. They range from classical Freudian psychoanalysis to hypnosis, drama, and poetry therapy to rolfing, orthomolecular psychiatry, and transactional analysis. For an overview of most modern therapies, see *The Psychotherapy Handbook,* edited by Richie Herink or *Shrinks, etc.* by Thomas Kiernan. (A useful pamphlet, *The Psychotherapies Today,* can be ordered for fifty cents from the Public Affairs Committee, 381 Park Avenue South, New York, New York 10016.) Remember that each therapist will view your problem through a special set of rules and perceptions, guided by his or her training and point of view. In essence, each therapist abides by a therapeutic religion, following its codes and rituals faithfully. It is up to you to decide which "religion" is best suited to solving your problem, as well as which one makes you feel most comfortable.

This section will deal with eight of the most common, widely accepted therapies now in use. They include: traditional psychoanalysis, psychiatry, cognitive, behavior/behavior modification, humanistic, group, family, and brief therapy. Although they can only be explained superficially in a limited space, the following discussion will provide you with a feeling for the rationale and style behind each type of therapy. The goals, assumptions, and methods of each therapy will be described, as well as how long it usually takes.

PSYCHOANALYSIS

Psychoanalysis, the mother of all "insight" therapy, was developed in the early 1900s by Sigmund Freud. Almost all types of modern therapy borrow at least a few theories from traditional psychoanalysis. This type of therapy is suited only to those who can afford the time (three to five sessions a week for a period of years) and money that orthodox psychoanalysis requires. It is also best only for those seeking intense personal understanding based on childhood traumas, fantasies, and sexual motives. Freudian analysts do not face their clients, who usually recline on a couch so that they are unable to see the analyst. These analysts also tend to be extremely passive, rarely offering insight or interpretation to clients.

Trained as a physician and specializing in nervous disorders, Freud developed his theory after trying to treat hysteria with hypnosis and concluding in discussions with patients that sexual conflict—desire versus guilt—was almost always the cause of their problems. His methods and theory have been modified and expanded upon by various disciples, who emphasized different aspects of the human psyche.

The goal of psychoanalysis is to uncover unconscious conflicts through free association (saying whatever comes to mind) to dreams, fantasy, and early memory, and through transference of the deep feelings these elicit to the analyst. Freud viewed the mind like an iceberg, only a small part of which—consciousness—is above water. The rest, the unconscious, lies below the surface. It is here, Freud believed, that the deepest passions, fears, and repressed ideas and feelings lie. (For an engaging description of the process of psychoanalysis, see Janet Malcolm's *Psychoanalysis: The Impossible Profession.)*

According to the tenets of psychoanalysis, the personality consists of three parts: the id, the ego, and the superego. The id contains the inherited instincts of sex and aggression and is the reservoir of all psychic energy. It reduces tension by satisfying the pleasure principle and is the seat of a person's sense of subjective reality. The ego deals with objective reality by obeying the reality principle. Often called the "executive" of personality, it controls actions and decides which of the instincts to obey. Finally, the superego represents the values and ideals of society. It inhibits the id by acting as the person's moral policeman. Neurosis, according to Freud, occurs in the ongoing conflict between these aspects of the psyche.

When we are unable to resolve conflicts between parts of the psyche, or when we must relieve anxiety, we deny reality through unconscious processes. The means by which we do so, Freud believed, is through defense mechanisms. With repression, we can force anxious or unwanted thoughts out of consciousness; with projection, we force them onto someone or something else; with reaction formation we replace an unwanted feeling with its opposite; with fixation or regression we get stuck in or go backward into an earlier stage of development.

Orthodox Freudian psychoanalysis, while still in use, has been supplemented by therapies developed by several of Freud's disciples. Most of them place less emphasis on the sexual origins of neurosis and each has its own distinctive focus. Therapy based on the work of Carl Jung, an analyst who broke away from Freud's circle, views personality in terms of its universal essence and symbolic meanings. To Jung the human mind contains "basic archetypes"—universal categories of experience such as Mother, Father, and Love—that comprise the *collective unconscious.* A major personal goal, according to Jungians, is to peel away the persona (the social mask we all wear) and develop into the true self. Jungian analysts are more involved with their patients than Freudians. Although they use free association, for example, they control and interpret meanings for clients. Relying heavily on imaginative interpretation of dreams, Jungians view dreams as symbolic of processes inherent in all human minds, rather than as symptoms of one person's problems. They also explain the source of neuroses to clients as well as the symbolic meaning behind those neuroses. When clients undergo what Jungians call a transformation, they are ready to become independent of the therapist. Jungian therapy is much more spiritual and mystical than Freud's self-enclosed theory.

Other types of analysis place greater emphasis on the social origins and social needs of personality. Analysts who follow Alfred Adler's theories emphasize individual psychology and each person's striving for competence and mastery. Adler viewed people as purposeful and goal-directed, not bound by irrational instincts as his former mentor Freud thought. He believed that neurotics are deprived of a sense of mastery and thus feel an "inferiority complex." Their neuroses are rooted in social factors, such as the family upbringing, birth order, and current experiences, rather than in internal mechanisms. The Adlerian therapist's goal is to interpret society to clients, to help them learn to trust and to develop feelings of self-worth. The Adlerian first gains an empathic understanding of the client's problem and then explains the client to herself. Later, she is encouraged to strengthen her social ties and interests. Adler's approach is quite outward-looking, especially compared to Freud's views.

Followers of Harry Stack Sullivan view personality as a function of interpersonal forces and the therapist as someone actively involved in the therapeutic process. A Sullivanian first listens to the client's problem, gains an understanding of the network of friends and social ties, and explains the problem in those terms. The therapist then does "reconnaissance," getting to know the social and personal history of the client by guiding and probing in two-way discussions. After a detailed inquiry focusing on the causes of the client's problem, the Sullivanian tests hypotheses about its causes. Finally, the therapist sums up what the client has learned and teaches her how to apply it to her own life.

Therapy as developed by Karen Horney, also a disciple of Freud, emphasizes basic anxiety as the root of most psychological problems. Her view is a feminist version of Freud's, looking at the psychology of women from the woman's point of view. She believed that basic anxiety develops when people grow up without the feeling of being loved and safe. Later on, their behavior is based partly on cultural stereotypes that teach them what is expected. (Good girls become meek and compliant; manly boys learn to be aggressive.) Horney also thought that there were typically American neuroses, stemming from the overemphasis in our culture on success, popularity, and being loved. Horneyan analysts believe that by bringing self-realization to their clients they can reeducate them to accept their real selves.

Psychoanalysis is especially suited to those who are deeply introspective and analytical and who favor an intellectual approach to their problems. According to analysts themselves, the ideal patient is between sixteen and fifty years old, well-educated, highly intelligent, articulate, and imaginative. Psychoanalytic patients, in any of theses branches, should also have a great deal of time (and money) to invest in a very lengthy process—the average "treatment" lasts five years.

In *Sleeper,* a movie in which the main character has been in suspended animation for two centuries, Woody Allen remarks upon awakening that "I haven't seen my analyst in two hundred years. He was a strict Freudian—if I'd been going all this time, I'd probably almost be cured by now."

PSYCHIATRY

Psychiatric therapy usually consists of a variety of analytic techniques, with more direct discussion between the therapist and patient than psychoanalysis allows. Because psychiatrists are licensed physicians and able to prescribe drugs, they place more importance than other therapists do on the use of medication to treat psychological problems.

The goal of psychiatric treatment is to relieve psychological symptoms with drugs, whenever possible, as well as to explore the source of the problem. In the new area of biopsychiatry, psychiatrists believe that many major mental illnesses are biological in origin. (For a useful summary of this field, see *Mind, Mood, and Medicine* by Paul Wender and Donald Klein.) Because schizophrenia and some kinds of depression run in families and because both can be successfully managed with drugs, most researchers think that they are related to a genetically based biochemical deficiency. The brain's 10 trillion cells pass impulses to each other by chemicals known as neurotransmitters, which can either stimulate another cell or diminish that cell's ability to respond. The amount and type of neurotransmitters in each person's brain can directly affect mood, appetite, sleep, sex drive, energy level, and even the ability to experience pleasure. Antipsychotic medication (major tranquilizers) can dramatically reduce the symptoms of schizophrenia. New drugs known as tricyclic antidepressants and monoamine oxidase (MAO) inhibitors alter the balance of the brain's neurotransmitters, making some depressed people feel happier and more energetic. (These drugs have no affect at all on nondepressed people.)

Although some experts feel that psychiatrists rely too heavily on drug treatment for psychological problems, there is growing evidence that many patients with debilitating mental illnesses experience relief that they never felt when treated only with traditional forms of psychotherapy (see Chaps. 19 and 20). Psychiatric treatment methods combine drugs with various forms of talking therapy. The treatment usually consists of one or two visits a week, for a period lasting between one and three years.

COGNITIVE THERAPY

Cognitive therapy is especially suited to articulate people who like clear-cut explanations and practical behavioral solutions for their problems. It combines verbal therapy with behavior modification. The most well-known proponents of cognitive therapy are Albert Ellis, who developed Rational Emotive Therapy (RET) and Aaron T. Beck, who constructed his own brand of cognitive therapy to treat depression and other emotional problems. (See *A New Guide to Rational Living* by Albert Ellis and Robert A. Harper; *Cognitive Therapy and the Emotional Disorders* by Aaron Beck; *Feeling Good* by David Burns.)

The goal of cognitive therapy is to change clients' ways of thinking, particularly their ongoing tendency to view themselves in negative and distorted ways. The theory behind cognitive therapy is quite simple: Altering cognitions (thoughts) is essential to change behavior. According to the cognitive therapist's point of view, faulty thought patterns or irrational beliefs contribute to most types of psychological disorders, because they usually produce painful and inappropriate emotional reactions and therefore interfere with people's ability to cope with life. Feelings of depression and hopelessness, says Beck, are the product of irrational thoughts, what he has called "automatic thoughts" or self-talk. He lists some of the attitudes that predispose people to depression: To be happy I have to be successful; to be happy I must be admired by all people at all times; if I make a mistake I am inept; my value as a person depends on what other people think of me; if no one loves me, I'm worthless; if somebody disagrees with me, it means he/she doesn't like me. Other maladaptive cognitions include all-or-nothing thinking ("If I don't get a date this Saturday, I will never get one again") and seeing life through a mental filter that notices only the bad things that happen.

Cognitive therapy breaks this vicious cycle (negative thoughts→depression→even more negative thoughts) by teaching patients to refute their wrong ideas and rationalizations, thereby altering their self-image. A depressed man thought that he was a failure in life because he had been divorced. His therapist asked the man if he knew other divorced people, which he did. Asked if they were also failures because they had been divorced, the client said that they were not. Eventually, the client began to see that his reasoning did not really make sense. Cognitive therapists teach their clients to be aware of their thoughts and to evaluate them objectively, a process that cognitive therapists sometimes refer to as "distancing." This allows the client to distinguish between what she believes to be true and what she knows to be a fact. A depressed woman, for example, may believe that it was her fault that it rained on the day she had planned the office picnic. Once she has distanced herself from this thought and realized that it was not her fault, the therapist will teach her "decentering," releasing her from viewing herself as the center of all events. Cognitive therapists also try to get clients to perceive accurately the rules or "shoulds" they set for themselves—"I should be a perfect friend," "I should never feel hurt," "I should always be happy," "I should be generous and considerate at all times"—and release them from this self-imposed tyranny.

Cognitive therapy is active, directive, and usually time-limited. Therapists who use Rational Emotive Therapy teach clients about the A-B-C-D-E progression. A stands for an *activating* event, such as parents refusing to lend their daughter the family car, even though they had promised to do so. B is her *belief* that this is awful and unfair and that her parents don't love her. C, the *consequence,* is that she feels angry and depressed, screaming at her parents and sulking for days. D is the *disputing* that the therapist does, challenging her belief by asking *why* not getting the car is so awful and if it really means that the teenager is unloved. E is the *effect* that the disputing has on the daughter. She begins to see the situation as it is—frustrating, but not proof that her parents don't love her.

Cognitive therapists assign homework to their clients, making them practice disputing and distancing, so that they take the part of the therapist. Clients sometimes keep a record of the A-B-C-D-E pattern as it happens in their lives, also known as a Daily Record of Dysfunctional Thought. Sometimes the homework involves actually doing something constructive, such as approaching someone they have always wanted to meet or telling a favorite person the truth about how fond they are of her.

Cognitive therapy is effective in treating some kinds of depression, but may be most effective for improving self-esteem, gaining confidence, or adjusting to life stresses such as losing a job or getting a divorce. There is an ongoing debate about whether it is more, less, or equally effective when paired with drug treatment (see *Feeling Good).* Cognitive therapists usually see patients once or twice a week for ten or twelve weeks, rarely longer than a year.

BEHAVIOR/BEHAVIOR MODIFICATION

Behavior/behavior modification is a straightforward system of therapy that, unlike most others, promises almost immediate relief from troublesome symptoms. It neglects the subtleties of human emotions, as well as underlying fears, motives, conflicts, and causes of the symptoms. It is best suited for people who are not introspective and who are troubled by a single phobia (e.g., of snakes), anxiety (e.g., of speaking in public), or an addiction (e.g., to smoking). It is not suited to those who seek self-exploration, heightened awareness of their motivations, or personal fulfillment.

The goal of behavior therapy is to change unwanted behavior by correcting faulty habits or removing the rewards that the behavior has brought. Thus, a behavior therapist has no need to consider internal mechanisms such as feelings or beliefs. This therapy evolved from the work of B. F. Skinner, who believed that all behavior is a function of its relation to the environment. He developed his science of behavior by studying animals, mostly rats and pigeons, whose entire repertoire of behavior he was eventually able to control. Using various kinds of positive reinforcement (such as food and water) and negative reinforcement (electric shock) he could get these animals to peck at disks, pull levers, walk in circles, or do just about anything he wanted them to do. Human behavior, said Skinner, is likewise determined. A little girl who is rewarded by attention every time she whines or cries will come to use whining and crying as a standard method for getting her way; a man who almost drowns (a negative reinforcement) may become permanently afraid of the water.

The theory behind behavior therapy is quite simple. All unwanted psychological symptoms are bad habits that have been learned. They can therefore be eliminated by simply teaching new, adaptive behavior. Because this approach sees all behavior as lawful and predictable, it also asserts that behavior can be controlled. (This was the premise of Skinner's fictional work, *Walden Two,* in which an entire society functions on the principles of operant conditioning and behavior control.) Thus, neurotic or deviant behavior is also controllable and can be changed through unlearning and reconditioning. Again, the only problem to a behavior therapist is the neurotic symptom; there is nothing else that needs to be probed, analyzed, or interpreted.

In general, behavior therapists ask standard questions when beginning to treat a problem. First, they decide what behavior needs to be changed. Second, they ask what events in the environment are maintaining the behavior. Third, they decide what environmental changes will modify or eliminate the behavior. And finally, they think about how the new behavior can be maintained over a period of time. A simple case might involve a woman who tends to overeat; the behavior that must be changed is eating too much. She does this whenever she has cookies in the house, passes a donut shop, or feels bored at home. The therapist might instruct her to stop buying cookies, change her route so that she doesn't pass any baked goods on the way, and tell her to take up a hobby or to go out more so that she is less often bored. To maintain these rather difficult new habits, a behavior therapist might ask the woman to keep a record of her daily eating habits and offer her some kind of reward (praise, a free visit, something other than food that she likes to have or do) every time she avoids eating unnecessarily.

Systematic desensitization is one of the most common behavioral techniques used to change phobias, in which anxiety has become a learned response. Desensitization involves a combination of relaxation training and a hierarchical organization of the anxiety-provoking stimulus. A boy who is bitten by a dog, for example, may develop a terrible fear of all dogs. A behavior therapist would present the child, in very small steps, with similar but less frightening objects. First, the child might play with a stuffed dog, and the therapist would have the child relax during the session. Next, he could play with a small puppy, moving up to a friendly, larger dog only when he is completely at ease. The ultimate test would be to have him approach a Great Dane without showing any signs of fear or anxiety. Sometimes therapists have their clients simply imagine the fearful stimulus, such as when they treat fears of flying or snakes. This method usually produces the same positive results.

Behavior therapists also use aversive conditioning, which involves the removal of a positive reinforcement and its replacement by a negative one. A woman who bites her nails, for example, is reinforced each time she does so by the relief of anxiety and the good feeling that it gives her. If she wants to stop this bad habit, a behavior therapist might have her wear a rubber band around her wrist and ask her to snap it hard each time she takes a bite or wants to. In time, that punishment may be sufficient to stop the bad habit.

Many behavior therapists claim that only ten to twenty sessions are needed to change most unwanted symptoms.

HUMANISTIC THERAPY

Humanistic therapy is also called "client-centered" or "nondirective therapy" and is based, for the most part, on the theories of Carl Rogers (see his book *On Becoming a Person).* In this setting therapist and client are like peers and interact a great deal. Humanistic therapy is probably best suited for people who like to be in control of a situation and who feel that they are just as competent as the therapist (if not more so). In most humanistic therapies, the client directs the course of therapy. The therapist's role is to be sympathetic and supportive of the client. In some ways, using this kind of therapist is like hiring an ideal mother.

The major goal of humanistic therapy is to build the client's self-esteem with empathy and unconditional support based on an intensely personal relationship with the therapist. It strives to allow clients to become more open to experience, with an absence of defensiveness, and in harmony with others. These values reflect some of the mores of the me-ism of the 1960s, the era during which this type of therapy achieved its greatest popularity.

Carl Rogers believed that the highest human need is for self-growth, or self-actualization. This state is attained, he said, by being sensitive to feelings rather than intellectual thoughts and by being acutely aware of here-and-now sensory experiences. Other important drives include the need for positive regard and the need for positive self-regard—learning to like others and oneself. If these drives are thwarted or learned incorrectly, the result is a deep dissatisfaction that motivates people to seek therapy. Humanistic therapists encourage positive self-regard in their clients by giving them unconditional support—the feeling that they are loved and respected *no matter what.*

The theory behind humanistic therapy reflects Rogers's generally optimistic view about the inherent goodness of people and his firm belief in the ability of psychology to help people. This has sometimes been favorably compared to the apparent coldness of behavior therapy or the rather pessimistic view of psychoanalysis. Humanistic therapy has a great deal of faith in people's self-reports of their feelings and views of themselves and downplays the importance of unconscious factors and defenses. Some critics have argued that people can and do deceive themselves and that they may not always know the truth about themselves.

Humanistic therapists almost always face their clients directly and actively participate in therapeutic discussions. Their method involves establishing a nonthreatening setting in which the therapist must be genuine, honest about feelings, dependable, and completely accepting. The therapist must be highly empathic to everything the client says. This method is clearly more feeling-oriented and less intellectual than many others. Therapists believe that these techniques not only allow clients to become more understanding and accepting of themselves, but also of other people. As they learn to think well of themselves, they learn to think likewise about the world around them.

In all of this lies the assumption that people who come to therapy lack unconditional support from important others—parents, teachers, relatives, friends. This is, therefore, the source of their neurosis. The client-centered therapeutic setting allows clients to uncover their own explanations and insights into their problems. Humanistic therapists usually see clients once or twice a week for periods ranging from several months to several years.

GROUP THERAPY

Group therapy, like humanistic therapy, reached the height of its popularity during the 1960s. It is especially popular for those people who have problems in relationships. Group therapy tends to be one of the least expensive kinds of therapy, since it requires less individual attention from the therapist. No specific therapeutic techniques characterize group therapy; instead, the background of the therapist running the group determines the school of thought on which it is based. Only the setting—self-revelation in a group—is unique.

The goal of group therapy is to expose maladjusted attitudes and behavior and help people learn to relate to each other in better, more productive ways. In conventional group therapy, each participant is both doctor and patient, since the group shares problems and interpretations communally. Each member is able, and usually encouraged, to comment on the problems and worries of every other group member. In this way clients are educated about the psychological theory behind common dilemmas, their own problems are demystified, and they learn by example that their problems are not unique (which in itself is often extremely comforting). The therapist who uses conventional group therapy almost always does individual therapy as well, and may sometimes recommend—for financial or therapeutic reasons (or both)—that a client switch from individual to group therapy. Most therapists believe that group therapy best suits those who tend to be passive in their interactions with other people, and who are unable to assert themselves or get along well in social settings. Because groups tend to mirror society, the therapist gets a relatively accurate view of how each client behaves in real social settings. Participation by every member is usually mandatory and encouraged by the leader.

Encounter groups, which became popular with Fritz Perls and his work at the Esalen Institute in California, are quick, confrontational versions of group therapy. Usually very brief—lasting only a day, weekend, or at most a week or two in residence—encounter groups stress the importance of brutal confrontation, honesty, "letting it all hang out," and the importance of touch. They often employ special exercises to induce trust (a member falls backward into the waiting arms of the rest of the group) or openness (everyone tells an important secret). Some encounter groups use psychodrama, in which each participant takes the role of herself and others play the roles of important people in her life. Variations of encounter groups include est, marathon, nude, scream, and meditation therapy.

A relatively new kind of group therapy is self-help groups, which may or may not be led by a mental health professional. These groups are geared to a very specific problem that everyone in the group shares, and are sometimes founded and run by the very people who want help in the form of social support. Self-help groups are devoted to overeaters, alcoholics, cigarette addicts, parents of murdered children, survivors of breast cancer, stroke victims, relatives of Alzheimer's patients, and just about any problem that is more easily dealt with in a group than alone. This practical group approach is designed to provide solidarity and support for traumatic life problems.

There are, however, several dangers of group therapy. First, some people become addicted to the therapy, neglecting to maintain attachments with their outside friends and family members. Second, groups often encourage a sort of tyranny that can be dangerously conformist. In one such group a man was persuaded to masturbate in front of everyone. This was supposed to be an act of "liberation," but the man felt humiliated and extremely distressed. Finally, much of what goes on in group therapy could be viewed as an invasion of privacy, in that everyone involved knows about everyone else's problems.

Most group therapy sessions involve from six to ten people who meet once a week for a period ranging from one time only to several years.

FAMILY THERAPY

First developed to treat schizophrenic children (in the mistaken belief that a disturbed family caused the illness), family therapy is most useful for people with specific, ongoing family problems—marital battles, disruptive children, the sickness of one family member.

The goal of family therapy is to treat the patient as part of a larger system. Family therapists seek to improve the functioning of the family as a system by creating better communication and improving on natural coalitions. The reason for doing this *en famille* is so that the therapist has the opportunity to see the family as it really functions, and not just as it appears in the eyes of one member of the family. Most family therapists believe that faulty values and behavior patterns encourage maladaptive behavior, especially in children. Diabetic children from disruptive families, for example, may learn to use their sickness to get attention. By not taking their medication properly, they initiate family upsets, thereby causing an acute diabetic attack, making the family problems even worse. In another family, parents may unconsciously reward their teenage children for delinquency or sexual promiscuity by bragging about their "bad son" or "sexy daughter," while vociferously denouncing the teenagers' faults. Observation and therapeutic insight for such families ameliorates their problems.

Several variations on family therapy include marital or couples therapy and sex therapy. Marriage therapists report that an astonishing number of couples never seem to have learned to talk to each other—they don't say what they think, want, or feel. The focus in this therapy is to teach couples practical skills: communication, realistic expectations, and adaptive styles of behavior. Couples therapists focus on behavior patterns and values in marriage, such as who sets the rules, who does what, and who expects whom to do what. Therapists try to get couples to say what they think, to give each other feedback (by finding out what each thought the other meant when making a statement), and to let them discover that even though they believe their spouse can read their mind, this is usually untrue. Some couples therapy involves weekend sessions called marriage encounter, in which couples are given various communication exercises. In one, for example, the purpose is to get couples to hold a sustained conversation. The pair lights a candle at bedtime and must talk to each other (without falling asleep) until it burns out.

Sex therapy is similar to marriage therapy in that the two major sources of sexual problems tend to be faulty communication and incorrect expectations. Therapists use the same techniques, such as helping couples learn what to ask for sexually, exploring with each other how they like to be touched, and to explore each other's sexual likes and dislikes (see Chap. 3).

Most family or couples therapy is much more direct and assertive than other types of therapy. Family therapists may forcefully intervene in the session by telling one member to be quiet or having the family change seats. Family therapists pay less attention to individual motives, fears, and feelings than they do to interpersonal perceptions and interaction sequences. They use role playing to get one family member to act out how he or she perceives another's behavior. Aside from weekend or two-week intensive sessions, most family therapy occurs once a week over a period lasting from several months to several years.

BRIEF THERAPY

Brief therapy evolved from simmering frustration with traditional, long-term therapy. Clients of therapists began to demand quick results that would be covered by insurance, which sometimes limits the number of sessions or the amount of time a patient can be treated. In addition, there was a growing need to treat clients quickly in emergency situations, such as after a suicide attempt or a family or personal crisis.

In brief therapy the client deals with only one central problem. Thus, the therapy is best for those who have a very clear idea of what their problem is, who have a strong desire to see it resolved quickly, and who may be a bit impatient with or skeptical about the nature of therapy itself. Since most research shows that the outcome of therapy does not depend on how long it lasts, brief therapy may be best if time and money are problems.

The goal of brief therapy is to resolve the problem within a short period of time and to prevent or intervene in a crisis situation. Therapists who practice brief therapy (most of whom also do longer-term therapy) believe that some kinds of focal issues—such as a conflict, crisis, specific problems such as phobias or relationship issues, can be resolved rapidly. Like group and family therapists, brief therapists' approach to their clients' problems depends entirely on the kind of therapy they practice. Brief therapy generally falls into four categories: psychodynamic, cognitive-behavioral, crisis intervention, and marital/family.

In psychodynamic brief therapy, which draws its theories and practices from traditional Freudian analysis, the client's goal is insight and character change. (For a description of time-limited dynamic psychotherapy, see *Psychotherapy in a New Key*, by Hans Strupp and Jeffrey Binder.) Therapists from this school interpret clients' unconscious wishes, fears, and dreams to resolve a very specific intrapsychic conflict in a short amount of time (usually fewer than twenty-five sessions). They direct the treatment to breaking current self-defeating patterns, not by harping on ones that occurred in the distant past. The key to this therapy is "dynamic focus," the idea that psychological difficulties represent a combination of cognitive distortions, behavioral habits, and self-defeating cyclical patterns of dealing with others. Brief dynamic therapy uses the therapist's relationship with the client to identify the sources of the client's problems.

An example of brief psychodynamic therapy, one that took eleven sessions, was the case of a twenty-two-year-old woman who had difficulty making decisions and feeling confidence in herself. The therapist took her history and found that as a child she had moved often, didn't know her father very well, and always tried to appear proper and smiling. She told the therapist she felt jealous of people in love; she seemed angry at her father and her own inability to fall in love. The therapist pointed out that her guilt was related to her aggressive feelings toward her parents, which she defended against by idealizing them. The therapist got her to face her anger and ambivalence, and she became more assertive, socially confident, and able to make important decisions.

Brief behavioral or cognitive therapy takes a much less internal, developmental approach. The goal here is simply to make the presenting symptom disappear. This therapy is best for anxiety disorders, mild depression, lack of assertiveness, and some kinds of sexual problems. For example, consider the case of a twenty-three-year-old teacher who enjoyed her work and did well except when she was observed by her supervisor. On those occasions she became extremely anxious, flustered, and panicky, which naturally resulted in a poor performance. The therapist first began a fantasy desensitization with the client, asking her to express the feelings that being observed gave her. She felt that she looked foolish, would be a disappointment, and would faint or lose control of herself. To rid her of this response to the supervisor's visit, the therapist had the teacher relax deeply while she imagined herself an hour before the boss's visit, half an hour before the visit, fifteen minutes before, her walk down the hall, her entrance into the classroom, her explanation of the visit to the students, and, finally, actually teaching the class while the supervisor watched. Her homework was to visit the supervisor, chat with him, and find out what he was looking for in his visits. After only ten treatment sessions, the teacher was performing as well under observation as she did while alone.

In crisis intervention the therapist's goal is to stabilize the client and teach her to deal with stress in constructive ways. Major crises that can be treated with this kind of brief therapy include the resolution of public crises such as for survivors of a kidnapping, earthquake, storm, or fire as well as personal crises such as divorce, loss of a job, serious illness, or a suicide attempt. Although treatments rarely last more than a week or two, these clients may be seen daily and their treatment might be supplemented with medication. Such clients must also be motivated and cooperate to the best of their ability.

Brief marital or family therapy strives to change family interactions in fewer than fifteen or twenty sessions. It is best for couples who need immediate help about a divorce or who have an urgent problem with a child, such as an arrest. This therapy is effective only if the family can communicate with a minimal amount of fighting and if they hold very few secrets from each other.

Becoming a Smart Therapy Consumer

In summary, here are the major issues to keep in mind if you decide to seek therapy:

- Take the time to select the best therapist for you.
- Choose a person you like and trust as well as an ideology that you respect; but keep in mind that, in practice, many therapies borrow liberally from each other and therefore may not seem as clear-cut as they do here.
- Try not to idolize your therapist's apparently superhuman qualities— they don't exist.
- Therapists, like dentists and doctors, can make mistakes. If you are not getting anywhere in therapy, it could be just as much your therapist's fault as your own.
- Realistic expectations for therapy will make the experience both more productive and more satisfying.
- If you are careful not to overestimate the benefits of therapy—"In one year I'll be more charming, attractive, and assertive, and glowing with high self-esteem"—you will be more likely to be satisfied with the results.

In many ways, the psychologizing of America is good. It reflects the fact that our needs have grown beyond food and shelter to higher ones of self-realization and understanding. In seeking to understand ourselves, we have a luxury not afforded to our grandparents or to people who must struggle for basic survival. Indeed, widely available psychotherapy can be spiritually liberating for women, who until very recently had to solve their problems by hysterical tree hugging or, more likely, by suffering in silence.

CARIN RUBENSTEIN holds a Ph.D. in social psychology from New York University. A former senior editor of *Psychology Today,* she has also written for *Family Circle, Discover,* and *Glamour.* Rubenstein is married to David Glickhouse and has a baby daughter, Rachel. She has always been a bit skeptical of psychotherapy and has never indulged in it herself. She dreads the day, twenty years from now, when her refusal to allow the baby to crawl off the edge of the bed or to eat magazine pages becomes fodder for Rachel's analyst.

Further Reading

Beck, Aaron. *Cognitive Therapy and the Emotional Disorders.* New York: International Universities Press, 1976.

Brim, Orville, and Kagan, Jerome, eds. *Constancy and Change in Human Development.* Cambridge, Mass.: Harvard University Press, 1980.

Brody, Jane. *Jane Brody's The New York Times Guide to Personal Health.* New York: Times Books, 1982.

Burns, David. *Feeling Good.* New York: Signet, 1980.

Buss, Arnold, and Plomin, Robert. *Temperament: Early Developing Personality Traits.* Hillsdale, N.J.: Erlbaum, 1984.

Ellis, Albert, and Harper, Robert. *A New Guide to Rational Living.* North Hollywood: Wilshire Books, 1975.

Frank, Jerome. *Persuasion and Healing.* Baltimore: Johns Hopkins University Press, 1973.

Herink, Richie, ed. *The Psychotherapy Handbook.* New York: New American Library, 1981.

Kagan, Jerome. *The Nature of the Child.* New York: Basic Books, 1984.

Kiernan, Thomas. *Shrinks, etc.: A Consumer's Guide to Psychotherapies.* New York: Dial Press, 1974.

Malcolm, Janet. *Psychoanalysis: The Impossible Profession.* New York: Knopf, 1981.

Rogers, Carl. *On Becoming a Person.* Boston: Houghton Mifflin, 1961.

Stratton, Joanna, *Pioneer Women: Voices from the Kansas Frontier.* New York: Simon and Schuster, 1981.

Strupp, Hans, and Binder, Jeffrey. *Time-Limited Dynamic Psychotherapy.* New York: Basic Books, 1984.

Thornton, E. M. *The Freudian Fallacy: An Alternative View of Freudian Theory.* Garden City, N.Y.: Dial Press, 1983.

Wender, Paul, and Klein, Donald. *Mind, Mood, and Medicine: A Guide to the New Biopsychiatry.* New York: New American Library, 1981.

Zilbergeld, Bernie. *The Shrinking of America: Myths of Psychological Change.* Boston: Little, Brown, 1983.

Index